giving
nature
a home

GARDENING
FOR WILDLIFE

New edition

A COMPLETE GUIDE TO
NATURE-FRIENDLY GARDENING

ADRIAN THOMAS

BLOOMSBURY
LONDON · OXFORD · NEW YORK · NEW DELHI · SYDNEY

Bloomsbury Natural History
An imprint of Bloomsbury Publishing Plc

50 Bedford Square
London
WC1B 3DP
UK

1385 Broadway
New York
NY 10018
USA

www.bloomsbury.com

New edition first published 2017

British Library Cataloguing-in-Publication Data
A catalogue record for this book is available from the British Library.

Library of Congress Cataloguing-in-Publication data has been applied for.

ISBN: HB: 978-1-4729-3857-2
ePub: 978-1-4729-3858-9
ePDF: 978-1-4729-3859-6

2 4 6 8 10 9 7 5 3 1

Design by Julie Dando, Fluke Art
Printed in China by C & C Offset Co. Ltd.

MIX
Paper from
responsible sources
FSC® C008047
FSC
www.fsc.org

To find out more about our authors and books visit www.bloomsbury.com. Here you will find extracts, author
interviews, details of forthcoming events and the option to sign up for our newsletters.

giving
nature
a home
rspb

For all items sold, Bloomsbury Publishing will donate a minimum of 2% of the publisher's receipts from sales
of licensed titles to RSPB Sales Ltd, the trading subsidiary of the RSPB. Subsequent sellers of this book are not
commercial participators for the purpose of Part II of the Charities Act 1992.

Contents

Foreword

When it comes to gardening for wildlife, it's up to you: you can do a little or you can do a lot. But what's important is to realise that everyone can do something for the wildlife that shares our gardens. And if everyone does their bit to help it really can make a difference.

Much of the UK's wildlife is having a tough time in the so-called 'countryside'. While conservationists work tirelessly to address conflicts and concerns, you can support their endeavours by trying to improve your own space for as many other species as possible.

So many of us in Britain are lucky enough to have access to a garden and these spaces already represent an incredibly valuable refuge, where many plants and animals have successfully adapted to prosper alongside us. It seems only right if we all try to enhance the space we have, to make sure it adds to the health of our world rather than detracting from it.

Adrian's book takes a very realistic, pragmatic and contemporary outlook on gardening for wildlife. This is a modern book for the modern naturalist and gardener, and it is a rich treasury of the information required to succeed in modest or ambitious plans. It provides the biological knowledge you need and sows plenty of original and imaginative ideas.

The calendar will keep you on your toes, the myth busting is fabulously reassuring, and the plans for small-scale habitat creation are very tempting and practically simple. Who wouldn't want to make their very own mini-cornfield?

Things might seem rosy in your garden already, but the wild world is a tough place to be, so please use this exciting new book to help conserve as much life as possible, and then you, your friends or family can all enjoy a healthier, wealthier community.

Chris Packham

P.S. Gardening for wildlife requires a bit of tolerance too, because it takes all sorts to make the world go round. Snails, slugs, wasps, flies, ants… they are all there to do their 'jobs' and without them your garden would be a poorer place. Try to avoid the 'P' word if you can; often it's humans who are the real 'pests'!

GARDENING FOR WILDLIFE

▲ Gardening is all about nurturing life; gardening for wildlife allows you to extend that to the creatures that share this planet with us.

▶ Gardening for wildlife can be great fun, offering you all sorts of little wild adventures without even leaving home! Yes, this is me. In my garden pond!

It's eight years since I began writing the first edition of *Gardening for Wildlife* and – with hand on heart – I can say that my passion for the subject has grown even more. I cannot tell you how much enjoyment I have had, what wonderful encounters with wildlife, all within a few feet of my back door.

In recent years, I have seen gardening for wildlife spread and blossom, and it is now central to the RSPB and its mission. All of us at the RSPB recognise that, if people are to care for our wildlife and try to save it, they need opportunities to get close to nature and to enjoy it as often as they can, and where better to start than in their own gardens.

At the same time, nature as a whole continues to struggle. As with wildlife in many other habitats, once familiar garden wildlife, such as Hedgehogs and Starlings, continue to decline and they need our concerted action if we are to turn the situation around. When you do things to make your gardens wildlife-friendly, you can feel proud that you are part of the solution.

So in this book we'll look at how to encourage many of the different species you can find in a garden. We'll go step by step through the creation of all sorts of mini habitats. And I've compiled a catalogue of more than 500 different garden plants that I know are not only great for wildlife, but look stunning in the garden too.

This new edition, with 48 new pages and a complete overhaul of the text and images, takes into account the extensive new research that has emerged in recent years, such as the RHS's Plants for Bugs study. I've also been lucky enough to work closely with the Wildlife Gardening Forum, of which the RSPB is a partner, which has allowed me to draw on the expertise of all sorts of experts in all manner of fields.

Since that first book, I've also had the privilege of visiting many more inspirational gardens around the UK, from Scilly to Shetland, where I've learnt a huge amount first-hand from other people's experiences. And I moved from my little garden – where I had enjoyed 15 glorious, transformative years – to one of an acre. It is the beloved former garden of two elderly sisters. It had become rather too much for them to cope with and I pledged to do my best to tend it back to its former glory and deliver a home for the wildlife they so adored there.

Use the book as you wish, but I would recommend that you read through the next section. In it we'll go back to basics, weeding out some of the wildlife-gardening myths that have sprung up and establishing exactly what gardening for wildlife is all about. Like all good gardening, preparing the ground well reaps rewards, and I think it might bring a few liberating surprises too.

Gardens are at last being seen as the brilliant and valuable wildlife habitat they are – or at least can be, with a bit of effort and encouragement. You can bring about profound improvement really quickly, so be bold, and enjoy all the benefits that giving nature a home brings.

Why We Should All Garden for Wildlife

The fact you've picked up this book probably means you have a good idea why you want to garden for wildlife – or indeed why you already do. But it is still worth reminding ourselves why it is such a good thing to do.

For some, it is about the sheer, simple joy of watching living things – connecting with nature, if you like – right on your doorstep. The lightning-speed precision of a Hummingbird Hawkmoth zipping from flower to flower; a House Martin constructing a dome from mud and saliva while hanging off the side of a house; watching a butterfly as it emerges from its pupa – there are endless jaw-dropping moments to be had with wildlife in a garden.

For other people, it's about the challenge of learning and perfecting the skills needed to be a 'good host' to our feathered and furry (and

sometimes shiny and hairy) friends. How can I encourage the Robins in my garden to breed? Why has my frogspawn gone cloudy? How can I entice more bumblebees? These and a million other questions are there to be asked and answered. Gardening for wildlife is an art and a science mixed with a healthy dose of old-fashioned nurture.

And then there are those who would like to do something good for the planet. I'm no prophet of doom, and I don't think humankind has totally trashed this world (yet), but you can't deny we've been having quite a wild party. In our gardens, however, we can ensure conservation starts at home. After all, we might like to think of our backyards as private property, but they are part of everyone's world. The air over your garden is directly connected to the air over the poles and the rainforests; and there are migrating birds that pass through your garden that, a few weeks later, will be feeding next to lions and elephants. By gardening with wildlife in mind, we can ensure our own little 'space' makes a positive contribution to the global environment.

At its very best, gardening for wildlife is all three of these reasons combined. Oh, and it's pretty good fun. I love it, and I hope you will too!

▼ It might be humble bumblebee to most people but, with the benefit of knowledge, you start to appreciate the complex lives they lead: the lives of queens, devoted daughters and – in this case – a self-serving male.

◄ If we take time to look, we find all manner of wild delights in gardens.

Myth busting

Ever since gardening for wildlife has seeped into mainstream gardening, a number of ideas have become rather entrenched that are either slightly off the mark or just plain wrong. I believe addressing them is vital and think you may find the truth quite eye-opening.

Myth 1: Wildlife gardens are great for wildlife; other gardens aren't

▼ All of these gardens will host wildlife, even if the gardener never intended it.

On the surface this myth seems to make perfect sense. Mr Smith at number 32 does nothing in his garden to help wildlife, and so his garden must be a desert for wild species. Mrs Jones at number 34, meanwhile, goes to huge efforts to help wildlife, and so her garden must be teeming with life. Surely? It would be terribly unfair if that wasn't the case.

The truth is that some of the gardens where nothing is purposely done to benefit it can actually be rather good for wildlife. Let me use the street where I used to live as an example. I gardened avidly for wildlife (no surprise there), but my garden was bounded by seven others in which no one else did likewise. They didn't even feed the birds. I had plenty of wildlife visiting my garden, and yet it visited theirs, too, and not just because 'my' wildlife decided to pop over the fence sometimes.

One of my neighbours never went into his garden, or rather 'jungle'. The trees were 40-foot high, and I couldn't even see his house. He didn't garden for wildlife or indeed garden for anything, but there was a fox den in his garden, which I didn't have, and there were Goldcrests, Chiffchaffs and Willow Warblers far more often than in mine.

Four of my other neighbours had lawns where kids and Scottie dogs played. My garden had no lawn whatsoever. Blackbirds visited their gardens as often as they did mine. On one occasion, I even saw a Red-legged Partridge and a group of Mallards on a neighbour's lawn, both of which remained dream visitors for me.

In fact, if you are to visit any garden – that's any garden, anywhere – you'll find wildlife in it. Whether it's a pretty, functional, urban or rooftop garden, home to some creature or other. Even gardens that have been paved and decked and sprayed to oblivion still support wildlife of some sort. Not a lot, but a bit.

Why is this important? Well, it reminds us that just because we might call a garden a 'wildlife garden' doesn't automatically make it great for wildlife.

The reality is every garden has wildlife in it; your challenge is to improve it, to make it even better for wildlife.

Myth 2: Wildlife gardening is something you do in only part of your garden

A garden fulfils many functions for us, and quite right too. Maybe you want to grow some vegetables. Perhaps a lawn is essential because you have a budding David Beckham in the household. For some it is a canvas to be painted with flowers.

If you were to analyse a garden, you might deduce that it has areas that are purely functional, such as paths and clothes lines: let's call those the function zone. Then there are parts where you enjoy yourself (the leisure zone), places where you grow things to eat (the production zone), and areas that you want to be beautiful (the aesthetic zone). Once all those bits are allocated around the garden, wildlife gets whatever is left over, right?

Well, you can play it that way if you want to, but once again wildlife doesn't seem to have read the rulebook. It strays cheekily out of the area that was designated for it, and you end up with Blackbirds on the lawn, butterflies in the borders, caterpillars in the cabbage patch and snails everywhere you don't want them.

So what am I saying? That we should just turn the whole

garden over to wildlife? Well no, and yes! Gardening for wildlife is not a case of abandoning all the other things you need a garden to be, not a bit of it. But we're clever creatures: we can squeeze multiple uses into one area if we try.

You want a shed? Great, its primary function is for storage, but with a sedum roof and a nest box nailed to the back, it's doing its bit for wildlife too. Perhaps you like to entertain guests on your patio? That doesn't mean that you can't train wildlife-friendly climbers up a pergola or have pots of nectar-rich plants there.

You don't have to compromise: you just have to be creative. With a bit of thought we can accommodate ourselves and wildlife throughout the garden at the same time. So prepare yourself for a bombshell: from this point on in the book, you won't find a single mention of the term 'wildlife garden' as it perpetuates the notion it should be a separate part of the garden.

The reality is that gardening for wildlife is about sharing our space with wildlife. Don't do it *anywhere* in the garden: do it *everywhere*!

◀ How refreshing to be able to dine *al fresco* within touching distance of wildlife rather than on a large sterile patio.

▲ You may want to keep your washing line away from your bird feeders, to avoid little accidents, but it and meadow butterflies can happily coexist on the lawn.

Myth 3: A garden fit for wildlife must be 'wild'

Perhaps the most pernicious of all the wildlife-gardening myths is the notion that neat and tidy is out, and shaggy and rambling is the order of the day. You would be forgiven for thinking that unsightly brambles and nettles are compulsory, that your borders should be weed-filled, your lawns straggly and your ponds shaped like a lumpy potato.

There are some excellent formal gardens out there that show why this does not have to be the case. One of my favourites is the Avenue Gardens in Regent's Park, London. With its strict symmetry, elegant urns and regiments of perfectly clipped evergreen columns, its primary purpose is to look good. It is so masterful in its planting and design and upkeep that I get goosebumps walking through it. But, for all that and despite it being in the centre of London, throughout the summer Avenue Gardens is alive with bees, butterflies and lots of other insects.

And yes, there are some species of animal that do like nettles and brambles, but – as we will see – there are plenty that don't. As for straight paths or geometric patterns or colour-coordinated planting schemes, wildlife doesn't mind one jot. I

think the key distinction here is between 'tidy' meaning 'orderly' (which is not a problem for wildlife) and 'tidy' meaning 'sterile' (which is a no-no).

The reality is that you can be as formal as you like in your garden and still make it a marvellous place for wildlife.

▲ A garden where nature has 'taken over' may seem great for wildlife, but it's not what most gardeners want. Fortunately, a good garden for wildlife doesn't have to be this way.

◄ In the Avenue Gardens in Regent's Park all manner of butterflies and other insects enjoy the nectar banquet, while we enjoy the glorious design and symmetry.

Myth 4: There is a blueprint for how to make a perfect garden for wildlife

What should a garden contain if it's to be as good as it can be for wildlife? Convention would suggest that there is just one way of going about it, one design to follow. Indeed, you might expect to find a diagram later on in this book showing you the bee's knees of wildlife garden design that you can follow to the letter.

I can save you flicking through because there is no such diagram. Wildlife isn't a single entity with a single set of needs. Even in gardens, there are thousands of different types of wildlife that you might like to help. And while what's good for the goose may be good for the gander, it isn't good for a grasshopper. Different species of wildlife need different things. Very different things.

WILDLIFE GARDENING: TRADITIONAL RECIPE

Ingredients
- Trees
- Pond
- Lawn
- Wildflowers
- Nest box and bird feeders

Method
Take one garden, preferably large.

Hopefully inherit one complete with trees, nice and mature (if not, you'll need to grow your own).

Make a hole in your mixture and add water.

Let your lawn rise until straggly.

Scatter liberally with wildflowers.

Decorate with a nest box and sprinkle with bird seed.

Hey presto!

To explain this more clearly, here's a plan of an empty garden, waiting to be made fit for wildlife. There are some fairly mature trees to start you off but, other than that, there's just bare soil – what a dream to begin with a bare canvas!

Let's follow the 'conventional' wildlife gardening recipe. We add log piles, berry-bearing bushes, a random-shaped pond and a wildflower-strewn meadow. Sure enough, we would soon see some butterflies and bees, Blue Tits and a few dragonflies. And there's absolutely nothing wrong with this if this is the garden you want. In fact it's fantastic.

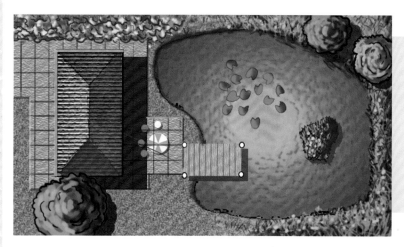

But what if we want to particularly encourage wildlife that lives in water? So we dig a pond that covers almost the entire garden. Moorhens will nest, frogs and newts will breed in profusion, and it will shimmer with dragonflies and damselflies in summer. Perfect…

…for them!

No, hold on, what about if now we're mad keen on butterflies and bees? So we fill in the pond, take out the trees that were casting so much shade, and stuff the garden with well-chosen flowers rich in nectar. We even have flowers in planters on the patio. There are no more Moorhens, but now the garden is alive with insects.

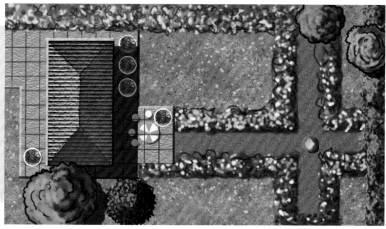

But what if we'd really prefer woodland wildlife, and would like more nesting birds? A carpet of Bluebells in spring would be nice too, and we'd like to encourage more moths. So we turn the garden into a spinney. After a while, sunlight becomes a rare commodity on the woodland floor and few butterflies visit. On the other hand, at night it is moth heaven (and great for bats), and there are now many more species of breeding bird.

The reality is there is no rigid formula for gardening for wildlife; there are thousands of possibilities that are in their own way brilliant for different sorts of wildlife.

Myth 5: You can attract wildlife to your garden

Oh come on, surely I'm joking now? Am I really saying after all this that there's actually no way of attracting wildlife to your garden? We might as well pack up and go home!

OK, I admit it, there is a nugget of truth in this myth and you *can* attract *some* wildlife to your garden. The scent from your flowerbed will waft to the bees a few gardens down the street; your lush oasis will be a beacon to birds flying over. But the issue here is the word 'attract'. It can imply that, by gardening for wildlife, you can magically draw in species from far and wide, which you can't.

Effectively wildlife needs to be within sensory distance to have any chance of being drawn in. No matter how good your gardening is, you are almost wholly reliant on what wildlife is living in your neighbourhood or accidentally stumbles upon your garden as it roves naturally. The skill is in making your garden so welcoming that your existing residents never feel like leaving, while when a creature happens to drop by, it thinks, 'Blimey, this is good', and decides to stick around. Your goal is to be the perfect host to the passing traveller and the present inhabitants.

The good news is that, given time, lots of wildlife will pass your way. It's what creatures are designed to do. Every year, a trillion new ones (give or take a million) are born and head out into the world to house hunt. Probably at this very moment, some animal is wandering across your garden looking for a new home.

If they don't find what they're looking for, they'll soon be gone, and you'll never know they visited. But if they find somewhere that offers them food, drink and accommodation, they're likely to be very grateful and stay put.

But lots of wildlife will never pass by. You may create the most wonderful habitats imaginable but if species can't get to them – maybe they shy away from people or don't like crossing roads – then your garden will never get visited.

The reality is you'll do the best job for wildlife if you understand which species are likely to visit your garden, and you give them the best welcome you can when they do.

▶ You might be very tempted to try to help Brimstone butterflies but, as they are not found north of Cumbria, there is no point trying if you live in Scotland.

Myth 6: You must grow native plants

This one is quite complex, so bear with me through to its conclusion. It starts with one of the most abiding myths – that if a plant is native, it must be great for local wildlife, but if a plant comes from somewhere else, it won't be.

On the surface this seems a logical argument. Pop into your local garden centre and it can seem like the United Nations of the plant world, where you can choose blooms from every continent. In contrast, most garden wildlife is 'home-grown'. Our wild creatures have evolved over millennia here on our shores, where they are adapted to using our native flora and not those recent imports from foreign parts .

The implication is that you must forsake all those exotic plants, which look nice and might grow well in your garden, for native plants that are often not as attractive or suited for cultivation.

But it's not as simple as it sounds. First, when is something 'native'? When it is naturally found in a certain country? The problem is that our boundaries are political rather than natural – a nation's border usually means nothing to wildlife.

Take the Scots Pine, so often listed as a 'native'. However, in the UK it is naturally found only in northern Scotland. If you live in Cornwall, you are some 800km away from its natural range. Conversely, you won't find the 'UK native' Pasqueflower, Hop or Field Rose growing naturally in Scotland – these are all species from south of the border.

There are also rather a lot of very familiar countryside plants, such as the Common Poppy, that you'd swear were native but aren't. They are what are called archaeophytes, brought to this country by early settlers.

So just because something is called 'native' that doesn't mean it's what the wildlife in your area is looking for or expecting.

The second problem is that 'foreign cuisine' can be really rather tasty, as we all know! Take bird food. Sunflower seeds are clearly adored by many birds. But not only are sunflowers native to the Americas, they have also undergone about 6,000 years of cultivation and then several trips into modern laboratories in order to generate big yielding hybrid cultivars. If you feed peanuts, it's the same story – they are South American in origin, and are now mass-produced from cultivars.

Also, the seed mixes that farmers are encouraged to grow in field margins to benefit declining farmland birds are a mixture of plants such as Wheat and Rye (which aren't even known as wild plants), Triticale (a man-made hybrid cereal), and Quinoa (a plant from Lake Titicaca in Peru). And it's not just seeds: there are plants that are happily visited here in UK for nectar and pollen but which originate in China, South America, Australia…

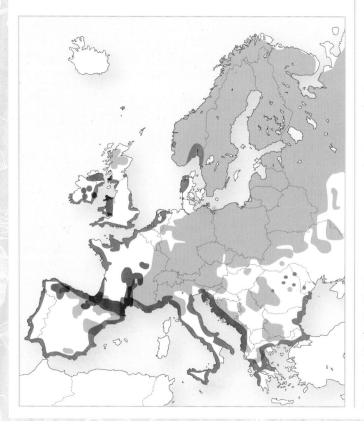

◀ Three plants native to the British Isles, but Scots Pine (green) is native only to parts of Highland Scotland; Welsh Poppy (orange) to parts of Wales, South-west Scotland and Ireland; and Yellow Horned Poppy (purple) is wholly coastal. None are likely to be native to where your garden sits.

So, the reality is that plenty of non-native plants are great for wildlife, while many native plants are actually not that good. The Biodiversity in Urban Gardens (BUGS) project provided some scientific proof for this. To quote Ken Thompson's excellent book on the subject, *No Nettles Required*, 'Most wildlife is almost completely indifferent…to whether plants in your garden are native or alien.'

In fact, it seems possible to create a stunning garden full of wildlife using only non-native plants.

But…

Before we start discarding all those native plants, there are some VERY important caveats.

The first is that some native plants are essential for certain wildlife. Some insects, for example, are so picky they will only eat one type of plant and that, of course, is almost always a native one. So if you don't have buckthorns, Brimstones won't breed, and if you don't have bedstraws you won't have Hummingbird Hawkmoths.

The second is to realise there are plenty of non-native plants that are absolutely rubbish for wildlife.

It is vital too that you never plant or carelessly discard non-native plants that are invasive in our countryside. Those causing the biggest problems are on pages 257–259.

Another caveat is that we still don't know the full picture about the relative value of native versus non-native plants. The Royal Horticultural Society's 'Plants for Bugs' project has given us some important indications, but there is still much more research to be done.

But nor should you underestimate the aesthetic appeal of some of our native plants. My beloved Red Campion is a prime example – who needs foreign blooms when you've got this stunner?

And, finally, there is still something morally compelling about growing the plants that would naturally be found where you live had someone not built a load of houses there. The Natural History Museum runs a great free website called Plants by Postcode to help you find the right species.

As I promised, the question of native plants versus non-natives is far from straightforward. But that doesn't mean that growing non-native plants and gardening for wildlife don't mix well. If you're careful, they most certainly can.

◀ The tightly packed seedhead of Quinoa is an energy-packed treat for many birds, even those that live far from its native Peru.

▲ Although some non-native plants do have wildlife value, there are great reasons to plant natives like this Red Campion.

So What *is* Gardening for Wildlife, then?

Busting those wildlife-gardening myths is useful because it reveals that we have much more freedom, more options, than we might otherwise imagine. But it also throws up lots of interesting questions, forcing us to consider what gardening for wildlife is really about. For example:

✿ If there is wildlife in every garden to start with, how can we be sure we are definitely improving on what is there already?

✿ If gardening for wildlife is best done in as much of the garden as we can, then how do we go about it?

✿ If a garden does not need to be 'wild' to be good for wildlife, what *can* it be like then?

✿ If the only species you're going to get in your garden are those that are likely to pass by, which ones are they?

✿ And if nativeness doesn't guarantee that a plant is good for wildlife, what does?

▼ This Starling seems delighted to have found these berries, but what will he need after they are gone?

To garden for wildlife successfully, clearly you need at least a little knowledge – and acquiring that can itself be very rewarding.

You need to know:

❀ which creatures you want to help
❀ if they are likely to visit your garden
❀ what their ecological needs are
❀ and how to fulfil those needs.

'Ecological needs'? Are you beginning to worry that this book is going to be all technical and daunting? Fear ye not! An 'ology' is, of course, just Greek for the study of something. And 'eco' means home. So, put simply, 'ecology' is just 'the study of home'.

What it means is that every plant and every animal has a wishlist of things – what we are going to call their home needs – that add up to their idea of the perfect home. For example, they will have 'food needs' throughout the year and for their youngsters as well. They will have 'shelter needs', which might include places that offer camouflage or the chance to escape from predators, or sites where they can survive cold and wet weather. They will have 'climate needs'. And they will want to find the right nursery in which to raise their young.

And that's what this book – and gardening for wildlife – is all about. It's about understanding the individual 'home needs' of different types of garden wildlife, and then using that knowledge to create ideal homes.

See yourself as the manager of a hotel. You want it to be a five-star establishment, and there will be some guests you are particularly keen to accommodate.

So you need to do a bit of research as to which guests are likely to travel your way, otherwise it could be a lot of wasted effort.

Once that's clear, you need to be sure what those guests need if their stay is to be a pleasant one. Do they need a pool? A gym? Do they have special diets? What do their kids like to eat? What type of room would they like?

Only then can you offer each of them exactly what they want and guarantee yourself very happy guests!

THE GARDEN HOTEL

Friendly Welcome for all Creatures

Large pool Nectar Bar

Restaurant – all diets catered for

Open to Non–residents

Short breaks/long-stay

No booking required

How Wildlife Sees Gardens

As we've seen, when it comes to gardening for wildlife you never start with a blank canvas: every garden has wildlife in it, it is already a 'habitat'. So it's worth us delving into what 'garden habitats' tend to be all about to get an insight into what wildlife is already using gardens, and why.

Now I don't think I need to tell you that you don't get Golden Eagles in gardens. Or Otters. Or hares, Curlews or seals. (Yes, I know that someone out there is going to email me to say that they do, but they are the exception and can rightly feel very smug about it.) Gardens clearly don't fulfil the home needs of every sort of wildlife.

Take birds, for example. Of the 250 or so regular British and northern European species, only about 30 are widespread in gardens. And butterflies? Of 60 or so species in the British Isles, only about a dozen grace our gardens regularly.

So why is that? Why do gardens satisfy some wildlife but not the rest?

Well, the first thing to understand is that we see our gardens in a very different way to wildlife.

We see it for what it means to us: a shed is somewhere to store tools; a lawn is a place for the kids to play; the patio a place to entertain friends; trees, hedges and fences are what offer us privacy.

How wildlife sees a garden is rather different. They are looking to see whether a garden offers them the things they need to survive. Check out this typical garden seen through their eyes...

© Bird Watching/Bauer Media.

Hard, flat rock everywhere: There are few places in nature where there are such large areas of unforgiving bare surfaces. Very few plants grow on it, but lichens do – it's still a habitat.

In the shadow of a monolith: Overlooking the garden is a great square lump of rock with vertical faces. It's hardly the most obvious wildlife habitat, but it heats up well in the sun (and is heated from within too), has overhangs and sometimes a few holes, and it creates shelter and shade.

A megadiversity of plants: What a huge number of different plants are grown in gardens – a single one can easily have more than 200 species. Many are from lands far away, or are hybrids and modifications you wouldn't find in nature.

An intricate mosaic of habitats: There are no big areas of anything – no great woodlands, no large meadows or fields, no big wetlands. Instead there are little bits of everything.

Water: There may be no huge lakes, but there is often moisture available in a pond or because humans water the ground.

Lots of food: Luscious tender plants, berries by the bucketful and piles of seed – yum!

© Bird Watching/Bauer Media.

Hidden dangers: There are some unusual dangers to catch out the unwary, such as giant cobwebs of netting and what looks like thin air but turns out to be hard as stone – windows.

Heavy grazing: A mechanical cow comes out nearly every weekend to graze the little meadows down to almost nothing.

Barriers: The garden is like a little box penned in by high thin 'walls', good as windbreaks but making it quite difficult to move into the next box unless you can jump or fly.

Disturbance: There aren't that many places to hide when you've got these humans wandering everywhere, dogs and cats running backwards and forwards, and metal monsters driving up and down the roads outside.

Trees, but where is the rotting wood? There are usually quite a few trees in gardens, but not much dead wood left to rot like it does in the countryside.

Fertility: How rich the soil seems here, so much better than in many wild habitats.

▶ On this aerial photograph, I've marked in imaginary territories of Blackbirds in pink, and the route a male Brimstone might take through sunnier areas looking for a mate in yellow. If a garden is like a room, clearly some creatures need dozens to fulfill their home needs.

Your garden is not an island

Now I want to zoom out from a single garden and look on a wider scale, with all the gardens and houses and roads laid out like a habitat jigsaw.

There's a very good 'gardening for wildlife' reason for doing this. We are conditioned to concentrate on our own garden because it's the only one where we have the right to do things and change things. But wildlife doesn't see the world one garden at a time; it has no idea what's yours and what isn't.

By looking at gardens in their wider context as nature might see them – houses, roads and all – we can understand how they compare to wild habitats in the countryside and get a feel for which wildlife communities are likely to find a suitable home here in our backyards.

Seen like this, it's not too hard to imagine why wildlife looking for an estuary or a mountaintop home is very unlikely to pitch down outside our houses. So what habitats are gardens like then? Well, gardens look a little bit like woodland, but the trees tend to be too small and sparse, and the habitat rather too bitty. Gardens also have plenty of grass, but compared to pastures and meadows they're more shaded and piecemeal. Gardens also have much in common with areas of scrub or newly planted woodlands where there are small

▼ From the air you can see that fields aren't much like gardens – they are too open and uniform. But then woodlands aren't like gardens either, being too dense and shady.

trees, open areas and disturbed soil. But gardens are also surrounded by lots of brick and tarmac.

The bottom line is that gardens are really rather weird habitats, not quite like anything else in nature. They are a crazy jumble: bits of this and bits of that. They are also rather a new invention (even though there are now millions of them) that haven't been around long enough for birds and animals to have evolved to live there and nowhere else. So the species that use gardens are actually successful invaders from a wild habitat.

Sure enough, the woodland element of gardens means that woodland wildlife aplenty has moved in such as Blue Tits and Robins, Speckled Wood butterflies and Foxes. But there is plenty of woodland wildlife that hasn't (yet) expanded into gardens such as many of the breeding warblers, fritillary butterflies and dozens of moth species.

Of the meadow wildlife, some ants, bumblebees and probing Starlings have successfully set up home in gardens, but creatures that need large areas of uniform grassland, such as grasshoppers and meadow butterflies, are rare while Skylarks are non-existent.

From scrubland comes spiders and shield bugs, but not Whitethroats and Stonechats. And in garden wetlands we find good numbers of amphibians and dragonflies, but few wetland birds or fish.

◀ Wildlife-friendly gardens often resemble a woodland glade, as here in Adrian Bury's wonderful garden in North Yorkshire, but they are clearly still a distinct habitat in their own right.

Getting your head around hectares

Many species need a certain area of habitat to survive, so in this book you will find I talk a lot about 'hectares'. One hectare (ha) is simple – it is the area of a square 100 metres by 100 metres. (In imperial measurements, one hectare = 2.47 acres.)

If that doesn't mean much to you (and area is notoriously difficult to visualise), then the pitch at Wembley Stadium (inside the white lines) is 105 metres x 68 metres which is about three quarters of a hectare. And in tennis courts? Well, about 40 tennis courts make a hectare.

▶ The pitch at Wembley looks pretty big compared to most gardens, but even one pair of small birds, such as Robins, often need a larger area of gardens than this pitch to raise a brood.

▶ Several species of shield bug, such as this Forest Bug *Pentatoma rufipes*, have made the transition to gardens well, or perhaps they never moved out after the diggers moved in.

Wildlife from 'wild' habitats is still moving into gardens as we speak. A hundred years ago, Blackbirds were a woodland species, but some pioneering birds made the crossover and found that gardens were almost perfect for them. Dunnocks did the same from an ancestral mountain home, and now Goldfinches are becoming ever more familiar. Who knows what will arrive next? Maybe Linnets will abandon their need for open spaces and come to see gardens as home; maybe Pine Martens will arrive hunting Grey Squirrels. Who knows?

Gardens it seems are the realm of the adaptable and the brave. The interesting thing is that for some species gardens have become their ideal homes, and some even like it more than where they originally came from.

In Summary

Over this chapter, we've seen why gardening for wildlife is important, we've debunked some of the myths, and we've looked at gardens as wildlife sees them.

In the next 80 or so pages, several hundred species of wildlife are lining up, waiting to impress you with their home needs, and hoping you will provide them with five-star accommodation. They have proved themselves adaptable enough to survive well in gardens, and there are enough fascinating species wanting a home to keep you occupied for a lifetime!

Deciding which you want to encourage is entirely up to you. If you love butterflies, or birds, or beetles, then you can garden for them. Or you can try to create particular habitats or encourage a whole range of species to visit.

So this is a good moment to pause and round up the headline facts that will ensure you are a great wildlife gardener:

▼ Bees know that they love Viper's Bugloss; your job is to know what they know.

✿ There is wildlife in every garden whether you garden for wildlife or not and, if we make careful decisions, we can improve our gardens for all of it.

✿ Wildlife gardening is something that can be done – and is best done – throughout the garden.

✿ A garden doesn't necessarily have to look wild to be good for wildlife.

✿ Gardening for wildlife is about making gardens so welcoming that nature's passers-by and existing residents want to linger.

✿ Each species of wildlife has its own particular criteria – its home needs – that add up to its ideal home.

✿ Because different species have different needs, there are all sorts of ways to garden for wildlife, each of which will benefit some wildlife but none that will benefit all.

✿ The more clued up you are about wildlife, the better you will be at helping it.

✿ Most wildlife needs more than just your garden – what surrounds your garden matters too.

✿ Gardening for wildlife is all about understanding:

– which wildlife uses gardens (it's a motley crew of adaptable species)

– which wildlife is local enough to you that it is likely to pass your way

– what the home needs are of that wildlife

– and how to fulfil those home needs

And that's what the rest of this book is all about!

THE RIGHT HOME FOR THE RIGHT SPECIES

So what wildlife does use gardens? Well, we know a lot more about that from the pioneering work done by the amazing Jennifer Owen who, for 30 years, tried to identify every species that she observed in her average, suburban garden in Leicester. She managed to find 2,673 species, including 94 species of hoverfly, 375 species of moth and 442 species of beetle. Her list even included several species of tiny wasp new to science! Who would ever have believed that gardens were so rich with wildlife?

In this section, we look at the wildlife commonly found in gardens – birds, mammals, butterflies, whatever – and discover what their particular home needs are, which will help you to decide which visitors you'd like to encourage.

In each species account, their **Distribution** will help you establish whether they live near you and consequently how likely they are to pass by your garden. Their **Habitat** and **Habits** tell you what type of environment they like to live in. You can see whether you already have the right types of landscape and vegetation in and around your garden, or if it's worth trying to create it.

If it looks like you've got a realistic chance of playing host to a species, you can check out their other home needs such as:

✿ what **Food** they need to find
✿ where they hide away to sleep and rest
✿ what they need for successful **Breeding**
✿ anything else they can't do without

Put all that together and you should have a good picture of what each species needs if they are to feel at home, and whether you think you can pull off those conditions in your garden.

Each species account finishes with a quick résumé, the 'So…' section, which sums up what gardeners can best do to encourage that species. The later stages of the book will then help you get on and achieve those things.

Note that this book doesn't aim to be an identification guide. If you want extra help, then the second edition of the companion *RSPB Handbook of Garden Wildlife*, by Peter Holden and Geoffrey Abbott, is a must.

UNWELCOME GUESTS

It is very likely that there are some species you most certainly don't want to encourage – the beleaguered Rat springs to mind, but there are several others that, in certain circumstances, may cause problems for other wildlife, for your neighbours, or for you.

I have included all of these species in the text, because understanding their home needs is just as important as it is for the species you do want to help. Only by recognising why unwelcome guests have chosen your garden can you know what not to provide or what temptation to remove.

◀◀ Every day, each animal – like this Blue Tit – instinctively seeks all the things it needs to survive. These aren't the 'nice to have' things that we humans fill our lives with – for wildlife, these needs are a matter of life or death.

◀ When you see a creature, such as this Weasel, in a certain place, it's there for a reason; understanding those reasons is the key to effective wildlife gardening.

Gardening for Birds

Of all the groups of wildlife that people like to help in the garden, birds almost always come top of the list. I'm sure that the woodlice, spiders and wasps of this world find that very unfair, but birds have a lot going for them: they are visible, audible, often pretty and regularly entertaining.

If that wasn't enough, they are often the gardener's friend, mopping up slugs, snails, aphids and insects. And the one extra thing about them that can make us wildlife gardeners very happy is that birds respond really well to the help we offer them. If you do the right things, birds will spend more time in the garden, new species will take up residence and several can easily be encouraged to breed.

The species entries that follow cover the home needs of about 50 of the most regular visitors to our gardens. They start with the 12 commonest garden birds as revealed in UK surveys, such as the RSPB Big Garden Birdwatch, and then work through another 40 species in field guide order. But let's sneak in some useful advice about the home needs of garden birds in general.

▲ Birds bring one of the most obvious of wildlife pleasures to the garden, in all their colours, patterns and behaviours.

- ✿ **Habitat**: Birds can be very picky indeed about what makes the ideal home. 'Trees' or 'lawns', for example, often aren't enough – they need the right kinds of trees or lawns.
- ✿ **Food**: Birds' diets can be surprisingly varied, more so than what you can provide on the bird table. Your gardening will have to deliver much of the menu, and a ready supply of insects is critical for more species than you might think.
- ✿ **Territory**: Breeding birds usually defend a territory. The better the habitat, the smaller the area they need, but even so it is unlikely that your garden will be large enough on its own. By understanding

how much room birds need, you will be able to see how much of their home range your garden can provide, and how many other good gardens they'll also need to use. Remember, one hectare (ha) is a bit bigger than a football pitch.

- ✿ **Nest site**: Having somewhere to nest may sound obvious, but it is interesting how often this is the missing or substandard ingredient in gardens. Nest boxes are the solution for only a few species; without your help the rest often have to make do with very poor and vulnerable places, or they are forced into moving out into the countryside when the breeding season comes.
- ✿ **Nesting material**: Note closely what material birds use for their nests – it can be hard for them to find what they need if we've gone and burnt, composted or thrown away all their preferred materials.
- ✿ **Broods**: In order to raise enough chicks to maintain the population, many species *must* raise more than one brood in a season. On top of this, many clutches of eggs are predated or the adults are disturbed before their eggs hatch, so to pull off just one brood the female may need to re-lay her clutch, often in a new location.

Birds and the law

All birds, their nests and eggs are protected by law, and it is an offence, with certain exceptions, to:
- intentionally kill, injure or take any wild bird,
- intentionally take, damage or destroy the nest of any wild bird while it is in use or being built,
- intentionally take or destroy the egg of any wild bird.

Blackbird
Turdus merula

A delightful and familiar presence in gardens, Blackbirds seem perfectly suited to our urban green spaces. With such a sublime song to boot, here's one species we all want to help.

HOME NEEDS

Distribution: Very common throughout the British Isles, except in north-west Scotland and mountain areas. Our resident birds are boosted by winter visitors from Scandinavia.

Habitat: Versatile, but basically a bird of the woodland edge liking a mix of bare ground, leaf-litter and short grass, plus the shade of bushes and trees. Once rare in gardens, they now thrive in them, even in city centres, although they do best in ones that are large, leafy and lawned. They like somewhere to bathe, too.

Habits: They feed mainly on the ground, hopping a short way and then stopping, and bolting back into cover if danger is sensed. They toss leaves aside or scratch at the earth to uncover prey.

Food: Insects and worms all year; berries and fruit in autumn. They take some seed from bird tables.

Roost: Thick cover, such as evergreen trees or climbers.

Breeding: They breed freely in gardens. The nesting territory can be as small as 0.2ha, but is usually 1ha or so. They nest in trees and bushes (conifers and deciduous) up against the main trunk, in climbers against a wall, inside sheds and outbuildings, or in low tangled vegetation. The nest is a well-constructed cup of twigs, grasses and stems on a bed of moss, lined with mud and fine grasses. They raise two to three broods, occasionally more. The three to five eggs in each clutch are laid March–July and are incubated for two weeks. The young fledge two weeks after hatching.

So... Make life easier for Blackbirds and help them rear more chicks by mulching flower beds with leaf-litter, keeping a mown lawn, planting fruiting shrubs and trees (especially dense, thorny ones), and by planting climbers against walls.

◄ Blackbirds, such as this beautiful, glossy male, love our 'glades of grazed grass' (AKA lawns) perhaps more than any other bird.

Robin
Erithacus rubecula

Familiar, approachable and inquisitive, the Robin is one of our best-loved birds. There's plenty you can do to help them, especially to encourage them to breed.

HOME NEEDS

Distribution: Very common resident throughout the British Isles, except in northern Scotland and the mountains.

Habitat: Found wherever there are relatively mature trees that offer cool shade, a moist woodland floor, sunny glades and perching posts. They are very fond of recently turned soil.

◄ The Robin's red breast is a powerful signal to rivals to back off, or prepare to fight.

Habits: Fiercely territorial throughout the year. They feed mainly on the ground, often watching from a low perch (such as a spade handle!) and then darting down to grab an insect. They don't turn over leaf-litter.

Food: Crawling insects such as beetles, ants and earwigs, quickly taking advantage when we (or other animals) dig. In autumn they eat some seeds and berries. At the bird table, mealworms are ideal, but they avidly take fat, although they struggle to cling to most feeders.

Roost: In dense cover such as Ivy or thick conifers.

Breeding: Maintains a winter territory of often less than 1ha, and a summer territory of 0.25–1.5ha. They nest in a hollow, be it in a wall, a tree, an open-fronted nest box or strange places such as hanging baskets! The nest is a bed of dead leaves topped with a cup of grasses, hair, moss and more leaves. They raise two broods (one in the north). The four to six eggs in each clutch are laid March–June and incubated for 12–21 days. The young fledge 10–18 days after hatching.

So... Gardens are great for Robins in winter but are often pretty poor in summer. If you can develop a shady woodland garden, increase the number of safe nest sites and boost your beetles, you stand a much better chance of hosting a breeding pair.

Blue Tit
Cyanistes caeruleus

If they were rarer, we'd be bowled over by the beauty of these little acrobats. It's probably the easiest bird to get to breed in your garden, and one of the most regular at bird feeders.

HOME NEEDS
Distribution: An abundant resident in lowland areas throughout the British Isles.

Habitat: Needs deciduous trees, especially oaks and birches, favouring sunny woodlands, parks, large gardens and hedgerows.

Habits: They work methodically from tree to tree, scouring branches and foliage for food, often dangling upside down. In winter, they wander in flocks with other tit species over an area of usually up to 10ha, although some are nomadic.

Food: Mainly insects and spiders gleaned from the trees, especially caterpillars in spring, but they also eat seeds, berries and nectar. Agile visitors to feeders, they take peanuts and sunflower seeds, and like to carry off large seeds to the safety of the trees – 'tit takeaways'!

Roost: In a hole in winter; often in dense foliage in summer.

Breeding: Territory about 0.5–1ha. They nest in a tree hole, preferably 2–5m off the ground, and willingly use a nest box or hole in a wall. The nest is a thick wad of moss, fine grasses, wool and hair. They raise one brood (occasionally two). The 6–16 eggs in each clutch (fewer in small nest boxes) are laid in April–mid-May and are incubated for 12–16 days. The young fledge after 16–23 days.

So... Provide a nest box with a 25mm hole and keep those peanut and seed feeders topped up, but don't stop there. If you want plenty of chicks to survive, you need trees full of insects. Go for leafy broadleaved trees, as large as you dare go.

◀ For a bird that is essentially a woodland species, the Blue Tit does incredibly well in gardens, but it does still need lots of trees.

Great Tit
Parus major

This bulky, strident tit with its cheery 'teacher teacher' song is not quite as common in gardens as its cousin the Blue, but is still a regular visitor to feeders and nest boxes.

HOME NEEDS
Distribution: A common resident throughout much of the British Isles.

Habitat: Likes deciduous trees and scrubby undergrowth, not too packed and with a few conifers, such as in woods, parks, gardens and hedgerows.

◀ The black line down the breast allows you to distinguish males (thick and solid line) from females (thin and patchy line, as here).

Habits: Forages through the trees, often low down in winter and even on the ground. Goes higher in spring to take caterpillars. Wanders about in small flocks in winter over an area of perhaps 4–8ha.

Food: Insects and spiders, especially moth caterpillars, beetles, flies and bugs. Also seeks berries and seeds in winter, including beechmast, hazelnuts and acorns. Takes peanuts and sunflower seeds at bird feeders.

Roost: In a hole (including nest box) in winter; in dense foliage in summer.

Breeding: A male defends a territory of 0.5–3ha. They nest in a tree hole, nest box or hole in a wall, making a nest similar to the Blue Tit's only even more luxurious. They raise one to two broods. The 5–12 eggs in each clutch are laid April–May and are incubated for 12–15 days. The young fledge after 16–22 days.

So... The advice is the same as for Blue Tits, but the nest box holes should be 28mm diameter. To offer a garden stuffed with tree-living insects is the five-star hotel that will mean more Great Tits can raise more chicks.

House Sparrow
Passer domesticus

From being the 'common or garden' bird, the House Sparrow's calamitous decline was one of nature's great mysteries. At last we know some of the things it needs to help it survive.

HOME NEEDS

Distribution: Common resident except in highland areas, but numbers are much reduced across almost all of the British Isles.

Habitat: Rarely seen far from habitation, they love allotments, stables and farmyards but are now found in far fewer gardens and are absent from many city centres.

◄ They may not be colourful, but there is something endearing about House Sparrows that perhaps we only appreciate now that their numbers are so depleted.

Habits: In the breeding season, they live in small colonies of up to 20 pairs, but in winter may band up in flocks several hundred strong, often in stubble fields. They enjoy gossiping sessions ('chapels') in thick hedges and are fond of dust bathing. They always like to be close to cover but will readily perch on buildings.

Food: Seeds, taken mainly from the ground, especially cereals and grasses, plus some berries such as Elder. Insects such as caterpillars and aphids are crucial for the chicks. At bird tables, they enjoy sunflower hearts and peanut granules.

Roost: In autumn and winter, they gather in flocks in dense bushes; otherwise they roost in the nest.

Breeding: In the colony, nest entrances need to be at least 30cm apart. They prefer to nest in a hole in a building or nest box, preferably 3m up or more, but sometimes build free-standing domes in trees and climbers made of woven dry grasses. They fill nest holes with hay, too, and line the nest with hair, wool and feathers, and with aromatic leaves to ward off parasites. They raise two, three or even four broods. The three to five eggs in each clutch are laid April–August and are incubated for 11–14 days. The young fledge after 11–19 days.

So... Put up several nest boxes (with 32mm diameter holes) a couple of metres apart from each other, keep supplementary feeding year-round and provide nesting materials. But above all, fill the garden with insects: plant a hedge and deciduous shrubs, have a vegetable patch, don't use chemicals... whatever it takes!

Starling
Sturnus vulgaris

Only now that its populations have plummeted do we fully appreciate the Starling's full-on personality and star-studded plumage. This is a red-listed bird in need of help.

HOME NEEDS

Distribution: Abundant but declining resident throughout most of the British Isles, with numbers boosted in winter by birds from the Low Countries, the Baltic States and Scandinavia.

Habitat: Found in many habitats wherever there are nesting holes and grassland but especially on farmland and in gardens. Tends to avoid mountains.

Habits: Highly gregarious, hyperactive and curious, they often pick around livestock or flock with thrushes and Lapwings. They also like to bathe communally.

Food: In summer, they seek insects such as leatherjackets, beetles, flies and flying ants, plus worms. In autumn, they gorge on fruit and seeds such as elderberries and cereal grains. At bird tables, they take bread, sunflower hearts, fat, pastry, etc and can hang at feeders.

Roost: Famous for large winter 'murmurations', with astonishing synchronised flock manoeuvres, prior to roosting in reedbeds, conifers (including cypresses), on building ledges and seaside piers.

Breeding: They breed in a loose colony, each pair defending its nest. The colony feeds over an area of 10–80ha. They nest high up in a hole, mainly in buildings, but also in trees, cliffs, and in larger nest boxes with a 45mm entrance hole. Inside they make a robust cup of twigs and grasses lined with hair, wool and fresh leaves. They raise one to two broods. The three to six eggs in each clutch are laid April–May and are incubated for 11–15 days. The young fledge 21 days after hatching and are independent 10–12 days later.

So... On top of supplementary feeding, provide an insect-rich lawn, an Elder tree and a fruit tree, and why not put up Starling nest boxes?

◄ Starlings find much of their food by probing in short grass, taking time out to preen and sing communally in trees and on overhead wires.

Chaffinch
Fringilla coelebs

A colourful and cheerful finch, usually top of the Big Garden Birdwatch charts in Scotland.

HOME NEEDS

Distribution: Abundant resident throughout almost all of the British Isles, with many more coming from Scandinavia in winter.

Habitat: In the breeding season, found wherever there are trees and bushes, but they really like a spread of big mature trees with lots of shrubs, and so do best in open woodlands and larger gardens. In winter, migrants will rove more widely on farmland.

Habits: A sometimes approachable bird, usually in small numbers in gardens, but larger flocks can build up in winter, especially on farmland.

Food: In winter, takes seeds of all sorts from the ground, including from cereals and grasses, the cabbage family and goosefoots. In summer, they are mainly insect eaters, taking aphids and caterpillars, and fly-catching in the trees. They are not very agile at feeders, preferring an open table or the ground, where they take sunflower seeds, rape seeds and linseed.

Roost: Alone, in a thick evergreen or thorn bush.

Breeding: The male defends a territory of 1ha or less but happily feeds outside it. The nest site is in a tree fork or out on a branch, most over 2m up and in a sunny spot. The neat, deep nest is a camouflaged cup of mosses and lichens, bound with spiders' webs and lined with feathers and hair. They raise one, sometimes two broods. The four to six eggs in each clutch are laid late April–June and incubated for 10–16 days. The young fledge 11–18 days after hatching.

So... A typical large garden, with a mature tree or two, a shrubbery and well-stocked bird table, suits them very well. If that 'mature tree or two' can become three or four, and if you can grow an area of seed-rich flowers, all the better.

◀ This is a natty male in his peachy breeding attire, but the white wing markings in the dark wing are the giveaway at all times of year for male and female Chaffinches.

Greenfinch
Carduelis chloris

Once a common sight at winter bird feeders, their numbers have been ravaged by the disease trichomoniasis (see page 59). Your hygiene regime at feeders is critical.

HOME NEEDS

Distribution: Found throughout most lowland areas of the British Isles, either as residents or moving short distances south and west for the winter.

◀ In winter, flocks of Greenfinches tend to sit high in trees. Then, when one bird drops down to food, the others are likely to soon follow.

Habitat: In the breeding season, they need a combination of trees and open ground rich in seeds, while in winter they sometimes move into farmland or coastal areas. Gardens suit them well.

Habits: In spring, males display in a weaving song flight above the trees, slowly beating their wings. Birds follow a daily routine visiting several feeding sites.

Food: Mainly large, hard seeds, taken from the ground, such as those of the cabbage family, cereals, docks and goosefoots. Will also eat berries including Yew, and rosehip seeds. Chicks are also fed insects, especially caterpillars, and spiders. At bird tables, they love sunflower seeds.

Roost: In winter, flocks gather at regular sites, often in dense evergreen shrubs or Ivy.

Breeding: Breeding pairs often nest in loose groups, with males defending just the area around the nest. They will travel quite a way to find food. The nest is built against a tree trunk or in the fork of a dense bush, small tree or creeper, deep in cover and often in conifers. It is a relatively large twig nest with grasses and mosses and lined with hair and feathers. They raise two broods. The four to six eggs in each clutch are laid May–July and are incubated for 11–15 days. The young fledge 14–18 days after hatching.

So... It's especially important to keep feeders clean, and use hanging feeders where possible. Keep feeding into spring when Greenfinches struggle to find natural food. Provide roosting and nesting sites by planting a shrubbery or dense hedge of evergreens or thorns, and by growing Ivy up a wall or tree.

Wren
Troglodytes troglodytes

What it lacks in size, this diminutive bird makes up for in volume. You can massively improve its fortunes in your garden by creating suitable nest sites and places to feed.

HOME NEEDS

Distribution: Abundant resident throughout the British Isles, only absent from uplands and open fields, but numbers are often low in gardens. Many die in cold winters.

Habitat: They prefer deciduous woodland with dense ground cover, especially along wet valleys, but are at home anywhere with tangled vegetation, rocks, log piles and thickets.

Habits: They behave rather like mice, exploring in, under and behind thick cover, rocks and logs, often near the ground.

Food: Small creepy-crawlies, especially beetles and spiders, but also bugs, small snails, flies, ants and woodlice.

Roost: Usually alone in vegetation such as Ivy, but groups may snuggle together in holes and nest boxes in cold weather.

Breeding: Males are territorial year-round, defending 0.5–2ha. Females wander blithely between males' territories. The nest is made in a hollow against a tree trunk, in a tree fork, bramble pile or hole in a wall, often low down. It is a well-hidden domed chamber of grasses, leaves and moss lined with feathers and hair. The male makes up to a dozen and a female chooses her favourite! A male with a good territory may mate with two or more females. Each female raises two broods. The five to eight eggs in each clutch are laid April–July and incubated for 12–20 days. The young fledge 14–19 days after hatching.

So... You need to offer lots of possible nest sites and thousands of spiders and insects, so grow dense thickets, make several log and stick piles, plant hedges if possible, and cloak walls and fences with climbers, preferably over a trellis.

◄ The shortest of wings and tail make nipping in and out of nooks and crannies all the easier for Wrens.

Dunnock
Prunella modularis

Dull in plumage, but not in character, this bird had an alpine origin but 200 years ago found a new home in gardens.

HOME NEEDS

Distribution: Resident and common throughout almost all of the British Isles, although scarce in the north and uplands.

Habitat: Anywhere there is dense, low cover in open habitats such as scrubby heaths, wasteland and hedgerows.

Habits: They spend much of their time on the ground, often deep in cover, hopping jerkily around and flicking their wings. They sunbathe regularly and get very excited when they meet each other. Males sing from prominent, though not high, perches.

Food: Spiders and insects such as ground beetles, weevils, earwigs, springtails, flies and caterpillars, plus worms and some weed seeds such as nettles, Yorkshire Fog grass and docks. May peck around underneath feeders and bird tables.

▲ The fine bill, streaky cheek and grey neck separate the Dunnock from the very similar female House Sparrow, but watch how it nervously flicks its wings constantly too.

Roost: Alone or with a partner, 1–2m up in a dense thorny hedge.

Breeding: Each Dunnock maintains its own small territory (less than 0.5ha) overlapping with up to five others, with whom it has a complex mating system and hierarchy that would get tabloid tongues wagging. The nest is well hidden in a thick bush and is a cup of twigs, roots and leaves. They raise two to three broods. The four to six eggs in each clutch are laid March–August and are incubated for 12–13 days. The young fledge 11–12 days after hatching.

So... This is one bird where it is definitely your gardening rather than what you put on the bird table that will help. A good dense thorny shrubbery or a native hedge will work wonders and serve almost all their needs. I hate to say it, but a patch of Brambles and nettles would be good too.

Collared Dove
Streptopelia decaocto

This delicate dove swept dramatically across Europe in the 20th century and is now a fixture in gardens almost everywhere, although numbers may be on the wane.

HOME NEEDS

Distribution: Common resident throughout most lowland areas of the British Isles.

Habitat: Needs a few trees or elevated perches, plus open ground for feeding, but otherwise it's more the availability of grain or seed that makes the difference, hence their love of farmyards and gardens.

▲ Collared Doves are prone to the disease trichomoniasis (see page 59), so keep bird tables clean.

Habits: They gather in small groups to feed on the ground. In spring, males coo monotonously from telegraph posts and high trees, and have a wing-clapping rise-and-glide display flight. They are often quite tame and a benign presence at bird tables.

Food: Mainly cereal grains, and will eat sunflower hearts at bird tables. They also eat weed seeds and a few invertebrates.

Roost: Usually in groups in dense evergreens or thorn bushes.

Breeding: A few pairs often nest within the same general area and share the same feeding sites. The nest, made of just a few sticks, is usually 2m or more up in trees, hedges and bushes, close to the trunk. They raise up to six broods a year. The two eggs in each clutch are laid March–October and incubated for 14–18 days. The young fledge at 15–19 days and are independent a week later.

So... Grow a tall hedge for nesting and provide grain-based seed at bird tables, or on the ground if safe from cats. Job done!

Woodpigeon
Columba palumbus

This portly pigeon is proving to be an adaptable bird in gardens, with populations on the increase.

HOME NEEDS

Distribution: Abundant resident or partial migrant throughout almost all of the British Isles, although scarce in the mountains and north-west Scotland.

Habitat: Very adaptable, surviving in most places with trees, especially liking farmland with woods and spinneys, but increasingly doing well in gardens.

Habits: Gathers, often in flocks, to feed on open ground or sometimes on the woodland floor, retreating to the trees if disturbed. In the breeding season, the 'lowing' song is much repeated, and males display by flying steeply up, wing-clapping as they do, then stalling and gliding down.

Food: Mostly plant material, especially cereal seeds, Ivy berries, elderberries, and leaves of clovers, peas, beans and cabbages. At the bird table, they take sunflower hearts, grain, biscuits, cake… and lots of it if given the chance! They have quite a thirst too.

Roost: Tall trees with thick cover such as conifers or Ivy, using the same site each night.

Breeding: Males defend a small territory of a tree or two. The unsophisticated twig nest is built in the fork of horizontal branches in a tree or high bush. They raise one to two broods. The two eggs in each clutch are laid February–November and are incubated for 17 days. The young fledge three to five weeks after hatching.

So... Now that they have learnt to feel safe in gardens, Woodpigeons don't need much more help. They can peck at peas, beans and cabbages in your vegetable patch, so be prepared to gently discourage them by carefully netting crops, and you can use scarecrows or dangle CDs that sparkle to startle them away.

◄ A real success story in gardens, Woodpigeons are now commonplace in the suburbs as well as rural areas. The white neck patch and plain closed wing tell it apart from the Feral Pigeon.

Mallard

Anas platyrhynchos

What a mixed relationship the Mallard has with us, sometimes ending up in the pot, at other times living cosily alongside us and taking full advantage of our handouts.

HOME NEEDS

Distribution: Resident across almost all of the British Isles, with more birds arriving in winter from eastern Europe and Scandinavia.

Habitat: They visit large, shallow waterbodies, whether flowing slowly or still, especially if there is plenty of bankside vegetation.

Habits: Often approachable, even tame, happily waddling about on land. They frequently gather in flocks. Males chase females in flight as part of courtship.

◄ Often seen on urban park pools, the Mallard is the only duck likely to visit garden ponds, and even then only large ones.

Food: Well, where to start? Grass, waterplants, seeds (especially cereal grains), insects (midges, mayflies, etc), worms, tadpoles, fish, even carrion, plus, of course, bread, rice and other human hand-outs. They pick food off the ground, from the water surface, or up-end while swimming, and will feed at night.

Roost: On the water's edge, especially on islands, by day or night.

Breeding: A wide range of well-hidden nest sites are used, from dense cover such as bramble thickets, to more open rushy clumps, the tops of pollarded willows or inside hollow trees, and they will use nesting baskets. They sometimes nest in gardens that don't have ponds – don't worry, they usually know what they're doing: leave well be. The nest is a grass cup stuffed with gorgeous thick down. They raise one brood. The 9–13 eggs are laid February–October and are incubated for 27–28 days. The young leave the nest when less than a day old, but do not fly until seven to eight weeks.

So… Supplementary duck food is available and is much more nutritious than sliced bread! But don't overfeed – duck droppings can enrich the water in ponds.

Pheasant

Phasianus colchicus

If you live near farmland, you may get wandering Pheasants under your feeders, especially if you feed grain to other birds. However, being a released gamebird, there is little need to encourage it.

HOME NEEDS

Distribution: Resident throughout most of the British Isles (except north-western Scotland). Populations are boosted by the huge numbers released each year for shooting.

Habitat: Woodland and woodland edge, and on farmland wherever they have access to thickets. They also need a good water source.

Habits: A social bird, with males establishing a clear pecking order. They spend most of their time on the ground, scratching and digging for food, and hate flying! They rarely move more than 1km from their birthplace. Males display from an open arena, loudly crowing and 'drumming' their wings.

Food: All sorts, but especially cereal grains and seeds, insects (beetles, flies and their larvae, etc) and worms, and plant food such as roots, shoots and berries. They are fond of acorns and blackberries.

Roost: Usually off the ground in trees or a thicket, and may spend much time sleeping.

Breeding: The male defends a territory of 0.5–5ha. The nest site is on the ground in thick vegetation, the nest being a barely lined depression. Females raise one brood. The 8–15 eggs are laid March–June and are incubated for 23–28 days. The chicks leave the nest on the first day and can fly short distances at only 12 days, but remain with their mother for 70–80 days.

So… If you live near farmland, you may get wandering Pheasants under your feeders, especially if you provide grain. A tray of water and a dense shrubbery for them to retreat into will also help.

◄ Refugees from the farmland where they are released, garden Pheasants can sometimes lose their natural nervousness and caution.

Grey Heron
Ardea cinerea

A tall and mighty fishing machine, only likely to be seen in larger gardens with ponds.

HOME NEEDS

Distribution: Found across much of the British Isles. Populations crash in hard winters.

Habitat: They like all sorts of shallow water that isn't too fast flowing, but they are surprisingly attached to trees and rarely found far from cover. They nest colonially, usually in big trees near water, so are an unlikely breeder in gardens.

Habits: Generally wary of people, they loathe coming near to buildings, but in London they are now much more tolerant and approachable.

Food: Half a kilogram of fish a day! They also take amphibians, Grass Snakes, dragonflies and small mammals. They feed alone, often at dusk and dawn but even at night, stalking or statuesque at the water's edge, catching their prey with a lightning strike.

Roost: Will rest on the ground near feeding sites by day or night.

So... Herons rarely come into gardens, but a garden pond stuffed with goldfish or froggy snacks is clearly very tempting to a Grey Heron flying over.

◀ With their dagger-like bill, enviable patience, and lightning reflexes, Grey Herons are master fishers, for whom goldfish inevitably present an easy and colourful target.

Should you wish to safeguard ornamental fish in your pond, there are various means of deterring Grey Herons.

✿ Netting the pond is the most effective method, but is unsightly.

✿ Scarecrows work well – with creativity, these can become a work of art.

✿ Herons like to land near water and then walk up to it, so extend two wires or ribbons all around the margin, one 20cm off the ground, the other 35cm, as a visible deterrent, not a tripwire!

✿ Placing a model heron at the pond edge is likely to draw others in, not scare them away.

Sparrowhawk
Accipiter nisus

A dashing bird of prey, this is the raptor most likely to be seen in gardens, even in cities.

HOME NEEDS

Distribution: Widespread resident throughout the British Isles (except north-western Scotland).

Habitat: Wooded countryside and farmland, but they cope well with urban environments.

◀ Sparrowhawks, with their orange eyes and barred underparts, can sometimes give fantastic close-up views in gardens – a mini-Tiger at work in our backyard jungles.

Habits: They hunt in low dashing manoeuvres along regular flightpaths, often close to the ground, nipping over hedges and fences to surprise their prey. They will also ambush prey from a perch. Usually seen singly, they spend much of the day resting and loafing. They fly above roof height to check out potential hunting sites, and they will circle high in spring to display.

Food: Birds, with the smaller male taking sparrows, buntings, tits and finches, and the female preferring thrushes, Starlings and doves but even taking Woodpigeons.

Roost: Alone in a tree, changing sites regularly.

Breeding: They hunt over an area of 1,000–5,000 hectares but defend a much smaller area for nesting. The simple stick platform nests are hidden high in conifers or large thorn bushes. They raise one brood. The four to six eggs are laid May–June and are incubated for 39–42 days. The young fledge after 24–30 days and are independent 20–30 days later.

So... Some people enjoy seeing them in gardens; others find it distressing. You can make things a bit more challenging for them by regularly changing the location of bird feeders, but remember that the presence of a top predator is always the sign of a healthy food chain and environment.

Kestrel
Falco tinnunculus

A rare garden visitor, this fabulous little falcon is famed for its precision-hovering over road verges, but its numbers are dwindling.

HOME NEEDS

Distribution: Resident or short-distance migrant across almost all of the British Isles.

Habitat: Open grasslands, such as downland and moorland, motorway verges and meadows. They also need safe perching places. A few pairs have adapted to city life.

Habits: Usually seen alone, they hover a few metres above the ground, sometimes beating their wings, sometimes just riding an updraught. They then plunge to the ground after prey. They sit for long periods upright on prominent perches such as tall buildings, telegraph posts, lamp-posts, bare trees and large rocks, and often choose to hunt in low light.

Food: Mainly voles, plus small mammals such as Wood Mice and a few beetles and other invertebrates. In urban areas, they will target small birds such as House Sparrows and Starlings.

Roost: In trees, on a cliff or on a building.

Breeding: Defends a small area around the nest, which is either an old Crow's nest or a rudimentary cup of twigs and grasses on a building ledge, in a nook in a cliff or in a nest box. They raise a single brood. The three to six eggs are laid April–June and are incubated for 27–29 days. The young fledge after 27–32 days but are not independent for at least another month.

So... Not easy to help in the garden, and if you encourage Kestrels in urban areas they will probably feed on garden birds. But if you have the space in a rural garden, turn lawns into meadows so that voles can thrive and then wait for the 'windhover' to come.

◄ While often confused with the Sparrowhawk, the Kestrel's hovering behaviour and love of open spaces and elevated vantage points is as much a giveaway as any plumage feature.

Moorhen
Gallinula chloropus

The easiest waterbird to cater for, whose families will keep you soundly entertained if you can give them a big enough pond to play in.

HOME NEEDS

Distribution: In lowland areas throughout the UK, wherever there are suitable bodies of water.

Habitat: Sheltered lowland pools, lakes, streams, ditches and rivers, including urban parks. They like at least some open water, so a tiny garden pond isn't enough. They also need abundant aquatic plants and thick cover at the pond margins.

◄ On city pools, Moorhens can become quite tame, but in rural areas they often remain shy and will scarper for cover – and even submerge – at the first sign of danger.

Habits: They usually live in pairs or family groups, spending most of their time either sculling jerkily across the water looking for food or clambering through vegetation at the water's edge. They sometimes potter about on land, never straying too far from the edge.

Food: A mix of plant material, mainly aquatic, such as duckweed, pondweed, rushes, leaves, seeds and fruit, plus some invertebrates such as molluscs, worms, spiders and tadpoles, and even carrion. They will peck at seed under bird tables.

Roost: In trees or in dense aquatic vegetation.

Breeding: A pair defends a linear territory along the water's edge, in which they breed and feed. Their nests are cups of twigs and stems lined with grasses and reed leaves, and are made in amongst dense pond plants or on a floating platform, or occasionally in waterside trees. They raise two to three broods. The five to nine eggs in each clutch are laid April–June and are incubated for three weeks. The young fledge at six to seven weeks.

So... Even though Moorhens don't need a huge lake, only a few of us have enough space for a large enough pond to fully satisfy them. However, you may live close to a ditch, canal or river, in which case a well-vegetated pond may become a nice addition to their territory, and they may even breed there.

Black-headed Gull

Larus ridibundus

This relatively dainty gull (compared to the robust Herring Gull) is familiar from sports fields and the seaside, and is a winter drop-in visitor to a few gardens.

HOME NEEDS

Distribution: Breeds across the British Isles but in a relatively small number of often large colonies in protected wetlands. In winter, they are much more widespread.

Habitat: In summer they are found on saltmarshes, shallow lakes and gravel pits. In winter, they are more catholic, visiting coasts, estuaries, gravel pits, reservoirs, urban park lakes, rubbish tips, playing fields and arable farmland, but only a few gardens.

Habits: A gregarious gull, often gathering by day to preen and bathe. They only come into gardens to scavenge kitchen scraps.

Food: They take mainly worms and insects, following the plough avidly. They also snatch food from the water surface or by shallow plunge-diving. They will circle high to take flying ants in summer.

Roost: In large flocks at sea, on estuaries and reservoirs.

So... Encouraging them into gardens by providing food may attract larger gulls and is probably best avoided.

◄ The Black-headed only retains a dark smudge behind its eye in winter, but the small build, red bill and red legs should give it away.

◄ The Herring Gull has a bill capable of ripping into unguarded bin bags, and has taken readily to nesting on roofs, which mimic its original cliff top home.

Herring Gull

Larus argentatus

The archetypal seagull, included in any child's drawing of the seaside, but now unfortunately sometimes coming into conflict with people as its breeding habits change.

HOME NEEDS

Distribution: In the breeding season they are found around much of our coast, although increasingly in cities; they travel widely inland in winter.

Habitat: They once bred predominantly on seacliffs but have undergone massive declines there. The rapid rise in rooftop populations, mainly in coastal towns, has not offset these losses. In winter, they are regular on beaches, rubbish tips, estuaries, sports fields and farmland.

Habits: A large, rather imposing and very gregarious gull, often loud and sometimes quite fearless of people. They make long feeding flights of up to 50km to find food. Problems can arise when pairs are nesting, including noise, fouling and ripping open rubbish bags. Also, if you stray near their eggs or chicks they see it as a threat and can dive-bomb to try to frighten us away. They generally avoid actual contact, but if people cower rather than fending them off, they can be bold enough to have a peck.

Food: Almost everything! They eat dead fish, shellfish and crabs on the tideline and at sea, but they are very adaptable and follow the plough for worms, scavenge fish offal in ports and grab human rubbish in the street, on beaches, in gardens and at dumps. They often harry and rob other gulls. But they don't eat bird seed or cling to feeders.

Roost: Outside the breeding season, many travel each evening to spend the night on reservoirs or the sea.

Breeding: They form large loose colonies on cliffs or rooftops. They especially like flat roofs, or will wedge their nest, made of grass, moss and seaweed, behind or between chimneys. They lay one brood of two to four eggs April–June, incubated for 28–30 days. The young fledge after 35–40 days.

So... Nationally, this is a declining bird that most certainly shouldn't be vilified. However, when gulls come into conflict with people, neither side wins. Do not feed them and use peck-proof bin-bags or put rubbish out in a closed bin. Restrict yourself to feeding bird seed in feeders for smaller birds.

If gulls are a problem on your property or you want to deter them from nesting, the only sustainable solution is to block potential nest sites. Use netting or anti-bird spikes, but do it in winter and not when the birds are actually nesting; remember breeding birds are protected by law.

Feral Pigeon
Columba livia

Its ancestors may have been wild Rock Doves living on cliffs, but our high-street pigeons are escaped or lost domestic pigeons and their descendants.

HOME NEEDS

Distribution: Common and sedentary resident throughout most urban and coastal areas.

Habitat: They need tall buildings or cliffs to perch and nest on, plus a source of fresh water. They especially like abandoned buildings, railway stations, under bridges and big public buildings.

Habits: They loaf in flocks on roofs, wheeling down to the ground to feed. In parks and city squares they can become incredibly tame, strutting and cooing around our feet.

◀ Any Feral Pigeon without a metal ring on its leg is likely to have been raised in the wild; those with rings are ones lost by their owner.

Food: They probably eat more human food than natural, enjoying everything from bread and chips to cheese, and feeding all night in well-lit areas. At bird tables they take most scraps and birdseed.

Roost: Under cover high on buildings.

Breeding: Can breed when less than a year old. They nest in loose colonies on ledges and in nooks and crannies, usually preferring elevated sites and building a rough cup of stems and roots. They raise five or more broods a year. The two eggs in each clutch are laid mainly February–November (but have been recorded in every month) and are incubated for 16–19 days. The young fledge at 25–35 days and are attended by their parents for up to another ten days.

So… Some people in urban areas, who see little other wildlife, are fond of pigeons; those who have to deal with their fouling of buildings, pavements and public places are not so keen. In gardens, they can provoke disputes between neighbours, so it is usually best not to encourage them. If so, use bird feeders that exclude pigeons and keep them out of potential nesting areas with netting as long as you are sure they are not nesting at the time.

Rose-ringed Parakeet
Psittacula krameri

This noisy, in-your-face, bright-green parrot looks set to stay – and spread. Urban myths surround its introduction – were they off the set of The African Queen, or escapees from Jimi Hendrix parties? Whatever the reason, numbers are booming.

HOME NEEDS

Distribution: This introduced species is found mainly in the London area, but is expanding into north Kent, Berkshire and Surrey. Another small population is well-established in south-east Kent.

Habitat: Although originally a tropical species, they are doing fine in urban and suburban gardens and parks, but need tall trees with nesting holes.

Habits: They travel widely during the day to look for food, often in groups, and rarely descending from the trees. Often very noisy, their squawk can be piercing.

Food: Largely fruits (apples, pears, grapes, etc), berries, cereal grains, seeds and nuts, but also flower buds and nectar. They readily take peanuts and seed mixes at bird tables.

Roost: In winter, they make long journeys daily to communal tree roosts where several thousand birds can gather. In the breeding season, they roost in or near their nest.

Breeding: Loosely colonial, a pair just defends their nest hole, which is either an old woodpecker hole or a natural one lined with just a few wood shavings. There is a single brood. The three to four eggs are laid January–June and incubated for 22–24 days, the young fledging at 40–50 days.

So… Be aware of the potential problems – as well as their noise and boisterous behaviour at bird feeders, they can strip fruit trees, and there are concerns that they may oust native hole-nesting species such as Starlings. Use feeder guards if you want to keep them from food.

◀ Parakeets are relatively dominant birds at the bird table, with a powerful hooked bill to boot.

Barn Owl
Tyto alba

Usually seen as a pale ghost in the half-light or headlights as it floats along verges and hedgerows, it's hard to find a bird with more charisma.

HOME NEEDS
Distribution: Resident if very scarce throughout most lowland areas of the British Isles, although a rarity in Scotland.
Habitat: Mainly farmland with scattered hedges, trees and small woods, especially where there are ample rough verges, margins and unimproved pasture. Often found on the edges of villages but not in urban areas. In gardens, rare in all but the largest.
Habits: They head out at dusk to hunt alone, slowly quartering grassy areas a couple of metres above the ground, hovering if something catches their eye (or ear). They sometimes pause for a while on the ground or a fence post. The screech call of the male is chilling.
Food: Small mammals, especially voles and mice, plus a few birds and amphibians.
Roost: By day in an undisturbed dark hideaway in barns and ruins, occasionally in bushes.
Breeding: A pair maintains a territory throughout the year of 40–250ha. They nest in a dark hole, often in a barn or ready-made nest box, sometimes in a cliff or quarry, but they need a big, flat floorspace. No nest is created within the hole. There is one brood, exceptionally two. The four to seven eggs in each clutch are laid April–August and are incubated for 30–31 days. The young fledge at 50–55 days and are independent a month later.
So... If you have a small garden, there's unfortunately little you can do. If you have a large rural garden, create a meadow; it will only provide a small part of their huge hunting territories but that could be critical. Barn Owl nest sites are often in short supply, so if you have the chance, erect a box either in an outbuilding or on a pole in an undisturbed part of the garden, facing east, north-east or south-east.

◀ Occasionally seen as a ghost in the headlights, the Barn Owl is almost white underneath, and has a fearsome screaming call. Populations are still perilously low, so help them if you can.

Tawny Owl
Strix aluco

Rarely seen but often heard, this is the hooting owl that kids like to mimic. It's a surprisingly frequent visitor to gardens with large trees, even in urban areas.

HOME NEEDS
Distribution: Resident across much of Britain, even to some altitude, but absent from Ireland.
Habitat: They need mature trees in woods, copses, churchyards, parks and large gardens.

◀ A master of camouflage in its daytime tree roost, many a time you will have been watched by a Tawny Owl without you knowing a thing about it.

Habits: They hunt almost exclusively at night, either in flight or from an elevated perch. Their short wings allow them to twist and turn, and they will plunge into bushes to catch roosting birds. Males mainly call in late autumn and spring. Can be highly aggressive at the nest.
Food: Small mammals and small birds such as sparrows, Starlings, thrushes and doves. Also amphibians, young Moles, plus some beetles, worms and even fish.
Roost: By day on a high branch, often up against the trunk; sometimes in holes. A pair will roost together in winter.
Breeding: A pair holds a territory all year, which can be as small as 5ha but usually 10–100ha. Many don't breed every year. When they do it is usually in a tree hole, or occasionally in a special nest box. There is a single brood, the two to four eggs being laid March–May and incubated for 28–30 days. The young fledge at 25–30 days, clambering from the nest when still down-covered, and are independent a month later.

So... If you increase the number of smaller birds and mammals in your garden, Tawny Owls will benefit, although be cautious about encouraging them to breed due to their aggressive nature.

Swift

Apus apus

If you live several storeys up, you are particularly well-placed to help these aerial masters and address their chronic shortage of nest sites and population decline. You may be rewarded by their exuberant screaming chases over the rooftops.

HOME NEEDS

Distribution: In summer, found across most of the British Isles.
Habitat: Uninterrupted airspace with insects. They come to land only to nest on cliffs and the human equivalent, tall buildings.
Habits: They arrive back from Africa in May and leave by early August, and have a lot to pack in to their three months here. They fly in loose flocks at a great height and for huge distances, chasing the best weather, and courting, mating and sleeping on the wing. When visiting their nest, which must have a clear flight line to it, they take several approaches to make a successful landing. Once inside, they can only shuffle about on their tiny legs.
Food: Flying insects and wind-borne spiders, but they avoid bees and wasps. Adults collect a ball of insect pulp in their throat to bring back to the young.
Roost: High in the sky most of the year, but in the nest through the breeding season.
Breeding: They nest colonially, up to a few dozen pairs in the local area. They mainly use flat internal roof spaces in old buildings or special Swift nest boxes, returning to the same site each year and making a modest nest cup of feathers and saliva. They raise a single brood. The one to four eggs are laid in June and incubated for 18–24 days, the young fledging after 37–56 days.

So... If you have a house wall where a Swift box can be placed, preferably under the eaves on the second storey or higher, it is sorely needed (see page 69). Maybe there is somewhere suitable at your workplace too. Playing tapes of Swift calls in May to attract them increases your chances of success.

◀ Let the RSPB know where you see Swifts flying low over houses in summer – we would like know to build up a better picture of where they are surviving.

Green Woodpecker

Picus viridis

It's a thrill if this charismatic joker, moss-green with a bold red cap and highwayman's mask, comes hopping about your lawn.

HOME NEEDS

Distribution: Localised resident throughout the British lowlands; absent from the far north of Scotland and from Ireland.
Habitat: Open deciduous woodland, parkland and orchards, with unimproved grassy areas.
Habits: They seek ants in warm grassy banks and in trees, and can be rather nervous, fleeing with a characteristic bounding flight and 'yaffling' call.
Food: Ants and their grubs are vital, licked up using their very long, sticky and sharp-tipped tongues. They will take other insects where available, including from behind bark.

▲ A woodpecker on a lawn may seem incongruous, but this is prime habitat for the Green Woodpecker, an ant-licking specialist.

Roost: In a tree hole.
Breeding: A pair defends a territory of 30–100ha. The nest is an unlined hole in a tree 30–50cm deep, the entrance 6cm wide; they either excavate their own or reuse an existing site. Each pair raises a single brood, the five to seven eggs being laid April–July and incubated for 17–19 days. The young fledge after three to four weeks.

So... You'll be hard pushed to encourage them into small or urban gardens, but if you live in the country or near suitable habitat, keep those lawns chemical free, boost your ant population and retain dead standing trees where possible. It is also worth trying a large nest box – although they may modify the box a bit for you!

Great Spotted Woodpecker
Dendrocopos major

The commonest woodpecker in gardens, but each visit is still exciting. It's quite easy to draw them onto your feeders, but your challenge is to fulfil even more of their needs.

HOME NEEDS

Distribution: Resident or short-distance migrant throughout Britain, but rare wherever trees are scarce. Very rare in Ireland.

Habitat: They like plenty of good-sized trees, especially a mix of deciduous and conifers.

Habits: They spend most of their time shimmying up branches and hammering out insects from the bark. They can cling well to bird feeders, but are often wary. Males drum in spring to attract a mate, often on resonant wood but sometimes on a telegraph post.

Food: Insects found in trees throughout the year. In autumn and winter, they take seeds from pine, spruce and Larch cones, and the fruit/nuts of Hazel, Hornbean, Beech and oak trees. At bird feeders they like peanuts, sunflower hearts and fat. They will take some bird eggs and nestlings in spring.

Roost: In an old hole or large nest box.

Breeding: The breeding territory is small, but they feed over a wider area. They hammer out a nest hole 3–5m off the ground in a dead or dying tree, often using the same one year after year. The entrance is 5–6cm wide and the chamber 30cm deep. They raise one brood. The four to seven eggs are laid April–July and are incubated for 10–13 days, with the young fledging 20–24 days after hatching.

So... Bird feeders are the easiest way to try to get regular visits. In addition, leave dead standing timber wherever possible (a real rarity in gardens) and, for the long term, plant suitable tree species, especially birches.

◀ A Starling-sized black-and-white woodpecker with a big blob of white on the wing is the Great Spotted. The sparrow-sized Lesser Spotted is now very rare.

Swallow
Hirundo rustica

A bird that country folk will know well and city dwellers almost never see – if you are visited by these harbingers of spring, treasure them.

HOME NEEDS

Distribution: Summer visitor from sub-Saharan Africa (and even South Africa) to most of the British Isles.

Habitat: Mainly farmland, often near water, and avoiding woods, uplands and urban areas.

◀ Swallows have a red face and deep blue throat band, unlike the House Martin which has a plain white underside and white rump.

Habits: They arrive here in April and May, and fly low and fast over grassy fields, especially around cattle and horses or over water. They only land on the ground to collect nesting materials. They are gregarious outside the breeding season, mixing with martins and gathering on wires. On migration, thousands pass along the coast, departing south in September and October.

Food: Flying insects, especially flies, plus flying ants, aphids and others.

Roost: In the breeding season, they roost in the nest or nearby. On migration, they drop into reedbeds, tall grasses and maize fields to spend the night.

Breeding: They often nest in small colonies, just a handful of pairs, with many returning to the same site each year. The nest is almost always in an open building such as a barn, stable, outbuilding or porch on a beam, ledge or shelf, and is a half-cup of mud and straw, lined with feathers. They raise two to three broods. The four to five eggs in each clutch are laid May–August and are incubated for 11–19 days. The young fledge 18–23 days after hatching.

So... If you live near open pasture, offer them a suitable nest site by leaving a barn window or outhouse door open. You will hopefully be rewarded with loyal repeat guests.

House Martin

Delichon urbica

To have House Martins nesting under the eaves was one of my childhood joys – their gentle night-time chatter just outside the window is a comforting sound of summer.

HOME NEEDS

Distribution: In summer, found throughout most of the British Isles, although numbers have fallen considerably. They migrate to Africa for the winter, although exactly where they go is poorly known.

Habitat: Birds of the air, they zip about high in the sky and only come down to earth to breed, collect nesting materials and drink. They are most frequent over habitation and areas of water.

Habits: They arrive in April and May, and spend much time flying around in loose flocks catching insects, only coming low if chilly weather forces insects down. Mud for their nests is collected from the ground. In autumn, large numbers pass along the coast and gather on wires, with most having left by early October.

Food: High-flying insects, especially flies and aphids but also beetles and flying ants, brought to their young in sticky blobs – lucky them!

Roost: Usually in the nest, arriving after dark, but some may sleep on the wing. On migration they will roost in the nests of other House Martins.

Breeding: They nest in colonies, most fewer than five pairs but some of several hundred. They build a virtuoso nest of 1,000 pellets of mud, lined with a few feathers, usually on buildings or bridges and at least 3m up on a vertical wall under the eaves. Pairs will reuse and repair the previous year's nest. They raise one to three broods. The three to five eggs in each clutch are laid May–August and incubated for 14–16 days. The young fledge 22–32 days after hatching.

So… If you have a high wall with eaves, put up an artificial nest. If one pair finds it, others will probably build alongside. Be prepared to wipe up droppings from the window sills beneath the nests, but it is a small price to pay for their company. Why not create a mud puddle for them on open ground too?

◀ House Martins need to be able to swoop up to their nest at speed and without hindrance – few will nest under the eaves of a bungalow, or where there are trees nearby.

Pied Wagtail

Motacilla alba

Rather energetic and restless, this is more a bird of driveways and roadside gutters than back gardens, but there's the chance you may be able to help it nest.

HOME NEEDS

Distribution: Resident throughout most of the British Isles, but they are only a summer visitor to higher ground and northern Scotland.

Habitat: Likes open places, often by still or slow-moving water such as lakes and canals. Also regular wherever the ground is bare or freshly turned, where vegetation is very short, or where flies are abundant, such as closely grazed pasture, ploughed earth, playing fields, seashores, sewage farms and farmyards. Around gardens, they visit large lawns, roads, roofs, car parks and paved areas.

◀ The fine bill of the Pied Wagtail gives away the insect-eating lifestyle, and the horizontal carriage is the mark of a runner, not a tree climber.

Habits: They walk and run across the ground, chasing small insects or picking them from the surface, their tail wagging relentlessly. They rarely perch in trees by day and are often quite tame.

Food: Mainly flies such as midges and craneflies, plus some beetles and aquatic insect larvae. They take a few seeds, especially in winter, so will scavenge under bird tables for fragments.

Roost: In the breeding season, they roost alone in their territory. In winter, they gather in large flocks in reedbeds, high-street trees and supermarket roofs, travelling many kilometres each evening to join the throng.

Breeding: A pair defends a territory of at least 3ha. They nest in holes or crevices, often in stone buildings or walls, frequently close to ground level. Their nests are cups of twigs and grasses, lined with soft feathers and wool. They raise one to three broods. The four to six eggs in each clutch are laid April–July and are incubated for 11–16 days. The young fledge 11–16 days after hatching.

So… A mown lawn and sunny bare-edged pond may prompt them to visit, but they will still probably prefer to spend time on your drive! If you are fortunate enough for them to be regular, you might try an open-fronted nest box to entice a pair to breed.

Grey Wagtail
Motacilla cinerea

Even longer and waggier-tailed than the Pied Wagtail, this denizen of fast water can sometimes stray into gardens in winter.

HOME NEEDS

Distribution: Found sparsely throughout much of the British Isles where they are residents or short-distance migrants.

Habitat: In the breeding season they are tied to fast-flowing streams where the water churns over rocks and weirs, especially those in wooded valleys with gravel bottoms and boulder-strewn margins. Some move into more lowland and even urban areas in winter but still near water.

Habits: As with the Pied, they hop, skip and jump along the water's edge. They can hover, and for a bird with such a long tail, they make surprisingly agile flying sorties after insects.

Food: All sorts of insects from damselflies to mayflies to midges, plus caddis flies and their larvae.

Roost: In winter they gather in small flocks, often in reedbeds.

Breeding: Few breed in gardens. Territories follow the course of a river, with most nests made in traditional sites next to water in bankside holes, cracks and crevices.

So... If you are fortunate to live alongside a stream, you may be visited regularly. For the rest of us, try a large garden pond with open stony margins and a bubbling water feature.

▲ In winter, when most Grey Wagtails are seen in gardens, they have lost their bright yellow underparts and black chin, but the yellow under the extra-long tail should give them away.

Waxwing
Bombycilla garrulus

What a bird! So elegant, so unpredictable – everyone wants a visit from a flock of these elusive northern wanderers.

HOME NEEDS

Distribution: They breed no closer than northern Scandinavia, but each winter they push south and west, reaching Britain annually, especially eastern counties. Numbers vary from almost none in some years to thousands in others.

◀ What a bird! With its wild crest, apricot-coloured suit and heavy eyeliner, if you attract a winter troupe of Waxwings you will be the envy of your neighbourhood.

Habitat: In winter, most likely to be seen in urban environments, from housing estates to supermarket car parks.

Habits: They are very gregarious in winter, their strange, high, bell-like call drawing in other Waxwings as they rove nomadically, almost desperately, in search of food. They often perch high in trees, and then zoom off to converge on berry-laden trees and bushes.

Food: They are berry and soft-fruit specialists, gorging on twice their body weight a day, with most food taken from a tree rather than the ground. Rowan berries are a favourite, but by the time they arrive in the UK few are left for them. Hawthorn berries (haws), crab apples, rosehips and almost any other berry are all taken avidly.

Roost: In trees.

So... There are so many other advantages of growing berry-bearing trees that you might as well go for it and plant as many as your garden will allow in the hope that one day you will be lucky.

Black Redstart
Phoenicurus ochruros

A perky little fella, like a soot-coloured Robin, this UK rarity has a curious penchant for rooftops and industrial landscapes.

HOME NEEDS

Distribution: A scarce migrant and winter visitor to English east and south coasts, with a few breeding in south-eastern England and the Midlands.

Habitat: They like rather dry, barren, stony places, avoiding trees, wetlands and lush vegetation, and have adapted well to rooftops. In winter in England, they visit undercliffs, coastal harbours and warehouses, while in summer they are found around factories, power stations and urban 'green' roofs. They made use of bombsites after the Second World War.

Habits: They hop and run over rocks and roof tiles, dashing to grab insects, quivering their rufous-tinged tail. One bird often remains faithful to a small feeding area. Males sing from elevated vantage points such as gable ends.

Food: Insects, such as beetles, ants, bugs and grasshoppers, plus spiders. They also take some berries and a few seeds.

Roost: Hole in a cliff or building.

Breeding: The territory can be as small as 0.5ha but up to about 5ha. The nest is built in a hole in a building, rock face or nest box. It is a cup of moss, leaves and plant stems, lined with softer material. They usually raise two broods. The five eggs in each clutch are laid May–June and incubated for 13–17 days. The young fledge 12–19 days after hatching but a family may stick together for several more weeks.

So... This is one species you are more likely to see on a summer European holiday, whereas in England you are very lucky if they visit your garden. However, if you live or work in an urban location in an area known for them and you have the chance to influence the development of 'green' roofs (see page 179), they are the best way of helping this unusual bird.

◀ A bit of a continental speciality, a few urban or coastal rooftops in Britain play host to this sooty little bird with a russet tail that it likes to shimmy repeatedly.

Fieldfare
Turdus pilaris

Bold and noisy, this attractive thrush with its exuberant 'chack chack' call is one of the evocative wild sounds of winter.

HOME NEEDS

Distribution: A winter visitor in large numbers, wandering nomadically throughout the British Isles.

Habitat: In winter, they like open farmland, preferably with grassland but also use stubble fields, and they are regular in orchards. They often perch in spinneys and tall hedgerow trees.

▲ It is often in the coldest weather that, with a few judiciously placed apples, we get our best chance to see Fieldfares in back gardens. Listen for the loud 'chacking' call.

Habits: In winter, they travel around the countryside in flocks sometimes several hundred strong, stopping in one area for a while, then moving on. They feed mainly on the ground, hopping about boldly, often with Redwings and sometimes Starlings, dashing to the refuge of trees and bushes if alarmed. In gardens, we see them most often in hard weather when hunger overrides nervousness.

Food: Insects, worms, slugs, berries and fruit. They are particularly fond of haws.

Roost: In flocks in thorny thickets, hedges and young conifer plantations.

So... When hard frosts come, put a few halved apples out on an open lawn not too close to cover and watch for these perky thrushes to arrive. If you have room to grow a Hawthorn, get planting!

Song Thrush
Turdus philomelos

Not too long ago, there were more Song Thrushes than Blackbirds in gardens. Not so now, so this rather reticent master-songster needs our help.

HOME NEEDS

Distribution: Resident throughout almost all of the British Isles, with more arriving in winter from northern and eastern Europe. Some British birds migrate south in winter.

Habitat: They need trees and bushes with grassy areas, damp soils and leaf-litter, so they enjoy woods, parks, churchyards and gardens.

Habits: They search for food, usually alone, close to the cover of bushes, hopping and then pausing to listen, and often flicking over leaves. The males' resonant, creative songs are delivered from a high vantage point.

Food: Markedly seasonal diet, taking worms in winter, caterpillars, beetles and other insects in summer, snails in late summer, and then fruit and berries in autumn such as currants, blackberries and elderberries. Snails are beaten against a favourite rock ('anvil') to extract the flesh.

Roost: Thick bush, usually on their own or in a pair.

Breeding: Each nesting territory can be as small as 0.2ha, but they will feed outside of that. The nest is built on a branch close to the trunk of a tree or shrub, in creepers against a wall, or sometimes in thick cover near the ground. It is a well-made cup of twigs, grass and moss, lined with a smoothed plaster of mud, dung and woodchips. They raise two to three broods. The three to five eggs in each clutch are laid March–August and incubated for 10–17 days. The young fledge 11–17 days after hatching.

So… Give them a garden full of worms, don't kill your snails, plant some berry bushes or a mixed hedge, and don't sweep up all that leaf-litter. If you can really enhance those nice moist and shady conditions, you have a good chance of enticing a pair to stay.

◄ Song Thrushes tend to winter in the same areas each year, so one in your garden one year may be the same you see the next.

Redwing
Turdus iliacus

A delicate winter thrush from Scandinavia and beyond, rarely seen in gardens until freezing weather strikes.

HOME NEEDS

Distribution: A winter visitor across most of the British Isles.

Habitat: During winter, they visit grassy fields, preferably with nearby cover such as hedges and woodland edges, and they also rootle among leaf-litter. Berry-rich hedges are favoured, and they will abandon inhibitions and come into parks and gardens in harsh conditions.

▲ The pale stripe over the eye and the 'bleeding' side separate the delightful Redwing from the similar Song Thrush.

Habits: Large flocks arrive by night in October and November when their thin 'seee' calls can be heard overhead. They rove around the countryside looking for good feeding sites, moving either when the weather changes or the food is exhausted. They usually feed on the ground, hopping and stopping across short turf, although they quickly fly into cover if disturbed.

Food: On arrival in autumn, they will gorge on berries and other fruit, in particular haws, but much of their time is spent looking for ground invertebrates such as beetles and their larvae, caterpillars, worms and snails.

Roost: In dense cover, such as evergreens, thorny thickets or dense woodland.

So… Be ready when cold weather comes to put out windfall apples on the lawn. If you have space for a Hawthorn or Rowan – or several – then there is every chance that your resident Blackbirds may leave a few berries for them.

Mistle Thrush
Turdus viscivorus

This is the thrush with a football rattle call and a song that can be heard for miles. You'll need a big lawn and tall trees to keep this one happy!

HOME NEEDS

Distribution: Resident throughout almost all of the British Isles, although rarely in large numbers.

Habitat: They need tall trees and large expanses of open, closely cropped natural turf, so they enjoy parkland and the grounds of country homes, orchards and a few large gardens. They also require berry-bearing trees in winter.

Habits: They hop purposefully across open short turf, chest out. Usually the only gatherings are of small flocks in autumn. The male sings early in the year, even in storms (hence the country name, 'Stormcock'), from the tops of tall trees. Pairs will guard favourite berry trees from all-comers in winter.

Food: Invertebrates through much of the year, especially beetles but also worms, slugs and flies. Favoured berries include Yew, Rowan, Ivy, Mistletoe, Purging Buckthorn and Holly.

Roost: In trees and bushes, often high up in evergreens.

Breeding: They defend a relatively small territory of 1–15ha, but feed over a large area in which other pairs may nest. The nest is built very high up on a thick tree branch, sometimes in a conifer, and is a large cup of twigs, moss and mud, lined with plenty of dry grasses. They raise two, sometimes three broods. The three to five eggs in each clutch are laid March–June and are incubated for 12–15 days. The young fledge 14–16 days after hatching.

So... Those of you with large lawns have the best chance of success, as long as they are rich in beetles. If you live anywhere near open meadows, parks or sports fields, you too can hope for a visit, so consider growing a fine Holly or Rowan on your boundary so that a pair may come to claim it.

◀ Notice how the breast spots on the Mistle Thrush are round on a white background, compared with teardrops on buff of the Song Thrush. It is unusual to see this larger cousin of the Song Thrush in small gardens.

Blackcap
Sylvia atricapilla

A warbler that comes to bird tables? It's a strange modern phenomenon from this curiously adaptable little insect-eater.

HOME NEEDS

Distribution: Common and increasing summer visitor to much of southern Britain; scarce but increasing in Ireland and Scotland. Some birds that breed in central Europe winter in southern Britain.

Habitat: In summer, a bird of mature deciduous woodland, rare but getting more frequent in large gardens. However, wintering birds in Britain are regularly seen in suburban gardens, especially in the south and west, and migrants turn up in many coastal gardens.

Habits: In summer, they spend much of their time in the treetops, but they need a good shrubby understorey too. In winter, they still require trees and shrubs but also come onto bird tables and feeders for food. They can be very loyal to an area of gardens for several weeks.

◀ A black topknot on grey is the adult male Blackcap's uniform; in females the crown is coppery.

Food: In the breeding season, they eat insects. They then switch to berries in later summer, enjoying elderberries, blackberries, currants, buckthorns, honeysuckles, Fig, Strawberry Tree, Ivy and more. They eat pollen in spring, such as Goat Willow. At bird tables, they are especially fond of fat and cut apples, but will take peanuts, cheese and coconut.

Roost: In dense cover.

Breeding: They defend a small territory, often less than 1ha. They nest low down in dense cover, often in bramble or nettle patches. They build a lovely cup of grasses, leaves and spiders' webs, finely lined with grasses and hair. They raise one, sometimes two, broods. The four to five eggs in each clutch are laid April–June and are incubated for 10–16 days. The young fledge 8–14 days after hatching.

So... In larger gardens, encourage them to breed by creating a woodland feel, full of a thick understorey where they can nest safely. In winter, many of us will be treated to a visit if we offer a constant supply of apple halves and fat balls.

Goldcrest
Regulus regulus

So small and seemingly vulnerable, you would never suspect that this fragile little bird can fly hundreds of miles over water or survive the Scottish winter.

HOME NEEDS

Distribution: Resident throughout much of the British Isles. Many more come here in winter from Scandinavia.

Habitat: In the breeding season, found mostly in mature conifers. They can survive where there are just a few, such as Yews in churchyards, but most live in plantations of spruce, Larch and fir. They are more widespread on migration when they visit mixed trees, including Sycamores, and shrubs in hedges and gardens where they often latch onto tit flocks.

◀ Don't mistake the Goldcrest, with its dark eye in a blank face, for the similar but much rarer Firecrest, a visitor to a few southern gardens in spring and autumn.

Habits: They need to eat almost constantly, and so flit about restlessly, usually high in a conifer. They sometimes seem in a world of their own, oblivious to our presence. In winter, they tend to stick to fixed feeding areas. Populations crash in hard winters.

Food: Insects such as springtails, bugs and moth caterpillars, spiders, plus a few spruce and pine seeds. They are very rare at bird feeders.

Roost: In dense conifer foliage, often several birds huddled together.

Breeding: They defend a territory of around 1ha, nesting high on the ends of conifer branches and building a warm ball of moss, lichens and spider silk entered through a tiny hole. They raise two broods. The 7–12 eggs in each clutch are laid May–July and incubated for 15–17 days. The young fledge 17–22 days after hatching.

So... Large conifers are the key if you want regular visits and breeding pairs; if not, they will visit garden hedges and Sycamores on occasions.

Spotted Flycatcher
Muscicapa striata

Few garden birds have declined as much as this one. If you have a chance, every bit of help for this perky tree-top bird is welcome.

HOME NEEDS

Distribution: A summer visitor from Africa throughout the British Isles, but numbers have plummeted for reasons poorly understood.

Habitat: They like big trees, usually deciduous, that offer open perches overlooking glades and sheltered airspace. They are fond of riversides, big gardens, cemeteries and parkland.

Habits: They arrive here in late spring, rarely before May. Much of the day is spent high in a tree on favourite exposed twigs ('snags'), launching after insects and looping straight back to the perch.

Food: A specialist in catching flying insects, especially flies, beetles and aphids. They may take caterpillars when rain stops play, and in autumn will eat berries such as Elder.

Roost: Poorly known.

Breeding: A pair has a territory of around 0.5–2ha. They build their nest on a ledge or in a nook, such as in Ivy or against a house wall, with shelter above but with a panoramic view. It can be at any height from ground level up to 10m or more. The nest is a loose cup of small roots and twigs, grasses, moss, lichens and feathers. They will take to an open-fronted nest box with a very low 'front wall'. They raise one to two broods. The three to five eggs in each clutch are laid May–July and are incubated for 10–15 days. The young fledge 10–17 days after hatching.

So... If your garden is like a sunny glade in a row of similar gardens, this could be just what a pair needs. Grow some dense climbers up your house wall, put some open-fronted boxes into gaps in the foliage, dig a pond and plant shrubberies or a meadow area to spawn insects, and keep your fingers well crossed!

◀ The catastrophic decline in Spotted Flycatchers may in part be due to problems on migration or on their wintering grounds in Africa. All the more reason to help them here, so that as many youngsters as possible set off on the hazardous journey.

Long-tailed Tit
Aegithalos caudatus

Perhaps the most endearing of garden birds, trooping through trees and bushes in family flocks and sometimes visiting feeders.

HOME NEEDS

Distribution: Common resident in lowland areas. Distribution rather patchier in the north and uplands. Populations can crash in bad winters.

Habitat: Deciduous woods with a good shrub layer, and areas of thick scrub and hedgerows. They are infrequent in most gardens, especially in cities.

Habits: In winter, they rove in tight-knit flocks of up to a dozen around a shared territory, often following hedgelines and rarely descending to the ground. In summer, they split into breeding pairs, often aided by young male relatives.

Food: Small insects, especially bugs and the eggs and caterpillars of moths. Increasingly, they are learning to take fat, peanuts and sunflower seeds at feeders.

Roost: They form a tight huddle along a horizontal branch in a big, dense thorn bush.

Breeding: The males of a flock find a nest site within their winter territory, so there can be several pairs within a 20ha area. Some pairs choose the fork of a tree, some nest low down in thorn bushes or gorse, and some high up in the outer foliage of conifers. The nest is an astonishing hollow 'dome', 16cm high, of moss, cobwebs, hair and lichen, lined with hundreds of feathers. They raise one brood. The 8–12 eggs are laid April–June and are incubated for 13–18 days. The young fledge 14–18 days after hatching.

So... Put out fat balls in winter, and grow trees, hedges and thorny bushes. If they choose your garden for breeding, offer some help with their nest building needs by emptying an old feather pillow!

◀ If it wasn't for its tail, this would be one of our smallest birds. Having a tiny body is a real problem in cold weather, especially for something that eats little more than insects.

Coal Tit
Periparus ater

An energetic little tit showing a close attachment to conifer trees and with unusual nesting habits.

HOME NEEDS

Distribution: Found across much of the British Isles, and quite common where habitats are suitable. Most birds are sedentary.

Habitat: A bird of coniferous woodland, especially spruce, but will use most mature conifers in gardens and churchyards. It is a common bird, too, in northern and western Sessile Oak and birch woodland.

Habits: Supreme gymnasts, Coal Tits will work their way systematically along branches to feed, often at great height, dangling from cones and investigating every spray of needles. They will sometimes hover to investigate the very outer foliage. They band together in winter with other tits, and are then most likely to be seen in gardens. Occasionally in winter they feed on the ground in woods.

◀ You can just make out the white streak down the back of the head as well as the buffy underparts that separate the Coal Tit from the larger yellow-bellied Great.

Food: Tiny insects and spiders, especially moth caterpillars and adults, plus bugs, small beetles, ants and flies. In autumn and winter, they take seeds of spruce, oaks, Beech, Sweet Chestnut and pines, and at the bird table eat peanut fragments and sunflower seeds. They will cache seeds and insects in gaps in tree bark, including squashing aphids together into an 'aphid pie'.

Roost: Varied, but especially among the snug outer sprays of conifer branches, in old bird nests or in a nook in a tree trunk, but rarely inside a hole.

Breeding: They defend a territory of 2ha or more. They make their nest in a hole in the ground or among tree roots, even among rocks, and only occasionally in a tree hole or nest box. The nest is a pad of moss lined with hair. They raise one, sometimes two, broods. The 6–12 eggs in each clutch are laid April–July and are incubated for 14–18 days. The young fledge 18–20 days after hatching.

So... If you have a mature pine or spruce in your garden, you may have resident Coal Tits. If not, a good range of feeders in winter among trees and bushes will often lead to regular visits.

Marsh Tit

Poecile palustris

A sneezing call is what usually alerts you to a Marsh Tit. Dull-coloured but with a dapper black cap, it is very much a woodland bird that hasn't moved into gardens in the way that Great and Blue Tits have. Its close cousin, the **Willow Tit** *Poecile montanus,* is even rarer in gardens.

HOME NEEDS

Distribution: Found in lowland England and Wales, avoiding urban and treeless areas and absent from Ireland and almost all of Scotland.

Habitat: Large areas of lowland deciduous woodland, preferably moist and with oaks and Beech.

Habits: They seek food in trees and shrubs, especially at lower levels and often on the ground, sometimes accompanying the tit flocks which pass through their territory.

◀ There is a risk of confusing Marsh Tits with male Blackcaps because of the tit's cap, but its white cheeks are a giveaway, as is the black chin.

Food: Insects and spiders in spring and summer, then turning to seeds, berries and nuts in winter, especially beechmast. At bird feeders, they take sunflower seeds, peanuts and hemp seeds.

Roost: Holes and nooks in trees, or sprays of conifer leaves.

Breeding: They defend a territory of about 1–5ha. They nest in a hole in a rotten tree or stump, rarely excavating it themselves, although they may enlarge it, and they occasionally use nest boxes. The nests inside are thick pads of moss, lined with hair. They raise one brood. The seven to ten eggs are laid April–May and are incubated for 13–15 days. The young fledge 17–20 days after hatching.

So... If you live very near large woods, then keep those seed feeders filled in the hope of seeing them, and do leave standing dead wood and put up a good array of nest boxes just in case it offers them extra nest site choice.

Nuthatch

Sitta europaea

A lively tree-dweller, scuttling up – and down – tree trunks, and often revealed by their excited piping calls.

HOME NEEDS

Distribution: Throughout much of England and Wales, but only as far as the Scottish borders and not in Ireland.

Habitat: Lowland woodland with lots of mature trees, especially deciduous, with dead and dying timber.

Habits: An incredibly sedentary species. They wend their way through the branches and trunks of their home ranges, winkling and hammering out food from crevices in the bark.

Food: Invertebrates such as beetles, flies, moths and caterpillars, plus tree seeds (beechmast, acorns, etc) in autumn and winter, which are cached if there is a glut. At bird tables they take seeds, peanuts and fat.

Roost: In holes in trees.

Breeding: They defend a territory of 2–5ha. They nest in holes in large trees, often many metres above the ground, or will use nest boxes. They line the nest with wood chippings and bark, and cement up the entrance with mud to the right diameter. They raise one brood. The six to eight eggs are laid April–May and are incubated for 13–18 days. The young fledge 23–24 days after hatching.

So... If you have plenty of big old trees around, keep the feeding station well stocked in winter, don't tidy old trees if it is safe to leave them and try putting up nest boxes for them.

◀ A rather compact body is what you need when most of your day is spent scurrying up and down tree trunks and noseying into every crevice around branches.

Treecreeper
Certhia familiaris

They live up to their name, expertly and endlessly shinning up mature trees.

HOME NEEDS

Distribution: A fairly common resident across almost the whole of the British Isles.

Habitat: They need lots of mature trees, visiting almost any species as long as the rough bark harbours insects, and so are mainly restricted to woodland, mature gardens and parks.

Habits: They endlessly search tree trunks and branches, often starting low and working up, even crawling beneath boughs. They sometimes travel with winter tit flocks, but hate crossing open space.

◄ The Treecreeper is bark-patterned above and snow-white below, with the most delicate curved little beak for winkling out its insect diet.

Food: Insects, especially beetles, but also flies and ants, plus spiders, caterpillars and moth eggs, and they collect aphids by squashing them together. In winter, they eat some seeds, including pine and spruce. They are very rare at bird feeders.

Roost: They snuggle into a depression in a tree trunk at about head height, sometimes communally, nibbling at a suitable site to make it a snug fit.

Breeding: They defend a territory of a few hectares. They nest behind loose bark, preferring oaks, willows, birches and elms, and will use 'nest boxes' that mimic this (a piece of bark strapped to a tree will do). Sometimes the nest is in Ivy or a tree hole. They drop dry wood, twigs, grass and needles into the nesting chink and line it with hair, lichens and moss. They raise one, sometimes two, broods. The five to six eggs in each clutch are laid April–June and are incubated for 12–20 days. The young fledge 13–17 days after hatching.

So… Nurture whatever large trees you have, and if you have the space for more trees, then get planting and help the Treecreepers of the future. If there are plenty of mature trees locally but few where the bark is flaking, then create artificial nest sites.

Jay
Garrulus glandarius

The shy dandy of the crow family that goes nuts for acorns.

HOME NEEDS

Distribution: Fairly common resident throughout much of the British Isles except the very far north of Scotland.

Habitat: Naturally a bird of dense, lowland woodland, mainly deciduous, but they will use conifer forests and some have moved into urban parks and gardens. They range more widely outside the breeding season, although rarely far from trees.

Habits: A shy bird, probably due to a long history of persecution. They live alone or in pairs, usually feeding on the ground near cover, probing about in the soil and leaf-litter, and burying excess food in moss or natural depressions in the ground for recovery later. They come to bird tables occasionally, and will even dangle from peanut feeders.

Food: Beetles, caterpillars, wasps, ants, fruit, seeds, carrion and scraps. In autumn, they are incredible acorn-hoarders, seen regularly flying to and from oaks. In spring, they raid nests for eggs, nestlings, small birds and mammals. Chicks are fed on caterpillars.

Roost: In dense cover.

Breeding: They defend a territory of 5–20ha. They nest in a tree fork, on a branch, or often in a thorny bush within a wooded area, building a rough cup of twigs well lined with mosses, leaves and grasses. They raise one brood. The four to seven eggs are laid April–May and are incubated for 16–17 days. The young fledge three weeks after hatching.

So… Their tendency to take birds' eggs and nestlings means they are not always welcome in gardens, but they are beautiful and an integral part of our natural woodland communities.

◄ The distended throat of a butterfly-winged Jay is a sure sign that it is transporting a crop-full of nuts to a winter hiding place. On the ground it is a perky salmon-pink bird, but watch for the white rump when it flies.

Magpie

Pica pica

A striking, adaptable and irrepressible bird that would probably be a great favourite were it not for its nest-robbing reputation.

HOME NEEDS

Distribution: Widespread and fairly common in suitable habitat throughout the British Isles, except where persecution is high.

Habitat: Farmland with unimproved, short, damp grassland and scattered trees, and along hedgerows and road verges. They have recently moved into many urban areas, large gardens and parks, but avoid extensive woods, open habitats and high mountains.

Habits: A sedentary bird, often seen in singles or pairs. Most are wary and keep close to cover.

Food: Opportunistic, picking most items from the ground or by probing, scratching or turning dung. Beetles are very important, together with spiders, flies, ants, leatherjackets, caterpillars, grasshoppers, carrion, scraps, and all sorts of seeds and fruits. They help clean our highways of road kill. They take some adult birds and many nestlings and eggs, especially of open-nest species, and will come to some bird tables for scraps.

Roost: In the nest or in trees nearby during the breeding season. In winter, they often use communal roosts in trees overhanging water.

Breeding: They defend a territory of about 5ha, nesting high in a dense or thorny tree, deciduous or evergreen. The nest is a big cup of sticks, usually with a roof, and lined with mud, dung, leaves, wool and hair. They raise one brood. The five to seven eggs are laid April–May and are incubated for 21–22 days. The young fledge 24–30 days after hatching.

So... If their predatory habits bother you, don't entice them with kitchen scraps intended for other birds and restrict your feeding to seed feeders. Importantly, give songbirds a helping hand by developing dense shrubberies and a surfeit of safe nesting sites.

◀ What dramatic evening wear, with white dinner jacket and extravagant tails. But are Magpies evil? No! It's meaningless to pin human moral codes on them; they are just trying to survive like every other creature.

Jackdaw

Corvus monedula

A perky and bright-eyed little crow, sociable, vocal and with a fondness for chimneys

HOME NEEDS

Distribution: Throughout the British Isles, mainly in the lowlands, but scarce in many urban areas. Many are resident, but in winter some move to lower altitudes, and some mainland British birds move to Ireland.

◀ Where there is one Jackdaw, you can usually be sure that their devoted mate is not far away, and probably several other pairs, too.

Habitat: They like areas of unimproved grazed pasture with groups of old trees rather than very open habitats or dense woods. Villages and country estates suit them well. They need an abundance of nest sites.

Habits: A sociable bird, mating for life and spending a lot of time interacting with other Jackdaws, either in trees or tumbling about in the sky.

Food: Omnivorous, taking grain, fruit, carrion, beetles, caterpillars, snails and more. They mostly feed on the ground, but will catch flying ants and ride the backs of sheep and donkeys looking for the insects they kick up. At bird feeders, they enjoy peanuts and can cling to hanging feeders.

Roost: In the nest in summer. In winter, they gather, often in large numbers, in traditional woodland sites.

Breeding: They form a loose colony. Each pair nests in a hole in a dead tree, wall or cliff, and they especially like chimneys and large nest boxes. They drop a pile of sticks into the hole and then make a rudimentary cup in it out of mud, dung, grasses and wool. They raise one brood. The four to six eggs are laid April–May and are incubated for 17–18 days. The young fledge about four to five weeks after hatching and are independent about five weeks after that.

So... Be aware of the risk of blocked chimneys if they nest there. They are big enough birds to dominate feeders, but apart from that they cause little problem in gardens and need little help. However, they won't turn their noses up at a nice new Kestrel nest box, thank you!

Rook
Corvus frugilegus

This is a rather fun, bare-faced, sociable cousin of the crows, whose nests dot countryside spinneys in the spring.

HOME NEEDS

Distribution: Resident across much of the lowland areas of the British Isles, bar most of northern Scotland.

Habitat: They need tall trees in copses and small woodlands for breeding, and open pasture and arable land for feeding, avoiding most urban areas, large forests and enclosed places.

Habits: They lead a busy social life in noisy, bustling breeding colonies (rookeries) of usually 20–80 pairs but they can be up to 1,000 pairs strong. The feeding ranges of neighbouring colonies overlap peaceably. They gather into large flocks in winter, and are most regular in rural gardens in harsh weather where they can be surprisingly agile at feeders for such a big bird.

Food: Beetles, worms, some caterpillars and leatherjackets, plus cereal grains, acorns and carrion. They almost always feed on the ground, winkling and probing in the soil or rooting through cowpats. They will cache excess food. They can be a problem in summer cereal crops, but equally may help reduce insect pests.

Roost: On the nest during the summer, but at other times they gather in woods with Jackdaws. Before going into roost, they perform tumbling flights known as a 'crow's wedding'.

Breeding: Each pair just defends its own nest, which is a wide platform of twigs containing a smaller cup of mud, leaves and twigs, lined with feathers and moss. They raise one brood. The three to six eggs are laid March–April and are incubated for 16–18 days. The young fledge 30–36 days after hatching.

So... A few large rural gardens bordered by tall trees may host a rookery. Otherwise, they will rootle around large rural lawns or drop in to scoff scraps. Few people do much to encourage them, but they rarely cause problems for gardeners.

◀ The bare white bill, purple gloss and shaggy trousers separate the Rook from the Carrion Crow, but they can be just as canny.

Carrion/Hooded Crows
Corvus corone/corvix

It can be hard to love crows. They look sinister, sound harsh and have a reputation for raiding birds' nests. They are, of course, just doing as nature intended, but it is often best not to encourage them.

HOME NEEDS

Distribution: These two closely related species share out the British Isles between them: the Hooded is found in north and west Scotland and in Ireland, the Carrion across the rest of Britain.

◀ They may be the same shape, but the all-black Carrion Crow (here) looks so different to the Hooded, which is also black but with a silvery-grey 'tank-top'.

Habitat: Open countryside with scattered tall trees, but also coastal areas and increasingly in cities and large gardens. In the north, they live on moorland too.

Habits: They tend to work alone or in small groups, strutting across pastures, tilled fields, stubbles, beaches, mudflats and parks, picking, probing, scavenging and investigating. Persecution has made them often wary of people, while small birds give them a wide berth.

Food: Omnivorous, taking plenty of insects such as beetles in spring and summer, plus eggs, nestlings, frogs, etc. In autumn, they will eat cereal grains. Carrion, such as road kill, is important in winter, and they will visit bird tables for scraps.

Roost: They gather in tall trees, often conifers, and sometimes on pylons.

Breeding: A pair's territory may be 15–50ha. They nest in the top of the tallest trees, building a stick (or bone!) foundation stuffed with moss, on top of which are twigs and roots with a wool, feather and grass lining. They raise one brood. The three to six eggs are laid April–May and incubated for 18–19 days. The young fledge 28–38 days after hatching and are independent after another three to five weeks.

So... Crows intimidate smaller birds, so you might want to be careful what you put out at bird tables so as not to draw them in. If they are a problem, exclude them by only feeding things like sunflower seeds in tubular feeders.

Tree Sparrow
Passer montanus

This is the unpredictable, shy, but ever-so-appealing, country cousin of the House Sparrow, and a species causing real conservation concern.

HOME NEEDS
Distribution: An uncommon and much declined resident in scattered lowland locations across central and eastern Britain and eastern Ireland.

Habitat: Mainly farmland where there are good mature hedgerows and copses, and often near water, sewage farms or the coast. A few come into large rural gardens but they are very rare in cities.

Habits: They are sociable all year, sometimes mixing with other sparrows and finches. Populations tend to fluctuate wildly, with colonies forming, flourishing and then disappearing just as quickly.

Food: Mainly small seeds of weeds and cereals, feeding on the ground in fields and usually close to hedgerows. At bird tables, they will take seeds but they can't de-husk sunflower seeds. In the breeding season they seek insects such as beetles, flies, grasshoppers and caterpillars.

Roost: Apart from late summer when they use dense trees and hedges near feeding areas, they tend to roost in or near their nests.

Breeding: They form a loose colony and are highly sensitive to disturbance. They nest in holes in trees, 2–5m off the ground, and readily take to nest boxes. They stuff the hole full of stems, leaves and roots, and line the nest cup with soft material including moss, wool and hair. They raise two to three broods. The two to seven eggs in each clutch are laid April–June and are incubated for 11–14 days. The young fledge 15–20 days after hatching.

So… If you have a big rural garden in a known Tree Sparrow area, then providing nest boxes, hedges, weedy vegetable plots and plenty of supplementary seed may reap very important rewards.

◀ It is only a lucky few who have Tree Sparrows in their garden – look for the warm chestnut crown and the black 'love mark' on the white cheek.

Brambling
Fringilla montifringilla

The Chaffinch's northern cousin is an exciting if erratic winter visitor to some fortunate garden bird tables.

HOME NEEDS
Distribution: A winter visitor from northern European breeding grounds to mainly eastern Britain, they arrive in varying numbers each year depending on the beechmast crop back home.

Habitat: They visit woodlands, especially mature Beech woods, and farmland with stubbles, usually staying close to the woodland edge or mature hedgerow trees.

◀ It's quite tricky telling Bramblings and Chaffinches apart, but see how the former's ruddy chest is sharply divided from its white belly, its wingbar and shoulder are rusty too, and there are freckles on its flanks. When it flies off, look out for its white rump.

Habits: They migrate from northern breeding woods in autumn, arriving in the UK from the end of September onwards, with most leaving again by March. They feed mostly on the ground and usually in flocks, regularly banding up with Chaffinches in late winter. A few sometimes end up in gardens where they will visit bird tables faithfully over several weeks. If a flock arrives, they can be quarrelsome but also nervous, taking flight into trees at the first sign of danger and then filtering back down again.

Food: Seeds, with a particular taste for beechmast, but also taking grass and cereal seeds, sometimes spruce seeds, and a few berries. They are adept at digging through snow to reach seed. At bird feeders they prefer open tables and the ground underneath where they are partial to sunflower seeds.

Roost: In flocks, preferring dense conifers and undergrowth, often many kilometres from where they may have fed.

So… Bird tables are your biggest hope of seeing Bramblings. Keep them well topped up with sunflower seeds and check out those Chaffinch flocks regularly in winter.

Goldfinch
Carduelis carduelis

Who says our garden birds aren't beautiful? This is a feisty little ray of sunshine, increasingly regular in gardens.

HOME NEEDS

Distribution: Fairly common throughout lowland areas, but only as far north as mid-Scotland. It is a partial migrant, with many British birds heading to France and Spain for the winter.

Habitat: Sheltered places, often with scattered trees, where favourite weeds grow tall and lush, such as open glades, downland, unimproved grassland, riverbanks, waste ground, thistlebeds, old allotments and large gardens. It is increasingly seen in cities.

Habits: This nomad wanders in tight-knit little flocks seeking out clumps of choice flowers that are coming into seed. Their jingling calls help others know where the food is and when it's time to move on. They are becoming more frequent at winter bird feeders.

Food: Small seeds, mainly from the daisy family (knapweeds, dandelions, thistles, etc) and Teasels, preferably half-ripe and picked straight from the plant where they are adept at clinging to stems and seedheads. They also eat pine, Alder and birch seeds in winter, buds and flowers in spring, and some caterpillars and aphids. In gardens, they enjoy nyjer seed and sunflower hearts.

Roost: In groups in dense trees and scrub.

Breeding: Pairs nest within earshot of another couple of pairs or so, and feed together in an area of 1–50ha. They nest on the swaying outer branches of trees, hidden by a branch above, and build a dinky cup of moss, grass and spiders' webs, lined with plush plant down. They raise two, sometimes three, broods. The four to six eggs in each clutch are laid May–August and are incubated for 9–14 days. The young fledge 13–18 days after hatching.

So... Seed feeders are your simplest way of holding their attention, but you can encourage them to breed, too, if you can offer suitable nesting trees and a good turnover of ripening wildflower seeds.

◀ Vibrant-costumed Goldfinches are beginning to like bird feeders as much as they like Teasels, brightening up even inner city gardens. I once saw one in the garden of No. 10 Downing Street (he says, name-dropping!).

Siskin
Carduelis spinus

A vibrant, streaky little finch that has recently become a regular sight at many bird feeders in early spring.

HOME NEEDS

Distribution: In winter they extend patchily across much of the British Isles. In summer they are a much more northerly bird, although their range expanded in the 20th century and some now breed in southern conifer plantations.

Habitat: They breed in extensive mature conifer forests, so they are usually only seen in gardens in winter. Their main winter haunts are Alders, pines and birches, often near running water.

◀ In some gardens, flocks of several dozen twittering Siskins can now gather in spring to feed up before heading back to their breeding woods. This is the male with a black crown, but all have the black-and-yellow striped wings.

Habits: They wander in hyperactive little flocks, sometimes with Lesser Redpolls, and often dangling in the treetops. They occasionally come to ground level, often to a pool or stream edge where seeds have collected. More are visiting garden feeders these days, mainly in spring.

Food: They feed their young on ripening spruce and pine seeds, and then in late summer take seeds from herbaceous plants and a few invertebrates, before switching their attention to Alder and birch seeds for much of the winter. They eventually end up at garden feeders, where they eat peanuts, nyjer seeds, hemp, linseed and sunflower hearts.

Roost: Communally in thick vegetation or conifers.

So... If you live near big forests, your garden may be visited throughout the winter. For most of us, keeping well-stocked feeders right into spring is our best chance of success as they begin to get hungry.

Lesser Redpoll
Carduelis cabaret

This acrobatic, buzzing little finch is an unusual but increasing winter visitor to garden trees and feeding stations. The 'poll' is the forehead, and is indeed as red as a ruby.

HOME NEEDS
Distribution: Much declined, it has a patchy distribution across the UK, although rare in southern parts in summer.
Habitat: In the breeding season, they are found in open woodlands with birch trees, plus young conifer plantations and heathy areas, but are very rare in gardens. In winter, many stay in their summer habitat but some move to riverside Alders and, increasingly, to gardens.
Habits: Gregarious, especially in winter, with jangling flocks of up to 30 dangling at the tips of fine branches.
Food: Throughout the winter, birch seeds are vital, which they extract with their very fine bill. They will also take Alder, Larch and spruce seeds. They sometimes feed on weed seeds on the ground, such as Tansy, nettle, thistles and Meadowsweet. They very occasionally come to seed feeders, especially nyjer.
Roost: In trees.

So... If you have space, plant a nice mature birch tree (or clump!). A stand of Tansy nearby, or a nettle-bed if you can face it, may give them extra options, but your best bet is to put out nyjer seed.

▼ Even in winter, the Redpoll retains the feature that earned it its name – a small, red mark on its forehead. Its streaky back and sides, wide pale wingbar and its little black chin also help to identify it.

▶ The female Bullfinch looks just like this male but with almost all the colour drained out of her. If you are lucky enough for a pair to take to your feeders, they may keep returning for weeks.

Bullfinch
Pyrrhula pyrrhula

The chubby male Bullfinch is one of the most vividly dressed birds, his mate a subtler version. This is a bird that has been struggling, so do all you can to help.

HOME NEEDS
Distribution: Sedentary throughout most lowland areas of the British Isles, though never common, and thinly scattered in the north.
Habitat: Large woodlands, whether mixed, coniferous or deciduous, with dense cover and sunny glades. They also like thickets and overgrown hedgerows. They often move into orchards in spring and, in winter, they mostly grace rural gardens.
Habits: Shy, retiring and unobtrusive, they are usually found in pairs or small groups, roving quietly through cover.

Food: Nettle seeds are an important part of the diet, so this is one occasion when nettles equals gardening for wildlife. In spring they love fruit blossom such as apples, plums and pears. In autumn and winter they take a wide range of seeds and berries including Ash keys and the seeds of goosefoots and docks. They take some invertebrates for their chicks, such as caterpillars and spiders, and occasionally come to feeders to take sunflower hearts.
Roost: Thick evergreens and conifers.
Breeding: Pairs don't seem to defend a territory. They nest 2–3m up in thick bushes and dense trees, often in evergreens and usually away from the main trunk. They build a cup of twigs combined with a mélange of moss, rootlets, grass, lichens, hair, wool and aromatic leaves. There are two to three broods; the three to six eggs in each clutch are laid May–July and are incubated for 12–14 days. The young fledge 15–17 days after hatching.

So... If you can, grow a thick, tall, native hedge, create a woodland garden with a good shrub layer, grow fruit trees, and develop a 'wild' area with a nettle-bed.

Yellowhammer
Emberiza citrinella

The male's 'little bit of bread and no cheese' song is a hallmark of country lanes – or *was* before numbers plummeted. It is a scarce winter visitor to mainly rural gardens.

HOME NEEDS

Distribution: Resident and widespread throughout much of Britain, but very rare in urban areas and the uplands, and disappearing in the north and west.

Habitat: They enjoy sunny and dry places with scattered shrubs and open ground, so are found in farmland hedgerows, downland and heathland. They visit just a few gardens in winter.

◄ A happy male Yellowhammer belting out his song. Females and winter males are duller with stripy heads, but retain the telltale chestnut rump, here hidden but best seen as birds fly away.

Habits: They feed on the ground in places where they can retreat quickly into cover. They gather in small flocks in winter, usually in stubble fields or where farm animals are fed.

Food: Mainly large grass seeds and cereal grains, plus weed seeds, tending to ignore oily seeds. They also eat a few insects such as beetles and caterpillars.

Roost: In reeds or in thick, low vegetation such as bramble thickets.

Breeding: Only exceptionally in gardens. In the countryside, they nest on or near the ground in thick cover or in gorse or other thick, low shrubs.

So... If you do back onto farmland, there is a chance you will draw them in if you plant a good thick hedgerow. Some rural gardeners are lucky enough to have them come to a well-stocked ground feeding station for finches and sparrows, especially on open ground near a hedge and away from the house.

Reed Bunting
Emberiza schoeniclus

A sparrow-like bunting with a fondness for marshy places. Numbers have declined, so consider yourself lucky if they visit your winter bird table.

HOME NEEDS

Distribution: Resident and widely scattered in lowland areas throughout the British Isles.

Habitat: In summer found in damp habitats with tall herbaceous vegetation, especially reeds, such as riverbanks, canals, saltmarshes and gravel pits, but also young conifer plantations. In winter they wander more widely, sometimes joining other small birds such as Chaffinches on farmland, and occasionally venturing into gardens to bird tables.

Habits: They spend most of their time feeding on the ground in dense vegetation or clinging to plant stems, but in gardens they may hop around under the bird table, on it or even on feeders.

Food: Mainly seeds, especially grasses and cereals, plus some from the chickweed, goosefoot and knotgrass families. They take insects when they can, such as caterpillars, midges and flies, and also spiders.

Roost: Usually in reeds.

Breeding: Almost never in gardens.

So... If you have a lake in your garden or a river running by it, you have a chance of seeing a Reed Bunting in the breeding season. If not, concentrate on feeding the common finches and sparrows with seed in winter and keep your fingers crossed and eyes peeled.

▲ This is a dapper male in breeding plumage with his black hood and white moustache. Females and winter males have weaker head markings but retain the pale moustache.

Migrants

As well as the long-term residents in your garden bird hotel, watch out for long-distance travellers that pitch up in the small hours desperate for a room. They're usually just after somewhere to bed down for a while, and maybe a spot of food.

Northern Europe is the flightpath for millions of these migrants. Many of them are insect-eating birds such as warblers and flycatchers that come here in summer when our countryside suits their home needs, but they then have to risk the long journey to Africa to escape our cold, insect-free winters.

They turn up in our gardens for two reasons. The first is as exhausted international arrivals. Some species migrate in giant leaps, so it is no wonder that they sometimes pitch down exhausted wherever they can after a night 'on the road'. A garden may not be ideal but it will certainly do for an hour or so.

The other occasion we may see them is at the end of the breeding season in late summer and autumn. Young birds that have been raised here don't just launch straight off for their wintering grounds but rove about a bit, getting their bearings and building up fat. Your garden may be a temporary stop-off

▼ It may be a common sight in summer farmland hedgerows, but a garden visit by a Whitethroat is a guest to savour.

in their adolescent wanderings. Some gardens are in much more favourable locations than others to receive these migrants. Anyone within a mile of the sea is well placed; anyone right on the coast is in migrant heaven.

The commonest migrants to expect are Chiffchaffs and Willow Warblers, and they often can't resist bursting into song while they're passing through. Whitethroats, Pied Flycatchers, Common Redstarts, Cuckoos and Turtle Doves are also all possible. You may even get birds well away from their normal habitat such as Reed Warblers in bushes instead of reeds.

HOME NEEDS

Migrants need the simple things you'd need on a short-stay after a long journey: food and somewhere to draw breath. They especially like dense cover, insect-rich habitats such as those around a pond, and anything that looks like a sunny woodland glade; in other words, many of the things that you do for other birds will benefit them too.

◀ Fresh in from southern Europe or northern Africa in spring, many an unobtrusive Chiffchaff will drop into gardens and stock up on insects for the day.

Rarities

Just a handful of species account for almost all of the birds seen in gardens. For example, of almost 10,000 bird records I logged in my garden over an eight year period, 91.5 per cent were of the top ten species, and 98.3 per cent were of the top 15. And just one bird record in every thousand individuals seen was of a species not covered in this book so far. But that just proves that, very occasionally, something unusual will turn up!

If you are lucky enough to have a very large or atypical garden or one in a prime location, such as on an island or headland, or with brilliant wild habitats nearby, you can expect to beat my strike rate for rare garden birds. If you have a very big garden, you may be able to create a habitat that goes beyond what we might normally think of as a true garden habitat – a large lake, for example – in which case you could have 'garden rarities' daily. But for most of us, the one in a thousand may even be one in ten thousand, or, heaven forbid, one in a million.

The good thing is that those moments are incredibly memorable. You stand agog at what fate has pitched out of the sky into your tiny patch of the world. It's like turning around on the train and finding you are sitting next to the Queen. I remember seeing a photo of a Bittern in a friend's garden. Bitterns live exclusively in reedbeds; this one was in an apple tree! It was a very cold winter, and presumably the bird was disorientated and exhausted, and just had to find somewhere to land.

Each year, there are stories similar to this as gardens play host to some of the rarest and most unlikely birds. If it happens to you, enjoy the moment – it may not happen again for a very long time! But is there anything you can do to enhance your chances of playing host to a rarity? Well, yes. By gardening for common bird species, you will create conditions that are likely to entice a stray to stay should it pass your way.

▼ It was an amazing day when I found one of these in my garden – a Yellow-browed Warbler. We know it must have come from deep within Russia – that's the closest they breed.

Supplementary Feeding

Putting out a bit of food is the single sure-fire way of bringing more birds into your garden. At times it can feel a bit like cheating, it's so easy.

To birds, it must seem like nature has created the most magical harvest. Mysterious 'pods' dangle from the trees, spilling an endless supply of highly nutritious seeds, while what to their eyes must look like flat-topped wooden stumps are topped with an food galore. Compared with the often-impoverished countryside, it can be a welcome feast.

Not that nature doesn't produce its own bird-food gluts. Think of Goldfinches visiting a stand of Teasels, thrushes flocking to berry-laden trees, or Green Woodpeckers unearthing an ants' nest. But rarely does nature produce something quite as bounteous as a bird-feeding station.

It would be nice if you could grow the seed to fill your feeders instead of having to plunder the productivity of land elsewhere, but the maths show how difficult it would be. Take sunflower seeds, for example. With good fertiliser and irrigation, farmers can get a yield of about 1,500kg of seeds per hectare. At this rate, a tennis-court-sized garden, if filled with sunflower plants, would yield about 39kg, which is less than the birds in my small garden get through in three months.

WHEN TO FEED

It was common practice when I was a kid to feed birds in the winter and not in summer. We now know that one of the key times in the year when many birds need it more than ever is through spring, right at the point when people often give up feeding. The RSPB's advice is that it is fine to feed all year round, if you like.

I'm sometimes asked if there are any downsides to feeding birds. Some people worry that it makes birds lazy, so much so that if you feed regularly but then go on holiday they will starve. Don't worry – they won't! If birds are hungry, they will follow their stomachs. Understand, too, that what may seem like 'your' pair of Blue Tits or five Greenfinches is usually just a fraction of many dozens of birds doing the rounds of your neighbourhood; they all probably know many other places to find food.

Another worry some people have is whether feeding garden birds makes them easy pickings for predators. This is a complex question, because while it is true that a feeding station will often receive regular visits by Sparrowhawks or cats, by feeding the smaller birds you actually keep them fitter and healthier and hence better able to survive not only predator attack but also disease and starvation.

The key to feeding garden birds is always to do it with care. Only put out as much as the birds need, follow the hygiene rules and always view it as supplementary food, just topping up what they will naturally find for themselves. If you do all this, then on balance the benefits of feeding should far outweigh any negatives. And of course buy your bird food from the RSPB, either from reserve shops, online, or by mail order. You are guaranteed top quality products grown and produced in environmentally friendly ways, and 100 per cent of the profits goes to conservation.

▼ Growing sunflowers is like having mini wildlife food factories, but you can augment what you produce yourself with extra supplies grown commercially.

Golden rules of bird feeding

✿ **Good hygiene is essential** A feeding station can attract large numbers of birds to a small area where diseases can spread. There is no point killing birds with kindness, so always follow the 'Birds and disease' guidelines below.

✿ **Feeding no-nos** Avoid the following: anything salted or cured; desiccated coconut; milk, and – in the breeding season – soft fat; whole peanuts, unless in a wire-mesh feeder; and bread that isn't finely crumbled.

✿ **Avoid mesh bags** Birds can get their feet and even tongues caught.

✿ **Feed little and often** Excess food can attract rats or go mouldy.

✿ **Feed somewhere quiet** Back gardens are usually better than front.

✿ **Reduce the predator risk** Feed high (in hanging feeders) if there are cats about. Ground feeding should be about 2m from the nearest bush – not so close to cover that cats can lie in ambush, but not so far that birds have nowhere safe to retreat to.

✿ **'Stepladders'** Many birds use key trees and branches to step down to feeders – watch the route they use and place your feeders at the foot of this 'ladder'.

Birds and disease

Just like us, birds are prone to all sorts of diseases, such as salmonella, avian pox and trichomoniasis. Watch for birds that are listless and fluffed up. Minimise the risks by:

✿ **Cleaning feeders and bird tables** every fortnight using mild disinfectant and hot water. We can catch some diseases from birds, although this is very rare, so wash feeders outside rather than in the kitchen sink.

✿ **Moving the location of feeders** every few weeks.

✿ **Digging over the ground** where seed has dropped.

✿ **Removing any food** that goes stale or mouldy. Never put fresh food on top of old.

✿ **If you see several poorly birds** in your garden, take the tough but responsible decision and stop feeding for at least a fortnight to allow the birds to disperse.

▲ Sometimes you don't need to be a genius to work out that your bird table is in a vulnerable position.

◄ Remember your own health, and wash your hands after handling bird feeders.

◄ I know, it's a chore, but regular cleaning of feeders is far better than risking the health of the birds you are trying to help.

▶ Hanging bird tables are an ingenious alternative to having to dig a pole into your flowerbed, but be aware they can get blown about in the wind.

▲ Modern polycarbonate feeders are great at keeping seed dry, and allowing you to feed the birds in raised locations where they are safer.

▶ By having to peck off small pieces of peanut *in situ*, these tits aren't at risk of choking their young on whole nuts.

How to feed

Seed feeders Hung from a tree or a pole, the clear polycarbonate tubes dispense seeds through small ports and keep them dry, and the wire mesh feeders are suitable for peanuts. Special nyjer seed feeders have smaller holes. The perches mean that only small finches and tits and ambitious Starlings and Jackdaws can get at the seed. Many can be fitted with a base tray to catch spilt food, although this also offers a perch for larger birds. Some feeders have suckers to stick them to windows; interestingly, feeding very close to windows is thought to cause fewer fatalities from birds striking windows than feeders a couple of metres away.

Bird table Simple is best – go for one with a surface area of about 40 x 40cm with a cleanable, smooth surface, a low rim to stop food blowing off, and gaps in the corners to allow water to run off. Avoid tables with a nest box built in – any taker will be

forced to defend it against the hordes of birds on its doorstep. Avoid tables with an integral water bowl as seed can fall in it and go mouldy. Leave the wood untreated if possible and erect it on a pole 120–180cm off the ground or hang it from a tree (but so you can still see onto it and reach it). Add a roof if you want to keep food dry but realise that it may inhibit some species from visiting, and the more elaborate the design, the more difficult they become to maintain and clean.

Live-food feeders Use a steep-sided dish (rather than one the mealworms can crawl out of!), preferably with a cover to keep the rain out, and place it either on a bird table or hang from a tree.

On the ground A mesh feeding table is a good idea, preferably raised about 5cm off the ground so that it can be cleaned more easily.

What to feed

Different birds eat different things, depending on what their beaks can handle and what they can digest. They have an uncanny knack of knowing what is good for them.

Although it is OK to put out various kitchen scraps, such as soaked breadcrumbs, crumbled pastry and broken biscuits, birds will do best if given proper bird food. For example, 100g of bread typically has around 200 calories, whereas 100g of sunflower seeds has more than 600.

There is a mind-boggling array of foods available, with many of them coming jumbled up in bird food 'mixes'. So which should you go for?

feeder mix

sunflower seeds

Top bird foods

Sunflower seeds Grown mainly in southern USA, China, India and Africa, they are well liked by many birds and are rich in protein and unsaturated oils. Black sunflower seed is softer husked than striped. Birds have to nibble the husk off and discard it, so use sunflower hearts or kibbled (coarsely crushed) hearts to cut down on the mess.

Peanuts Grown mainly in China, India, Nigeria and USA, peanuts are high in protein. Only feed whole peanuts from a wire mesh feeder (young birds can choke on large pieces), or buy peanut granules or 'nibs'. Only buy peanuts that are certified nil-detectable for aflatoxins, a fungal poison that is lethal to birds.

Nyjer (or niger) seed *Guizotia abyssinica* Fine seed that is usually imported from Africa or Asia. Especially liked by Goldfinches, Siskins and Redpolls.

Mealworms, the larvae of the Flour Beetle, are about 48 per cent protein and 40 per cent fat. You can buy them dead and dried, or keep them live in the fridge in sealed tubs fed with bran – either way they don't smell! Even larger are Waxworms, the larvae of the Greater Wax Moth. Both types are excellent for Robins and thrushes that need insect protein, but only feed live or soaked mealworms in spring and summer, rather than dried, as the chicks need the moisture.

Earthworms can be bought live in pots, but why not nurture your own in the garden?

Fat Usually available as cakes and balls of animal fat (suet, sometimes rendered as tallow) but sometimes of vegetable (soya) fat. Don't use polyunsaturated fat or butter, which can smear feathers, but grated cheese is fine. You can buy fat impregnated with seeds, berries or 'insects' (usually mealworms). Peanut cake, made with suet

peanuts

and peanut flour, is very nutritious. Only make home-made fat balls in winter, as the fat softens and goes off in warm weather (commercial fat balls are specially formulated to stay hard).

Fruit, such as raisins and sultanas, is ideal for thrushes and Robins. They are best fed on the ground unless you have pets, in which case feed from a table. Store windfall apples in autumn and put them out through the winter.

Grit/oystershell Gives female birds a source of calcium in spring to help them form eggs.

OTHER SEEDS AVAILABLE, OFTEN IN MIXES, INCLUDE:

Canary seed Small starchy seeds from an annual grass native to southern Europe but now grown mainly in Canada and Argentina.

Hemp As in cannabis. Used to be widely available as birdseed, often causing a rather dodgy crop to grow underneath the feeders!

Maize (Sweetcorn) Usually comes kibbled, cut or flaked.

Millet A number of unrelated grass species with small seeds, including Red, White, Yellow and Japanese. Enjoyed by House and Tree Sparrows, and Reed Buntings.

Oats Feed as dry porridge oats or as pinhead oats (the inside of the oat grain).

Peas Sold as 'pea chips' or split peas.

Rapeseed from Oil-seed Rape.

Rice Cooked is more readily taken than uncooked.

Sorghum/Milo/Milo maize A heavily cropping tropical grass.

Wheat Starchy, relatively low-calorie food, enjoyed by pigeons and doves.

nyger seed

canary seed

oats

table mix

Drinking and bathing

Most birds need to drink, and most need to bathe in water to keep their feathers in good condition. The solution? A birdbath! But have you ever bought one, brought it home, and then found that nothing ever seems to visit it? There could be a very good reason for that, so here are the tricks to help guarantee a steady stream of bathing beauties to your garden boudoir.

▲ Getting its feathers wet makes a bird very vulnerable, but they have to wash sometimes. Providing water in a safe location with good visibility is therefore crucial.

▶ Shallow is the rule when providing water for birds – it means birds like this Song Thrush are more likely to visit.

The golden rules of birdbaths

The puddle rule. You can pick up birdbaths from almost any garden centre, with designs to suit all pockets and tastes, from mock Grecian to modern art. But many, far too many, are designed for what we want to look at and not for what birds want to use. Garden birds like to bathe in shallow puddles (and are scared of deep water), so think of an ideal birdbath in those terms. Choose one that has gently sloping sides and is no more than about 5cm deep in the middle. So many on the market have sides that are too steep and water depths that are too deep.

Wide is best. It will allow a whole troop of Starlings to have a wild communal bath together, spray going everywhere. Try to get a birdbath at least 30cm in diameter.

Place it carefully, not too close to cover and not too far away. Birds are especially vulnerable during and after bathing. It is fine to place it on the ground if your garden is rarely visited by cats, but if Tiddles is a regular visitor, either use a birdbath on a pedestal or even a hanging dish, although they are usually rather small.

Frozen birdbath? Never apply salt or antifreeze (don't laugh, it has been known). The tip to float a ping pong or tennis ball in it (where the motion of the ball in the wind keeps an area unfrozen) works only in the lightest frosts. Your best solution is to tip out the ice and start again each morning with tepid water.

Quality will make life easier for you. Pick a birdbath that is easy to clean and that won't shatter in a frost.

Tap water is fine. Birds don't demand bottled spring water!

Keep it clean. Birds will spoil the water quite quickly. I like to give mine a quick sploosh out with the hose pipe every few days, and a good clean with dilute disinfectant followed by a thorough rinse is good practice.

And remember, often birds can get all the water they need from the food they eat, and when they can't do that they can always get it from beads of dew or from rain, puddles, gutters or all sorts of places – after all, a sparrow's sip isn't very big. Many small birds will even bathe in dew.

So if you are not visited constantly, don't give up, for there are two times when that birdbath will repay whatever money you have spent on it:

1. During very hot weather, when there's no dew and other water supplies have dried up, and

2. In very cold weather, when all other water is frozen.

So do invest in or make a birdbath, keep it filled and clean all year so that birds know it's there, and when they really need it, it will be a lifesaver.

How to make a birdbath

Here is the cheapest, easiest and most successful way I have found to give birds the perfect place for a wash-and-brush up.

You'll need:
* A galvanised dustbin lid. (Even buying the full dustbin is usually cheaper than a birdbath!).
* Four bricks
* A small amount of gravel

1. Place the bricks in a square, just smaller than the size of the dustbin lid.
2. Turn the dustbin lid upside down on the bricks. Check it is level and steady
3. Place a layer of clean gravel 2-3cm deep in the lid.
4. Fill with water to the brim. The water in the middle should be no more than about 5cm deep.

It's as simple as that!

In my dustbin-lid birdbath, I've had hours of entertainment as birds arrive and splash and thrash to their hearts' content. Blackbirds, Robins, House Sparrows, tits: often several different species visit at the same time and have a whale of a time.

If cats visit the garden, it is possible to raise the birdbath up using more bricks. You can even put a ring of holly clippings on the ground around it to deter tender-toed moggies.

Dust bathing

In hot dry weather, House Sparrows, Dunnocks and Wrens will wallow about in dust, throwing clouds of it over themselves. It probably helps get rid of mites and other parasites, and soaks up excess natural oils in the feathers. Try creating your own dusty area in part of a south-facing flowerbed.

▼ See how this House Sparrow (and his friends) have created little craters through their vigorous dust bathing.

Artificial nest sites

There's something very rewarding about watching a Blue Tit pair shuttle backwards and forwards taking green wriggling caterpillars to an unseen but twittering brood inside a little nest box that you made (or at least erected).

Nest boxes are often necessary in a garden because the natural tree and cliff holes that they mimic just aren't available, either because trees are too young, old trees have been removed, or modern building standards have forced us to seal up every possible hole in our roofspaces, walls and soffits.

Several people have asked me why the box they put up so lovingly has had no takers. Don't worry, it's probably no reflection on you – not every box gets used in its first or even second year. But it might be the wrong box in the wrong place, so hopefully this section will enable you to check that you did everything right.

But understand that, while you can feel good about putting up bird boxes, you must never then sit back thinking 'job done', because:

✿ **Boxes only serve a very limited number of species.** All those birds that don't use boxes (ie most of them) need your help just as much. Check out all their home needs and you'll see that unless you also offer all the thorny-bush, fork-of-a-tree, thick-evergreen nest sites and more, your accommodation portfolio is very limited indeed.

✿ **And there's no point having somewhere to raise your young if there's not enough food.** You need to create the right habitat to go with your box. A house with an empty larder is not a home!

What species will use boxes?

Very regular: Blue Tit
Regular: Great Tit, Robin
Regular, but could really do with lots more boxes please: House Sparrow, Tree Sparrow, House Martin, Starling
Would be more regular if the right boxes were put up: Swift
Sometimes: Great Spotted Woodpecker, Wren, Spotted Flycatcher, Pied Wagtail, Nuthatch
Special big boxes only: Owls, Jackdaw, Stock Dove

If you have any species other than these using boxes in your garden, you can feel the warm smug glow of knowing you've got something special.

▲ Blue Tits have by far been the most willing occupants of artificial nest boxes – but there are plenty of other species to try and encourage.

◄ Birds know how to spot an 'ideal home' when they see one.

▶ Having a pair of birds move into a home you've provided and raise a family is hugely rewarding, but remember this is your cue to meet their other home needs too.

The golden rules of bird boxes

CONSTRUCTION

Size matters Different species need different size boxes. Check out the size chart (page 68). Precision isn't required but close approximations are!

Materials Select exterior wood at least 15mm thick, preferably 18mm, from a Forest Stewardship Council-certified source. Alternatively 'woodcrete' boxes are available, a mix of wood shavings and cement.

It's got to be snug Ensure the joints are tight so that no rain can seep in and make sure there are drainage holes drilled in the base.

Don't make it too jazzy! You don't have to stick to a boring brown box, but don't make it so obvious that predators will spot it a mile off. How

about going for chic camouflage? Avoid nest boxes incorporated into bird tables, which can give the prospective homeowners a real headache trying to defend their territory.

No chemicals please You can treat the outside of a box with a water-based preservative, but inside should be untouched, rough wood.

Birds demand security Use a metal guard around the hole to keep Great Spotted Woodpeckers and Grey Squirrels out. And no perches beneath the hole, please – that's just an invitation to predators.

Don't put straw in nest boxes It can harbour the spores of aspergillosis, which causes lung infections in birds. Use hay or let them fill it themselves.

◄ When you see what's going on inside a nest box, you can see why the depth of the cavity is important – if the box isn't deep, the stretching chicks, raised up on their bed of moss, would be vulnerable to predators reaching in through the hole.

▲ Boxes don't have to be wood – here's one made from a substance called woodcrete – but all the rules about dimensions, drainage and location still apply. Metal is a definite no-no for nest boxes – it would get too hot.

LOCATION, LOCATION, LOCATION

Choose your location carefully A quiet part of the garden is ideal – next to your front door might be good for you but not for them. Above head height is usually better in gardens where cats are a problem, but some species do like to nest low down. You can put boxes near each other, but Robins and tits are territorial and only one box will be used per species in most gardens. The exceptions are House and Tree Sparrows, Starlings, Swifts, House Martins, Swallows and Jackdaws, which will nest colonially. Most birds need a clear flight path in.

A sunny aspect? No! To avoid fried chicks, most boxes should be placed facing somewhere between north and south-east.

Don't harm trees when erecting the box Fix the box to the tree using wire threaded through rubber tubing, or at a push use galvanised screws.

When to put it up? Autumn is best, to allow birds to familiarise themselves with it, but there is no absolute rule. Just be prepared that if you put one up in spring, it may not be used until the following year.

LOOKING AFTER YOUR BOX

Clean it out every couple of years, anytime from September to January, but I recommend September or October, as later in the winter birds are more likely to be using the box for roosting. Remove the nesting materials using gloves and discard any unhatched eggs (which is quite normal). Blast the inside of the box with boiling water to kill parasites. Let it dry thoroughly before putting it back up.

And don't look in the box while it is in use! Your only safe way to see what is going on is to install a box with a little remote camera.

Spring bedding sale... As well as feeding birds, do you put out nesting materials in spring? Feathers, sheep's wool, human hair, hay, dog and cat combings – all will be gratefully taken back to the box.

◀ Here I've tied my homemade Blue Tit box to a tree rather than hammering in nails, although I'll still need to go back to loosen the wires as the tree grows.

◀ Oops. How to break all the rules of a nest box: close to feeders, swaying in the wind and sun, and the wrong dimensions! Yet, amazingly, this box was used by Blue Tits, presumably because nothing better was available.

Nest box size chart

Whether making your own box or buying one, here are the all-important sizes you need to encourage different species. Brilliant small boxes are available to buy very cheaply, but if you do want to make your own, use galvanised nails or screws. For hole nest boxes, you will need a special drill bit designed for the purpose, without which making that hole is a bit tricky! All timber should be 15mm thick at least, and the box draughtproof.

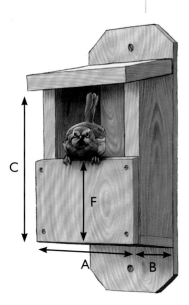

NEST BOXES WITH ROUND HOLES

The depth from the hole down to the base of the box is crucial. I see far too many boxes for sale that are just not suitable. If the box isn't deep enough, it is that much easier for a predator to reach in and get the nestlings, that's if the box ever gets used in the first place.

Species	A x B x C	D	E
Blue Tit and Coal Tit	15 x 15 x 20cm	25mm	13cm
Great Tit and Tree Sparrow	15 x 15 x 20cm	28mm	13cm
House Sparrow and Nuthatch	15 x 15 x 20cm, or a terrace of 3 boxes together.	32mm	13cm
Starling	18 x 15 x 25cm	45mm	17cm
Jackdaw	30 x 30 x 40cm	150mm	20cm
Great Spotted Woodpecker	15 x 15 x 40cm Fill the box with a block of balsa wood or stuff with wood chippings.	50mm	28cm
Green Woodpecker	18 x 18 x 45cm Fill the box with wood chippings.	60mm	35cm

NEST BOXES WITH AN OPEN FRONT

Although some bird species prefer a nest box design like this, you can imagine how vulnerable the chicks and eggs are inside. The placement of these kinds of boxes is crucial – in open view just isn't suitable. So don't go putting them on a bare tree trunk as you would with a tit box, but hide it well behind thick vegetation or in among creepers.

Species	A x B x C – all 15 x 12 x 20cm	F
Robin	Place low in thick cover.	10cm
Pied Wagtail	Works best set into a wall.	10cm
Wren	Place low in thick cover.	15cm
Spotted Flycatcher	Place with good shelter above but good visibility.	6cm

Unusual boxes

All of these are proven to work, but all will require tall ladders, a head for heights and, in the case of the larger boxes, considerable strength to hoick them to their required position.

▼ Swift

By far the best option is a specially-made hollow brick that can be inserted into the shell of your building. Alternatively, and more easily, fix wooden (or woodcrete) boxes under the eaves, but they are much less frequently used.

▼ Swallow

A moulded shallow cup for a beam in an open outhouse or barn.

▼ House Martin

A moulded deep cup on a backing board with a half-circle entrance, 60mm wide and 25mm deep. Place under the eaves (so that the top of the cup is tightly closed) with a clear flightpath in, and not aligned over a doorway, path or window because of their droppings.

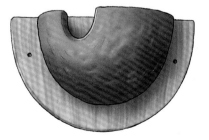

▼ Treecreeper

A slim wedge-shaped box with a 25mm radius 'quarter circle' in the top back corner. Front of box 15 x 20cm, and 10cm deep at the top. Alternatively, strap a piece of bark to a tree.

▲ Kestrel

A box (usually wooden, but moulded version shown), about 30cm wide x 30cm high x 50cm deep with overhanging canopy, half-open front and a broom-pole perch jutting in front. Site either in a tree or even on a tall pole.

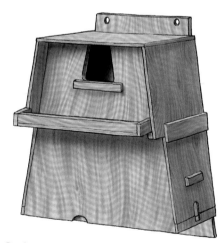

▲ Barn Owl

Usually a large wooden box, 45cm wide x 45cm high x 60cm deep, with a 23cm x 23cm hole and a 'patio' area. The inside has a dark 'back room', without which the adults feel too vulnerable. Shown is an alternative, with entrance at the top. Place in an undisturbed outbuilding up on a beam or in a tree.

Gardening for Butterflies

Running the birds a close second in the popularity stakes, butterflies seem to have it all – beautiful colours, a gentle manner and the evocation of lazy, summer days. How could you fail to want more of them in your garden?

As a gardener, you can make plenty of quick and easy gains, boosting both the number of species and the number of individuals that you regularly see in your garden.

Because they are so popular, and because different species require noticeably different things, the following pages look at the 21 commonest garden species in more detail, starting with some of the most glamorous and obvious ones, but it is worth us first taking a quick peek at the most important needs that all butterflies share.

▼ Nectar is the obvious home need for butterflies, but choosing the right flowers is a skill, and delivering all their other needs is an added and exciting challenge.

HOME NEEDS

Distribution: About 60 species of butterfly are recorded regularly in the British Isles, but this is just a fraction of the 380 recorded in Europe. I'm afraid the further north you live, the fewer species you will find: some that are as common as muck in southern England are completely absent in Scotland, and several species never made it to Ireland either.

Habitats: Most butterflies are countryside lovers in places where habitats are, by and large, semi-natural. Many are restricted to special habitats such as chalk downland or extensive ancient woodland.

Habits: Some species are migratory, covering huge distances so you will never be able to give them a year-round home. Others live in tight-knit colonies where each individual may only need a few square metres of good habitat, but can only survive if all its friends have their own few square metres too. It means that a colony may need far more space than your garden alone can offer.

Shelter: During the day, butterflies are just as keen sun-worshippers as we are, so they will often congregate in warm sun-traps. The adults also need somewhere to rest overnight or escape from the rain. The caterpillars are also vulnerable, often hiding deep in grass, and when they pupate they are little more than mush trapped in a bite-sized case and so need somewhere undisturbed while they undergo their amazing transformation. And all butterflies must survive the winter in some form, with many hibernating as caterpillars but a few enduring the dark, cold nights as adults.

Caterpillar foodplants: The most important food to provide for butterflies is that for their caterpillars. They are leaf eaters, but are fussy, often only eating those of one particular plant species.

Adult nectar plants: Be aware that butterflies don't always need nectar – some are much more intent on finding a mate. But those that do like to drink have clear preferences in terms of the flowers they visit, so pick your plants carefully. Many brochures and garden centres highlight plants they claim are good for butterflies, but you can't always believe the hype. See page 82 for a plant list that is based on proven observation, not wishful thinking. And always remember that butterflies like to have their favourite flowers planted en masse, not just the odd one here and there.

So... Gardening for butterflies involves creating sunny hotspots and filling them – yes, *filling* them – with the right nectar flowers and the right caterpillar foodplants for the right species.

Red Admiral

Vanessa atalanta

This is one of our largest, most familiar and striking butterflies, and there's plenty you can do to give them a helping hand.

HOME NEEDS

Distribution: A strong migrant, reaching most of the British Isles each year from southern Europe, but numbers vary.

Habitat: Found in almost any flower-rich habitat, such as hedgerows, unimproved grasslands, woodland rides, coasts, heaths and riverbanks, with sunny gardens a favourite.

Habits: A bold butterfly, easy to watch, often basking in the sun. The first migrants arrive in spring, with more waves of immigrants following. By autumn, 'home-grown' youngsters mix with newcomers, and some attempt to migrate back to the Continent.

Flight season: Those seen in early spring have often overwintered. Migrants arrive from April and can then be seen in any month, usually peaking in autumn, with a few seen as late as December.

Hibernates as: Adult, in rather open locations such as tree trunks, but only a few survive our winters. Some caterpillars are also now surviving in milder parts of the country.

Caterpillar foodplants: Stinging Nettle, especially sunny beds with vigorous growth. May sometimes use Annual Nettle and Pellitory-of-the-wall. The caterpillars fold nettle leaves into a tent where they feed, but they are heavily parasitised by ichneumon flies.

Adult nectar plants: As the year progresses, they come ever more readily to nectar, especially Ivy, Hemp Agrimony (and other *Eupatoriums*), *Verbena bonariensis*, Michaelmas daisies, Marjoram, *Escallonia bifida* and Iceplant. Also uses Red Valerian, *Abelia*, Devil's-bit Scabious, Coneflower, Teasel, brambles, thistles and *Lysimachia clethroides*. They are fond of over-ripe blackberries, apples and plums, will sip at sap and love banana mush!

So... This is one occasion when you might consider gardening for nettles! If not, then a good spread of its preferred nectar flowers and a dollop of mashed banana will work wonders.

◀ To attract Red Admirals in autumn, pummel a ripe banana within its skin until it feels mushy, cut some slits along it, and put it out in a sheltered sunny position – they will stay for hours drinking the juice.

Peacock

Inachis io

Four eyes stare unblinkingly at you from this striking and noisy – yes, noisy – butterfly.

HOME NEEDS

Distribution: Found throughout much of the British Isles except in mountain areas and northern Scotland. It is scarcer in the north but increasing its range.

Habitat: Mainly a butterfly of sunny, flower-rich woodlands and hedgerows, coming frequently into gardens, especially rural ones.

Habits: A wanderer, travelling short distances to find food and nettle-beds. In spring, they feed in the morning and then males take up territory in suitable warm corners to wait for a mate. In autumn, they nectar greedily, somewhere near a spot they have chosen to hibernate. They can 'hiss' if startled, flashing their eye-spots to try to scare you.

◀ One of the first butterflies of spring, Peacocks often bask on bare ground to soak up the weak sun.

Flight season: Overwintering adults emerge on warm spring days from March onwards and can still be on the wing in June. The summer brood emerges from July onwards, hibernating from September.

Hibernates as: Adult, in hollow trees and crevices in walls.

Caterpillar foodplants: Stinging Nettle – females lay large egg batches on vigorous plants. The caterpillars spin communal webs but are prone to attack by parasitic wasps. They pupate in trees.

Adult nectar plants: Especially thistles, *Inulas* and Iceplant. Also Michaelmas daisies, dandelions, *Abelia*, *Osmanthus*, Marjoram, *Lysimachia clethroides*, gayfeathers, Teasel, *Verbena bonariensis*, Purple Loosestrife, Red Valerian, lavenders, brambles, knapweeds, Coneflower, Hemp Agrimony and spring blossom such as sallows and Blackthorn.

So... Another butterfly for which you'll need a meaty nettle-bed in a choice position to get them to breed. Providing the adults with plenty of nectar in both spring and autumn may be your preference!

Small Tortoiseshell
Aglais urticae

Once a common butterfly, their populations have nose-dived especially in the south due to a parasite, so give them what help you can.

HOME NEEDS

Distribution: Throughout the British Isles, where it was once abundant but is now much reduced.

Habitat: Wherever there are nettle-beds and flower-rich habitats, so this is a butterfly of farmland, scrub, waste ground and gardens.

◀ It is a joy to see adults: a parasitic wasp is thought to have played a large part in the species' decline.

Habits: In spring and summer, they wander the countryside, looking for suitable nettle-beds where the males set up territory and watch attentively for females. Some even migrate northwards.

Flight season: Overwintering adults fly during March–May. The first brood then emerges in June–July, and in the south these lead to a second brood in August–October that then hibernates.

Hibernates as: Adult, in sheds and barns. It is too warm in houses, so release them if they get in.

Caterpillar foodplants: Nettles – Stinging and Annual. Females carefully choose fresh growth on large, sunny, sheltered beds for batches of up to 100 eggs. The caterpillars spin a communal web, but can succumb to ichneumon wasp and tachinid fly parasites.

Adult nectar plants: They feed avidly, especially in autumn, on thistles, Michaelmas daisies and Iceplant, but also Ivy, Red Valerian, Coneflower, Water Mint, Marjoram, dandelions, Tansy, Hemp Agrimony, knapweeds, lavenders, brambles, zinnias, Common Ragwort, Inulas, Common Privet, hedge veronicas, *Verbena bonariensis*, scabiouses, Coltsfoot and blossom such as sallows and Blackthorn.

So… Getting them to breed isn't easy. You need a large nettle-bed in a sunny position, and you also need to cut it back in midsummer to provide fresh growth. Providing nectar is far easier – fill those flower borders with the suite of beautiful flowers they love.

Comma
Polygonia c-album

The loss of so many hopfields where they once bred has dented the fortunes of this golden butterfly with ragged-edged wings, but, encouragingly, it appears to be on the rebound.

HOME NEEDS

Distribution: Southern Britain as far as Yorkshire; not present in Ireland.

Habitat: They like to be near trees, so prefer woodland edges and country lanes, coming regularly to gardens.

Habits: Solitary; they wander around their local ranges without ever straying too far, spending time basking in the sun, up in a tree or even on the ground.

Flight season: They emerge from hibernation in March–April, find a mate, and the females then lay their eggs. The earliest caterpillars of this brood to pupate emerge as a brighter-coloured summer generation in July–August and produce an autumn brood. Late spring caterpillars hatch in August–September.

Hibernates as: Adult, in the dry parts of woods.

Caterpillar foodplants: Hop and Stinging Nettle.

Adult nectar plants: Feeds most avidly in autumn, favourites being Ivy, Michaelmas daisies and Iceplant. Also uses *Inulas*, *Verbena bonariensis*, brambles, thistles, lavenders, Coneflower, globe thistles, scabiouses and Hemp Agrimony; in spring, they visit Blackthorn and sallows. Special favourites are over-ripe blackberries and plums, on which they will guzzle until drunk. They also drink sap.

So… Grow Hop plants and let them scramble through hedges and trees. The funky caterpillars usually pupate dangling under the leaves, and so you can watch the life cycle from egg to adult. Back this up with a range of nectar plants and rotting fruit and you should be well rewarded.

◀ Soaking up the sun, the Comma is a splash of deep orange on a spring morning, but when it closes up its jagged-edged wings it looks just like a dead leaf.

Large White
Pieris brassicae

This is one butterfly that can really be a menace in your vegetable garden, but give it nasturtium to distract it and you can learn to love it.

HOME NEEDS

Distribution: Throughout the British Isles.
Habitat: Gardens, allotments, farms and sunny woodland rides. Very common in gardens.
Habits: They wander freely from garden to garden, with resident populations boosted by immigrants from southern Europe. The females are egg machines, laying clumps like massed tiny orange skittles on the underside of cabbage leaves. The black-and-yellow caterpillars feed en masse, turning plants to a skeleton. They taste of mustard, which puts birds right off, but it doesn't deter parasitic wasps one jot; their larvae grow inside the living caterpillars.
Flight season: The spring generation flies April–June, the second generation from late July–September, and often there is a third generation in autumn.
Hibernates as: Chrysalis.
Caterpillar foodplants: Cultivated brassicas (cabbages, sprouts, kale, broccoli, Oilseed Rape), and also Nasturtium.
Adult nectar plants: They mostly feed in summer and autumn, especially on *Verbena bonariensis*, Red Valerian and lavenders, plus Marjoram, thistles, scabiouses, knapweeds, Teasel, burdocks, dandelions, brambles, Dame's Violet, ragworts, Michaelmas daisies and hawkbits.

So... If you have cabbage-growing neighbours, obviously refrain from spawning thousands of Large Whites. But if there's no-one to upset, grow a sacrificial cabbage or some nasturtium in the flower border and enjoy following the life cycle. If they are a problem in your vegetable patch, monitor your plants and wipe any eggs off the leaves with your fingers for an easy organic solution.

◀ The extensive black tips of the upper forewing (which here show through to the underside like grey-green shadows) separate the Large White from the Small.

Small White
Pieris rapae

The Small White often gets lumped in with its big cousin, the Large, under the title 'cabbage white'. However, while the Small White's caterpillar also munches at cabbages, it differs in that it is less destructive, and is edible to birds and beetles.

HOME NEEDS

Distribution: Throughout the British Isles.
Habitat: Gardens, farms, sunny woodlands, especially in nice sheltered spots. Common in gardens.

◀ For a butterfly that looks so similar to the Large White, the Small has quite a different strategy when it comes to laying its eggs.

Habits: Like the Large White, we see a mix of locally bred Small Whites plus migrants from further south. Males and females wander nomadically, and the eggs are laid individually. The green caterpillar doesn't store up poisons like the Large White but, at first, hides deep in the plant's heart and later relies on its camouflage. However, they are discovered by many predators including tits, thrushes, harvestmen and beetles.
Flight season: The first brood flies April–June; the second from late July–September. There is often a third brood in autumn.
Hibernates as: Chrysalis.
Caterpillar foodplants: Cultivated brassicas and Nasturtium, and they will use wild brassicas such as Garlic Mustard and Charlock.
Adult nectar plants: As Large White, plus forget-me-nots.

So... Whatever you do to help the Large White will work for the Small. So go on, grow sacrificial cabbages in among your prize dahlias and create quite a talking point!

Painted Lady
Vanessa cardui

A glamorous if unpredictable visitor, all the way – would you believe it – from Africa! If you want proof that nature knows no boundaries, here it is.

HOME NEEDS

Distribution: In a good year, they can seem to be everywhere; in a bad year, few reach us.

Habitat: They like warm, dry, open habitats such as downland, sunny woodlands, dunes, flowery meadows and gardens.

Habits: Painted Ladies never hibernate. Instead, huge numbers hatch in North Africa in the spring and head north across Europe, breeding as they go. However, almost none survive our winters.

Flight season: With a good wind from the Sahara, the first arrive in February, but few usually reach us before May. Subsequent generations can then be seen right through till October.

Hibernates as: It doesn't!

Caterpillar foodplants: Almost always uses thistles, such as Musk, Spear and Creeping.

Adult nectar plants: Nectars freely, especially from summer onwards, at *Verbena bonariensis*, Red Valerian, knapweeds, scabiouses, Teasel, Marjoram, Ivy, Iceplant and thistles.

So... It is tempting to grow thistles for the caterpillars, but they are such a pernicious and widespread weed that you are excused if you don't – hopefully some are growing nearby. Instead, offer loads of good nectar sources for the adults as a good compromise.

◀ 2009 was a bumper year for the Painted Lady, with millions emerging from the Atlas Mountains in early spring, and sweeping north into almost every garden in Britain.

Brimstone
Gonepteryx rhamni

Possibly the 'butter-coloured fly' that gave us the word 'butterfly', this is a real harbinger of spring in southern areas.

HOME NEEDS

Distribution: Has a distinctly southern and lowland range in Britain, with few found north of Yorkshire or Cumbria. Has a scattered distribution in central Ireland.

◀ Brimstones only ever settle with their wings closed. This is the female, almost white with a hint of limey-yellow, but even the males don't reveal their sunshine-yellow upperwings until they fly.

Habitat: Sunny woodland glades and rides, hedgerows and country lanes. Fairly common in gardens.

Habits: The males emerge from hibernation on warm spring days and rove nomadically along hedgerows and woodland edges seeking the pale females, who wait coyly in the undergrowth. They have a brief, ecstatic, soaring courtship, after which the female goes seeking buckthorn trees. Adults roost by mid-afternoon.

Flight season: Hibernators emerge March–June. The summer generation flies August–September.

Hibernates as: Adult, often in the evergreen cover of thick Ivy, Holly or brambles.

Caterpillar foodplants: Purging Buckthorn and Alder Buckthorn only. The eggs are laid on young trees in sunny situations.

Adult nectar plants: In spring, they visit woodland flowers such as Bluebell, grape hyacinths, Primrose, Cowslip and sallow blossom. The summer brood feeds more avidly, using Teasel, Purple Loosestrife, thistles, scabiouses, knapweeds, Runner Bean and Betony.

So... If you live in the right area, growing one of the caterpillar's two foodplants is nigh on compulsory for a wildlife-friendly gardener! Also train Ivy up a tree for hibernation, and grow a range of the right nectar flowers in your border. Look, too, for a wilder, sunny spot where you can grow a flush of Teasel and Marsh Thistle.

Green-veined White
Pieris napi

Easily dismissed as just another 'cabbage white', the Green-veined is a delicate, innocuous butterfly that seeks choice wild weeds rather than your prize cabbages for its caterpillars.

HOME NEEDS

Distribution: Throughout the British Isles except in the highest mountains and Shetland. They are uncommon in urban areas, and rarely abundant anywhere.

Habitat: Damp sheltered hedgerows, ditches and woodland rides. Fairly common in gardens.

Habits: On hatching in spring, the males flutter weakly in search of females. Once mated, the female seeks out tender leaves of the caterpillar foodplants in a trembling, dithering flight, oblivious to your approach. Eggs are laid singly, so there are no infestations of caterpillars as with Large White.

Flight season: The first generation flies April–June, the second July–August. There is sometimes a small autumn emergence, and northern and upland populations may have just one generation in June–July.

Hibernates as: Pupa.

Caterpillar foodplants: The leaves of Garlic Mustard, Lady's Smock, Hedge Mustard, Charlock and Watercress. Various other crucifers are sometimes used.

Adult nectar plants: Not especially big drinkers, but they will use a range of plants including Garlic Mustard, Lady's Smock, Dame's Violet, Honesty, Bugle, Field Scabious, brambles, *Verbena bonariensis*, Hemp Agrimony and Marjoram. They sometimes sup from muddy puddles for minerals.

So… Growing clumps of the caterpillars' foodplants in a sheltered, damp part of the garden is almost certain to be successful.

◀ The 'green veins' in their name are on the underwings, but even seen from above the veins appear as a delicate grey tracery and are characteristic.

Orange-tip
Anthocharis cardamines

A beautiful butterfly, the first male indicates that spring is here, the last signals that spring is over.

HOME NEEDS

Distribution: Throughout much of the British Isles, but scarce in the north, and absent from most upland areas. Uncommon in towns.

Habitat: Country lanes, open woodlands and edges, ditches and wet meadows. Fairly common in rural gardens.

◀ The female Orange-tip (top) lacks the bright wing markings of the male (below), making her even less conspicuous to add to her already secretive nature.

Habits: The males hatch on warm days in April and May and wander for miles along hedges and ditches in search of shy females. They form more cohesive loose colonies in the north. Once mated, the females quickly seek out large, vigorous foodplants to lay their eggs, one per plant. The caterpillars eat the flowers and developing seedpods.

Flight season: April–June.

Hibernates as: Pupa.

Caterpillar foodplants: Garlic Mustard and Lady's Smock.

Adult nectar plants: Lady's Smock and Garlic Mustard, plus can also be found at a range of mainly woodland flowers such as Bugle, Pignut, forget-me-nots, Wild Strawberry, Primrose and Bluebell.

So… It is all down to that duo of caterpillar foodplants: if you don't have either growing lushly in damp, sheltered places, any visits the adults make will be flying ones!

Holly Blue
Celastrina argiolus

You can easily help this radiant and high-flying beauty breed in southern gardens, even in city centres.

HOME NEEDS
Distribution: Throughout England and Wales as far north as the Lake District. In Ireland, mainly in the east and south.
Habitat: Shrubs, woodland edges and gardens in sunny sheltered locations.
Habits: Flits alone over the tops of bushes, wandering from garden to garden and easily vaulting the tallest of hedges and fences. Alights on sunny leaves. Rarely comes down to ground level except to sip minerals from muddy puddles. Populations fluctuate wildly due to the caterpillars being attacked by a type of small parasitic wasp.

◄ A rare glimpse of the upperside of the Holly Blue. It usually settles with its wings closed revealing the distinctive silvery ground colour underneath, flecked black. This is a male – the female has thick black tips to the upper forewing.

Flight season: Two generations: April–June and July–August. In warm years, there can be a small third generation in October in the south. Sometimes in the north there is just one extended generation.
Hibernates as: Pupa.
Caterpillar foodplants: The spring generation usually lays eggs on Holly, where the caterpillar feeds on flower buds, leaves and old berries. Second generation eggs are laid mainly on Ivy, the caterpillar feeding on the young berries, but also on Dogwood, Spindle, gorses and Snowberry.
Adult nectar plants: They only occasionally visit flowers, such as Hemp Agrimony, Mexican Orange Blossom and Green Alkanet, spending far more time drinking honeydew from the tops of trees.

So... For almost guaranteed success within their range, grow female Holly bushes in a sunny place, with a male bush nearby to ensure berries are formed, and allow Ivy to scramble into a sunny position where it can flower and fruit.

Common Blue
Polyommatus icarus

A stunning jewel of a butterfly. Although it is the commonest blue in the countryside, it is quite difficult to cater for in gardens but well worth the effort.

HOME NEEDS
Distribution: Scattered throughout most of the British Isles, but scarcer in the north. However, much of the countryside is now unsuitable for it.
Habitat: 'Unimproved' grassy places in the lowlands, such as downland, old pasture, verges, quarries, dunes, open woodlands and clifftops, with areas of long and short grass. Uncommon in gardens.
Habits: They live in colonies spread over half a hectare or more, with only a few individuals wandering beyond its boundaries, and rarely fly higher than knee height. Males defend their own personal patch from atop grasses and flowers, waiting for rivals or females to pass. At night, colonies often roost communally, heads downwards on grass stems.
Flight season: In the south, the first generation flies mid-May–mid-June, the second late July–September, with sometimes a small third generation in October. In the north, there is often only one generation, flying during June–August.
Hibernates as: Caterpillar.
Caterpillar foodplants: Mainly Common Bird's-foot Trefoil leaves. Also uses Black Medick, Lesser Trefoil, Common Restharrow and Greater Bird's-foot Trefoil. Eggs are laid on young fresh growth.
Adult nectar plants: Common Ragwort, Marjoram, Common Bird's-foot Trefoil, knapweeds and Devil's-bit Scabious.

So... The key is to have enough flower-rich grassland full of Bird's-foot Trefoil to support a colony. So you either need a garden large enough, or for your mini-meadow to augment meadows and verges nearby, in which case why not get cooperative with your neighbours?

◄ A dazzling male. Female Common Blues are brown above, with usually just a hint of blue where the wings meet the body.

Speckled Wood

Pararge aegeria

The wings look as if dappled with weak sunlight, perfect for this shade-loving butterfly.

HOME NEEDS

Distribution: Common over much of southern Britain and throughout Ireland, but absent from most upland areas and in Scotland except for a patchy distribution in the west and the Great Glen.

Habitat: Deciduous woodlands, preferring a fairly closed canopy where shafts of sunlight spotlight the woodland floor and small areas of woodland grasses grow. Fairly common in gardens.

◀ A typical posture for a Speckled Wood, wings open in a sunny sheltered position among the leaves of a tree, looking as dappled as the light around it.

Habits: They live in loose colonies where males guard a sunbeamed territory, either taking up static sentry duty or patrolling up and down, waiting for a female to venture out. All spend lots of time up in the canopy.

Flight season: The first generation flies April–June, with those that overwintered as pupae emerging first. There is a second generation in late summer and often a third in autumn, with such extended emergence periods that adults can be seen on the wing in almost every week from April to October.

Hibernates as: Caterpillar or pupa.

Caterpillar foodplants: Generally coarse wild grasses such as Cocksfoot, False Brome and Yorkshire Fog.

Adult nectar plants: Occasionally comes to brambles, dandelions and Hemp Agrimony, ripe blackberries and windfall fruit, but happiest at honeydew.

So... Do you have big, deciduous trees where you can create the feel of a patch of woodland and grow native coarse grasses sparsely underneath? It doesn't really matter which trees – in my garden, they're very happy with honeydew-rich Sycamores.

Gatekeeper

Pyronia tithonus

Resplendent in chocolate and gold, this familiar face of high summer along southern country lanes has a bit of a weakness for Marjoram.

HOME NEEDS

Distribution: In a sharp divide, they are common (but declining) south of the Pennines but absent from most of northern England and all of Scotland. In Ireland they are only found in the south.

Habitat: Grassy places with bushes, especially hedgerows, woodland rides and scrubby downland, and where the grasses grow tall. Fairly frequent in gardens, but scarce in urban areas.

Habits: Males flutter slowly along hedgerows within their loose colony looking for females, rarely leaving the cosy shelter of sunny shrubs. In a good year, there can be hundreds in choice habitats. Males and females often sit soaking up the sun and taking nectar, while in woodland they fly to treetops for honeydew.

Flight season: Mid-July–August.

Hibernates as: Caterpillar.

Caterpillar foodplants: A range of wild grasses including bents and fescues, ie not what most people have in their lawn. They especially like tall patches of grass growing in the sunny lee of bushes.

Adult nectar plants: They adore Marjoram, but are also partial to Common Ragwort, Common Fleabane and brambles. They will use scabiouses, knapweeds, lavenders, sea hollies and thistles. The only have short proboscies, so can't feed from tubular flowers.

So... If Gatekeepers breed in suitable habitat nearby, then a few are likely to potter through your garden each year, and a Marjoram plant or two will be much appreciated. If you have space for a mixed hedge next to a meadow area, there is every chance they will adopt the garden as part of their colony's home.

◀ This female Gatekeeper is feeding on the much-favoured Common Fleabane. Similar to the Meadow Brown, note the telltale orange patch on the rear upperwing.

Meadow Brown
Maniola jurtina

It may be the commonest butterfly of meadows – in fact probably the commonest butterfly full stop – but changes in the countryside mean that numbers are not what they used to be.

HOME NEEDS

Distribution: Widespread and abundant resident throughout the British Isles except the highest mountains and the far north.

Habitat: Warm grasslands where wild grasses grow fairly tall interspersed with wildflowers, such as in hay meadows, verges, woodland rides and hedgerows. They regularly wander into gardens, although rarely get a chance to breed there.

◄ They might be one of our dullest-coloured butterflies, but if a colony forms in your garden it is a sign that you are well on track to creating a healthy meadow habitat. This is a female; males lack the orange patch on the upper forewing.

Habits: They live in large colonies, the males bobbing through the grasses looking for females, even in dull weather.

Flight season: One long season June–October.

Hibernates as: Caterpillar, deep in the grass.

Caterpillar foodplants: Medium and fine-leaved wild grasses such as bents, fescues, False Brome, meadow-grasses and ryegrasses.

Adult nectar plants: They are especially fond of knapweeds, scabiouses, Creeping Thistle and brambles, also coming regularly to ragworts, Red Valerian, Tansy, Common Fleabane, lavenders and Marjoram, and sometimes at Coneflower and Hemp Agrimony.

So... Yes, you can grow flowers in your borders that will waylay an individual or two wandering from their colony, but creating a wildflower meadow is the big goal and could mean that you entertain dozens and their offspring.

Ringlet
Aphantopus hyperantus

This dark-chocolate butterfly is easily mistaken for the Meadow Brown, until you bend down and spot the exquisite chain of eye-spots all the way down its underwing.

HOME NEEDS

Distribution: Found throughout much of the British Isles, although absent from north-western England and northern Scotland. Infrequent in urban areas.

Habitat: Moist tall grasslands, often with some shade as in woodland rides or along hedge-side ditches, and especially on clay soils. Uncommon in gardens.

Habits: A colonial species, males bob weakly through tall grasses in search of females, even in cloudy weather, often pausing to rest on grass stems and leaves. The females drop their eggs seemingly randomly into tall grasses while in flight!

Flight season: Late June–early August.

Hibernates as: Caterpillar.

Caterpillar foodplants: Coarse wild grasses such as Cocksfoot, False Brome, Common Couch and Tufted Hair-grass.

Adult nectar plants: Not the most eager of feeders, but uses brambles, thistles, Saw-wort, Hemp Agrimony, and will sometimes come to *Inulas*, Tansy, Coneflower, ragworts, scabiouses, Wild Privet, knapweeds and sea hollies.

So... A few clumps of the Ringlet's preferred grasses won't satisfy a colony, and you will need to be within spitting distance of an existing population for a few individuals to stray into your garden and set up home. But if you are in a suitable damp location and have the space, then let wild grasses grow tall along hedgerows and around bushes.

◄ Ringlets take the idea of adorning yourself with false eyes to the extreme. It is designed to startle predators, or make them peck at the wing rather than the vulnerable real eyes.

Wall Brown

Lasiommata megera

This is a sun-worshipper extraordinaire, seeking out the best-baked spots to raise its body temperature. You'd think it would be doing well with climate change, but its range has shrunk dramatically, so help is welcome.

HOME NEEDS

Distribution: A scattered resident throughout much of lowland England, Wales and Ireland, but now much declined and absent from many inland areas in the south. In Scotland it is only found in a few southern coastal areas.

Habitat: Unimproved grassy areas where the vegetation is short, the terrain bumpy, and there is exposed bare ground and rocks, such as coastal cliffs, grassy heaths, wasteground and downland. Fairly regular in sunny gardens in core parts of their range. Males perch, wings open, on sunny tracks, stones and, of course, walls. If disturbed, they fly strongly for 20 metres or so, before dropping back down. Females lay their eggs where the turf is broken.

Habits: They live in loose colonies of just a few dozen individuals.

Flight season: Two generations, May–June and July–September, with an occasional third brood in warm years in October.

Hibernates as: Caterpillar in the grass.

Caterpillar foodplants: Wild grasses such as False Brome, Cocksfoot, Tor-grass, Yorkshire Fog and Wavy Hair-grass.

Adult nectar plants: Not a huge drinker, but they will come to knapweeds and scabiouses, and sometimes to ragworts, hawkbits, Common Fleabane, Red Valerian, lavenders and *Verbena bonariensis*.

So... This is yet another grassland species where a typical ryegrass lawn is not what the butterfly is looking for. Instead, give them a sparse wild meadow in as sunny a microclimate as possible, with bare, sun-baked areas.

◀ The Wall Brown is rather like a Speckled Wood with the pale areas coloured orange, but the habitats they live in are quite different. Here one is enjoying its preferred sunbed of bare rocks.

Small Copper

Lycaena phlaeas

This is a bright, bold and energetic little gem, but another of those species whose caterpillars have very picky tastes and whose numbers are much declined.

HOME NEEDS

Distribution: Throughout much of the British Isles, though scarcer in the north and upland areas.

Habitat: Warm, dry places such as heaths, downland, road verges, dunes and quarries, preferring areas with quite sparse vegetation. Uncommon in gardens.

◀ Look carefully and you will see that this Small Copper is resting on one of its food plants – Sheep's Sorrel, with its inconspicuous tiny red flowers.

Habits: The male is a little bundle of brightness, buzzing around his small territory, which is often within a larger area used by a dozen or so adults. He waits on a prominent stem or grasshead and then launches himself to intercept any insect that passes, seeing them off in a quick aerial dog-fight, unless it is a female willing to be wooed!

Flight season: The spring generation flies May–June, followed by a summer generation in August, and in the south a third generation September–October.

Hibernates as: Caterpillar.

Caterpillar foodplants: Common and Sheep's Sorrel.

Adult nectar plants: Especially likes Common Ragwort and forget-me-not species, but will also come to Marjoram, Devil's-bit Scabious, Tansy, thistles, goldenrods, Michaelmas daisies, Yarrow, *Verbena bonariensis*, heathers, Common Fleabane and Iceplant.

So... They occasionally stray into gardens, but you are most likely to succeed if you can turn your lawn into a sunny, sorrel-rich meadow for a whole colony.

Small/Essex Skipper
Thymelicus sylvestris/lineola

Here are two almost-identical butterflies with almost-identical home needs. You will need to get on your hands and knees to tell these little fellas apart!

HOME NEEDS

Distribution: The Small is found throughout England and Wales as far north as Northumberland; the Essex's range is south-eastern, only reaching as far north as the Midlands. Both are extending their ranges northwards.

Habitat: Unimproved, sunny grasslands where the grasses grow tall, such as meadows and road verges. They are uncommon in gardens.

Habits: Both live in colonies that can cover an extensive or relatively small area (but usually still larger than most gardens!). Males set up little territories, often on the lookout from the top of a grass stem, flying out speedily at knee-level to check passing insects. Females wander between the grass stems laying eggs, resting or nectaring.

Flight season: Late June–August for Small; July–August for Essex.

Hibernates as: Caterpillar for Small; egg for Essex.

Caterpillar foodplants: Wild grasses: Yorkshire Fog for the Small, Cocksfoot or Creeping Soft-grass for the Essex, with both sometimes using several other wild grasses.

Adult nectar plants: Not especially big drinkers, but they feed at a wide range of flowers including knapweeds, hawkbits, Iceplant, Marjoram, Common Ragwort, vetches, thistles, scabiouses, Ox-eye Daisy, clovers, brambles, catmints, lavenders and Teasel.

So... The creation of a fairly large mini-meadow full of wild grasses is your real goal here, although you will probably need to be close to an existing colony to be successful.

◄ The key to telling Small Skippers from Essex is the tip of their antennae – in the Small they are orangey underneath; in the Essex they look as if they have been dipped in black ink. This is the Small – it's ludicrously difficult, isn't it!

Large Skipper
Ochlodes venata

A golden whirlwind of early summer that, like the other skippers, holds its tiny wings in a curious 'pop-up book' fashion.

HOME NEEDS

Distribution: Widespread across England and Wales, and just over into the Scottish Borders, where its range is expanding.

Habitat: Anywhere where its preferred grasses grow tall and undisturbed in the sunny lee of shrubs, so is widespread along hedgerows, woodland rides, verges and unimproved grasslands. Uncommon in gardens.

◄ A little bit easier to identify than Small and Essex, the pale 'windows' in the wings of the Large Skipper show up well here with the light shining through.

Habits: Lives in small colonies. Males perch on conspicuous vantage points, such as sunny leaves, to wait for a female to come by, zooming out to intercept any butterfly that passes. At times, often in the morning, they will also patrol actively seeking mates. The females carefully lay eggs on grass leaves. Both males and females will bask in the sun and take nectar.

Flight season: Late May–August.

Hibernates as: Caterpillar.

Caterpillar foodplants: Coarse wild grasses, in particular Cocksfoot, but they will eat False Brome, Tor-grass and Purple Moor-grass.

Adult nectar plants: They are big fans of brambles, and also regularly visit Marsh and Creeping Thistles and the knapweeds, plus geraniums, buttercups, vetches (eg Tufted Vetch, Meadow Vetchling), clovers, hawkbits and lavenders.

So... You either need enough space for a whole colony – maybe half a hectare – or for your garden to augment an existing colony. Let native grasses grow tall on the sunny side of bushes, with a bit of bramble scrambling through to make them extra happy.

Rarities

Just as with birds, it is always possible that your garden might one day entertain a butterfly that is out of the ordinary. Your best chance is if you live near to one of the 'special' butterfly habitats, places where the really picky species live. Such butterflies might be rather attractive guests to hope for, but they are ever so difficult to please!

The most amazing butterfly habitat we have is chalk and limestone downland. There is something about the richness of the plant life and the warm, sunny slopes that keeps a whole range of rare species happy. If you live on or very near downland and can recreate some of these conditions, you stand a good chance of seeing species such as **Chalkhill Blue** *Polyommatus coridon*, **Adonis Blue** *P. bellargus*, **Brown Argus** *Aricia agestis* and **Dark Green Fritillary** *Argynnis aglaja*.

Another fantastic habitat is ancient coppiced woodland. If you live in the south with such a haven nearby, a **White Admiral** *Limenitis camilla* might come soaring and swooping around your garden like a caped superhero, along with its sidekick, the golden **Silver-washed Fritillary** *Argynnis paphia*.

If you have mature oak trees in your garden, it is quite possible that you are host to a colony of **Purple Hairstreaks** *Neozephyrus quercus*. If your tree-climbing days are over, then spotting them skipping around the canopy will require some high-summer neck-craning, or you could try to tempt them down to ground level with some choice bramble flowers.

Another species that can match the Painted Lady as a great explorer is the **Clouded Yellow** *Colias croceus*. It travels to us all the way from the Mediterranean and North Africa, sometimes by the thousand, although good years come by seemingly randomly and are peppered by several years of dearth. 1877 – now that was a year to remember, although 1996 is perhaps fresher in our memories!

Another good bet for a visit to some gardens is that flying chequerboard, the **Marbled White** *Melanargia galathea*. It lives in southern unimproved meadows and downs, but the odd one or two are prone to undertaking a bit of garden exploration. The **Small Heath** *Coenonympha pamphilus*, with its endearing habit of leaning right over to hide its shadow, is not quite such a strong flyer but may also make it from dry meadows into some gardens.

◀ If you live near to woodland in southern Britain, there is every chance that a spectacular Silver-washed Fritillary may come wafting into your garden, and will even pause if you have butterfly-friendly flowers – a moment to treasure.

▲ The Chalkhill Blue does what it says on the tin – it is a blue that lives on chalky (or limestone) hills, such as the North and South Downs, Chilterns and Cotswolds.

Top 20 flowers for butterflies

Here is my pick of the best garden flowers for butterflies, with the species that are likely to use them. Remember to grow them en masse and in a sheltered, warm and sunny location for an even better chance of success.

Marjoram
Origanum vulgare
– Gatekeeper
(left), Meadow
Brown,
Common Blue,
skippers, Red
Admiral, Painted
Lady, Small
Tortoiseshell,
Small Copper.

Ivy
Hedera helix
– Red Admiral,
Comma, Painted
Lady (left).

**Verbena
bonariensis**
– whites, Red
Admiral, Painted
Lady, Small
Tortoiseshell,
Peacock, Small
Copper, Small
White (left).

**Buddleja x
weyeriana** –
Red Admiral,
Small Tortoiseshell,
Painted Lady, Small
Copper (left),
Peacock, Comma,
Brimstone,
whites. (*Buddleja
davidii* is now not
recommended.)

Black Knapweed
Centaurea nigra
– Gatekeeper,
Green-veined
White (left),
Meadow Brown,
Common Blue,
Brimstone, Small
Tortoiseshell, skippers,
Painted Lady,
Peacock, whites.

Bramble
Rubus fruticosus
– Red Admiral
(left), Small
Tortoiseshell,
Peacock, Comma,
Speckled Wood,
Gatekeeper,
Meadow Brown,
Ringlet, skippers.

Field Scabious
*Knautia
arvensis* – Red
Admiral, Painted
Lady, Small
Tortoiseshell,
Meadow Brown
(left), Brimstone,
skippers, whites.

**Devil's-bit
Scabious**
*Succisa
pratensis* – Red
Admiral, Painted
Lady, Small
Tortoiseshell,
Meadow Brown
(left), Common
Blue, Small
Copper, whites.

**Hemp
Agrimony**
*Eupatorium
cannabinum* –
Red Admiral, Small
Tortoiseshell,
Peacock,
Speckled Wood,
Meadow Brown,
Ringlet, Holly
Blue, whites.

**Michaelmas
Daisy**
Aster novi-belgii
(singles only)
– Red Admiral
(left), Small
Tortoiseshell,
Peacock, Small
Copper, whites.

**English
Lavender**
*Lavandula
angustifolia*
– Small
Tortoiseshell
(left), Peacock,
Meadow Brown,
whites.

Marsh Thistle
Cirsium palustre
– Gatekeeper,
Meadow Brown,
Brimstone (left),
whites, skippers,
Small Copper,
Red Admiral,
Painted Lady, Small
Tortoiseshell,
Peacock, Ringlet.

Iceplant *Sedum spectabile* – Red Admiral, Small Tortoiseshell, Peacock, Painted Lady, Comma, Small Copper.

Blackthorn *Prunus spinosa* – Comma, Small Tortoiseshell, Peacock.

Red Valerian *Centranthus ruber* – Red Admiral, Small Tortoiseshell, Peacock, Meadow Brown, whites.

Tickseed *Coreopsis verticillata* – whites, Gatekeeper, Small Skipper.

Goat Willow (Sallow) *Salix caprea* – Peacock, Small Tortoiseshell, Comma, Brimstone.

Common Fleabane *Pulicaria dysenterica* – Gatekeeper, Meadow Brown, Brimstone, Common Blue.

Lady's Smock *Cardamine pratensis* – Orange-tip, Green-veined White.

Coneflower *Echinacea purpurea* – Red Admiral, Small Tortoiseshell, Peacock, Meadow Brown.

Top 10 plants for butterfly caterpillars

Actually you've got a bargain – I've given you ten and a whole host of grasses too.

Stinging Nettle
Urtica dioica – Red Admiral, Small Tortoise-shell, Peacock, Comma.

Hop
Humulus lupulus – Comma.

Garlic Mustard
Alliaria petiolata – Green-veined White, Orange-tip.

Lady's Smock
Cardamine pratensis – Green-veined White, Orange-tip.

Purging Buckthorn
Rhamnus cathartica and **Alder Buckthorn** *Frangula alnus* (illustrated) – Brimstone. Note the caterpillar on the midrib.

Holly *Ilex aquifolium* (illustrated) and **Ivy** *Hedera helix* – Holly Blue.

Common Bird's-foot Trefoil
Lotus corniculatus – Common Blue.

Nasturtium
Tropaeolum majus – Large White (that's its caterpillar), Small White.

Native grasses, such as Yorkshire Fog (left), Cocksfoot, False Brome, bents, fescues and meadow-grasses – skippers, Ringlet, Meadow Brown, Gatekeeper, Speckled Wood.

Butterfly houses

You may see wooden boxes on sale that are described as hibernation boxes for adult butterflies. They tend to have narrow vertical slits at the front and a hollow rear. But do they work?

Let's say that there isn't much evidence that they do! This perhaps isn't surprising when you consider that there are only five species that regularly overwinter in an adult state in northern Europe: Brimstone, Comma, Peacock, Small Tortoiseshell and, recently, Red Admiral. Of these, the hibernation boxes perhaps best mimic the hollow tree hibernation sites naturally sought by the Peacock. So if you do use these boxes, just be aware that there are very few butterfly species they could possibly work for, and maybe spend your money on some nice butterfly nectar plants instead?

Gardening for Mammals

Considering the close relationships we have with so many mammals – as pets, fluffy toys, cartoon characters – they rarely seem to be high on the wildlife gardener's target list. That might seem a little strange given that we ourselves are mammals – surely we would want to help any warm-blooded, furry, doe-eyed creature that came our way?

The problem is that many species are either unobtrusive, nervous and nocturnal, or just a bit of a nuisance. There are also rather few species; even a good garden for mammals might only host half a dozen species compared with perhaps 25 bird species. And there is also the problem that the larger mammals tend to occupy such large home territories that one garden can only fulfil a small part of their home needs.

But here's the good news: anyone whose gardens are visited by mammals such as Badgers,

Red Squirrels, Hedgehogs or, if you're very lucky, Dormice or even Pine Martens, will probably get more excited by them than any other wild creature that visits the garden. On top of this, several small mammals are important links in food chains. In short, mammals are definitely worth the effort.

Oh, and understanding all those home needs is indispensable for those times when you want to know how not to encourage a particularly unwelcome guest!

▲ A rare glimpse in daylight of a House Mouse that, like most mammals, is more often a denizen of the night.

▶ Experiences with creatures such as Hedgehogs can be some of the most rewarding for the wildlife gardener.

Hedgehog
Erinaceus europaeus

This snuffling ball of prickles is an adored and welcome garden visitor that urgently needs our help, having declined from 30 million in the 1950s to less than a million now.

Most people only see Hedgehogs when they have been killed on the roads, but they face many other dangers including less food in the countryside, garden fences making travel through urban areas difficult, and poisoning from slug pellets (especially after eating slugs that have eaten pellets). They are also at risk from bonfires, getting trapped in netting, drowning in steep-sided ponds, and being killed by Badgers and sometimes dogs and Foxes.

◄ Hedgehogs' well-known defence strategy is to roll into a ball, spines facing out. Unfortunately for them, it is no deterrent to a Badger.

HOME NEEDS

Distribution: Thinly spread throughout most of the British Isles.

Habitat: Hedgerows, unimproved grasslands, woodlands and orchards, but also some rural and suburban gardens.

Habits: Nocturnal, they wander for up to 3km a night in search of food using their keen sense of smell and good hearing. They can climb low walls and fences if necessary, but gardens can turn into an energy-sapping assault course. Daytime is spent in one of several 'nest' sites in their patch.

Territory: They don't guard a territory, but individuals stay within home ranges averaging about 10ha for females to 30ha for males. The home ranges of different Hedgehogs will overlap.

Hibernation: November to March, rolled in a ball of leaves under the shelter of log piles, bramble patches, sheds etc. Here the temperature is constant and cool without being cold.

Food: Invertebrates, especially beetles, worms and caterpillars, with some slugs and millipedes, but apparently very few snails or woodlice. They can be opportunistic, even taking carrion.

Supplementary feeding: Dog or cat food (including biscuits) with a shallow bowl of fresh water are ideal. Cows' milk is too rich and avoid bread, which is hard to digest and low in protein.

Breeding: The female gives birth in a sheltered nest similar to that used for hibernation. She has one or two litters, May–September, with two to five hoglets per litter. They are independent at about eight weeks.

So...

✿ Ensure your garden is good for worms, beetles and moths.

✿ Provide small amounts of supplementary food and water.

✿ Create stick piles that have room for a Hedgehog to crawl in underneath, leave leaf piles around the garden in autumn, and build or buy a Hedgehog house.

✿ Create easy routes in and out of the garden – ideally remove fences and replace with hedges, but at the very least liaise with neighbours to cut 'passageways' under fences.

✿ Make sure that they can scramble easily out of ponds should they fall in.

HEDGEHOG HOUSE

✿ Site in a quiet, sheltered part of the garden. Partly bury in leaves and branches.

✿ An entrance tunnel, about 30cm long, prevents attack by Badgers or Foxes. The tunnel should be about 15cm wide and high, and can be external or (as in the design in the photo) within the box.

✿ Aim for a main compartment about 30cm high x 30cm deep x 50cm wide. Precision is not required!

✿ Half-fill with dry leaves and hay.

✿ Ensure there is good ventilation.

✿ Watch the entrance at dusk to see if it is being used rather than being tempted to open it, which can make the occupants abandon home.

Squirrels

The tale of the two species of squirrel is rather a cautionary one.

The **Red Squirrel** *Sciurus vulgaris* is native to Britain and Ireland. It is the Squirrel Nutkin of Beatrix Potter, a bounding high-wire expert of the tree tops with ruddy fur and wispy ear-tufts in winter.

◀ The Red Squirrel is a gorgeous deep auburn, with silver hints. Some Greys can have a reddish tinge in their fur, but never like this!

The **Grey Squirrel** *S. carolinensis* was introduced into the UK from North America a hundred years ago. It spread rapidly: there are now thought to be over 2.5 million, mainly in England and Wales.

Unfortunately, the Greys brought with them the squirrelpox virus. They are largely immune to it, but Reds are not. Also Greys can digest unripe acorns and nuts, which Reds can't. And Greys tend to dominate fights with Reds. The result? Wherever Greys turn up, Reds are usually eliminated within 20 years.

Both species damage trees by stripping bark, but it is the Grey that most often enters roof spaces and chews cables, and it redefines what makes a bird feeder 'indestructible'! Both species also take a few eggs and chicks of nesting birds.

HOME NEEDS

Distribution: Reds are now restricted to the pine forests of Scotland, plus a few places in Ireland, Northumberland, the North West, Wales, the Isle of Wight and Poole Harbour. Greys are found throughout most of England, Wales and Ireland, but are absent from the Isle of Wight, and from most of Scotland bar the central belt. Schemes are underway to try and halt the Grey's spread.

Habitat: Both species need plenty of large trees, such as in woods, parks and mature gardens. Greys prefer oaks, Beech and Hazel; Reds are most at home in Scots Pine, but in the absence of Greys survive well in deciduous woods.

Habits: Generally solitary, both species are diurnal and spend most of their time high in the branches, leaping from tree to tree along the slimmest of branches. The Grey comes to ground more regularly than the Red. Neither species hibernates.

Food: Reds take the seeds, bark and sap of Scots Pine, plus ripe hazelnuts and beechmast, and fungi. Greys eat hazelnuts, acorns, beech mast and chestnuts, plus cereal grains and fruit. They will raid birds' nests, and they cache surplus food in autumn, digging small pits in the ground. In gardens, they are particularly fond of peanuts.

Breeding: Both species maintain territories of 2–10ha. They build nests, which are called dreys, high in trees. They are round balls of twigs and pliable stems about 30cm across high in a tree and usually lined with grasses and leaves. Here they sleep and breed. Greys are less skilled at drey building, and will often use a hollow tree. Reds breed twice a year, in early spring and mid–late summer; Greys can breed twice in the same seasons, but often only manage one litter. Reds have 3–8 kittens per litter, Greys 1–7, with the kittens independent at 3–4 months in both species.

So...

❀ Go in with your eyes open if you want to encourage squirrels – be fully aware of the problems first.

❀ Don't provide supplementary food where both Greys and Reds are present – this may help the transmission of squirrelpox. Clean feeders well and often, too.

❀ If you live in a Red Squirrel area, plant Scots Pine instead of oaks, Beech or Hazel, which will favour the Red.

❀ If you live across a road from prime squirrel habitat, don't feed them. (I'll leave you to imagine why!)

❀ If Grey Squirrels are getting into your roof spaces, erect a strong wire mesh (25mm mesh or less) over the holes to exclude them, once you are sure there are no adults or babies inside.

◀ Although they are a problem for the Reds, many people still love Grey Squirrels and no wonder given that they are so approachable and entertaining.

DISCOURAGING GREY SQUIRRELS AT BIRD FEEDERS

Grey Squirrels are masters at getting to bird food, using agility, cunning, determination and brute chewing power in equal measure. To defeat them, view it as a battle of wills and ingenuity where you will sometimes lose. Here are some ideas:

❀ Hang feeders on a very fine line strung above head height between two trees/stakes; you can even thread empty plastic drinks bottles either side of the feeder as rotating slippery baffles.

❀ Put feeders inside a very strong 'guardian' cage.

❀ Use anti-squirrel plastic domes above and below pole feeders, and grease the poles with vaseline.

❀ Turn up the heat! Sprinkle chilli powder or Tabasco on bird food, the stronger the better (but don't get confused and use curry powder: it won't work). Squirrels hate it; birds don't seem to mind.

❀ I strongly recommend the clever feeders available that use the squirrel's weight to close access to the food.

❀ Some people part-solve the problem by giving squirrels their own feeding areas, deflecting them from bird-feeding areas. Just be aware that this may encourage squirrels to stay in and around your garden, putting bird eggs and chicks at greater risk.

◀ This is the Squirrel Buster bird seed feeder, where the weight of a squirrel causes the strong outer cover to drop down over the seed ports. Yes, ingenuity is an essential ingredient when trying to outwit squirrels.

Hazel Dormouse

Muscardinus avellanarius

Who could resist a golden Dormouse, the little sleepy-head of the animal world? They are rare and elusive visitors to rural gardens near woodland, where any help you can give them is welcome.

◀ It's rare to see a Dormouse in daylight, but if you do the wonderful ginger fur and all over cuteness give it away.

HOME NEEDS

Distribution: Widespread but decreasing in southern England with few found further north than the Midlands.

Habitat: Copses, thick hedgerows and coppice woodland, especially with Hazel, Honeysuckle and brambles. They are rare in gardens and don't come into buildings.

Habits: Usually nocturnal, they scamper through shrubs, rarely coming to ground. Nest-makers extraordinaire, they hibernate for up to six months in winter in a ball of grass, leaves and moss under leaf-litter, while in summer they sleep by day up in a tree in a golf-ball-sized nest woven out of grass and Honeysuckle bark. They happily use Dormice boxes, which are like tit boxes but erected with the hole facing inwards and held clear of the trunk by a couple of batons.

Food: Nuts (especially hazelnuts), seeds, bark, fruit (especially blackberries), flowers (especially of brambles) and insects. A few have started visiting garden bird feeders, even in daylight.

Breeding: Females raise two litters of three to five young in June and August–September in a large nursery nest.

The law: They are fully protected, and you need a licence to handle them or to inspect nest boxes where Dormice are known to be present.

So... If you live next to woodland in the south and have the space, plant a mixed native hedge and lots of Hazel, grow plenty of brambles and Honeysuckle too, and create a 'coppice rotation', cutting back a proportion of the trees each year.

Bats

If one group of animals has suffered a poor press going back hundreds of years, it is the bats. It's what happens when you only come out at night, are a tad on the ugly side and have a tropical cousin that drinks blood. If it wasn't for Batman giving them a PR lift, they'd be stuck with associations of witchcraft, Dracula and Meatloaf albums.

The reality is that these tiny, vulnerable creatures rarely cause us any problems. They are clean and sociable, and many species have suffered drastic population declines. They even help us, cleansing the night skies of insects, catching them by emitting high squeaks beyond our hearing range and homing in on the tiniest of echoes that bounce back off the insects' bodies. It's a skill that guarantees they will never get caught in anyone's hair, despite popular fears.

There are 17 species of bat breeding in the British Isles, ten have been recorded in Ireland, and the number of species thins out rapidly as you head north. They are very difficult to identify by sight, and you need a licence to observe them at their roosts, so the best way to tell them apart is to use a bat detector, which makes their unique sounds audible to us.

Many species are rare, and some are far more regular around gardens than others. The most frequent visitors are probably **Common Pipistrelle** *Pipistrellus pipstrellus*, **Soprano Pipistrelle** *Pipistrellus pygmaeus*, **Serotine** *Eptesicus serotinus* and **Brown Long-eared Bat** *Plecotus auritus*, but there's always the chance of something rarer, especially in southern rural areas.

Different bat species share many aspects of their lifestyles and behaviour, and there are things that you can do in the garden that will benefit whatever species may be around, so the following is a broad summary of bat needs.

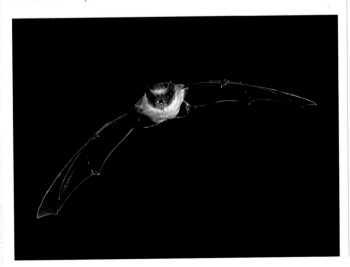

HOME NEEDS

Habitat: Bats can be found almost anywhere in lowland areas, but are mainly associated with woods, hedges, orchards, parks, pond and lake margins, and sometimes cliffs and meadows.

Habits: Bats emerge from their roosts at dusk. They are creatures of habit, most flying along set routes, working one good patch for a while before moving on to the next. They may travel as far as 5km from the roost before returning. They often take rests during the night, clinging to trees or walls while they digest their food. Different species tend to fly slightly differently: the two species of long-eared bat, for example, flutter close to trees, pipistrelles loop and wheel at about head height, while **Noctules** *Nyctalus noctula* fly high in straight lines and make steep dives. Bats can live for up to 30 years if lucky. Owls and cats are their principal enemies. Oh, and humans when we undertake house repairs.

Food: All our bats eat night-flying insects, such as non-biting midges, caddis flies, lacewings, beetles, moths and others, and need to eat thousands each night to survive. The two species of long-eared bats are able to snatch caterpillars off leaves. Several species grab insects from the surface of pools, and many will drink this way – batting about is thirsty work.

Hibernation: Bats choose different roosts at different times of year, and their needs are very particular indeed. In winter, they demand somewhere dark, undisturbed, humid and cool, but not cold. Just a few caves, cellars, mines, barns and hollow trees meet these exacting criteria, and few houses are suitable. Inside, they hibernate upside down from November to April. If disturbed, they use up precious amounts of fat and are less likely to survive. They do sometimes emerge briefly during mild spells, however, to hoover up some winter insects.

Breeding: In most species, the males court the females and mate in autumn. In the spring, females gather together in a maternity roost where they will bear their young. Males go somewhere quieter! This is the main time when nest boxes or attics get used by some species. Almost all adult female bats have just one pup a year, in June or July, which will be weaned within about six weeks.

So... To encourage bats:

✿ **Dig a pond.** They support heaps of insects, and bats will drink from them, swooping low over ponds soon after dusk.

◀ Bats are the masters of night-time flight, using echolocation to locate and catch prey, although not always out of the air, as you might have thought.

- ✿ **Grow plants that encourage insects.** Your nectar- and pollen-rich flowerbeds will do the trick nicely.
- ✿ **Plant trees.** Not only are they great for hosting insects, but they offer sheltered feeding and ultimately may provide roost sites (many years down the line!).
- ✿ **Don't nuke insects with pesticides** – let nature be the natural pest-controller.
- ✿ **Put up bat boxes.**

Bat boxes

Bats are fussy blighters. Unlike Blue Tits, which can move into a new nest box the moment you turn your back, bats can take years to find either the box or the courage. Even then, they may only visit for a few weeks each year when the temperature in that particular box is 'just so'.

There are several different types of box on the market. It doesn't matter whether they are box-shaped, wedge-shaped or circular, or whether they are wooden or woodcrete, but the larger the better and there are some definite rules to follow (below). You can make your own, but I have found it very difficult to get hold of untreated timber and it is just as cheap (and much easier!) to buy good-quality ready-made boxes on the market.

The golden rules of bat boxes

When I said they were picky, I wasn't lying!

Making a good entrance If the entrance is at the rear of the underside of the box, there should be a roughly hewn or grooved backboard beneath it. The bats will land here and crawl in. If the entrance is low down at the front of the box, it should have a little lip to land on but no more. The entrance slit should be no more than 2cm 'high'; it can be as little as 13mm for pipistrelles.

◀ On 'land' bats are particularly awkward and vulnerable, barely able to shuffle on flat surfaces and dangling from hooked hind claws on vertical ones.

It's got to be snug It should be made of wood at least 2.5cm thick, and the joints must be well sealed – bats abhor draughts. A box split internally into vertical cavities offers more space, insulation and microclimates.

No chemicals please Wood *must* be untreated because bats are very sensitive to chemicals. That doesn't just mean woodstain – much timber is soaked in preservatives these days.

A bit of rough The wood surface must be rough on the inside – you try hanging upside down on smooth timber!

Location, location, location The box should be at least 3m off the ground on the wall of a house or tree trunk. Place it near a line of trees, but with a clear flightline up to the box. Try to have several boxes in a cluster facing different directions. Unlike bird boxes, some can be in full sunlight, but some cover above is ideal.

To check if your box is being used, look for small, dry, black droppings underneath the box entrance, and watch at dusk to see if anything emerges. If you're really lucky, you'll see streams of them.

◀ This is a typical bat box, which is about the same dimensions as a Blue Tit box. Bats land on the 'ladder' (the grooved backboard at the base) and crawl up through the tiny slit into the box.

Bats and the law

Bats are incredibly well protected – imagine how rare they'd be if they weren't! It is an offence to kill, injure or capture them, to deliberately disturb them, to handle them without a licence, or to damage, destroy or obstruct access to a known roost whether it is in use or not.

Red Fox
Vulpes vulpes

Isn't it amazing that a wild dog – and a very attractive one at that – still survives throughout most of western Europe. Even more amazing, it finds a place to call home in the middle of many of our cities.

Be careful when deciding whether to encourage Foxes as they can, on occasion, cause problems. They have been known to attack kittens (although rarely adult cats), and will kill small pets such as rabbits and especially chickens, if poorly housed. They can also dig holes in lawns and flowerbeds when looking for worms, and will root through rubbish bins if the lids aren't secure, but blame is perhaps too easily placed at their door for some issues.

HOME NEEDS

Distribution: Widespread, found in all but the highest mountains and smaller islands.

Habitat: Once a woodland dweller, they can now be found in almost any habitat and have adapted brilliantly to cities where they are often at their highest densities.

Habits: A pair (dog and vixen) holds territory throughout the year, as little as 20ha in cities but 1,000ha in remote locations. They may share the territory with females from the previous year's litter, but they usually roam it alone, mainly at night, looking for food. They then lie up by day in thick cover or underground. They mark their territories with scats (dark twisted faeces), pungent urine and secretions from scent glands.

▲ This sunbathing cub was one of a litter raised in a den under a large logpile in my garden. Having resident Foxes is often no problem in a larger garden; most of the time, you wouldn't know they were there.

Food: They have an appetite for almost anything – carrion, small mammals, small birds, worms, beetles, fruit (they love blackberries) and kitchen scraps.

Breeding: In January, the top-ranking female in a territory will come into season. During courtship and mating, she will make chilling howls. She chooses a den in which to give birth, called an earth. This can be a hole she digs or finds or even under a shed. A single litter of 1–5 cubs is born in late March–April. The mother will move them if they are disturbed. At 6–9 months, they disperse, and many will breed in their first year.

Threats: Foxes are most at risk from dogs, cars and disease, especially sarcoptic mange. This is a skin mite that causes intense irritation leading to scratching, fur loss and often death.

So... Be careful if planning to put out food for Foxes. It can attract unwanted extra guests such as cats, dogs and rats, and the Foxes can become overly tame and approachable. But if you feel that a little food is justified, try the occasional peanut butter or dog-food sandwich.

DISCOURAGING FOXES

✿ Don't overfeed birds, which encourages Foxes to mop up the surplus.
✿ Keep pet rabbits, chickens, etc in secure cages.
✿ Board up gaps under sheds.
✿ Keep rubbish in closed bins.

Badger
Meles meles

Like the Fox, it is a miracle that a mammal as large as the Badger has survived in our busy world. Elusive, attractive and amusing, watching them can be a real thrill.

However think carefully before encouraging them because these are fruit-chomping master diggers, which can cause problems in gardens. They can raid vegetable and soft fruit crops, dig holes in lawns and damage fences. There is also considerable sensitivity over Badgers because of the risk of them transmitting bovine tuberculosis to cattle, prompting both local culls and calls for more widespread ones.

HOME NEEDS

Distribution: They are found throughout most of the British Isles,

◀ Badgers tend to emerge after dark, following regular routes and forming well-worn paths. Here they forage for food, as opportunists rather than out-and-out hunters.

peanuts, fruit and raisins, but only put out a little – Badgers should not become reliant on it – and ensure it is Badgers that are taking the food, not rats or cats. Don't feed sugary food or milk.

DISCOURAGING BADGERS

If Badgers are a problem, don't leave bird food on the ground overnight, secure rubbish bags in closed dustbins and consider using solar-powered electric fencing around your vegetable plot. Excluding Badgers using normal fencing is difficult – those paws were made for digging.

but are scarce in upland areas and northern Scotland. They are surprisingly common considering how infrequently they are seen, and they survive well in some urban areas.

Habitat: Usually in deciduous woods, copses and hedgerows near a mosaic of open pasture, arable fields and orchards. They prefer lighter soils, where digging burrows (setts) is so much easier.

Habits: Social groups (clans) of 5–8 adults live in communal setts where they sleep by day. The setts are built into banks and slopes or under tree roots and have several entrances and up to 300m of tunnels leading to various sleeping and breeding chambers. Earth is mounded up outside the entrances, often mixed with spent bedding. Youngsters sometimes use smaller, outlying setts – what you might call sub-setts – to hang out in. The badgers emerge after dark to forage, following regular routes and forming well-worn paths. In winter, they sleep out cold periods, relying on their autumn fat deposits to see them through.

Territory: Rural Badgers have a strict territory, maybe 50ha, marked with latrines. Urban Badgers are rather more chilled and mix more freely.

Food: A forager rather than hunter, earthworms are staple in the diet, but fruit is important in autumn. They also take everything from beetles, slugs, moths and small mammals to bulbs, beech mast, acorns and seeds. They even dig up bee or wasp nests. In gardens, they can raid rubbish bags if given the opportunity, and can cause havoc in carrot crops and soft-fruit beds.

Breeding: Adults (boars and sows) mate in summer with a single litter of 2–3 cubs born in a nesting chamber in February. Cubs stay underground for 6–8 weeks, are weaned at 12 weeks but remain close by their mother into autumn or winter. They live for up to 12 years.

So... If Badgers visit your garden, and you judge there is little risk of conflict with neighbours or farmers, the natural way to encourage them is by letting them access your lawn, where they can find earthworms, and to plant fruit trees, where you can let the windfalls lie where they land. The best supplementary food is 'wet' dog food,

Stoat *Mustela erminea*
Weasel *Mustela nivalis*

These streaks of quicksilver, with their tiny legs and sinuous bodies, are widespread in the countryside throughout most of the British Isles (although the Weasel is absent from Ireland). They live in hedgerows, scrub and unimproved meadows but are rare visitors to gardens.

They need a den snuggled among tree roots or woodpiles and a ready supply of mice and voles; Stoats, being the larger of the two species, also catch rabbits. Weasels are small enough even to fit into rodent burrows.

So... if you have a garden fit for plenty of small rodents, then Stoats and Weasels may follow.

▲ Agile and lithe, both the Weasel (above) and the Stoat have long thin bodies, warm brown above and white below, but only the Stoat has a black tip to its tail.

MICE AND VOLES

Unless you have a prowling cat, you'd probably never realise that mice are commonplace in gardens, and voles sometimes so. Their nocturnal habits and shy nature mean that we rarely see them in the open.

Gardening for them has knock-on benefits: they are prey for owls and Kestrels, while their burrows are prime nesting sites for bumblebees, sometimes even for nesting Coal Tits, and they are used by hibernating lizards and Slow-worms.

Mice

HOME NEEDS

Distribution: Three mice species are commonly found in gardens. The **Wood Mouse** *Apodemus sylvaticus* is found throughout the British Isles, the **Yellow-necked Mouse** *A. falvicollis* is only found in southern England and Wales, and the **House Mouse** *Mus musculus* lives pretty much everywhere.

Habitat: Wood and Yellow-necked Mice are very similar, inhabiting woodlands, hedges and gardens and rarely coming into houses. The House Mouse lives up to its name, much preferring old houses and sheds and only going outside when the weather is warm enough or if it needs to move home.

Habits: Wood and Yellow-necked Mice live fairly blameless lives (as far as we're concerned) apart from playing merry hell with your sown pea seeds and seedlings. They dig burrows, inside which they create breeding chambers that they line with hay, and larders where they stash food. Above ground, they create a network of little runways through vegetation and leaf-litter. House Mice are more of a nuisance, eating our food, gnawing at wood and cables, and building nests out of loft material, newspapers, etc. They can squeeze through gaps 1cm high, and can run up seemingly smooth internal walls.

Food: Wood and Yellow-necked Mice eat seeds, fruit and berries, plus some insects and small snails. They will readily climb onto bird tables at night. House Mice are pretty omnivorous, especially liking bird food… and your food.

Breeding: All mice can have multiple litters a year, up to ten in the case of the House Mouse.

So… Wood Mice and Yellow-necked Mice are worthwhile visitors for the garden food chain. Give them woodland areas, log piles, dense vegetation and uncut meadows. House Mice are best deterred through good household hygiene and food storage.

▲ Bank Voles (above) and Field Voles have small eyes, half-hidden ears, a snub nose and a short tail, unlike mice which have prominent eyes and ears, a long pointed nose and a tail as long as their body.

Voles

HOME NEEDS

Distribution: The **Field (or Short-tailed) Vole** *Microtus agrestis* and the rather russety **Bank Vole** *Clethrionomys glareolus* are found throughout most of Britain but not Ireland, while the **Common Vole** *M. arvalis* is only found in Guernsey and Orkney.

Habitat: They prefer the dense cover of undisturbed, ungrazed grasslands, hedgerows, scrub and woodlands and some rural gardens, with the Field Vole generally preferring damper habitats.

Habits: Like mice, they too make burrows and have runways, predominantly through long grass. They don't enter houses, but they can chew the bark of young trees. They don't hibernate, and suffer losses in harsh weather.

Food: Field and Common Voles eat stems, roots, leaves, bark and the seeds of grasses and sedges, while the Bank Vole also eats berries and fruit.

Breeding: Four to five litters of five to six young, March–November.

So… Turn an area of lawn into meadow, and make a wildlife sunbed (see page 99) nearby, under which they are likely to make neat nests from dried grass and moss.

Shrews

These hyperactive, short-lived, tiny mammals may look mouse-like but are insectivores, related to Hedgehogs. Although rarely seen, you* can hear their high-pitched squeaks as two meet and squabble in the undergrowth (*until about the age of 40!)

There are four species in the British Isles: the **Common Shrew** *Sorex araneus* and **Pygmy Shrew** *S. minutus* are widespread, although the Common never made it to Ireland, while the **Greater** and **Lesser White-toothed Shrews** *Crocidura russula* and *C. suaveolens* are found in the Channel Islands, with the latter also on Scilly. The Greater White-toothed has a habit of entering outhouses and even occupied buildings. They are all similar in nature.

HOME NEEDS
Habitat: Rough pasture, hedgerows, dunes, open woodlands, rocky shores and some gardens. Shrews will live in larger and more rural gardens.
Habits: They lead rather solitary lives, scurrying through their small territory along runways hidden in thick grass, or even underground in shallow tunnels. They hunt by day and night, turning over leaves and soil, and taking regular rests in nests. They fall prey to owls, but their musky smell makes them unpopular with mammal predators. They don't hibernate in winter, when many die.
Food: It's 'eat, eat, eat' all day and all night for shrews. They take insects and their larvae, spiders and woodlice, with the larger species enjoying a few worms.
Breeding: Mainly May–August, raising up to five litters of four to ten young in hollow nests of grass and leaves. Young are independent within eight weeks.

So... Shrews may set up home in your garden if you create areas of meadow and hedgerow, especially if you live near open countryside.

◀ Shrews are easily told from mice by their narrow pink snout, tiny eyes and barely visible ear.

Mole
Talpa europaea

Much despised, Moles can undermine vegetable plots and cause gardeners to tear out their hair. But if the problems they cause in a garden are only aesthetic, hopefully they can be tolerated.

HOME NEEDS
Distribution: Most of Britain but not Ireland.
Habitat: Grasslands, but surprisingly they also live in woods where they are less conspicuous. They come into large gardens near open countryside. Sandy soils are much less favoured.

◀ Molehills are where a Mole has had to extend its tunnels to find food; in areas where feeding is good, you rarely see signs of digging. However, they sometimes come to the surface at night to look for worms.

Habits: They dig their famous tunnel systems close to the surface and extending perhaps 100–200m for each mole. Here they live alone, defending their territories aggressively, although a few tunnels appear to be communal Mole 'highways'. Moles charge up and down their tunnels looking for food, eating and sleeping in four-hour shifts round-the-clock.
Food: Predominantly worms, but also any other juicy soil creature that drops into the tunnels, which act like pitfall traps.
Breeding: Males go in search of females in early spring. Females raise one litter a year of three to four young in a nesting chamber underground or within an extra-large molehill, lined with dry grass and leaves. The youngsters are then chucked out after five to six weeks and wander above ground through the grass in search of a territory. Many are taken by Tawny Owls at this stage.

So... If you have large grasslands with plenty of soil-life that hasn't been blasted by pesticides, you may well find that one day a mole appears – or at least a molehill does. If your urge is 'to get rid', resist the temptation. It is usually a thankless task. Use the aerated soil heaps as a gift for elsewhere in the garden, rake them thinly over the lawn as a dressing, or better still leave them in place as a fine microhabitat where solitary bees may nest and Robins and thrushes can feed. Go on, be brave!

◀ The dog-sized Muntjac – this is a buck I photographed in a Norfolk garden – are perhaps the most regular deer species in British gardens these days.

Deer

If you have a rural garden, especially a large one near to woodland, you have a good chance of being visited at night by deer. If this is the case, you don't need me to tell you what they're capable of doing, be it chomping prized trees up to 'browse height' or munching choice rose bushes and vegetables. The two most likely species are the elegant **Roe Deer** *Capreolus capreolus* and the dog-sized **Muntjac** *Muntiacus reevesi*.

HOME NEEDS

Distribution: The Roe Deer was persecuted almost to extinction by the 18th century, but is now doing well across much of rural Britain. The Muntjac was introduced to Woburn Abbey just over 100 years ago, and is increasing across much of southern lowland England and Wales.

Habitat: Both species are animals of dense woodland, conifer as well as deciduous, feeding in rides, glades and adjacent farmland.

Habits: Roe Deer move about singly, in pairs or very small groups, with twin fawns born May–June. The 'barking deer', as the Muntjac is sometimes known, lives singly or in pairs. Both hide away by day in woodlands and copses with a thick understorey, and can jump well.

Food: Dawn and dusk are favoured feeding times. Roe Deer browse tree twigs, brambles, roses, Ivy and some grass and flowers, and can destroy trees when they nibble the bark or when the males rub the velvet off their horns against tree trunks ('fraying'). They will also eat the tips of heathers and young conifers. Muntjac feed on a wide range of succulent ground flora, will nibble at bark and dig up and eat Bluebells. Both move onto autumn-sown cereal crops to feed in winter.

So... A few people tolerate and even enjoy seeing deer in their gardens, but for most the damage they do outweighs the delight. You could try one of the many homespun deterrents, such as human hair and scented soap, but the only guaranteed strategy is a deer-proof fence no lower than 1.5m, and with a mesh no larger than 10cm square. Protect trees with guards, staked at the base.

Rabbit
Oryctolagus cuniculus

They may be cute, but their endless nibbling plus their ability to breed like, erm, rabbits make them considerable pests of agriculture and gardens alike.

HOME NEEDS

Distribution: Native to western mainland Europe, but introduced to the UK in about the 12th century and to many other places in Europe, they are now widespread in the lowlands. The disease myxomatosis was introduced into Britain in the 1950s and wiped out 99 per cent of the population in two years, from which they are slowly recovering (and sometimes relapsing).

Habitat: They are found wherever there are grassy and flower-rich feeding areas near to dense cover, preferring sandy or light soils. Small gardens are often too disturbed.

Habits: Generally sedentary, they live in a social hierarchy of two to three bucks and three to four does plus youngsters. They usually dig a warren of burrows, but sometimes live above ground in dense thickets and between boulders. Most activity is at dawn and dusk.

Food: Vegetarians, but busy ones! One rabbit can eat half a kilo of food a day, mainly grass, wildflowers and cereal crops. In the garden, their love of carrots is no myth, and many other young plants and vegetables are fair game, as is some tree bark.

Breeding: The does have four to six litters, February–July, with two to eight kits per litter. Youngsters are sexually mature at three to four months.

So... If rabbits are raiding your cabbage patch, fencing is the answer. Use a 60cm wire fence, buried 5cm or so under the soil, with a maximum 2.5cm mesh. Trees can be protected with guards.

Brown Rat

Rattus norvegicus

I'm a firm believer that almost all wildlife has a place in the garden – all that is required in some cases is a bit of understanding. However, in the case of rats, the welcome ends. They're not evil, they don't mean to cause problems, and remember that their success is entirely down to us. But they're still rarely welcome!

HOME NEEDS

Distribution: Throughout. Humans brought them as stowaways from Asia in the 18th century.

Habitat: They live in our shadow everywhere – under floorboards, in sewers, in grain stores, in some compost heaps. They also find a home along seaweed-strewn rocky shores and even in hedgerows.

Habits: Quite a social animal, they live in small colonies and often build a good network of underground burrows. They can climb, swim and especially jump, but spend most of the time on the ground, and are most active at night. They seem to be able to gnaw through almost anything and create frequently used runways, marked with greasy smears from their skin glands. They don't hibernate and are cautious of any new object, making them very difficult to catch. Their urine carries the Weil's disease (leptospirosis) bacteria, which we can contract causing jaundice and kidney failure.

Food: Originally a grain-eater, they have become a super-scavenger, even existing (apologies if you're eating) on human faeces.

Breeding: They are prolific breeders, raising three to five litters a year of four to ten young in a nest made of grass, paper, etc. The young leave the nest after three weeks and are sexually mature after three months.

So… Rats probably pass through every garden at some point; your job is to ensure they don't want to stay. So store bird food securely, only feed birds using rat-proof feeders or only put out enough food in the morning to last the day, and avoid putting meat, dairy or cooked products on compost heaps. If you do all this but still end up with rats, put vegetable peelings and waste fruit in a sealed compost bin, liaise with neighbours in case the problem stems from there, and ultimately be prepared to call in the professionals.

◀ Undeniably cute, Rabbits are nevertheless usually an alarming sight in gardens, given their capacity to eat almost anything in the flower border!

▶ Whereas indoors he is only Tiddles, a loved pet and companion, outside he is loose in the natural world where his hunting instincts can be practiced on rodents, birds, reptiles and amphibians.

Cats

The number of domestic cats in the UK is astonishing – perhaps as many as 10 million – and although many don't kill garden birds and other animals, many do. The wildlife body-count is huge.

Although there is no evidence that this causes declines in any species at the wider population level, it can still be very distressing to see cats making a kill, even if it's your own cat, and there are various things you can do to decrease the number of creatures it brings home.

If you own a wildlife-catching cat:

✿ Fit it with a bell on a properly fitted collar with a quick-release buckle – it makes stalking in silence difficult and can substantially reduce predation.

✿ Keep it in from before dusk until after dawn when birds are most vulnerable.

✿ Have it neutered to prevent additions to the feral-cat population.

If you don't own a cat but want to reduce their visits to your garden:

✿ Buy an electronic cat deterrent. These motion-activated devices can be placed anywhere in the garden and emit a high-pitched noise that cats hate.

If cats visit your garden regularly:

✿ Place bird tables and feeders carefully, away from ground cover and preferably high, and use seed trays to prevent food from falling to the ground and tempting birds down to the ground.

✿ Make sure that you offer wildlife plenty of opportunities to escape from cats, such as dense, thorny bushes and log piles.

✿ Consider using plastic spikes along fence tops, if safe to do so.

Gardening for Reptiles and Amphibians

When I was about six, we sacrificed a corner of the lawn and dug a pond that was almost as deep as I was tall. Once filled, frogs arrived as if by magic, and every year we would watch for the first frogspawn, marvel as it hatched, delight at the wriggling tadpoles, and watch in wonder as they grew stumps that turned into legs.

What made the experience all the more powerful was the fact that frogs were one of the few wild creatures I was able to touch. Many found themselves pounced upon and temporarily cupped in my little hands. Some I now suspect were actually trying to get away from the pond but found themselves ceremoniously carried back 'where they belonged'. How they must have cursed me!

Reptiles and amphibians seem to create these kind of vivid memories for people. Interactions with them are often rare, but when they happen, they are filled with curiosity and delight. I love to lie awake on spring nights listening to toads gently bleating out their love songs.

So it might seem a shame that we have just a fraction of the almost 200 reptile and amphibian species found in Europe, but the few we have will give you much pleasure and are well worth gardening for.

▲ Barely bigger than a thumbnail, a young Common Frog – freshly emerged from the pond – may then spend the rest of its adult life in your garden if conditions are right.

▶ The Common Lizard is a really attractive creature to have visit your garden. To see them you will need to creep up quietly – a heavy-footed or swift approach will see them dart for cover in the blink of an eye.

SNAKES

Few of us see a snake from one year to the next and yet age-old fears live on – I'm sure some of you are shuddering at the very thought of snakes in your gardens. Others are probably getting very excited at the prospect!

In reality only larger gardens tend to be suitable for snakes. But if you do have a chance to encourage them, please do, for these are amazing, rather shy and misunderstood creatures which are struggling as many of their favourite habitats are lost.

▼ The sight of a snake might evoke primitive fears in us, but the Grass Snake is harmless, easily told from the Adder by its yellow collar and lack of zigzag markings down its back.

Adder
Vipera berus

Readily told by the zigzag line down its back, the Adder is very rare in gardens. It has a venomous bite that is dangerous to pets, children and the elderly, but it is a shy creature that only attacks if severely provoked.

HOME NEEDS
Distribution: Widely if thinly spread throughout much of mainland Britain, but absent from Ireland.
Habitat: They occupy a surprisingly wide range, favouring heathland especially, but also sunny hedgerows, open woodlands, riverside meadows, downs, dunes and moors. They are rare in gardens unless near these habitats. They like to warm themselves beneath sheets of corrugated iron or roofing material.
Habits: They hibernate throughout the winter, often in groups, underground in holes, burrows and among tree roots. The males emerge on warm days from late February onwards and bask. Females emerge a month later, and they all then move to preferred breeding habitats up to 2km away. Here rival males do the 'dance of the Adders', which is actually a wrestle for supremacy.
Food: Small mammals (voles and mice), plus some amphibians, lizards, etc. Young Adders eat insects.
Breeding: They first breed when three to four years old. Mating is in late April–early May. The 6–12 young develop inside the mother and are born live in very late summer or even delayed until spring.

So... Few gardeners have the chance to encourage them, and be mindful of children and pets if you do. Offer quiet undisturbed places, especially warm woodland gardens and places with heathland plants, with plenty of rodents to catch.

Grass Snake
Natrix natrix

A large non-venomous snake with prominent yellow and black markings on the head. They may lunge if provoked, but are more likely to roll over and play dead, their tongues lolling out.

HOME NEEDS
Distribution: Found throughout much of southern England and Wales and some as far north as southern Scotland, but rare in the north and absent from Ireland.
Habitat: Mainly wet meadows, riverbanks and damp woods, but some drier hedgerows too. A secretive visitor to a surprisingly large number of rural gardens.
Habits: They hibernate in burrows and under large log piles, emerging in March or April. Surprisingly, they are good swimmers, often hunting in water and even able to stay submerged for half an hour.
Food: Frogs, toads and newts, plus some fish. Young Grass Snakes eat young amphibians and insects.
Territory: They may cover a wide area, even as large as 100ha.
Breeding: Males mature at three years, females at five years. After mating in spring, females lay about 30 sticky eggs in June–July in rotting vegetation such as sunny compost heaps and decomposing leaf piles, where the heat helps incubate the eggs. Several females often choose the same spot. Incubation lasts six to ten weeks, with the young hatching August–October.

So... This is a relatively easy snake to help. Create a pond fit for amphibians, a nice undisturbed rotting pile of vegetation in which the snakes can lay their eggs, big half-buried log piles where they can hibernate, and ensure they can slither easily under garden boundaries.

LIZARDS

Both the Slow-worm and the Common Lizard are more common than people realise, and both eat garden pests, so these are visitors well worth welcoming.

Slow-worm
Anguis fragilis

Seemingly part snake, part lizard and part worm, Slow-worms are harmless, legless lizards we rarely see but which probably visit many gardens.

HOME NEEDS
Distribution: Found throughout much of Britain but absent from Ireland and upland areas.
Habitat: They like lush, moist vegetation warmed by the sun, so are found along hedgerows, woodland glades, scrubby areas, waste ground and heaths, and they adore open, undisturbed compost heaps.
Habits: They keep very much out of sight, slipping gently through the grass and undergrowth or even burrowing through loose soil and roots. They don't often bask in the open, but are very fond of soaking up the heat beneath a corrugated sheet or rubber mat. They are especially vulnerable to cats.
Food: Slugs, worms, some snails, plus other small invertebrates, hunting often at dusk.
Hibernates: They overwinter underground in burrows or cavities, October–March.
Breeding: Young Slow-worms take several years before they breed. Females give birth to 6–12 young in spring, each in a membrane from which they quickly wriggle free.

◄ With attractively polished bronze skin, Slow-worms can grow up to 40cm long and may live up to a decade. They can make a good dent in your slug population, so cherish them!

So… This is definitely one species that will benefit if more of us make Wildlife Sunbeds (opposite), giving them somewhere that is snug and safe from predators. Alternatively, build an open compost heap that they can crawl into and out of, have corridors of lush vegetation and try to resist killing all those slugs!

◄ Adult Common Lizards come in a range of colours and patterns, such as this one freckled with gold; their young are almost black.

Common (Viviparous) Lizard
Lacerta vivipara

Common in the countryside but infrequent in gardens, they are the closest you will get to having little dinosaurs in your garden!

HOME NEEDS
Distribution: Widespread but scattered across the British Isles.
Habitat: They like all sorts of habitats where there is undisturbed ground cover with plenty of sunlight and humidity, so are found on heaths, hedgebanks, sunny woodlands and in a few gardens.
Habits: They are sedentary, rarely straying more than a few metres from home. They bask avidly in spring and autumn, choosing a log, wall or fenceline to soak up the sun and raise their body temperature. On hot days they stay undercover.
Food: Insects and spiders, caught by day and by sight using the lizards' lightning speed.
Hibernates: Underground in a frost-free hole, usually November–March.
Breeding: Young are born June–September, with usually six to ten live young to a litter, each wrapped in a membrane from which they break almost instantly.

So… Give them safe sunbathing platforms facing south – logs, rocks or wildlife sunbeds (see p 99) – near to lush vegetation where they can hunt. Build rock piles, preferably including boulders loosely buried deep in the soil under which they can rest overnight and hibernate.

How to make a wildlife sunbed

Reptiles, being cold-blooded, need to warm up before they can get going in the morning (I know the feeling). People who study wild snakes and lizards use this fact to their advantage by putting out corrugated sheets, either of iron or of modern roofing materials. These sheets warm up in the early morning sun much quicker than the surrounding vegetation, and the reptiles have an uncanny knack of finding them. All the scientists have to do is then wander from sheet to sheet, gently lifting them up to see who is warming their cockles underneath.

If it works in the countryside, I wondered why we don't do more of that in gardens. So I now have four sheets in my garden, under which I expected to find Slow-worms but instead I discovered Grass Snakes! Not only that, but under one I have a huge ants' nest. It is fascinating; lift it up in the morning and usually a consignment of ant larvae and pupae have been brought to the surface for a warm-up, but by afternoon, they have usually all been taken back underground.

But my favourites are the Field Voles which nest under the sheets, creating little domed nests out of dried grasses.

If you feel like giving it a go, here's how to make your sunbed.

1. Buy a sheet of bituminous corrugated roofing material from your local DIY store. It normally comes in 2m x 1m sheets, so it may be too big for your car and you may need to get it delivered. You could use iron sheets but they can rust terribly and develop jagged edges, so roofing material is much safer to use with children.

2. I then cut the sheet into two 1m x 1m squares, which don't look quite so obvious when placed in the garden, and are easier to lift and lower without risking hurting the creatures underneath. Whatever you do, don't try to saw the roofing material! The bitumen covering will just clog the teeth of the saw in moments and you won't be at all happy. Use a Stanley knife instead, pushing through into a soft surface like a lawn.

3. I then drill a couple of holes and thread some string through as a handle. It means I don't have to put my hand underneath the edge of the sunbed to lift it up, very important if there is any chance that you have Adders using your garden.

4. Then put your sheets out in sheltered locations around the garden. I spread mine in a range of sunny and half-shady positions, as different creatures like different conditions.

5. When lifting the sheets, do so slowly and gently, look for just a few seconds, and then gently lower it back down. Ration yourself to looking only once a week or so, or your residents may get twitchy about being disturbed too often.

AMPHIBIANS

These much-loved species have the incredible ability to survive both in water and on land, the adults often breathing through their skin as much as with their lungs. We also get to witness the miracle of metamorphosis from spawn to tadpole (or eft) to adult. Oh, and they are good pest-controllers into the bargain.

Common Frog
Rana temporaria

It's hard not to like frogs. Big pop-up eyes, a wide smile and a penchant for munching on slugs make these leaping pond-dwellers all-round favourites.

HOME NEEDS

Distribution: Found throughout most of the British Isles from sea level almost up to the snow line.

Habitat: They use all sorts of undisturbed habitats wherever there is unpolluted shallow fresh water nearby (preferably without fish) and some shady moist places. They will breed in the same pools as toads and newts.

Habits: Sedentary by nature, they spend much of the year out of water, rarely moving more than 1km from the breeding pond. They find food among thick damp vegetation, and shelter in moist places such as log piles and among rocks.

Hibernation: October–February, usually in the mud at the bottom of ponds and ditches, where they breathe through their skin, but occasionally in damp, dark, sheltered locations out of water such as deep leaf-litter and log piles.

Food: They eat slugs, worms, flies, beetles and other insects, catching faster creatures using their whip-like tongue. The tadpoles eat algae, neatly cleaning the sides of ponds.

Breeding: Frogs breed by their third year, and migrate back to

▼ When a pond develops a large frog population, as here in my tiny suburban garden, the surface can become a mass of bodies during the mating season.

their pond by night in February or early March. There, the males chorus to attract females. Pairs join up, males claiming a female by climbing on her back in a tight grip (amplexus). Females often lay more than 1,000 eggs in clumps of floating spawn. The eggs hatch after 10–21 days. Froglets leave the pond from about late June.

Threats: Spawn is eaten by newts and can be killed by late frosts. Tadpoles are eaten by dragonfly nymphs, diving beetles, newts, fish, Blackbirds, Crows, Grey Herons and Mallards. Froglets succumb to Hedgehogs and garden birds, and adults to Grey Herons, Foxes and cats. Many adults are also killed on the roads, and some die during hibernation if the pond freezes and vegetation rots under the surface. The big killer, though, is disease.

So... A pond is essential – make sure there are shallow areas in sunshine and plenty of aquatic vegetation. But don't ignore their other needs. In particular, damp meadow areas full of insects and slugs and moist sheltered flowerbeds are important, as are hideaways under rocks, bricks or logpiles. The best time to clean out ponds is October, in between breeding and hibernation, and check meadows and long grass before mowing.

FROGS AND DISEASE

There have been some devastating outbreaks of disease in some parts of the country in recent years, in particular the ranavirus, which is thought to have been brought in from North America. It is untreatable, with large numbers of Common Frogs, some Common Toads and even newts dying each year, usually in the heat of midsummer. They become lethargic and emaciated, and can develop secondary infections and lesions. To reduce the risks, don't move frogspawn between ponds, which can transfer the disease, and if you suspect frogs have the disease in your garden, report it to www.gardenwildlifehealth.org.

◄ Frogspawn is usually laid in shallow, sunny water. The higher the temperature of the water, the faster the spawn tends to hatch.

Common Toad
Bufo bufo

Toads inspire so much affection that each year, all over the country, volunteers spend many cold spring evenings helping them cross roads safely as they migrate back to their breeding ponds.

HOME NEEDS

Distribution: Throughout much of Britain but absent from Ireland.

Habitat: They live in surprisingly dry (although not overdry) habitats throughout much of the year, including woodland, hedgerows, scrub and rough grasslands, but need access to a shaded and moist hollow by day such as under a log or stone. They breed in a pond, often quite large and deep, and do well in ponds with fish because toadpoles taste awful. ('Toadpole' isn't a real word, but it ought to be.) They are scarcer in gardens than Common Frogs, and rare in urban gardens.

Habits: Generally nocturnal and solitary, they wander slowly through vegetation and leaf-litter looking for prey, before returning to their regular daytime hideaway. They hibernate October–March underground in a mouse burrow or under a woodpile or compost heap, sheltered from frost and predators. Males emerge by early March, females somewhat later. They are preyed upon by Grass

Snakes, but most deaths are on roads, during the stress of courtship, or are caused by disease.

Food: Insects (such as beetles and ants), spiders, worms, snails and some slugs. Toadpoles feed on algae.

Breeding: In spring, males and females migrate back to traditional breeding ponds, which can be 1km away. Here males call and wrestle, often at night, and when they find a female, climb on her back in a tight grip. Females then stay in the pond just long enough to lay their eggs. Each female can lay up to 8,000 eggs. The eggs hatch after 10–20 days into toadpoles, which are black and gregarious; they then metamorphose and leave the pond when only just over 1cm long.

So... A pond, of course, is key – the bigger you can make it the better. Make sure there are some aquatic weeds, such as Hornwort, and shallow areas in the sun. In addition, you need to make it easy for toads to actually get into your garden and to the pond – those Hedgehog Highways under fences are just the ticket. Add plenty of good feeding areas (leaf-litter, moist tall grass, flower borders and shrubberies), and a wide range of undisturbed retreats including log piles (half buried if possible), compost heaps and jumbled bricks.

◄ Unlike the clumps of frogspawn, toadspawn is laid in long strings wound around waterweed (top). 'Toadpoles' (bottom) are blackish-brown, much darker than the brown and grey of Frog tadpoles.

▲ The warty skin, the swollen poison gland behind the eye, and the lack of a dark, smooth cheek-patch are the easy ways to tell a toad from a frog. But beware, frogs in particular come in all sorts of colours!

Newts

Even small garden ponds are likely to harbour a newt or two. Looking rather like swimming lizards, they might not have caught the public imagination in the same way frogs and toads have, but newts still have plenty of character.

In the UK, their profile would be even lower were it not for the large, rare and protected **Great Crested Newt** *Triturus cristatus*, which grabs the headlines when its presence stops wildlife habitat being lost to 'development'. You need a licence in the UK to collect or even handle them.

Few people realise that newts can actually be watched relatively easily. The secret is a special Newt-watching Device (NWD). Battery operated, they come in a range of colours and sizes, and are sold under the name 'torch'.

HOME NEEDS

Distribution: Your garden is most likely to support the **Common Newt** *Triturus vulgaris*, often called the Smooth Newt, which is widespread throughout the British Isles. Don't discount finding the **Palmate Newt** *Triturus helveticus*, however, especially in western Britain (but not Ireland). It looks much like the Common, but has an unspotted throat and males have webbed back feet. Finding the Great Crested is not out of the question in Britain (although again Ireland misses out).

Habitat: In the breeding season, the Common enjoys still, shallow pools and even ditches and flooded tyre tracks, preferably neither too exposed nor shadowed. The Palmate especially likes pools in broadleaved woodlands, while Great Cresteds like water depths of

at least 50cm. Once the breeding season is over, newts leave the water and head to all sorts of grassy and leaf-litter habitats.

Habits: In water, they tend to live on the bottom. Great Cresteds form leks where the males gather to display at night. Out of water, adults hide by day and emerge at night to rove through the undergrowth looking for prey. It is unusual to see a newt away from water even though they spend much of their lives on dry land. The adults are predated by snakes, Hedgehogs, cats and small mammals, and the larvae ('efts') by frogs, toads, dragonfly larvae and water beetle larvae.

Hibernation: November–February, in a damp sheltered nook such as under log piles or rocks or among tree roots.

Food: Adults eat insects, slugs, worms and small snails. The efts are carnivorous and eat aquatic insect larvae, small freshwater crustaceans, and are notorious for eating frogspawn and tadpoles.

Breeding: Adults usually return to their breeding ponds on wet nights during February–April, the females laying 200–400 eggs, stuck individually to waterweeds. The frilly efts hatch after one to four weeks and live alone, with some overwintering before metamorphosing into adults.

So... A pond is clearly a vital thing to provide, but they also need all those out-of-water hunting habitats and suitable places to hide and hibernate. So dig a pond, create log piles and rock piles, and make sure you have areas of uncut grass, deep leaf-litter and thick ground vegetation.

◀ It may seem odd to see a newt out of water, but they spend more of their year on land than in water. This is a female Common Newt heading back to her breeding ditch in spring.

▲ A male Common Newt (above), in breeding dress and with a fiery belly, has a crest all along his back, but it is nothing like the wild spiky crest of the Great Crested Newt.

Make an amphibian hibernaculum

If you needed somewhere dark to sleep for weeks on end during the winter where you wouldn't dry out, where you wouldn't freeze, but wouldn't get too warm either, and where predators couldn't get at you in your dozy, vulnerable state, where would you go in a garden?

That's the challenge facing our amphibians. Some Frogs elect to swim down to the mud at the bottom of ponds, but many of them and also our Toads and newts try to find somewhere drier to wriggle down into, preferably a little way underground.

If you've made a logpile, that may do the trick, or they may snuggle into the base of a compost heap or even under a shed. But the following design is thought to offer some of the best conditions for them.

1. You'll need some chunky waste materials such as lumps of hardcore, broken bricks and old logs – the kind of things that are lying around in many gardens.

2. If you are on free draining soils, dig a hole about 30–50cm deep in a shady location; if you can, make your hole a metre or so across. If you are on really wet, impermeable soils, don't worry about this step.

3. Now fill your hole with your bulky material, or on wet soils just pile it all up on the surface. Keep going until you have quite a mound. Aim for the pile to be stable, with lots of possible entrance holes into a labyrinth of different-sized chambers and passageways. Small newts and froglets can wriggle into gaps barely a centimetre across; large toads may need ones 6–8cm or so wide. It doesn't matter if your hibernaculum looks rough and ready but if you want you could aim for some architectural merit in how you arrange everything.

4. If you dug soil out, you can sprinkle some back onto the pile, but you don't want the rain to swill too much of it into the cracks and crevices which might clog up all those chambers you created.

5. As a finishing touch, you could sprinkle some wildflower and wild grass seed on and around the pile so that the amphibians have some cover as they enter and leave their winter dormitory. It will also help bind together any soil you put on the pile.

It should now last for several seasons, and some amphibians may even return to it year after year.

◀ Prepare an area of shady ground – this is a great way to use a forgotten corner of the garden.

◀ Dig a hole – if amphibians can get underground in winter, the conditions are much more constant.

◀ You could just create a random mound, or you could get creative, like my 'Froghenge'.

◀ Fill with large rocks, making sure there are lots of different sized gaps for everything from large Toads to tiny Froglets to wriggle into.

Gardening for Bees

How many types of bee can you name? Honeybees, yes. Bumblebees, of course. Doing well so far. How about the Red Mason Bee, which is the one that nests in those tube-filled wooden boxes you see advertised. Any more? (Rack those brains!) If you're anything like I was before I started gardening for wildlife, you will be struggling.

Amazingly more than 250 species of bee have been recorded in the British Isles. Granted, not all of them will find their way into your garden, but you could easily host 20 or more, especially if you live in the south. Smaller bees can seem a bit of a 'specialist' subject, but I recommend you get to know and love bees of all sorts as they are vital for pollination. With a little wildlife gardening know-how and a keen eye, you will start to recognise some of the less well-known species and witness all sorts of astonishing behaviours.

LONERS, SOCIALITES AND SNEAKY INTRUDERS

It is worth understanding the basic differences in lifestyles between the main groups of bees.

The one we are most familiar with is the Honeybee. There is just one species, living in a 'megasociety'. Effectively, it is a totalitarian monarchy with each colony having an all-female workforce collecting food, providing security and dutifully serving their lone queen, albeit with the occasional bloody coup thrown in. Most of the colony survives the winter.

Bumblebees also have female-dominated societies, but only their queens survive the winter and then raise new workforces in the spring, single-handedly at first.

The solitary bees, which make up 90 per cent of all British bee species, do indeed lead pretty solitary lives. The females emerge, find a male and mate, and then go off alone to construct a small nest, lay their eggs and abandon them to nature. Some solitary species do form clusters of nests, but there is no cooperative behaviour between the adults.

Finally, on the edges of bee society are the parasitic bees. They behave rather like a Cuckoo does, creeping into the nest of another bee species, laying their eggs and scarpering.

With so many species, there are inevitably further differences of lifestyle, and we will look at those in more detail, but it is possible to pick out some general bee needs that apply to almost all species.

HOME NEEDS

Distribution: It is the usual story as with other groups of wildlife – there are more species the further south you live. But you can expect some bees almost anywhere.

Habitat: Sunny, sheltered flower-rich places are paramount, so meadows, hedgerows, orchards, warm coastal areas, woodlands and gardens are key.

Habits: Life for a bee largely consists of flying about in search of food in warm sunny weather, with different species flying at different times of year.

Food: All bees exist on a strict diet of nectar and pollen, and feed their grubs on the same. Their endless roving from bloom to bloom makes them vital pollinators. Almost all species show preferences for the types of flower they visit, determined by the shape of their tongues and the time of year they fly. Most prefer to visit big clumps of their preferred flowers.

Breeding: Every bee starts life in a specially constructed cell in a sheltered nest of some sort, often a tunnel or hole. Here, the grubs are provided with a stash of baby-food and go through a process of pupation before emerging as an adult.

So... Bottom line, we need to grow a range of bee-friendly flowers over a long season, and provide a range of different nest sites.

▲ If you look closely, you will find that many bees that you have previously passed off as just Honeybees are in fact a whole range of different species, such as this mining bee.

SOLITARY BEES

The eyes of the wildlife world are at last opening to the delights of solitary bees. I can't take you through each of them species by species, as there are over 200 and some are very difficult indeed to identify, but I've split some of the most familiar species into five groups to help get you started.

Short-tongued bees

These are primitive bees, including the small black and hairless *Hylaeus* bees, and the many *Colletes* bees, which are like small honeybees with prominent white and dark bands on their hairy bodies. The autumn-flying Ivy Bee *C. hederae* first arrived in Dorset in 2001 and is now spreading fast.

HOME NEEDS
Habits: *Colletes* bees carry pollen back to their nests on their hairy legs; *Hylaeus* bees, being hairless, have to transport it in their stomachs.

Food: They have very short tongues rather similar to a wasp, and so can only feed at flowers where the pollen and nectar are easily reached. Popular flowers include brambles, Masterwort, Mignonette, heathers, Ox-eye Daisy, *Anthemis*, Yarrow, Tansy, ragworts and Iceplant, and Ivy for the Ivy Bee.

Breeding: *Hylaeus* bees nest in small hollow plant stems, making the cells from their saliva. Most *Colletes* bees nest in loose soil, digging a burrow. *C. daviesanus* burrows into soft mortar, but rarely causes structural damage.

◄ One of the most distinctive of all garden bees with its silvery fur waistcoat, the Ashy Mining Bee *Andrena cineraria* loves nesting in bare banks of soil.

Mining bees

These include the *Andrena* and *Halictus* groups of bees, smaller than the Honeybee and which usually have furry bodies.

HOME NEEDS
Habits: Many live solitary lives but some have a degree of social organisation. Most carry pollen on hairs on their legs.

Food: These bees have a pointed tongue and so can reach into slightly deeper flowers than the short-tongued species. They are important pollinators of fruit trees, plus a wide range of flowers including Wild Strawberry, Lesser Celandine, lupins, daisies, dandelions, clovers and sallows.

Breeding: Most burrow into soft, sandy soil, with the Tawny Mining Bee *A. fulva* digging into your garden lawn and creating a little pyramid of soil with a hole in the middle. It is no problem unless you like your lawn to be a bowling green.

◄ The Ivy Bee is one of the 'plasterer' bees, which nest in warm, dry soils and paint the inside of their nesting burrows with saliva.

◄ Several species of solitary mining bee, such as this Early Mining Bee *Andrena haemorrhoa*, are frequently found in gardens.

◄ Feeding on *Inula hookeri*, this is one of the leafcutter bees, with a mainly dark body above but concealing a bright yellow underside.

Mason and leaf-cutter bees

The masons are named for their building skills rather than for forming secret societies! The leaf-cutters live up to their name. All are usually quite small and dark but with a bright yellow belly.

HOME NEEDS

Habits: They carry the pollen back to their nests on their hairy bellies. If you love your rose plants, look away now, for leaf-cutter bees cut neat circles from the edges of leaves, and you may see them flying back to their nests with the disc of leaf slung beneath them.
Food: All have long tongues and can delve deep into tubular flowers. Favourites include Borage, geraniums and grape hyacinths.
Breeding: They often build their nest cells in beetle holes in wood or excavate their own holes in soft mortar. Leaf-cutters roll up their leaves to create cell walls within their burrows. The familiar **Red Mason Bee** *Osmia rufa* has both a spring and a summer generation.

◄ A Wool Carder Bee, with yellow markings along the edge of her abdomen, sits on the furry leaf of Lamb's-ear. The plant will provide her with both the 'wool' to build her nest and nectar from its flowers.

Wool Carder Bee
Anthidium manicatum

This is a large bee well worth watching out for in the south, with yellow spots down either side of its body.

HOME NEEDS

Habits: The females carry home giant balls of wool, which they harvest from the leaves of furry plants such as Lamb's-ear, foxgloves, woundworts and dead-nettles. They will guard a favourite clump from all comers.
Food: Tubular flowers, such as those used by the masons.
Breeding: The wool is used to create the cells within their burrows.

◄ The male Hairy-footed Flower Bee really lives up to its name, and is a good starting point for getting hooked on the world of solitary bees.

Flower bees
Anthophora

If you don't know the Hairy-footed Flower Bee *Anthophora plumipes*, you're missing a treat. It and its rarer cousins are smaller than bumblebees but just as furry, and are real characters.

HOME NEEDS

Habits: The Hairy-footed emerges in early spring, the ginger males (with characteristic white furry faces) and the black female (with red hind legs) are really obvious as they dart from flower to flower, skillfully hovering and making a high pitched buzz.
Food: All sorts of flowers, often at ground level, such as Ground-ivy, lungworts and Green Alkanet.
Breeding: Big numbers can gather to nest in soft mortar and cob walls.

So... Encouraging solitary bees from any of these groups is all about two things: providing the right flowers where they can collect food – which are often different from the flowers used by larger bees – and ensuring that they have suitable places to nest. The greater the diversity of their favourite plants, the more solitary bees you will have.

Making nest sites for solitary bees

The vogue for creating solitary bee 'nest boxes' has been one of the big steps forward in wildlife gardening in recent times. The science has moved on considerably, but at the same time people have realised that they can let their imagination soar, and all sorts of wonderful creations have emerged.

I certainly hope you're willing to make a nest box, but don't let your ambition stop there. Try encouraging several many more types to breed in your garden by creating the five different types of nest sites:

◀ With nest sites for solitary bees, you can let your imagination run riot. If you want, you can open up a whole mega-wall of holes.

1. For species that nest in hollow plant stems:

❀ Gather any old dried stems that are hollow, such as Angelica and Alexanders, plus bamboo canes, reeds, etc.

❀ Cut into 15cm lengths. Ensure that tube is not blocked at 'nodes' along the plant stem – bees can't bore through those barriers.

❀ Wedge them tightly in a container, such as a wooden box or tin can, preferably with a slight overhang to keep the rain off.

❀ Fix firmly to a sunny fence or wall, facing between SE and SW (don't hang it from a tree).

❀ If there is the risk of tits or Great Spotted Woodpeckers raiding the box, cover the front with chicken mesh, which will still allow the bees through but will inhibit the birds.

2. For species that nest in holes in wood:

❀ Take a piece of untreated hard wood or log (avoid softwoods such as pine) and go mad with all your drill bits, peppering its surface with holes of different diameters from 2–8mm width.

❀ If using a log, go in through the bark rather than in the cut face.

❀ Drill in as deep as you can go, with the holes slightly sloping upwards so they won't fill with rain.

❀ Make sure the entrances of all the tunnels are nice and smooth – bees avoid jagged splinters, which might tear their wings.

◀ Here I've used drilled logs, hollow stems and reed stems to give a range of different tube diameters.

❀ Fix in a sunny position facing between SE and SW, and ensure it is stable and not rocking about in a wind.

3. For species that burrow into pithy plant stems:

❀ Take lengths of raspberry cane, bramble stem, Elder or sunflowers and fix them upright to your beewall in a sunny position.

4. For species that nest in nooks and crannies:

❀ Create a low wall (of bricks or rocks), held together with a dry mortar, in a sunny position.

◀ By building a mound of soil and then cutting a vertical face on the south side, I've created a bank that various mining bees can use.

5. For species that nest in the ground:

These could turn out to be the most important habitats to create in gardens for solitary bees, but the science of how to make them is still in its infancy – you are welcome to innovate. Just think about where the bees might breed in the wild – in beds or banks of very poor bare, sandy and gravelly soil. Use that as inspiration for creating a bank of sandy soil, at least 10cm deep, in a warm, sheltered sunny position, where little vegetation can take hold. You could try holding the sand together with a little bit of cement.

Follow the advice closely and success is almost assured. You may not always see the bees go in, but you should see tell-tale signs, such as blocked burrow entrances. If the mums aren't at home when you look, try checking your flower borders to see if they are out at work.

These nest sites may also be used by several species of solitary wasps, which are useful pest hunters around the garden.

Bumblebees

What adorable creatures bumblebees are. With their portly little bodies and fluffy, striped jumpers, they have got bags of character. You will almost certainly have success in encouraging bumblebees to use your garden. Not only are they entertaining, but bumblebees in general are having a hard time in the British countryside, so they are well worth the effort.

◄ Not all bumblebees are chunky with black and yellow stripes – this Common Carder Bee *Bombus pascuorum*, a common garden visitor, is a gingery colour, but has the typical 'teddy bear' fur of a bumblebee.

HOME NEEDS

Distribution: There are just 25 different species of bumblebee in the British Isles, but only about half a dozen of them are common in gardens. Many have a strong southerly bias to their range. Identification can be difficult – queens differ in size and colour from the female workers, which are variable and differ from the males.

Habitats: Flowery meadows and downland are their most important habitat, but gardens can be pretty good for some species.

Habits: We usually encounter bumblebees blundering around the flower borders. They can forage even in quite dull weather.

Food: All species have relatively long tongues compared to most bees, but some have very long ones, and most species show distinct preferences for certain species of flower.

Breeding: The life cycle for this social species starts with lone queens emerging from hibernation in spring and seeking out suitable nest sites. Some species use old mouse burrows, ideally full of bedding. Others nest at the base of bushes, in tussocks of grass, in holes in walls, or beneath sheds, log piles or compost heaps. The Tree Bumblebee will take over empty bird boxes. Once installed, the queen starts by making a little wax cup that she fills with nectar to keep her going through hard times. She then collects pollen, moulding it into a little lump on which she lays her first eggs. She

broods them, and feeds the grubs from when they hatch until they pupate. They then emerge as worker females. The queen can now stay at home while her industrious first brood harvest more food for yet more daughters until the colony contains up to 150 workers. By late summer, some of the grubs emerge as males and new queens. They fly the nest, mate, and all, apart from the old and new queens, die before winter.

So... Because bumblebee colonies are often on the go from early spring right through to late autumn, a supply of nectar and pollen is essential throughout. It is a good gardening challenge, and there are some sure-fire plants that will keep bumblebees in love with your garden (see pages 110–111).

Offering a choice of nest sites is clearly also vital. A good mix would include hedges and shrubberies, log piles and areas of tussocky grass, or you could try making them a home…

Bumblebee boxes

I'm not going to lie to you – getting bumblebees to nest where you want them to is notoriously difficult. It seems that we struggle to see things through a queen bee's eyes. A bumblebee box aims to recreate a mouse burrow leading down to a dark, dry chamber with some bedding material. Here are two models to try:

✿ **The 50p home-made model** – a half-buried clay plant pot, topped with a slate to keep the rain out and fed by 30cm of buried old hosepipe well-skewered for drainage. Put a ball of dry moss and grass inside.

✿ **The £20 proprietary model** – a wooden box full of bedding such as dry moss and grasses with a small entrance hole 18–25mm across. Place facing south at the base of a bush or hedge.

◄ There are a whole range of 'bumblebee homes' you can buy. You may be lucky, but the evidence shows that the chances of them being occupied are very slim.

Honeybee

Apis mellifera

The Honeybee is, throughout much of Britain, effectively a semi-domesticated animal rather than true 'wildlife', imported from Europe and beyond. In a very few places, some of the original native, dark Honeybees are thought to survive. Nevertheless, it is such a well-loved creature, an important pollinator, and of course the source of honey, that most people still love to encourage them in gardens, whatever their origin.

The life story of the Honeybee must rank as one of the most astonishing in nature. It involves a mother and up to 40,000 daughters work in perfect cooperation to maintain a colony that persists year on year.

Populations have been declining alarmingly (so-called Colony Collapse Disorder), the reasons for which are poorly known. Possible causes include a parasitic mite, malnutrition and pesticides. With Honeybees estimated to pollinate about 80 per cent of flowers, they are crucial for horticulture.

HOME NEEDS

Distribution: Thanks to domestication, they are found throughout almost all of Europe.

Habitat: Anywhere with access to flower-rich habitats, such as meadows, orchards and some horticultural crops. Wild or feral colonies need large hollow trees.

Habits: They live in large colonies usually in a hive tended by beekeepers. Almost all are daughters of the one giant queen who pumps out pheromones to keep the colony united. The workers spend most of their lives tending to the nest and larvae or collecting food. The colony has to forage over a huge area, up to 20,000ha, with workers travelling up to 12km. They have special dances that signal to fellow bees where good food sources are. By winter, many of the workers perish, but a core of the colony survives, relying on stores of honey and pollen to see them through.

Food: Wildflowers in profusion, plus lime trees, fruit trees, clover meadows and garden flowers.

Breeding: In the nest, the sheets of honeycomb are divided into perfect hexagonal cells. Some cells are a store for honey and pollen, others are nursery chambers. The queen, having mated with several males (drones) on an autumn honeymoon flight, has enough sperm to last three years. She roams through the nest, fed by diligent housemaids, and lays up to 1,000 eggs a day, one per cell.

Each egg hatches after five days, and the workers secrete a special baby-food, royal jelly, for the larvae's first three days. For the next two, the larvae are fed nectar and pollen, and the workers

▼ This Honeybee pauses for breath on the flower stems of Borage before recommencing the arduous food collection job she performs for the queen.

then cap the cell and the larvae pupates. Eight days later, a new worker emerges to join the labour force.

In summer, the workers construct slightly bigger cells, prompting the queen to lay unfertilised eggs that emerge as drones. Larvae in extra-large cells are fed bumper amounts of royal jelly and become virgin queens. When the first of them hatches, either the old queen will flee to set up a new nest with a loyal coterie (a swarm), or a virgin queen will head out to mate with drones and return to oust the flagging old matriarch.

So... By growing as many top bee plants as possible (see pages 110–111), you will have the workers rushing back to the colony and dancing the good news that your garden is the best!

Beekeeping

With honey being so scrumptious and with a colony producing up to 30kg a year, it is no wonder that people (and a certain Pooh Bear of very little brain) have long been tempted to take advantage, sealed honey jars were even found in Tutankhamun's tomb.

At first, early civilisations raided wild nests, destroying them for the honey. Over time, swarms were collected and placed in artificial hives, and the Honeybee became domesticated, but it is only 200 years since modern hives were invented that allow honey to be collected without destroying the colony.

If you want to take up beekeeping, start by joining your local beekeeping society and use only proper hives that can be inspected and cleaned. Start-up costs for equipment are about £300–500, it does require time and skill, and you will get stung, but the rewards are sweet (groan).

Top flowers for bees – season by season

There are plenty of flowers that bees will use; unfortunately, there are many, many more that are absolutely useless, and I browse through some plant catalogues despairing at the sheer dearth of good bee plants that are available to buy (even if some little wildlife icons on seed packets appear to be telling, or selling, us a different story).

So here are my top choices, season by season, of the groups of flowers that are some of the very best for bees.

Through a range of excellent studies in recent years, we are learning more and more about which varieties really are the very best. Even within one plant family that may be noted for its attractiveness, there can be some that are excellent for bees through to others that are only OK.

Nevertheless, I stand by my broad recommendations, for within those groups there are very few flowers that you would think of as 'bad for bees'.

And, remember it's not only the species of plant that is key. For the best results:

❀ try to ensure that something is in flower to provide bees with nectar and pollen throughout the year, from the point the first queen bumblebees emerge in very early spring, until honeybees are gathering their last stores for the winter

❀ ensure the flowers are in sheltered, sunny positions wherever possible

❀ strive to have a range of different flower shapes, from deep-throated flowers to those with a flat 'table-top' as this will help the widest range of bee species. Smaller solitary bees in particular need those more open flowers.

❀ plant flowers in drifts – bees do best if there is a mass of the same sort of flower so that they can just hop from one to the next.

Spring: February–May

Apples *Malus*

Hellebores *Helleborus*

Willows and sallows *Salix*

Crocuses *Crocus*

Lungworts *Pulmonaria*

Winter heathers e.g. *Erica carnea*

Dead-nettles *Lamium*

Oregon-grapes *Mahonia*

Barberries *Berberis*, **Blackthorn** *Prunus spinosa*, **cherries** *Prunus*, **Corydalis**, **Columbine** *Aquilegia*, **currants** *Ribes*, **dead-nettles** *Lamium*, **grape hyacinths** *Muscari*, **Ground Ivy** *Glechoma hederacea*, **lavenders** *Lavandula*, **Norway Maple** *Acer platanoides*, **Snake's-head Fritillary** *Fritillaria melegaris*, **wallflowers** *Cherianthus*, **Winter Honeysuckle** *Lonicera purpusii*

Midsummer: June–July

Alliums

Limes
(the tree, not the fruit!) *Tilia*

Sages *Salvias*

Bellflowers
Campanula

Rosemary
Rosmarinus

Scorpion weeds *Phacelia*

Cranesbills
Geranium

Thymes
Thymus

Agastaches, **Alder Buckthorn** *Frangula alnus*, **Blackberries and raspberries** *Rubus*, **Borage** *Borago*, **clovers** *Trifolium*, **comfreys** *Symphytum*, **Deutzias**, **fennels** *Foeniculum*, **foxgloves** *Digitalis*, **germanders** *Teucrium*, **globe thistles** *Echinops*, **hedge veronicas** *Hebe*, **hemp-agrimonies** *Eupatorium*, **Honeywort** *Cerinthe major*, **knapweeds and cornflowers** *Centaurea*, **lavenders** *Lavandula*, **Marjoram** *Oreganum*, **scabiouses** *Scabiosa/Knautia/Succisa*, **Teasel** *Dipsacus fullonum*, **viper's buglosses** *Echium*, **Yellow Rattle** *Rhinanthus minor*

Late summer/autumn: August –November

Catmints
Nepeta

Dahlias

Iceplants
Sedum

Coneflowers
Echinacea

Globe thistles
Echinops

Bee-balms *Monarda*, **Buddleja x weyeriana**, **Cardoon** *Cynara*, **Devil's-bit Scabious** *Succisa pratensis*, **Ivy** *Hedera helix*, **Lavenders** *Lavandula*, **Michaelmas daisies** *Aster/Symphiotrichum*, **sneezeweeds** *Helenium*, **woundworts** *Stachys*, **heathers** *Erica* and *Calluna*

Gardening for Dragons and Damsels

▼ Damselflies tend to hold their wings closed behind them. This is a male Banded Demoiselle.

A sunny summer's day lounging by the edge of a pond may sound idyllic to us, but it's pretty scary if you're a fly. It needs to keep alert if it is to evade the jazzy but rapacious dragonflies and damselflies that patrol the airways above the water like fighter planes.

'Dragons' have chunky, almost pencil-thick bodies. They include the large green- or blue-marked **hawker** dragonflies, the chasers and skimmers with rather flattened bodies, and the rather stumpy and often red or yellowy **darters**.

'Damsels' in comparison are bantamweights, with slender fragile bodies and tissue-paper wings. Most are marked with green, red or blue.

▼ Dragonflies, such as this female Broad-bodied Chaser, hold their wings out flat.

On the next page we look at some of the specific home needs of the commoner garden species, but here is a little insight to them as a group.

HOME NEEDS

Distribution: About 40 species breed in the UK, split almost equally between dragons and damsels, with fewer the further north you are.

Habitat: Water is key for much of a dragon's or damsel's needs, but different species have different preferences. Some like it moving; some prefer still. Some can cope with acidic water; some need neutral or alkaline. Muddy bottoms might be desirable or they might need gravel. The list goes on: minimum surface area, ideal depth, water temperature, levels of dissolved oxygen, amount of aquatic vegetation – all impact on the species that you will find. You are fortunate if your garden pond is visited by even five species, but if you live near to prime dragonfly habitats such as wet

▼ On emerging from the water, the larval skin splits and the adult crawls out, pausing to pump up its crumpled wings.

heathland, rivers or fens then you could play host to a bumper number of species.

Habits: The larval stage, which are called nymphs, lurk around underwater, breathing using gills. Here they overwinter, some species taking two to three years to mature. At well-defined times of year, depending on species, the nymphs leave the water, clambering up plant stems, and shed their skins to emerge as adults. Most now leave their birthplace and spend time away from water before finding a new water-body to breed. Some adults even migrate huge distances each year to reach our shores.

Food: Nymphs are ferocious predators and catch all sorts of underwater creatures, many larger than themselves. Some dragon nymphs can even bag small fish. Adults target flying insects such as flies, midges and mosquitoes. Some damsels are taken by dragons.

Breeding: Males gather at water-bodies to wait to grab a mate. In some species, the male will hold onto the female while she is egg-laying and even in flight to ensure no rival steals her away. Some females drop the eggs casually into the water; others choose their spot carefully, inserting the egg into the stems of aquatic plants or submerged logs.

So... Pond size is important, the larger you can make it the more species are likely to visit. You want your pond to be rich in aquatic life, so make sure it gets sunshine, and include areas at different depths including lots of shallow areas. Have plenty of submerged and emergent plants, an underwater log or two, and good insect-hunting habitat nearby, such as sheltered hedgerows and flowerbeds.

Emperor (female, egg laying)   Broad-bodied Chaser (male)   Common Darter (female)

Common garden dragonflies and damselflies

Brown Hawker *Aeshna grandis*
Distribution: Much of lowland Britain, and spreading north. **Habitat:** Most water-bodies, including garden ponds. **Habits:** This amber-winged large dragon is often seen well away from ponds. **Flight season:** June–October.

Migrant Hawker *Aeshna mixta*
Distribution: Southern England and Wales. **Habitat:** All sorts of ponds and lakes with some vegetation. **Habits:** Groups gather around treetops and hedgerows in autumn. **Flight season:** August–October.

Southern Hawker *Aeshna cyanea*
Distribution: England, Wales, and small populations in Scotland. **Habitat:** Stagnant, shady, woodland ponds, faring quite well in gardens. **Habits:** Quarters to and fro along sunny corridors, often checking out people. **Flight season:** July–September.

Emperor *Anax imperator*
Distribution: Southern Britain. **Habitat:** Large ponds with plenty of vegetation, but will come to quite small garden ponds. **Habits:** Flies high and mightily over the water; females lay eggs on floating vegetation. **Flight season:** June–August.

Broad-bodied Chaser *Libellula depressa*
Distribution: The southern half of Britain. **Habitat:** Small, shallow, sunny ponds. **Habits:** Quite approachable, often coming back to a favourite perch. **Flight season:** June–July.

Common Darter *Sympetrum striolatum*
Distribution: Almost all of the British Isles. **Habitat:** Many waters, and will even use small ponds with few plants. **Habits:** Approachable, often basking on fences and slabs. **Flight season:** July–October.

Large Red Damselfly *Pyrrhosoma nymphula*
Distribution: Throughout the British Isles. **Habitat:** All sorts of ponds, but especially well-vegetated ones. Common in gardens. **Habits:** Perches on pond vegetation and then flies out to intercept rivals. **Flight season:** April–August.

Azure Damselfly *Coenagrion puella*
Distribution: All of British Isles bar northern Scotland. **Habitat:** Small ponds with vegetation and shelter. **Habits:** Darts low around pond margins. **Flight season:** May–August.

Common Blue Damselfly
Enallagma cyathigerum
Distribution: Throughout the British Isles. **Habitat:** All sorts of water-bodies. **Habits:** Often flies way out over open water. **Flight season:** May–September.

Blue-tailed Damselfly *Ischnura elegans*
Distribution: Throughout the British Isles. **Habitat:** All sorts of ponds including small and new ones. **Habits:** Flies weakly among low vegetation. **Flight season:** May–August.

Other species you may be lucky enough to see include:
Common Hawker *Aeshna juncea*, Four-spotted Chaser *Libellula quadrimaculata*, Ruddy Darter *Sympetrum sanguineum*, Banded Demoiselle *Calopteryx splendens*, Emerald Damselfly *Lestes sponsa* and Red-eyed Damselfly *Erythromma najas*.

Southern Hawker (male)   Large Red Damselfly (female)   Blue-tailed Damselfly (male)

Gardening for Moths

As a child, I could identify every species of butterfly that visited my garden. Moths, on the other hand, I blatantly ignored. As far as I was concerned, they were drab, boring and unidentifiable.

So it was an eye-opener when, two decades later, I started moth trapping in my tiny suburban garden. The technique is to lure them at night with special lights and then release them unharmed the next day. In one summer's night, a tiny garden can easily catch 200 moths of 30 species. And I started finding things like this…

But not all moths are nocturnal. Every year the RSPB get dozens of phone calls from people saying they have a hummingbird in their garden, hovering at flowers and sucking nectar through its beak.

It's this, the **Hummingbird Hawkmoth** *Macroglossum stellatarum*, with its amazing tongue, and there are other funky daytime species too.

As its name would suggest, the Garden Tiger was once a common sight in gardens, but numbers have declined dramatically. Climatic changes may be responsible for the falls as the Garden Tiger caterpillars' food plants – garden plants – remain common.

It's an **Elephant Hawkmoth** *Deilephila elpenor*; I had no idea that shocking-pink, fluffy monsters were out there in gardens.

And I love this one, the **Buff-tip** *Phalera bucephala*, designed to look like a broken twig. What amazed me most was that these are common garden species, but without trapping them you just wouldn't know that they are there.

If I still haven't won you round to moths' charms, then there's another reason to love them – their importance in the food chain. For many bird species in particular, moths are vital. Tits, Goldcrests and many others eat not only the adult moths but their eggs, caterpillars and pupae. Bats, of course, eat moths, too, and long-eared bats even pluck caterpillars off leaves.

It all adds up to the conclusion that you've just *got* to garden for moths, and the great thing is that there is plenty you can do for them.

HOME NEEDS

There is a mind-boggling myriad of moths. More than 2,400 species have been recorded in the British Isles, about a third of which are the so-called 'macro moths', which are generally at least the size of a 5p piece and often much bigger. The 'micros' in comparison are usually very small indeed, and very difficult to identify.

Picking out the home needs for each and every moth would, of course, be a long read, but we can at least make some good general observations.

Distribution: There are moths to be found pretty much everywhere. The number of species thins the further north or the higher you go, but these places have their own specialities.

Habitats: Moths occupy almost every habitat you can think of. They are perhaps most numerous in woodland, but there are moths on the coast, in wetlands, in mountains, and there are plenty that find a good home in gardens, even in urban areas.

Habits: Most moth species fly by night. Without the heat of the sun to warm them up, many of them have to vibrate their wings vigorously before they can get airborne. Damp cloudy nights are often best. Why many species fly towards lights is still not fully understood, but it may be that the construction of their eyes makes them think they are flying away from them. Many wander widely, ending up in unsuitable habitats, and some are even long-distance migrants.

Roost: Every moth must hide away before daylight comes in a place where birds won't find them, so plenty of dense vegetation is vital.

Food for the caterpillars: Different moth caterpillars eat different things, from plant leaves to flowers, seedpods, dead leaves, algae, roots and living wood. If we take all the common macro moths in the British Isles and those which are more local, but which turn up in gardens, just under 400 species in all, we find that:

- About 20 per cent of species aren't fussy, eating all sorts of herbaceous plants
- About 15 per cent eat the leaves of all sorts of broadleaved trees, without restricting themselves to one species
- And about 7 per cent eat wild grasses.

All the rest are specialists, eating just one particular family or species of plant. If you don't have that plant in your garden, that's it, the moth can't breed there. Some of the key plants are trees – especially willows, birches, poplars, hawthorns, oaks and Blackthorn. Now you can see why so many insect-eating birds spend so much of their time in trees. In terms of herbaceous plants, bedstraws are popular. Beyond that, there are more than 100 different plant species that each have their own specialist moths. And that doesn't even begin to take account of the micro moths.

Food for the adults: Some adult moths need to drink sweet liquids, but many don't – some don't even have functioning mouthparts. For those that do, top tipples are the fermenting juice of overripe blackberries, the nectar of Ivy, sallow catkins, ragworts, Red Valerian, honeysuckles and campions, and aphid honeydew.

Breeding: Much of the adult male moth's life is spent searching for a mate in the dark; the females sit waiting to be found, often pumping out scent. Once mated, the females have to find the right plants in the dark on which to lay their eggs.

◀ The Mint Moth *Pyrausta aurata* is a familiar visitor to the herb garden – the adults nectar on mint and Marjoram flower, the caterpillars eat the leaves.

▼ The Cinnabar caterpillar is a familiar sight on ragwort in summer – the yellow and black stripes signal that it is very unpleasant to eat, and so there is no need for it to hide.

▼▼ You can tell the finger-sized caterpillars of hawkmoths by the 'thorn' on their rear end. This is the Privet Hawkmoth, which feeds on privets, ash and various other shrubs.

Home needs, moth by moth…

OK, maybe that's a bit ambitious. But at least here is a starter guide to some of the main groups of macro moths.

Six-spot Burnet

Burnet moths *Zygaena*

Boldly patterned red and dark metal-green, and with black hockey-stick antennae, the three common species fly by day in midsummer. They live in colonies in flower-rich meadows where their caterpillars eat bird's-foot trefoils and clovers, and the adults nectar at knapweeds, scabiouses and Viper's Bugloss.

Geometrids

Mostly nocturnal, this is a large family of slender-bodied moths that tend to hold their wings out flat (apart from the group called the thorns, which hold them in a 'V' or even 'up like a sail'). This family includes groups of moths such as the carpets, pugs and waves, of which many different species visit even small gardens. It also includes the master of camouflage, Willow Beauty *Peribatodes secundaria* (above), and the common and distinctive Magpie Moth *Abraxas grossulariata*. These moths fly weakly, expending little energy, so few need to nectar at flowers and some are able to emerge in midwinter. Their 'looper' caterpillars have a gap between the front three pairs of true legs and the two pairs of hind legs (prolegs) that

allows them to crawl quickly by looping their rear end up behind their front end.

Helping Geometrids is all about helping their caterpillars, a great many of which feed on woody plants, especially native trees and shrubs.

Hawkmoths

Guaranteed to wow the kids, these are the giants of our insect world, with the **Privet Hawkmoth** *Sphinx ligustri* having a 12cm wingspan. As its name suggests, its caterpillar feeds on Garden and Wild Privet. Other common and no less dramatic species include (with caterpillar foodplants in brackets): **Poplar Hawkmoth** *Laothoe populi* (poplars); **Lime Hawkmoth** *Mimas tiliae* (limes, elms); **Pine Hawkmoth** *Hyloicus pinastri* (Scots Pine); **Small Elephant Hawkmoth** *Deilephila porcellus* (bedstraws); as well as the two we've already seen (both on page 114), **Elephant Hawkmoth** (bedstraws, willowherbs and garden fuchsias) and **Hummingbird Hawkmoth** (Lady's and Hedge Bedstraws). The caterpillars of all of them are impressive.

Adult hawkmoths (bar Privet and Lime) feed at tubular flowers such as honeysuckles and Tobacco Plant. Hummingbird Hawkmoths feed at Red Valerian, lavenders, *Verbena bonariensis* and fuchsias. They set up feeding rounds, returning to the same plant every hour or so over several days.

Lime Hawkmoth   Privet Hawkmoth

Prominents and kittens

These are rather chunky moths that sit with their wings held like a ridge-tent over their backs. The prominents are named after the little knobs along the rear edge of the moths' forewings, which poke up when they are resting. They include the **Swallow Prominent** *Phoesia tremula* and the **Pale Prominent** *Pterostoma palpina*. The kittens are so called because of their supremely furry bodies, the largest of which is the **Puss Moth** *Cerura vinula* (oh, how I love moth names!)

These moths don't feed as adults, so again nurturing them is all about satisfying the needs of their hungry caterpillars, which feed on tree leaves, each species having particular favourites, with birches, willows, oaks and Aspen particularly favoured.

Willow Beauty   Magpie Moth

Pale Prominent   Swallow Prominent

Tiger moths

The **Garden Tiger** *Arctia caja* has wings that are more leopard-print than tiger-like. The day-flying **Cinnabar** *Tyria jacobaeae*, whose familiar yellow-and-black caterpillars feed on ragworts, is sometimes mistaken for the Garden Tiger. The **Ruby Tiger** looks quite different – its body is even brighter red than its wings. Its caterpillars are 'polyphages', meaning they eat all sorts of plants.

Garden Tiger   Ruby Tiger

Noctuids

This is a very large group of mainly night-flying moths, most of which have rather chunky bodies and hold their mottled brown and grey wings flat over their backs or like a ridge tent. These are fast and furious flyers, and need pit stops at flowers and honeydew to refuel. Two very common species are the **Large Yellow Underwing** *Noctua pronuba*, which you are likely to flush from long grass while mowing, and the **Angle Shades** *Phlogophora meticulosa*, which is very distinctive, having folded wing edges that look like origami.

Large Yellow Underwing   Angle Shades

So... Gardening for moths: top things to do

Plant a tree. If you have a large garden, you can't do any better than an oak. If you have a small garden, a hawthorn, fruit tree or willow would be great.

Plant a mixed native hedge. This is a way of growing trees without them becoming huge. You may not generate quite the same mass of leaves and branches, but you can pack in loads of different species and hence accommodate many moths.

Vegetation, vegetation, vegetation. The more you have, the more caterpillars your garden is likely to support.

Grow climbers up walls. Ivy is the best because it will provide nectar, too, but any dense climber offers great places for moths to hide by day.

Don't use pesticides.

Plant a wildflower meadow. Burnet moths will be the obvious sign of success, but you might be lucky to get a day-flying Burnet Companion or Mother Shipton, and think of all those species whose caterpillars feed on wild grasses.

Grow nectar plants for the adults. You'll need to get out with a torch to see them being used, but that's a mini-adventure in itself.

Grow an area of Rosebay Willowherb. It's an attractive flower, some adult moths love it for its nectar, but if you then get Elephant Hawkmoth caterpillars, you are so going to thank me!

Rosebay Willowherb

Gardening for Minibeasts

There is a whole host of smaller garden species that might not, at first, seem like worthy recipients of your hospitality. Many of them, however, turn out to be fascinating in their own right and often these species are crucial items on the menus you hope to serve up for your larger garden guests.

▲ Even some dramatic-looking creatures that make it into gardens, such as this longhorn beetle, are not familiar enough to the general public to have a common English name: this is *Strangalia maculata*.

After all the glam and attention-seeking celebrities of the garden-wildlife world – the A-list birds, beauty-queen butterflies and character-actor amphibians – the supporting cast often don't get much of a look in. Most are small or even tiny, many are nocturnal, and some are decidedly ugly or even alarming.

Many are also ridiculously hard to identify, a frustration given that we humans delight in being able to give a name to everything (and tend to ignore those we can't).

But while they may not have quite the allure of their larger brethren, these creatures and 'lesser' plants are certainly not 'extras'. Nature, as we know, is one large interconnected web, where the smallest creatures underpin complex food chains. Take away the creepy crawlies, fungi and mosses and our garden wildlife hotel loses its foundations and comes crashing down.

▲ Some insects that everyone has heard of, such as the grasshoppers, are actually quite rare in gardens, and need hard work on your part if they are to flourish there.

In fact, this section doesn't even start to delve into the microscopic world, where, for instance, small lumps of soil are stuffed with hundreds of mites and springtails, thousands of tiny worms (nematodes), not to mention billions of bacteria.

But that still leaves us plenty of fascinating minor beasties that we can watch out for, get to know and try to help.

I realise that studying even one particular group of these to the point of precisely understanding their home needs is often a life's work, but there are plenty of general principles we can apply to help satisfy them.

▶ Even many species that aren't our favourites, such as this sarcophage fly, are both visually impressive, and an important part of the garden food chain.

Grasshoppers and bush-crickets

These have long been popular little insects, perhaps because they don't bite, their jump is amazing, and they make funny percussive noises in the grass and bushes ('stridulation').

All have the characteristic long-jumper back legs, so the simple way to tell the two groups apart is that grasshoppers have short antennae, bush-crickets have *huge* ones. Unfortunately, most gardens don't seem to be great habitats for them, but see that as your challenge!

HOME NEEDS

Distribution: These are mainly insects of sunny climes, with only about 30 of Europe's 650 species making it to the British Isles and only about 10 in Scotland. The few likely to turn up in gardens are **Speckled Bush-cricket** *Leptophyes punctatissima*, **Oak Bush-cricket** *Meconema thalassinum*, **Dark Bush-cricket** *Pholidoptera griseoaptera*, **Meadow Grasshopper** *Chorthippus parallelus* (right) and **Common Field Grasshopper** *Chorthippus brunneus*.

Habitats: Grasshoppers like open, sunny, undisturbed meadows where the grass grows quite long; bush-crickets live up to their name, liking thickets and hedgerows. Individual species have subtly different preferences.

Habits: They live to a large extent in sedentary colonies, where the males set up a territory by singing. Grasshoppers are usually active by day, bush-crickets most often at night. Bush-crickets in particular are difficult to find – try homing in on one singing and you will discover their ventriloquial powers. Most grasshoppers can fly; many bush-crickets can't, although the Oak Bush-cricket most certainly can and is attracted to lit bedroom windows.

Food: Grasshoppers are vegetarian, eating wild grasses and some low-growing plants. Bush-crickets are usually partly or mostly carnivorous, eating caterpillars and other insects, although the Speckled Bush-cricket is partial to a bit of bramble or Raspberry leaf.

Breeding: Females lay eggs in or near the ground, or they insert them into plant tissue or behind bark. Most species winter as eggs, all the adults dying as winter draws in. They hatch as miniature versions of the adults in spring and moult up to ten times to reach maturity by late summer.

So... Why are grasshoppers and bush-crickets not a common sight in summer gardens? In the case of grasshoppers, lawns are usually too manicured for them to survive. In the case of bush-crickets, our shrubberies aren't always a match for a good bramble thicket, but as both the Speckled and Oak have pitiful songs maybe we overlook them. If you can, turn your lawn into a sunny meadow and create a woodland garden, and success may come leaping your way.

◀ The ridiculously long antennae on this grasshopper-like insect mark it out immediately as a bush-cricket (in this case a Speckled with its tiny and useless wing cases).

▲ It is only by late summer that grasshoppers and their allies reach full size, like this Meadow Grasshopper. They will have moulted up to ten times by this stage.

Beetles

This is an almighty group of insects with all manner of body types and sizes, colours and life-styles. In the British Isles alone there are about 4,000 species, and most gardens will host hundreds of these.

The one thing they all have in common is that they have jaws they use for munching. Many adults have a rather rounded shiny 'shell' formed by the leathery forewings, which is a fantastic protective carrying-case for the delicate hindwings, which are used for flying. Famous groups of beetles include ladybirds, stag beetles and cockchafers, but there are also (deep breath) tiger beetles, ground beetles, dor beetles, dung beetles, longhorn beetles, leaf beetles, weevils… I could go on!

Some beetles are serious pests of crops or foodstores, but most are pretty, innocuous or even useful, either for us gardeners or for other wildlife. Think of the aphid-eating ladybirds, or just have a look through the diets of many of our favourite garden birds and you will see how many feature beetles and bugs in their diet.

Despite all their differences, fulfilling these generic home needs will ensure you have a wide range of beetles using your garden, and then we'll look in more detail at some of the best loved species.

HOME NEEDS

Distribution: Beetles are everywhere, but generally there are more species to the south and east of the UK – cold, damp conditions don't suit them well.

◀ When we think of beetles, we tend to focus on the larger and more colourful species, but many such as these pollen beetles are small and easy to overlook – except as here when they gather en masse.

◀ Soldier Beetles, such as this *Cantharis rustica*, visit flowers just like the Thick-kneed, but are there to hunt other insects.

Habitat: There's a beetle for every habitat, but heathland, undisturbed flower-rich grasslands and especially woodland generally hold the most species, but gardens can be almost as rich.

Habits: Many are nocturnal. Even those that aren't are often great at hiding, either by being well camouflaged, by living nocturnal lifestyles or by tucking themselves away among leaf litter, in deep vegetation, or in the soil. Most prefer not to fly, spending life on their feet, either on the ground or in vegetation.

Food: Some beetles use their biting jaws to eat plants, others to devour other creatures, and some to bore into live or dead wood. Most have larvae that are like maggots-with-legs with the same biting jaws (and tastes) as the adults.

Breeding: Most species survive the winter as eggs in the soil or behind bark.

So… Although beetle lifestyles are varied, if you aim to deliver these basics you will encourage a wide range of species and hence benefit the whole food chain above:

✿ **Plants, plants, plants.** Whether trees, shrubs, climbers, flowerbeds or meadows, pack in whatever you can. Many of the vegetarian beetles have very picky needs, requiring a single plant species, so having more types of plant should mean more beetle diversity. Plant choice is also important – good old hawthorns or oaks are probably among the best for supporting lots of species.

✿ Provide plenty of **rotting wood**.

✿ Use **mulches**, especially of **leaflitter**, for them to rove through.

✿ **Compost heaps** are great for both debris-eaters and predator beetles.

✿ And, of course, **don't use insecticides**.

One species of native ladybird that seems to have coped relatively well with the arrival of the invasive Harlequin is the Seven-spot, which can still be seen in large groups in spring, fresh out of hibernation.

Ladybirds

Perhaps the best loved of all groups of beetles, most of the 40 or so British species of ladybird not only look pretty funky but are also inveterate chompers of aphids, both as the familiar adults and as the rather aggressive-looking larvae, so they are well worth encouraging.

Common garden species include the **Two-spot** *Adalia bipunctata*, the **Seven-spot** *Coccinella 7-punctata*, and the black-spots-on-yellow **22-spot** *Psyllobora 22-punctata*.

To meet their home needs, clearly don't obliterate your aphids with chemicals, and also provide somewhere for adult ladybirds to hibernate – a good, diverse garden, with clumps of tall grasses, hollow plant stems, leaf litter and old trees should do the trick.

Sadly, the most frequently seen ladybird in most parts these days is the **Harlequin** *Harmonia axyridis*. Like a mutant ninja ladybird, this Asian import will happily munch on its smaller cousins. It arrived in 2004 in southern England, and has spread at alarming speed northwards, reaching Scotland within five years. At present there seems little we can do to combat them.

Here is one ladybird that proves that not all are aphid munchers – this is the 22-spot Ladybird, which feeds on mildews.

Stag beetles

Being our largest beetle – with males up to 7.5cm long and sporting dramatic 'antlers' – the **Stag Beetle** *Lucanus cervus* has lots of fans. It is found in southern England, where numbers are thought to be declining. I am lucky enough to have Stag Beetles breeding in my garden, and it is quite a sight at dusk on a summer's evening to have the adults pass by in a flight best described as 'lumbering'. The prime home need is rotting tree stumps such as those of old fruit trees. It is here that their white, bloated larvae will munch on their high-fibre, low-calorie diet for up to three or four years before emerging. You can create ideal conditions by burying a log of a suitable tree species, with the top just poking out of the ground.

▲ The male Stag Beetle is our largest beetle, with ferocious looking 'antlers' that are used in head-to-head bouts with other males. If you are lucky enough to see one in the hand, I have always found them to be gentle giants.

▼ Stag Beetle larvae are almost as impressive as the adults, but are rarely seen as they need to stay deep within their rotting log or else they would make an easy and satisfying meal for many a predator.

◀ The Bloody-nosed Beetle can often benefit from a helping hand. They can't fly, and walk very slowly, so any that stray onto paths or roads risk being squashed without a kindly lift to safety.

Bloody-nosed beetles *Timarca*

Handle these black, neatly-domed beetles and they will exude their own blood to desperately try and fend you off, hence their name. They are found in open grass habitats in the southern half of the UK and are peaceful vegetarians, feeding on bedstraw leaves. If you don't have bedstraws in your garden, you won't have the Bloody-nosed beetles, showing how even beetles can have very particular home needs.

Thick-kneed Flower Beetle
Oedemera nobilis

Once you've seen the males of this green, metallic beetle, you'll never forget them, for they are the original winner of the knobbly-knees competition. Only their hind legs have the swollen joints. You can find both sexes nibbling pollen at all sorts of summer flowers, from scabiouses to bindweeds. The larvae live in hollow plant stems, another reminder not to hack back everything to the ground at the end of autumn.

◀ This is the male Thick-kneed Beetle – the females have much more shapely legs!

Wasp Beetle *Clytus arietus*

This beetle almost matches the Stag in terms of dramatic looks, with its black and yellow warning markings. It is quite harmless, despite its large size. Its larvae live in *dry*, dead wood such as willows and birches (showing how your log piles shouldn't just be in damp, shady corners), while the conspicuous and fearless adults visit flowers.

◀ The stunning Wasp Beetle is not at all related to wasps or hornets but has evolved the same yellow-and-black warning colours.

PROBLEM BEETLES?

A few beetles can be a bit of a nuisance for gardeners. Perhaps the most infamous is the Vine Weevil *Otiorhynchus sulcatus*, a regular in the top ten of garden pests. The root-chomping larvae are the main problem, especially in containers.

Meanwhile, two accidental imports are creating quite a stir: the bright-red Lily Beetle *Lilioceris lilii* from Asia can devastate lilies and other bulbous plants, while the Rosemary Beetle *Chrysolina americana* from southern Europe, metallic green with red stripes, is spreading like wildfire. Just pick off the adults if their nibbling is badly damaging your plants.

However, for most problem beetles, including the Garden Chafer *Phyllopertha horticola* and Cockchafer *Melolontha melolontha* whose larvae feed on plants roots, the best answer is a healthy, wildlife-rich garden where nature will find a balance.

◀ Cockchafers can be seen as a menace because their grubs eat plant roots, but that's where grub-eating Starlings and Rooks come into their own, nature's own pest control.

True bugs

When I say 'bug', I mean the group of insects called the Hemipterans (literally, the 'half-wings'), also known as the True Bugs, rather than 'bug' as in 'any creepy-crawly'. They are a bit beetle-like but are even more diverse in form and lifestyle, with over 1,800 species in the UK including familiar groups such as the shieldbugs and aphids, but with a whole host of others such as flatbugs, barkbugs, groundbugs, damselbugs, mirid bugs and, yes, more. See also page 129 for some very familiar water bugs, such as the pond skaters and backswimmers. And those noisy churring cicadas that lull you to sleep on tropical holidays? Yes, those are bugs too.

One common feature of all of them is that they have mouthparts shaped like a sharpened straw. This helps explain what aphids are doing when they cluster along your stems: each of them has pierced the stem and is merrily supping away as the plant tries to pump fluids up to its leaves.

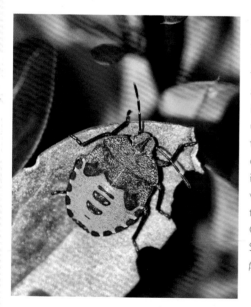

◄ Bugs tend to grow in stages (instars), shedding their outer skin and expanding into their new one underneath. Each time they can look quite different – this is a late instar of what will become the all-green Common Green Shieldbug *Palomena prasina*.

Froghoppers and their relatives, the leafhoppers, are bugs, too; they hold their wings above their back like a ridge tent. They are plant eaters, and are quite abundant in gardens, with different species associated with particular plants. But it is the globs of froth exuded by froghopper nymphs with which we are most familiar – often called cuckoo spit, it is a protective cloak of bubbles within which the nymph can grow.

Shield bugs live up to their name thanks to their distinctive shape. There aren't many widespread species, and they are commoner in the south.

◄ This is the fairly common Dock Bug *Coreus marginatus*, which feeds on dock and sorrel leaves and seeds.

HOME NEEDS

With so many species of bug, found in so many habitats, there are inevitable endless permutations of home needs. However, this is one group of species that will just automatically benefit from all the other things you do for wildlife in the garden.

So... Lots of plants of lots of different types and a lack of insecticides will mean lots of bugs and that, in turn, will mean lots of food for other wildlife.

PROBLEM BUGS

Being predominantly plant eaters, it is inevitable that some may cause us some grief when we are trying to grow a lovely plant and they think we are providing dinner.

Aphids are perhaps the biggest culprits. There are dozens of species: green ones are known colloquially as 'greenfly'; black ones as 'blackfly'; white ones as...yes, you get the picture. But they are most definitely bugs, not flies.

But aphids do have their uses. Many exude a sweet liquid called honeydew, which is harvested by ants and drunk by various butterflies and other insects. Aphids are also important in the diet of ladybirds, hoverfly larvae, lacewings and some birds. A world without them would be much the poorer, so just tolerate them if you can, and work hard to have a garden full of their predators to keep their numbers in balance.

Scale insects and mealy bugs are also true bugs, again sucking away at plants, but are perhaps most of a problem with houseplants and in the greenhouse. Focus on having a rich, varied ecosystem in your garden and if a plant is really susceptible to problem bugs, take that as a sign to try growing something else.

Flies

Why, oh why, would anyone want to garden for flies? Horseflies, bluebottles, mosquitoes, midges, dungflies – it is hardly a roll call of sought-after or cherished wildlife, and I can't see *The Wildlife Gardening Guide to Flies* being a best seller.

Time for a spot of public relations on their behalf. Or at least on behalf of the wildlife that *does* love flies. For without flies, Swallows and House Martins, wagtails and warblers, and, of course, Spotted Flycatchers would all go rather hungry. In fact, flies feature heavily in the diet of species ranging from dragonflies to amphibians, and are vital links in many food chains.

When you think about it, how many of them actually bother you? Houseflies, yes, and if you live in the north and west I'll agree that tiny midges can be hugely irritating. But there are more than 5,000 species of fly in the British Isles alone, and the vast majority of them never make a nuisance of themselves.

I will deal with the rather fun hoverflies separately, but here is a quick overview of some of the other prominent members of the fly family and their home needs.

HOME NEEDS

Different flies live very different lives, so pinning down home needs for them all would be a challenge. They do share some similarities in their life cycles, however. All lay eggs, which then hatch into legless larvae. These usually live quite a different life from the adults: some live in water, some in soil, some in live animals and others in plants, but most live as maggots in decaying matter, animal or vegetable.

◀ Lacewings are not true flies, but like hoverfly larvae they too eat aphids, making them the gardener's friend. Hoverfly larvae even camouflage themselves using the empty skins.

▼ Bee-flies are one of the signs of spring. Like small bumblebees with hair-thin legs , they hover in front of low-growing spring flowers such as lungworts and primroses to suck nectar with their tusk-like probosces, and then seek out the nests of bees where their grubs feed on bee larvae.

The larvae then pupate – many pupae can still wriggle. When they hatch into the adult, most, but not all, flies can fly! Their mouthparts are adapted for sucking, the only problem for us being that some are sharp enough to pierce before they suck. But at least you now know that it is impossible to be bitten by a mosquito – you just get sucked by a very sharp straw!

So... Gardening for flies equals gardening for other wildlife. Although different fly species have such different needs, if you do the following you will create a garden where fly-eating wildlife will be happy:

* ❀ Make a pond
* ❀ Create compost heaps
* ❀ Don't use chemicals
* ❀ Grow plenty of flowers
* ❀ And don't worry – few flies will trouble you!

▼ Many of the metallic flies such as this 'greenbottle' have maggots that undertake the rather unsavoury job of clearing the landscape of dead creatures, and so deserve our gratitude.

DISCOURAGING UNWANTED FLIES

Houseflies can be limited through good kitchen hygiene, while midges and mosquitoes are most prevalent where water has turned stagnant. This tends to happen in open water butts, buckets, and ponds where organic matter such as leaves has been allowed to accumulate.

Hoverflies

Have you ever stood in the garden in a sheltered spot and watched a hoverfly live up to its name? It is an astonishing feat as it hangs motionless in the air, wings a-blur, somehow coping with any gust of wind. Suddenly, it will dart off, maybe to intercept a rival, often to then return to its little mid-air territory.

◄ Drone-fly *Eristalis*: This group of 10 species are very common and are very similar in size, colour and shape to Honeybees. Their larvae are called 'rat-tailed maggots' and live underwater, eating detritus.

Rather fewer people notice hoverflies in the flower border, not because there are none there but because of their excellent disguise. Many bear the yellow and black 'danger' colours of bees, wasps and hornets, and some are even fluffy to pretend to be bumblebees. It is enough to fool many birds, which avoid eating them rather than risk being stung, when actually the hoverflies are totally defenceless. And it fools us too; on many occasions I have heard people noting the number of 'bees' visiting flowers when they are looking at these impersonators.

It means that, compared to bees, hoverflies are little celebrated for the pollination services they bring, but they ought to be.

There are some 280 or so species in the UK, and a good, wildlife-friendly garden can be home to 25 species or more. Jennifer Owen in her Leicester garden found 94 species over 30 years!

◄ Bulb-fly *Merodon equestris*: Bearing an uncanny likeness to a bumblebee, its larvae burrow underground to feed on the bulbs of flowers such as daffodils.

▼ Marmalade Hoverfly *Episyrphus balteatus*: This is the commonest of the many species that have black-and-yellow wasp-like markings. Their larvae are aphid eaters, crawling along plant stems like little pale maggots hunting their prey.

HOME NEEDS

Distribution: Found in every garden, there are more species in the south, but some rarities are only found in the north.

Habitat: Especially fond of sunny, sheltered habitats with lots of flowers.

Habits: Adults spend a lot of time at flowers, tending to prefer those that have an open, 'table-top' shape.

Food: The one thing that people do know about hoverflies is that their larvae eat aphids, which is of course a Brownie point in most gardeners' eyes. What may therefore surprise you is that, while this is true for many species, there are some hoverflies whose larvae actually feed on rotting vegetation or bulbs, or find tiny morsels in the mud in ponds, or even live as scavengers within the nests of social bumblebees and wasps.

So...

✿ Grow lots and lots of flowers, especially those in the carrot ('umbellifers') and composite (dandelion- and daisy-type) families

✿ Dig a pond

✿ Create sheltered, sunny glade like habitats.

◄ Hornet Hoverfly *Volucella zonaria*: Large enough and convincing enough to fool people that it is indeed a Hornet, like all hoverflies it is harmless. It has a fascinating lifestyle, the larvae live in wasps' nests, acting as cleaners or dining on wasp larvae.

Ants

The fact that they form almost the entire diet of Green Woodpeckers is surely a good reason to want more ants in your garden. No? How about the fact that ants mop up all sorts of troublesome creepy-crawlies that would otherwise ravage your crops and flowers?

Actually ants are a mixed blessing because they also farm aphids, guarding them from predators. And, of course, no sunbather wants ants in their pants, and no cook wants them marching across the kitchen. But hopefully you can find a little place for them in your lives.

HOME NEEDS

Distribution: There are about 50 ant species in the British Isles, with fewer the further north you go. Common garden species include the **Black Garden Ant** *Lasius niger*, **Red Ant** *Myrmica rubra*, **Yellow Lawn Ant** *Lasius umbratus* and **Yellow Meadow Ant** *Lasius flavus*.

Habitats: Ants are mainly creatures of warm places, with the greatest number of species on sandy heaths and open grasslands. Some are found in woodland.

Habits: Ants live in colonies, with a social structure matched only by the social bees and wasps. It's a utopian world of queens and their pheromone-controlled daughters, living in a ramshackle underground palace of corridors and chambers. A colony can persist for many years, with queens living three or four. Some species sting with formic acid, some spray the acid, and most also nip with their mouths.

Food: Most species eat a range of plant and animal matter, such as seeds, nectar and caterpillars. Many will climb trees as well as making ground raids. Worker ants that have found food lay a trail of scent for comrades to follow. Ants also milk aphids for honeydew, even taking them back to the nest to tend them.

Breeding: The queen sits within her chamber laying eggs, which workers take away to hatch, feed and guard. Many emerge as new workers, but in late summer there is a synchronised hatching of winged males and virgin queens. These fly up into the sky where they are eagerly picked off by wheeling Starlings, Swallows and gulls. The mated queens that survive come back down to start a new colony.

So... Ants do little damage in the garden, are very difficult to eliminate and are eaten by more garden birds than you'd realise, so tolerate them if you can. Brush the Yellow Meadow Ants' little soil mounds back into the lawn if they offend you (if not, they make extra microhabitats). If you get Black Garden Ants in your kitchen, then an ant scout has found sweet food and it is time for you to get cleaning!

Wasps and Hornets

I bet the mention of wasps makes you think of those that plague your picnics, determined to get at your jam sandwiches. Yes, they can be a nuisance, but that is just a handful of species whereas there are an astonishing several thousand others that have no interest in you whatsoever.

They include ichneumon wasps, potter wasps, digger wasps. Most are small and solitary, and they just get on with their slightly grim lifestyle of catching insects, immobilising them with a quick sting and laying an egg on them so that the developing larvae can then feast on fresh meat. If you garden for other insects, solitary wasps will come.

Some tiny wasps lay their eggs in plant tissue, which prompts the plant to produce strange tissue called galls, within which the larvae feed. Oak apples, spangle galls on oak leaves and 'robin's pin-cushions' on roses are all caused by wasps.

◄ The Hornet is our largest wasp, and looks quite menacing as it steams about over flower borders looking for insect prey. They rarely sting humans, however.

The wasps that worry us most are the stinging social wasps (including the Hornet *Vespa crabro*). They use chewed rotten wood to build football-sized, papier-mâché nests underground, in attics and sheds, or in hollow trees. These wasps have a similar colony structure to Honeybees, with a single queen and a large daughter workforce. The big difference is that worker wasps catch insects for their larvae (usefully getting rid of a lot of pests for us in the process). The adults drink sugary liquids, usually nectar, but will happily lap up soft drinks. It is only when they have become tipsy on the juices of rotting windfalls that they can become a nuisance and you should treat them with caution.

◄ Solitary wasps, such as this digger wasp, tend to be parasites, often laying their eggs on the caterpillars of butterflies or moths.

Spiders and harvestmen

Just the thought of gardening to benefit spiders may seem sheer lunacy to some people. The case for their defence is a compelling one, however, unless you are a complete arachnophobe:

✿ They trap or grab millions of insects each year, many of which are pests of crops
✿ They are themselves vital food for many garden birds.
✿ Spiders' webs are used by some birds such as Long-tailed Tits and Goldfinches to help build nests.

HOME NEEDS

Distribution: There are more than 600 species of spider in the British Isles. Many species are tiny, but they all have eight legs and a distinct waist. Harvestmen are cousins of the spiders, but with a simple rounded body and with just 23 species in the British Isles.

◀ Harvestmen can't spin silk, and so hunt on foot. They have very long legs, but so do some spiders, so the way to tell them apart is that they have just one main body section, whereas spiders have two.

◀ The Wasp Spider – here the large and dramatic female – is a recent arrival in southern England, but is fast spreading northwards.

As with so many other groups of creatures, the further north you are, the fewer species to expect, but most gardens can expect to host dozens.

Habitats: Sunny woodlands, hedgerows and meadows are key habitats, especially near water, but there is a species for almost every habitat. The **Woodlouse Spider** *Dysdera crocata*, for example, is a common species of log piles and brick stacks.

Habits: There are several groups of spiders with quite different lifestyles. The most familiar are the orb-weaving spiders that spin the famous spiral webs and need suitable structures from which to hang them. There are many other ways of using silk, however, with many spiders just creating sticky mats or irregular scaffolding.

There are plenty of spiders that don't use silk, hunting instead on foot. These include jumping spiders and wolf spiders. There are many that hunt at night, too, while the crab spiders sit and wait, often camouflaged in flowers, to ambush prey.

Food: The web-spinning spiders mainly target flying insects, but many of the hunting spiders will target other creepy-crawlies, too, and there are some spiders that specialise in hunting other spiders.

Breeding: Most spiders and harvestmen live for just one season and die at the start of winter. The females leave behind eggs either in a silk sac or in the soil or rotting wood. The eggs hatch in the spring as miniature versions of the adult, and usually soon disperse, either on foot or blown on strands of silk, called 'ballooning'. A few species live for more than a year and seek warm sheltered places to spend the winter, such as in your bedroom!

So... Gardening for insects equals gardening for spiders which equals gardening for birds. Provide spiders with vegetation, trees, standing water, log piles, hedges – all will boost the numbers in your garden with you hardly noticing them.

◀ This Nursery-web Spider *Pisaura mirabilis* is a common garden spider, hunting on the ground for prey. During mating, the male offers the female a gift to distract her and avoid being munched by his bride.

Woodlice

Woodlice are those familiar little creatures that cluster under logs and bricks looking like miniature, silver, armoured tanks with articulated shells. Expose them to the light and there's panic in the ranks. They have their uses in the wildlife garden, especially in the compost heap.

HOME NEEDS

Distribution: There are five widespread species in the British Isles – the **Common Rough Woodlouse** *Porcellio scaber*, the **Common Shiny Woodlouse** *Oniscus asellus*, the **Striped Woodlouse** *Philoscia muscorum*, the **Common Pill Woodlouse** *Armadillidium vulgare* and the **Common Pygmy Woodlouse** *Trichoniscus pusillus*, with about 30 rarer species and every chance that one or more of these may be present in your garden.

Habitat: Woodlice are crustaceans, related to the crabs and shrimps, but they have found a way to survive on 'dry' land by hiding in dark, moist places such as under the bark of dead wood, in compost heaps, and among rock piles.

◀ Turn over any brick or log that has been lying around for a while and you are likely to find harmless woodlice, such as this Common Woodlouse *Oniscus asellus*, one of your unpaid gardening helpers.

Habits: They tend to be gregarious, emerging only after dark on damp nights and rarely travelling far. Woodlice are eaten by various spiders, shrews, toads, and just a few birds such as Wrens.

Food: They eat large amounts of dead leaves and other spent organic matter, helping hugely in the decomposition process.

Breeding: Females have an internal, fluid-filled brood pouch where they incubate their eggs.

So... With a compost heap, log pile or 'habitat' pile, you should have all the woodlice you need, a little army helping to ensure that you don't end up knee-deep in dead plant matter.

Millipedes and centipedes

They have lots of legs, yes, but there are more to these little arthropods than that. Centipedes are important venomous predators of the micro-world, and millipedes help in the decomposition of plant material.

HOME NEEDS

Distribution: There are close on 50 species of both centipedes and millipedes in the British Isles, with at least some species in most areas of the country.

◀ This is a particularly impressive centipede I found under rotting logs in my garden, which was about 5 cm long. The commonest species are typically 3 cm long or less.

Habitat: They all need to keep out of sunlight in moist dark places such as in the soil, leaf-litter, under logs and stones, and in compost heaps.

Habits: Centipedes are flat, fast, fanged carnivores, hunting prey at speed and grabbing victims with pincer-like, venom-pumping front legs. Millipedes in contrast are generally slow-moving, burrowing vegetarians, with some looking like worms with hundreds of legs, others like woodlice, and others like centipedes!

Food: Centipedes eat caterpillars, spiders, small snails and worms; millipedes mostly eat decaying plant matter.

Breeding: They all lay eggs in the soil; very few show any level of parental care after that.

So... If you create a compost heap, develop a woodland garden, apply leaf-litter as mulch to your flowerbeds and build a log pile, you should be well away.

◀ Turning over logs is probably the best way to find millipedes – this one in my garden looked rather like a miniature vacuum cleaner hose on tiny legs.

Pond creatures

Beneath a pond's surface is a universe in its own right where, throughout the warmer months, all of life's trials are played out fiercely, day and night.

Earlier in this section we covered the headline-grabbers of the pool: the amphibians, dragonflies and damselflies. There are then usually a dozen or so other types of aquatic wildlife that are easily visible in an average garden pond, coming from all sorts of different animal groups. Here are the commonest with a brief summary of their home needs.

Water beetles and their larvae

The big daddy of them all is the **Great Diving Beetle** *Dytiscus marginalis*, which can grow up to 35mm long. Both the adults and the larvae are ferocious enough to kill newts, tadpoles and goldfish. There are several smaller species of diving beetle, all still top predators. Even the several species of **whirligig beetles** *Gyrinus*, spinning crazily across the surface, are actually hunting prey.

True bugs

The four UK species of **backswimmers** *Notonecta* (below) are also formidable predators for their size. They swim upside-down, skulling with their long back legs and clutching an air-bubble to their chest. They catch prey using a venomous bite (they can give us a sharp nip, but the venom is designed for tiny creatures), and are good flyers.

There are several types of **pond-skater** *Gerridae*, which do as their name suggests – the long middle legs provide propulsion, the back ones steer and the front ones grab prey through the surface.

The **Water Scorpion** *Nepa cinerea* is a chunky beast up to 20mm long, stalking just under the surface and poking its spear-like rear end through the surface as a snorkel.

Water-boatmen are true bugs which rove the bottom eating plant particles and algae.

Flies

Mosquitoes lay their eggs in rafts on the water surface. Their larvae and bull-headed free-swimming pupae hang down from the surface and wriggle off at your approach.

Midge larvae live in the mud of stagnant water and include the little red maggots (bloodworms) of non-biting *Chironomid* gnats.

The **rat-tailed maggot** is the larva of the **Drone-fly** *Eristalis tenax* and lives in stagnant water with a long breathing tube of a tail.

Caddis-fly larvae

Several species crawl about on the pond bottom, eating tiny fragments of whatever they can find and hiding in little home-made cases.

Molluscs

The **Great Pond Snail** *Lymnaea stagnalis* with its pointed spiral shell and the **ramshorn snails** *Planorbis* with their coiled discs are grazers, munching through algae.

Crustaceans

Gammarus is a genus of what are sometimes called '**freshwater shrimps**' that are very common in ponds, wriggling about in the debris on the bottom and eating detritus, but they are strong if apparently lop-sided swimmers when disturbed.

The **waterlice** or **hoglice** of the genus *Asellus* are like small underwater woodlice with overlong legs. They too are cleaners, sifting through the pond's 'rubbish'.

There are two groups of fascinating microscopic crustaceans that are abundant in ponds. The name 'water flea' doesn't do justice to the genus *Daphnia*, which cluster in large shoals and when magnified look like limbless, see-through jellybabies with horns. *Cyclops* is a club-shaped swimmer with four big horns, one eye, and egg sacs dangling from the hip. They all filter microscopic plankton.

So... All of these creatures have subtly differing needs, but you can accommodate many of them by creating a large pond with parts in sun and parts in shade, with deeper areas and plenty of shallows, with different substrates such as pebbles and gravel, and plenty of aquatic vegetation. However, keep rich organic material such as soil and leaves to a minimum if you want to reduce the risk of stagnant conditions and algal blooms.

◄ Backswimmers are powerful, upside-down rowers, but they are also good flyers, just like the other pond bugs. In fact, the only creatures you need to introduce to ponds are pond snails, because everything else will find its own way there..

Earthworms

Earthworms are the unsung heroes of your garden. Their design is simple – a muscular tube that eats its way through the soil. Earth and dead leaves go in the front end, travel down the gut and come out the other end partially digested. Each worm alone makes little difference, but a million or so per hectare in good habitat move mountains of soil and are vital for the decomposition of organic matter.

This activity is hugely beneficial to plants: it aerates the soil, aids drainage and gives roots channels they can easily penetrate. Worms also help break down organic matter making it more available to plants, and they bring essential minerals back to the surface in their wormcasts.

And, of course, worms feature in many creatures' diets. To thrushes, Badgers, Hedgehogs, shrews and amphibians, they are not a delicacy but the main course. Worms are clearly worth nurturing.

HOME NEEDS

Distribution: There are about 25 species of earthworm in the British Isles. They are quite difficult to identify, but most are widespread in suitable habitats.

Habitat: Different species tend to live in slightly different habitats, with species such as the **Garden Earthworm** *Lumbricus terrestris*, **Anglers Red Worm** *Lumbricus rubellus* and the **Long Worm** *Allolobophora longa* living under lawns and grasslands, and the **Brandling Worm** *Eisenia foetida* and **Cockspur Worm** *Dendrodrilus*

rubidus in compost heaps, where huge numbers can gather. Worms can be found in most fertile soils apart from those that are very acidic, sandy or waterlogged, with good populations in undisturbed habitats such as unimproved grassland and woodland. Regular turning of the soil exposes them to predators, leading to far smaller numbers in such places.

Habits: Earthworms tend to live in the top 25cm of the soil, going deeper only in dry or cold weather. They usually remain active for most of the year.

Food: Large bits of organic matter are ingested together with soil particles and bacteria. Some worms come to the surface to yank big leaves down into their tunnels where they can soften them and munch in peace.

Breeding: Earthworms mature after about a year, and can then live for ten if they can avoid your Blackbirds! They are hermaphrodite, finding a mate in late summer either on the surface or within a burrow. They lie alongside each other, head to toe, and exchange sperm. Each then lays a cocoon of about 20 fertilised eggs in the soil.

So... Building up a healthy population of earthworms is clearly great for wildlife in the garden. Lawns, meadows and undisturbed woodland floors are preferable to turned soil, which is in turn better than concrete, gravel and decking. A compost heap that worms can get into will help too. In the vegetable patch, leave a fallow plot in your crop rotation.

It is best to clear autumn leaves off a lawn as they will otherwise smother and kill the grass, but a top-dressing in autumn that includes sieved leaf-mould and soil will help worms no end.

WORMS AND LAWNS – NUISANCE OR FRIEND?

I realise that not everyone loves the humble worm. Groundsmen and aficionados of 'the perfect lawn' see them as a curse because of the casts that *Allolobophora* worms leave on the surface. Some people find these unsightly, and they do offer a place for weeds to germinate. As a result, worm-killing chemicals are still widely used, but the tragedy is that these kill *all* earthworms, not just those that make casts. A lawn without worms will then need much more spiking and fertilising than one with, and will be far worse for wildlife in general. Anyway, it is no big deal to brush the wormcasts in once dry, so I'd like to think that everyone can learn to love the worm and all the benefits it brings!

◄ A good compost heap can squirm with tangled masses of Brandling Worms.

Slugs and snails

▼ Slugs and snails – such as this Large Black Slug – tend to be one of the gardener's biggest nightmares. For creatures that move so slowly, they manage to get everywhere under cover of darkness to cause havoc.

So what are you going to do to encourage slugs and snails in your garden? (Cue: shrieks of horror from aghast readers whose strawberries, hostas, potatoes, etc, they endlessly devour.) Don't worry; read on to find ways of controlling them without harming other wildlife.

But I'm going to be brave and start with a little plea: they are a natural part of our environment and a key link in food chains. Clearly the countryside survives with them, so maybe if we understand their home needs we can work out how to better live with them.

HOME NEEDS

Distribution: Snails and slugs are found pretty much everywhere, but the number of species thins out quickly as you head north.

Habitat: Of the 80 or so species of snail in the British Isles and 30 or so slugs, most live in damp habitats such as woodland, but a few have found ideal conditions in our gardens. Snails are especially common on lime-rich soils, as the minerals there are important building materials for their shells.

Habits: Slugs and snails are molluscs, the group that includes seashells, but they have evolved to survive on land. Nevertheless, they still need damp conditions, and so escape becoming sun-dried by hiding by day under logs and stones and, in the case of many slugs, burrowing deep into the soil. In very dry spells, snails will seal themselves into their shells with a dried layer of mucus. Most people don't realise that some species, such as the attractive yellow-and-brown whorled **Brown-lipped** *Cepaea nemoralis* and **White-lipped Snail** *C. hortensis*, are more help than hindrance, preferring to eat dead and rotting vegetation or fungi rather than living plants. See them as friends!

The main problem species are:

Garden Snail *Helix aspersa*, the big one up to 40mm across with brown flecks

Strawberry Snail *Trichia striolata*, a small, rather flattened snail to 14mm diameter

Grey Field or **Netted Slug** *Deroceras reticulatum*, grey with darker flecks to 40mm long, which prefers feeding on the surface

Garden Slug *Arion hortensis*, to 30mm long, dark with a pale stripe down the side; a burrower

Keeled or **Budapest Slug** *Tandonia budapestensis*, to 60mm, with an orangey stripe down the middle of the back, also a burrower, and **Large Black Slug** *Arion ater*, up to a whopping 200mm long, often black with an orange stripe along the foot, and really just a problem with seedlings.

Breeding: Slugs and snails are hermaphrodite, with every individual having both sets of sexual organs. All are able to mate with any other of their species and all then lay eggs. These are deposited in loose soil, 30–80 at a time, up to six times a year, and are pale, rather jelly-like and round.

COPING WITH SLUGS AND SNAILS

❀ Grow plants that snails and slugs avoid; many herbs and other aromatic plants are an ideal place to start.

❀ Place slug and snail hideaways (rock and log piles, compost heaps) away from vulnerable plants.

❀ Seedlings are most at risk, so propagate them indoors and plant them out when well advanced.

❀ Grow vulnerable vegetables in raised pots, and harvest potatoes early.

❀ Use cloches made of plastic drinking bottles pushed into the soil around small plants.

❀ They don't like anything that dries their mucus, so lay barriers of crushed eggshells, soot, sharp sand, bran, woodash and human hair. None are guaranteed to work, but all should have some effect.

❀ Lure them with their favourite things, such as upturned half grapefruits or wilting cabbage leaves, and then relocate them to places where they aren't a problem.

❀ Use copper tape and sheets of matting impregnated with copper to give them a mini-electric shock.

❀ If you must kill them, give them a nice way to go! Sink jars full of bitter ale into the ground. Keep the rim 2cm above the soil surface to avoid killing ground beetles, and cover with a raised stone 'lid' to avoid the risk of tipsy Hedgehogs and pets.

Gardening for Mosses and Fungi

You won't find pots of moss or packets of fungi spores for sale in garden centres. In fact, they are more likely to crop up in the 'problem' sections of gardening books. But they are all part of the amazing web of life in gardens.

Mosses and liverworts

▲ They may not have flowers and grow no more than ankle deep, but up close many mosses form attractive cushions, a mass of green starry foliage.

Together, mosses and liverworts are primitive plants known as the bryophytes. They form mats or cushions of short, dense, green growth, and there are plenty of species to get to grips with if you want to become a bryologist, with some 763 mosses in the British Isles at the last count, and around 300 liverworts. The British Bryological Society has an excellent online field guide and atlas.

Mosses are usually quite feathery, whereas liverworts are either 'lobed' like fleshy growths or have tiny pairs of leaves either side of the stem. In terms of their value for wild animals, mosses are a key nest-building material for many birds. However, it is probably the ability of bryophytes to colonise wet places where other flowering plants can't grow that makes them special. Here, they create a whole new habitat for you, a mini wet forest where tiny creatures can set up home.

▼ Moss is an important building material in many bird nests. Here, the moss in an old nest, possibly a Blackbird's, has continued to grow.

HOME NEEDS

Distribution: We do very well for mosses and liverworts, with the British Isles hosting two-thirds of all European species, and this is one group of wildlife where there are more species in the north, west and in the mountains.

Habitat: Mosses and liverworts need moisture, and so many can be found in damp, shady woodlands, stream-sides and peat-bogs, but wet lawns suffice for some species. They absorb water across all their surfaces, and in fact don't have roots. This means that they can grow on rocks, walls, tree trunks, fences and sand dunes. Some species grow in winter when the weather is at its wettest. Many like undisturbed places but a few are quick to colonise tilled fields or burnt ground. Different species are often adapted to a particular pH – the level of acidity or alkalinity – of the soil or rock they grow on.

Breeding: Neither mosses nor liverworts have flowers, but instead they produce microscopic spores, often in stalked capsules.

So... Provide the damp, shady places they like, using logs, rocks and landscaping to create dips and hollows. Then let nature do the rest. Once they have colonised, just let them be.

COPING WITH MOSSY LAWNS

'Moss' (and I quote a leading gardening encyclopaedia) 'is almost always undesirable in a lawn'. The reason seems to be cultural for there's actually nothing inherently 'wrong' with mossy lawns.

If you do have moss in your lawn and don't want it, the short-term solution is to kill it, but this ignores the reason why it is there in the first place. It is there because you were fulfilling its home needs without even trying, be it poor drainage, compacted soil or pH levels more suited to moss than grass. If you don't address these, moss will always be a problem.

So ditch the chemicals and identify the underlying issue. 'Top dress' with sand and scarify the lawn as required, and ensure your lawn fulfils the home needs of grass and not of moss. Alternatively, relax and enjoy a mossy lawn – it is possible!

Fungi and lichens

Fungi are a bit weird – they aren't plants and they aren't animals. Lichens are weirder still – they are a plant and a fungus living together. Both are likely to arrive in your garden of their own accord, and if they find what they need, they will stay and grow.

Many fungi help break down dead matter, while lichens usually indicate that the air quality is good. They also help life establish in bare environments. And both can provide extra food and extra mini-worlds for your garden wildlife.

◀ These bracket fungi attached to the side of a tree are the Birch Polypore *Piptoporus betulinus*. One of our commonest species, it still has precise home needs – it only grows on birch trees.

FUNGI: HOME NEEDS

Distribution: There are thought to be more than 12,000 species of fungi in the British Isles alone, with some to be found almost everywhere.

Habitat: Fungi live in all sorts of habitats, but the greatest number of species prefer damp woodland and unimproved meadows.

Habits: There are all sorts of fungi, from moulds and mildews to blights and slime-moulds, and many that attack plants. The ones we're most likely to be interested in as gardeners are those that produce mushrooms and toadstools. For these species, most of their lives are spent as a mass of tiny threads, hidden away, preparing for their big show. Then, at the right time of year, they suck up water by the bucketload and in a big fanfare throw up their familiar fruiting bodies.

Food: Some fungi are saprophytes, living off dead organic matter such as spent leaves, fallen trees and animal droppings. Some are parasitic, eating live material. And some form amazing relationships with trees and other plants in which the fungal threads invade the very heart of the roots and help themselves to sugars that the tree

has produced, but in return draw up quantities of moisture and minerals from the soil that the plants couldn't hope to absorb alone.

So… Encourage fungi by providing damp conditions and plenty of fungi-food such as log piles and rotting tree stumps in leaf-littered woodland gardens. An unfertilised, untreated lawn or meadow is also perfect.

LICHENS: HOME NEEDS

Distribution: Found almost everywhere, with plenty in some of our wildest environments such as exposed coasts and mountaintops. There may be more than 1,800 species in the British Isles alone.

Habitat: Undisturbed places, often where other plants can't grow, such as rocks, tree bark, pavements and roof tiles, and especially alkaline surfaces, such as limestone. They prosper best in damp conditions, but hate polluted air. If you've got lots of lichens, breathe deeply – you're living somewhere special. Fortunately, the cleaning up of industrial emissions has helped some lichens return to cities.

Habits: Lichens are a complex slow-growing partnership between an alga and a fungus. It is difficult to know if both get equal benefit out of the relationship but it seems to be a pretty friendly affair. The fungus creates a protective shell and anchors the partnership down while the alga does much of the food generation. You can get crusty lichens, scaly ones and bushy ones. Several species of moth caterpillars specialise in eating lichens.

Food: Lichens get nourishment thanks to the algae photo-synthesising, and by absorbing water and minerals through their surface. Even when living on bark, they don't steal food from the tree itself.

So… There's a big element of patience in gardening for lichens, for they live life slowly. Fortunately, most of our gardens have been around longer than we have and many lichens will be there already. Find them, enjoy them, and hold back from scrubbing roof tiles and paving slabs.

◀ Encrusting branches with its bright yellow flakes and orange cups is one of our commonest lichens, *Xanthoria parietina*. It can survive even in cities where the air is polluted, unlike most lichens.

CREATING DIFFERENT HABITATS

If the previous section was all about understanding the home needs of different wildlife, then now is the point where you can use that knowledge to create the right garden accommodation to encourage the wildlife you'd like to entertain.

❀ We will look at the headline habitats you can create, such as woodland gardens and wetland gardens, and how to go about it.

❀ We'll see how to garden for wildlife in big gardens and small gardens and on balconies and patios too.

▲ Garden tools – yes, your signal that this is the part of the book where we start to put our muscles into action as well as our brains!

❀ And there are ideas and advice for things to do in all those bits of the garden that you might previously have thought were useless or out of bounds for wildlife.

ONE LAST, VITAL THING BEFORE YOU START…

It's time to get out the camera. If you take plenty of photos and some notes *first*, you will be able to look back and see how much your garden has changed thanks to your efforts. You will find that it makes the rewards all the greater.

◄ Gardening for wildlife isn't about exactly replicating wild habitats; it's about using them as an inspiration for different areas, such as here in the flower border.

◄ Your home can sit right at the heart of all sorts of homes for wildlife.

◄◄ Gardening for wildlife isn't about exactly replicating wild habitats; it's about using them as an inspiration for different areas, such as here in the flower border.

Making a Woodland Home

There is something about trees that resonates deeply with us. Perhaps it is their magnificent size; maybe we see in them something of our own lives in their change from slender youngster to proud adult to wrinkled veteran; or perhaps it is how they signal the seasons, from the fresh green hope of spring to the flash of autumnal fireworks?

Whatever the reason, they offer something quite profound for garden wildlife: they open up 'room'. Or, more precisely, 'rooms'. They turn a garden from a wildlife bungalow into nature's hi-rise luxury hotel. The sheer volume of eatable material and the vast surface area they offer is astonishing, and they achieve this 'perched on a pole', a trunk that takes up only a square metre or often less of actual floor space. It's an incredible way of maximising opportunities for the wildlife that likes and needs trees.

It can also be cheaper and easier than many people think. In fact, a little sapling can cost less than a pot plant. It is also something that I believe can be done in any garden; even the smallest gardens can develop their own little bit of woodland heritage. Yes, it takes time, but the key thing is to enjoy the journey as your flimsy little knee-high trees 'get their feet down' and, year by year, thrust ever skywards. Ultimately, it is a legacy for future generations, of people and of wildlife, to enjoy.

◄ The Speckled Wood only feels at home in the dappled light of the woodland, as do a huge number of moths.

KEY SPECIES

— Almost all garden birds, but especially, woodpeckers, thrushes, tits, Starling, pigeons and finches

— Speckled Wood butterfly

— Bats

— Squirrels

— Wood Mouse

— Dormouse

— Many bee species

— Many moth species

— Many beetle and bug species

— Many spider species

— Many moss, liverwort and fungi species

◄ The soaring trunks and spreading branches are the five-star skyscraper hotel of gardening for wildlife.

▲ Mosses flourish in the damp shade under trees, a lush microjungle for minibeasts, where the spreading buttress of tree roots offers ideal natural cavities for mice, and even nesting tits.

The inspiration

An ancient woodland – one that hasn't been ploughed for 400 years or more – is a glorious place to look for woodland-garden inspiration. It is a glimpse of the time when the Wildwood covered much of northern Europe. This is the awe-inspiring oak woodland at RSPB Dinas in mid Wales.

It is a compelling thought that once upon a time most of our gardens were probably part of this giant forest. They probably still carry a bit of this 'memory' in their soils and in some of the creatures that live there. Why not reinstate a little bit of the Wildwood now in your garden?

A mature tree may have more than 100,000 **leaves**, every one a launch pad, hiding place or salad for all sorts of insects.

The **trunk and main branches** are the main highways for wildlife, offering a huge surface area made even larger by the bark's ruts and folds. Mosses and lichens create a miniature jungle here, Ivy clambers up, woodpeckers drum holes and beetles bore under the bark.

The **blossom** of many trees offers pollen and nectar, followed by a great harvest of **seeds, nuts or fruit**. A tree is a supermarket as well as a hotel.

In the dappled shade underneath the canopy, smaller trees and shrubs create an **understorey**, yet another suite of rooms in this grand hotel.

Dead wood is just as vital to wildlife as the living tree, and that includes dead and dying branches on the tree itself. Here, all manner of beetles and dead-wood creatures live and breed, and fungi take hold.

In the **crown** of the tree, wildlife must have a head for heights and be able to cling on in a buffeting wind. But life-giving sun is aplenty, and they are safe from ground predators.

Thousands of smaller **branches and twigs** form miles (no exaggeration) of minor byways for insects, and safe perches and nesting sites for birds.

In the wild, as old trees die and fall, they open up sunny, sheltered **glades**. Flowering plants that need the light grab their opportunity, insects buzz, and large grazing animals, such as deer, may keep the glade open for years.

It is a different world depending **which side of the tree** you get up on. On the north side of the trunk it is cold and dark, it is dry on the east out of the prevailing wind, and warm and damp on the south and west.

Every year, falling leaves deliver a free **mulch** to the shady ground beneath. Part fertiliser but also part weed-suppressor, this windfall offers yet another microhabitat in which many creatures can prosper.

Down on the **woodland floor**, there can be a glorious carpet of flowers that bloom early before the canopy closes over.

Unseen underground, the **roots** spread out as wide as the tree itself, many of them close to the surface. Most are entwined with fungal threads in a cooperative partnership.

How to make your woodland: step by step

1. Think ahead…a long way!

Planning for the future If you plant the wrong species in the wrong place, you may find yourself having to start again (with an axe!) ten years down the line. So identify how much room you have for trees to grow and spread, and imagine how they might change the look and feel of your garden, and where they will cast their shade. Think if they will eventually affect buildings, roads, street lights, overhead cables, or underground pipes and services.

Choose the right species Focus on how tall *and* wide a tree is said to grow, if it is right for your soil and climate, and, of course, make sure you select ones that will provide the home needs you want.

The sooner you start, the better!

2. Seeds, saplings or specimens?

How you actually start off your trees is down to you, your budget and your levels of patience.

Planting from seed If you can afford the wait, this is the cheapest and ultimately most rewarding option – they will be *your* 'babies'. Collect seed locally, knowing the trees will be well suited to where you live. Big seeds, such as hazelnuts and acorns, can be planted directly into pots of compost and do best if nicked with a knife to trigger growth. Berries should be soaked until the seeds can be

extracted from the pulp; then sow them in compost under a layer of grit. Most tree seeds need scarifying before they will germinate, which means chilling them for several weeks in a bag of sharp sand in the fridge or leaving them out over winter in a cold frame.

Bare-rooted trees These are young trees dug up in winter while dormant, their bare roots wrapped in polythene for delivery. Plant them out as soon as possible and don't expose the roots to the air for more than a few minutes. Some are sold as single slender stems only a year or two old called whips, and are a great and incredibly cheap way to start; it's how I do it.

Root-balled trees These are delivered with the roots in a ball of soil within hessian sacking and can be pretty big (and expensive). They are best planted in autumn or spring.

Container-grown trees The most expensive way to start, they can be planted at any time of year but do best if planted in autumn or spring. You may need some well-muscled friends to help extract the heavy rootball.

3. Planting your tree

Dig a big hole! It should be two to three times wider than the container or rootball. Lower in the tree, ensuring that it sits at the same level as it did in the container. If planting a bare-rooted tree, form a mound in the base of the hole and spread the roots over the top. You can mix in some well-rotted compost with the removed soil, but it isn't essential. Fill the hole back in, treading in firmly. Then water well.

Most young trees need staking – a wooden stake hammered in at an angle of 45° is ideal. Anchor the tree to the stake with a soft cord such as rubber tubing, tied in a figure of eight. You might also want to use a tree guard if you are visited by rabbits or deer.

4. Caring for your woodland

The first year is crucial In particular, young trees need lots of water. Even then, a few young trees may not 'take'.

Mulch Cover the ground around the tree with 5cm depth of well-rotted compost, keeping it clear of the young trunk. It will keep moisture in and weeds out.

Pruning Most young trees won't need much. You may at some point, however, want to 'lift' the canopy, removing lower branches to let more light onto the woodland floor. Eventually large trees may need dangerous or inconvenient branches removing or their height reducing. When this happens, call in a tree surgeon.

Enjoy the gradual change The trick is to relish each step as your woodland grows rather than hanging on for your final vision to be achieved.

◀ When planting, take care to ensure the tree is vertical, and lay a stake across the hole to check it will be at the same level in the ground as it was at the nursery.

Creating woodland's layers

To create all those different microhabitats that make up a natural woodland, we need to do more than just plant what will become the big trees – we need to create all the layers, so that there is all the variety, microclimates, food and homes for wildlife.

The Shrub Layer As long as the canopy isn't too dense, you can plant an understorey of smaller trees and bushes. In a native woodland, these are often dominated by Hazel, Holly, hawthorns, Field Maple and Elder, but there can be smaller shrubs too such as Spurge Laurel, Mezereum and Butcher's Broom. In your garden you have the chance to be even more adventurous, using non-native shrubs that are also well able to survive in the dappled shade between larger trees, such as Oregon-grapes, Flowering Currant and viburnums.

The Field Layer Beneath the shrubs, a bed of flowering bulbs and herbaceous plants grabs the limelight before the trees break into leaf in spring. Most herbaceous border plants sold in garden centres tend to be sun-worshippers, but if you look hard, you will find plenty of exciting wildlife-friendly plants that will tolerate or even delight in a shady position.

TOP 20 WILDLIFE PLANTS FOR THE WOODLAND FLOOR

Bluebell, English	Monkshood
Bugbane	Pendulous Sedge
Bugle	Primrose
Burdocks	Red Campion
Columbines	Violets
Cranesbills, eg *Geranium sylvaticum*	Wild Strawberry
Dead-nettles, eg *Lamium maculatum*	Wood Forget-me-not
Ferns	Woodland grasses
Foxgloves	Wood Sage
Lungworts	Yellow Archangel

The Ground Layer Unless some creature has been having a bit of a rootle about, few woodlands have a ground surface that is just bare earth. Instead, it is covered with a mouldering layer of dead leaves, bits of twig, decaying logs and flakes of bark. You can mimic this when you start your woodland area by putting down a thick mulch of bark chippings. Then, if you rake leaves off your lawn in autumn, you can sprinkle these here, too. Over time, it will begin to look and feel like a rich woodland floor.

The Climbers Finally, crawling up the natural scaffolding of trunks and branches, climbers such as Ivy and honeysuckles add yet more variety to the food and habitat on offer. Plant these about 30cm (12 inches) from the base of more mature trees, leaning in. Some people are horrified at the thought of letting Ivy loose on a tree, and I understand why, but a good healthy tree will cope, just as they have over thousands of years.

TREES FOR A VERY SMALL WOODLAND GARDEN

It is possible to create something that has the essence of woodland in the smallest of gardens. Select trees that are naturally small, such as Japanese Crab *Malus floribunda* which grows to 4 m or so, or, even smaller, *Malus sargentii*. There are then some tree cultivars that have been bred specially to be dwarf such as the weeping Goat Willow 'Kilmarnock'. For a *really* small garden, then you can't go far wrong with one of the fruit trees that has been grafted onto a dwarfing rootstock.

Growing a tree in a large pot slows down growth. Hollies and Yew do especially well and can be pruned like topiary. Fruit trees are also ideal for this, but almost any tree can be tried. They will, however, need plenty of water and a thick mulch.

Or grow 'two-dimensional' trees, trained up and along walls and fences as cordons or fans. Apples and pears are the ideal subjects, giving you flowers, fruit and nesting habitats for birds between branch and wall.

▶ Foxgloves are one of those woodland plants native to Britain that are so glorious in flower they look straight out of the garden centre.

CREATING A SMALL WOODLAND GARDEN

It is possible to create something that has the essence of woodland even in small gardens. Here is my own example from where I used to live in what was called Woodlands Close. As with many road names, its origins were clearly ancient history for there were no woodlands to be seen, but at least my small front garden contained three mature Sycamore trees, and I was determined to put back a bit of what might once have been there.

The Sycamores cast a deep shade across almost the entire garden and, when I first moved in, the ground beneath the trees was just a bed of thin weedy grass and some wind-blown rubbish.

I set about planting a native hedge around the outside while, deep within my 'woodland', I planted young trees of different sorts under the canopy. I then introduced a wide range of woodland perennials beneath them, and added a bark path edged with old branches, plus a couple of stick piles. I drilled a birch stump with holes and 'planted' it upright in the ground; it soon became the nesting place for solitary wasps.

The woodland garden became an oasis of shade where Blue Tits nested, where Wrens sang and which hummed with insects in summer.

▶ My woodland flowers at their best in April and May, with beds of Red Campion, *Lamium maculatum*, comfreys and geraniums seizing their moment before the closing of the canopy. Later in the season, woodland gardens inevitably look rather tired and dark, but by then thoughts can turn elsewhere in the garden.

▲ In very early spring, Snowdrops and pink Mezereum buds ensure your mini woodland is a 'must see' part of the garden.

▲ By March, Wild Daffodils take centre stage. Although not the best for wildlife, they help add to the complex network for woodland creatures to explore and hide amongst.

▲ The trunks of the trees are perfect for bat and tit boxes.

BRINGING DEAD WOOD ALIVE

Few gardens naturally have dead wood lying about the place (fences don't count – dead wood needs to be untreated and rotting to be good for wildlife!). In fact, it is one of the things that people tend to compulsively clear up. As I always say, it is not the tidiness that is the problem; it is when the things that have been tidied then get thrown away or burnt that wildlife loses out. A good garden for wildlife can be incredibly tidy, as long as it isn't sterile.

So when it comes to making a 'dead wood pile', you can be as slapdash or as nitpickingly precise in how you arrange your materials. You can make it look as if dropped from a great height and left where it landed, or you can use your creative flair to turn it into a piece of art.

Notice how I'm not calling it a 'log pile'. I want you to see any dead wood, including bark or sticks, as fair game. Dead wood can be used in all sorts of places and in all sorts of ways: the only limit is your imagination.

▲ Log piles offer a complex world of decay mixed with a labyrinth of dark and damp gaps and cracks. No garden should be without one!

How to make a dead wood pile

1. Find some logs Should you ever need to have existing trees in your garden removed, keep anything that gets cut down. Keep a watch out, too, for any neighbours having tree work done and get straight round there to see if any are going begging. They'll probably be delighted! Oh, and remember to tell them why you want it, to help spread the good word about gardening for wildlife. If all else fails, order a delivery. Try to source logs that come from near where you live: there are likely to be all sorts of creatures already inside the logs, and so will be well suited to your local climate and environment.

2. Choose a site – or several Don't imagine that a dead wood

◄ Lying or standing up; half buried or piled high – get creative with your logs to create homes for all sorts of creatures and a talking point for visitors. Just remember to keep your back straight!

pile has to be somewhere dark and dank. Build one in a sunny position and you'll get a totally different range of creatures use it than one deep in shade. In particular, solitary bees and wasps do like sunbaked wood.

3. Then over to you and your artistic flair Arrange the logs in any way you wish, whether that be the natural look, or orderly perfection. But do consider part-burying some of them as some creatures much prefer rotting wood underground, especially Stag Beetle larvae. And why not even dot interesting-looking bits of dead wood among your flower borders.

4. Don't forget the brash 'Brash' is another word for thin sticks, stems and twigs, which too often gets forgotten when creating a dead wood pile. Chunky logs are great, but they create rather a coarse network of large nooks and crannies. In a stick pile, the maze of spaces is much more complex. I have a hunch that in the cat-dominated garden world, a large stick pile may provide the best nesting site for Blackbirds, Robins, Dunnocks and Wrens, and a brilliant place for Slow-worms, too. In fact, because so few people bother to make a brash pile, it may be one of the most useful things you can create for wildlife, so I urge you to give it a go.

5. And finally, add flowers A log or brash pile is a perfect climbing frame for a clamberer such as a clematis or blackberry (wild or cultivated), adding yet more wildlife value. Or push earth into some of the gaps and plant woodland flowers such as Primroses and Bugle. Plus of course grow some nectar-rich flowers around its base. What a wonderfully diverse habitat you will have created.

Making a Scrubland Home

In the countryside it's known as 'scrub'; in the garden it's a 'shrubbery'. Whatever you like to call it, these are sunny areas filled with bushes, and they can be brilliant for wildlife.

What distinguishes a bush from a tree is an inexact science, but they are usually smaller and so don't dominate or shade the garden quite as much. Their many woody stems usually emerge from near the base, unlike the single trunk of a tree, giving them greater breadth low down, and so they create a strong framework of the garden's design around which the kaleidoscope of your flower borders can emerge, dazzle and fade. Bushes often like to show off a bit themselves, too, delivering displays of shape, texture and colour.

Wildlife, while no doubt admiring our creativity, is more concerned with what shelter and food the bushes can offer, and the shrubbery can be very generous indeed, fulfilling the home needs for a wide range of creatures. For a selection of shrubs that work well for plenty of wildlife, see pages 208–214.

KEY SPECIES

- Blackbird
- Song Thrush
- House Sparrow
- Bullfinch
- Yellowhammer
- Robin
- Dunnock
- Wren
- Several bee species
- Brimstone, Holly Blue and Gatekeeper butterflies
- Hedgehog
- Wood Mouse
- Amphibians
- Many moth species
- Beetles and bugs
- Many spider species
- Bush-crickets

The inspiration

Small birds can disappear into the **dense, thorny tangle** of branches and leaves. Predators struggle to find or reach their nests and they have sanctuary from people too.

The **network of branches** is a great place to sling your web if you are a spider.

Good wildlife shrubs offer **nectar and pollen** by the bucketload…
…and then turn into a harvest festival of **fruit and berries**.

Down around their long 'skirts' are pockets of **shelter and warmth** where plants grow lush and butterflies congregate.

Around their **crowns**, bushes are warm and sun-soaked.

Some **evergreen shrubs** mixed in among the deciduous ones will offer early nesting sites and winter cover.

The sheer volume of **foliage** offers good portions for moth caterpillars.

The **ground** beneath the shrubbery is dark, cool and damp, and just right for anything that likes moseying through a bit of humus-rich leaf-litter.

How to make your shrubbery: step by step

1. Choose your shrubs carefully for your soil and location

As with most plants, there is a shrub for each situation, but get it wrong and you'll have an unhappy plant on your hands. Check for things such as how much sun they like, what soil they prefer, and whether they are a bit on the tender side and need to be out of the wind.

2. Prepare the ground

Most shrubs need a fertile, moisture-retentive soil, so fork in loads of compost.

3. Planting

You can plant out container-grown shrubs at any time, but those that are bare-rooted are best planted in mild weather in winter, while root-balled shrubs should be put in between autumn and early spring.

Plant it in a hole twice as wide as the roots, and ensure you plant the shrub at the same height in the ground as it sat in the pot. It is unlikely to need staking.

Water it well and continue to do so regularly until it is established. Light watering promotes roots to grow too near the surface, so give them a good long soak.

4. Aftercare

Mulch well in spring with well-rotted compost. It gives them a hearty meal and retains moisture, but keep the mulch clear of the stems.

Pruning can seem a bit of a black art, but focus on a little formative pruning when the shrub is young to help establish a good shape, and then in subsequent years just take out dead or crossing branches. A good rule of thumb is to prune spring-flowering shrubs immediately after flowering (next year's flowers will be on stems that they grow this year) and to prune summer-flowering shrubs in late winter or early spring.

If you need to, move established shrubs in the autumn by digging up the complete root ball.

And remember don't just wait for the 'end effect' – enjoy your shrubbery all the way through its evolution. In the early years why not plant the gaps between the shrubs with herbaceous plants, and then let the shrubs come into their own?

◄◄ A shrubbery can often create the feel of a mini woodland glade, but often also has the benefit of really good, dense and varied cover.

◄ With judicious pruning, some shrubs can be rejuvenated time and again, ensuring the shrubbery doesn't become 'tired'.

A potted shrubbery

Some shrubs will do just nicely in pots on the patio or balcony. Give each one as big a pot as you can and 'top-dress' it every couple of years by carefully removing the top 5cm of soil and replacing it with fresh compost. It's then just a case of plenty of water (potted plants dry out very quickly), keep the pot weed free to remove competition and repot the shrub occasionally.

◄ Pots can help stunt the growth of bushes, making them even more suitable for a smaller garden, but they do need a lot of TLC.

Hedges

There is, of course, one other brilliant way of creating a shrubbery, and that is to line them up like soldiers to guard your boundary, in other words, a hedge. Isn't it amazing that plants that, if left to their own devices, would grow into trees are malleable enough to be repeatedly chopped and snipped into such a neat shape?

And can you imagine the difference a hedge makes to wildlife? As well as it providing shelter, food and security, many creatures can climb through it or along it. In contrast, imagine you're a small creature trying to find your way through or over a six-foot high fence or wall; for anything that can't fly or do the pole vault, it must be a nightmare!

There are more good reasons why you should plant a hedge: they filter the wind rather than block it, so are less prone to being blown over than a fence; they can be very long lived; and those that are thorny make an excellent security cordon.

So why don't people plant hedges around their gardens anymore? Why are so many gardens divided into inaccessible boxes of regulation fencing?

Well, I think there are two main reasons. Firstly, people want instant privacy and security and it only takes a day's work for a fence to go up for instant seclusion. I do understand that, and unless you've got money to burn, there is no way of planting an instant, impenetrable hedge. However, hedges do form a substantial boundary far quicker than people imagine.

But the other reason is the assumption that it must be both costly and difficult to plant and look after a hedge. Wrong! The cost of buying bare-rooted hedging plants ('whips', which tend to be 50–70cm tall) is less per metre than fencing, they can be put in just as quickly, and you'll never have to touch a creosote tin again.

▲ Imagine how much poorer it would be for wildlife if this boundary was a plain, solid fence or wall instead of this glorious 'line of life'.

Even the annual trim for most garden hedges is only half a day's work a year.

So, go on, planting a hedge is one of the best things you can do for wildlife. Don't think that it even has to be along your boundary, you can use them to divide up even quite a small garden into discrete areas.

HOW TO PLANT A HEDGE

You will need to plant a bare-root deciduous hedge in winter (November–March); evergreen hedges can go in earlier (September) to start to settle in.

1. Choose where will it go and decide what type of hedge you want Do you want one that is trimmed immaculately, a formal hedge, or will it be wilder and woollier like one in the countryside. And how tall do you want it to grow? See my guide opposite.

2. Measure the length Then buy about 10 plants for every 3m of hedge, or double that if you intend to plant a double row (see No. 5, below).

3. Dig a strip of soil, 1m wide, where the hedge is going to go Remove all weeds. Dig a trench in the middle about 50cm wide and 50cm deep.

4. If using bare-rooted whips, keep them in the plastic bag until ready to use Those roots may be asleep, but they're very vulnerable to drying out.

5. Now plant your whips Use a taut string if you want to ensure the plants are in straight rows. One at a time, plant the whips 30–40cm apart, making sure for each that the junction between the stem and the roots is at ground level. If you want a thicker hedge (which I recommend), plant in a double, staggered row, the two rows 30cm apart.

6. Now I need you to be brave! Take secateurs and lop off at least the top half of each whip. It will prompt the whip to grow branches close to the ground, ensuring you get a thick hedge top to bottom. Trust me, be brutal!

7. Water and mulch Give your new hedge a drink now and again in dry weather throughout its first two years. Keep the ground beneath them well mulched to stop weeds.

8. If rabbits are a problem, put tree protectors (cheap plastic wrap-around tubes) around each plant.

9. Aftercare By Year 3, your hedge should start to mesh together. By Year 5 it will look and feel like a proper hedge. Trim it annually in winter, or cut one side one year and the other the next to give the hedge a chance to flower and set fruit on the uncut side.

HEDGING PLANTS

Here is your guide to the best plants to use for wildlife-friendly hedges:

Beech *Fagus sylvatica*

When closely planted, Beech whips make an excellent hedge, up to 6m tall if you really want, retaining their dead leaves over winter on any branches below 3m and so offering good shelter for several garden birds.

Escallonia rubra var. *macrantha* (below)

Evergreen. From Chile, this shrub makes a great hedge in mild coastal areas growing up to 2.5m tall. In June, it is thick with dangling, pink, tubular flowers, enjoyed by Honeybees and bumblebees. Throughout the year, its dense structure offers nest sites for Blackbirds, places for House Sparrows to gather (called 'chapels') and hideaways for other small birds.

Field Maple *Acer campestre*

Deciduous. You don't often see this grown as a single-species hedge, but it can be really attractive. Give it a bit more width and height than e.g. Hawthorns.

Hawthorns *Crataegus*

Deciduous. This is possibly the best hedging plant for wildlife, and the staple within a mixed species hedge, tolerating extensive and repeat pruning. It is quick growing, and the dense, thorny structure is better security than any fence. You can keep it pegged back to about 1.2m tall or let it expand to 2m or more, and it can be shaped tightly or left to be more 'loose' and natural.

Hazels *Corylus*

Deciduous. Not typically one to use as a formal hedge, and rather more blousy and less dense in structure than many of the other hedges, this can make a big and soft hedge.

Holly *Ilex aquifolium*

Evergreen. It makes a lovely dense hedge, easily up to 5m tall but much lower if you wish, that responds well to pruning, allowing you to keep the shape very neat. There are plenty of variegated cultivars to choose from but the deep green of the simple native works a treat.

Hornbeam *Carpinus betulus*

Closely planted whips create a brilliant hedge thanks to their fine mesh of branches and habit of retaining low-level dead leaves through winter. Can be pruned to be 4m tall or more. A mature hedge offers nesting and roosting sites for birds such as Blackbirds.

Privet *Ligustrum vulgare*

Semi-evergreen. Watch out because the plant usually sold for this purpose is the invasive *L. ovalifolium*. Instead, hunt down the native species. It makes a wonderfully neat and dense hedge, up to 4m tall, which is very quick to establish.

Yew *Taxus baccata* (below)

Evergreen. Makes a wonderful dense formal hedge, to 5m or more if necessary, and surely the most pliable to your whim and fancy! So if you want a hedge that will cope with being sculpted into a living arch, a cube or an elephant (I've seen it done!), Yew is the one for you. And what a fine nesting and roosting site for birds it is, whatever its shape. Trim annually in late summer.

The mixed-native hedge

Use about 50 per cent Hawthorn with a mix of any of the other native species, and maybe a Spindle, Dog Rose or Burnet Rose thrown in, for that look and feel of a rich and varied wild hedge. You can include Blackthorn but just be aware of its tendency to sucker.

Making a Wildflower Meadow Home

There's a deep nostalgia for flower-rich meadows, provoking visions of Impressionist paintings, Merchant Ivory films and young lovers skipping through tall grasses a-buzz with butterflies, bees and grasshoppers.

OK, cut! There's little chance of seeing a meadow like this these days. Most of the green fields out there are just monocultures of specially-selected Ryegrass cultivars that have been boosted by powerful fertilisers, sprayed with weedkillers, and cut early and repeatedly for silage.

The UK's national Habitat Action Plan for lowland meadows cites a 97 per cent loss of flower-filled pastures in the 50 years to 1984, and there has been a continued destruction since, with perhaps less than 15,000ha remaining in the UK (in a nation that covers 24 million hectares). What were some of the richest habitats for creatures, such as bugs and beetles as well as bees and butterflies, are now restricted to nature reserves and forgotten corners. Don't blame farmers: it's the result of advances in technology and a postwar agricultural policy demanding efficiency and productivity.

In your garden, however, you have the chance to recreate the essence of the wildflower meadows of old. They are difficult habitats to create, but don't let that put you off. Even to do a bit will help, and it is proven to be a lifeline for wildlife such as sparrows.

KEY SPECIES
— House Sparrow
— Tree Sparrow
— Goldfinch
— Yellowhammer
— Most butterflies (including Meadow Brown – right)
— Hedgehogs
— Voles and shrews
— Many bee species
— Many moth species
— Many beetle and bug species
— Many spider species
— Many hoverfly species
— Grasshoppers
— Earthworms
— Wild meadow flowers

◀ Wildflower meadows can enliven even quite small spaces, and needn't be confined to distant parts of the garden.

The inspiration

There are few wildflower meadows that have survived intact into the 21st century, but those that do are usually under conservation management, and they are well worth a visit just to admire the amazing sense of nature at her richest.

The types of wild flowers that grow, and the creatures that use them, differ according to the soil type and climate. It is as though there is not one type of wildflower meadow but a massive family of them, each slightly different. Learning these idiosyncrasies, and translating them to suit your garden, is an important tool.

Visually, wildflower meadows are something of an **informal tapestry**, delightful in their randomness rather than being orderly.

Freed from the endless nibbling of animals (or mowing machines), plants throw up their flowers offering **pollen, nectar and seeds** to a whole range of butterflies, bees, beetles and birds.

In the wild, livestock are brought onto meadows to graze, usually in early spring or late autumn. Their hooves churn the ground a little, so that there is **freshly turned soil** where the seeds of annual plants such as the Yellow Rattle can germinate.

Because it is never dug or ploughed, **perennial plants** that don't like being disturbed can become established. Wildflower meadows are THE place for orchids.

Unlike garden lawns, meadows contain **many grass species**, each with their own particular character and favoured wildlife.

Long stems create a **mini jungle** that is moist and shady near the ground. Down here a varied community of beetles and caterpillars tuck themselves away, and larger creatures such as voles and shrews can scurry.

After all this lushness and colour of spring, meadows then turn to summer patterns of yellowing waving seedheads, which can be just as attractive and evocative.

The **poor soil** means that grasses can't dominate in the way they do when they have fertilisers to give them a boost, and the number of different flowers in a small area can be huge.

How to make a wildflower meadow

In this section I will show you two different ways to make a meadow. However, first I'm must emphasise how critical it is to understand the difference between a wildflower meadow and a bed of cornfield annuals. The latter is often called a 'meadow' but isn't, and the reason why that is important is because it is created and looked after in a very different way to a real meadow.

In simple terms:

❀ **A wildflower meadow** is predominantly made up of wild grasses, interspersed with a range of mainly perennial flowers. It does best on poor soil, and is managed by mowing.

❀ **A cornfield annual mix** doesn't contain grasses and is mainly made up of (you guessed it!) annual flowers. It is fine for a rich soil, and is managed by clearing the bed each autumn, cultivating the soil and re-sowing.

If you thought meadows were masses of poppies and other colourful flowers, you've come to the wrong place! Hop across to page 152.

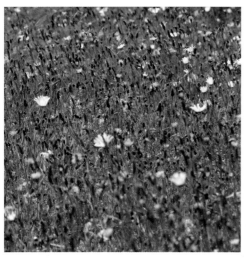

◀ A true wildflower meadow – permanent wild grasses dotted with a myriad of mainly native perennials.

▶ This is NOT a meadow – this is a cornfield annual mix.

Meadow method 1: making from scratch

Difficulty level: **Difficult, but not impossible!**

This method involves taking an area, be it a lawn or flower border, right back to bare, weed-free subsoil and sowing from seed. To me, this is the A-level of wildlife gardening: take on this challenge and you can feel very proud indeed.

1. Choose your area

It should be somewhere sunny. The larger the area, the more successful it is likely to be. Then measure it carefully in square metres – you will need to know this for buying seed.

2. Choose your type of meadow

You have two choices, both beautiful in their own way.

Spring meadows bloom with Lady's Smock, Cowslips and bulbs and are at their best between April and June. They are then kept relatively short the rest of the year, giving you back your 'lawn'.

Summer meadows come into their own in July and August with many species of butterflies winding their way through the yellowing grass stems and nectar-rich flowers, before the hay is cropped late in the season.

Once you've made your selection, stick to it!

3. Prepare a bed of bare, poor soil

Meadow plants need a soil that is low in nutrients. I mean it – it should be really awful. If yours is rich, which is likely, prepare to do something drastic. The best method is to completely remove the top 5–10cm of topsoil or turf in July or August and start with a blank canvas. As you might guess, this is pretty drastic stuff, and you'll need somewhere for all that topsoil and turf to go.

Then allow the bare ground to 'rest' for a couple of weeks. As weed seeds germinate, get rid of them with either a hoe or flame-thrower, depending on how dramatically you like to garden.

◀ Broadcasting seed is a wonderfully primal thing to do – your dual aim is to get an even coverage but at the suggested grams per metre square.

▶ A path mown through your meadow is inviting, it keeps your feet dry after rain and dew, and you'll find your Blackbirds use it as much as you do.

While you wait, buy the right seed for your soil, and the right amount for sowing at 4 grams per square metre in a ratio of one part wildflower seed to three parts meadow grasses. Never buy anything that includes ryegrasses! And here's the secret – make sure it includes Yellow Rattle. This lovely little annual plant, with hooded yellow flowers that bumblebees enjoy, taps into the roots of grasses, reducing their vigour and allowing other flowers to have their day in the sun.

4. In early September, sow your wildflower seed mix

Rake the soil until you have a fine tilth. Then broadcast the seed evenly. To help, you can mix the seed with silver sand to bulk up the small amounts involved and to help you see where you have sown.

Rake in the seed very lightly, and firm it in gently by shuffling over it. Water with a fine spray if conditions are dry, and if necessary protect from birds by erecting strings festooned with flapping plastic bags or dangling CDs.

5. In the first spring, mow your meadow

Cut it to 5cm as soon as the grasses have reached 10cm high, removing the clippings. Make sure the mower blades are sharp so as not to uproot the tender young plants.

6. Year 1: cut every 6–8 weeks

Remove the clippings, and hand weed any nuisance weeds such as dandelions, nettles and docks. You will not get flowers in the first year, and be warned, a meadow does not look like a bowling green, even when cut.

7. Year 2 onwards

Spring meadow Don't mow until late June or early July. Then cut to 5cm, leaving the clippings to dry in situ for a few days so that they can shed their seed, and then remove and compost them. Mow every few weeks for the rest of the growing season (usually to late autumn), always removing the clippings.

Summer meadow Mow in late March/early April to 5cm and remove the clippings. Then leave until August or even September, and mow again to 5cm, and once again in late autumn if there has been some regrowth. Top up with a bit of Yellow Rattle seed if needed, which needs to be sown in autumn.

Mowing in both of these options may require a sickle or scythe (ideally) or failing that shears or a strimmer. Be mindful of frogs and other wildlife when you cut.

As I say, real meadows aren't easy, but be brave, keep at it, experiment, and enjoy every success you have.

◀ Richard Brown of the Scythe Association demonstrates how speedy and efficient mowing can be done the traditional, and quiet, way.

Meadow method 2: the liberated lawn

Difficulty level: Easy or very easy

If the thought of ripping up your lawn and digging down to subsoil is too much to contemplate, this solution, while not as rich in wildlife, will give you many of the benefits for a lot less pain, and a lot less time with the lawnmower!

This method is all about freeing your lawn from its usual prison sentence of repeated cutting. I've seen it done in gardens across the country, and it looks great.

1. For starters, just leave the mower in the shed for a month

This is the simplest technique, leaving the lawn uncut for a few weeks at some point in the summer. The grass will grow long and, in all likelihood, there will be some herbaceous plants tucked away among the grasses that will now get their turn in the limelight. Typical lawn 'weeds' include dandelions, Daisy, Self-heal, Black Medick and various speedwells. For a few glorious weeks, a whole wildlife community will delight in the mini jungle. Then resume your usual cutting routine.

◀ By adding a range of plug plants including Common Bird's-foot Trefoil and (here) Lady's Bedstraw, Simon and Mark have further increased the diversity of plants and hence wildlife.

◀ Here in Findon Valley, West Sussex, Simon Dannatt and Mark Taylor have used the 'liberated lawn' method to turn their back and front lawns into meadows. Without having to dig up the original lawn, but by reducing mowing and introducing Yellow Rattle seed, their lawns are now alive with bees in high summer.

2. Take it further, treat it like a real meadow

Adopt one of the following mowing regimes.

For a spring meadow, don't mow at all until late June or early July. Then 'mow', leaving the clippings to dry in situ for a few days so that they can shed their seed, and then remove and compost them. This first mow may need to be with a sickle if the grass is too high for a lawnmower. Then mow every few weeks for the rest of the growing season (usually to late autumn), always removing the clippings.

For a summer meadow, mow in late March/early April with the mower raised to its highest setting, and remove the clippings. Then leave until August or early September, and mow again on highest setting, and once again in late autumn if there has been some regrowth.

3. With both of these options, resist all temptation to use fertilisers, top-dressings and weedkillers

Do rake out the thatch and moss if necessary, but always remove the grass cuttings. You are trying to reduce the fertility bit by bit, to allow the flowering plants a chance to compete against the vigorous grasses.

4. Spice it up with plug plants

It is certainly worth planting some low-growing meadow flowers as 'plugs' (young plants grown in individual modules). Top plants to try include Bird's-foot Trefoil, Cowslip and Field Scabious.

5. Use the secret weapon – Yellow Rattle

Scratch the surface with a rake in autumn to create a mosaic of bare patches among the turf, and sprinkle with Yellow Rattle seed.

MAKING A LIBERATED LAWN LOOK LOVED

If it is the untidiness of a wildflower meadow that puts you off, there is a brilliant solution. All you need to so is impose some discipline by mowing neat lines around the edges of your meadow areas to create clearly defined shapes, and by cutting paths through the middle. Kids will love running along the paths, you'll still save plenty of time, and it will clearly signal to anybody peering over the fence that you haven't let things go and that you are most definitely in control in a rather daring and modern way!

▶ With selective mowing, this is both a wildlife-friendly garden but also one that is clearly loved.

Flowers and grasses for wildflower meadows

Use this table to pick a mix of seeds that's right for your garden and the type of meadow you want to have.

	Clay and damp soils	Sandy soils	Chalky soils	Spring meadow	Summer meadow
Grasses					
Crested Dog's-tail	Y	Y	Y	Y	Y
Crested Hairgrass		Y	Y	Y	Y
Common Bent	Y	Y	Y	Y	Y
Meadow Barley	Y			Y	Y
Meadow Foxtail	Y			Y	Y
Quaking Grass		Y	Y	Y	Y
Red Fescue	Y	Y	Y	Y	Y
Sheep's Fescue	Y	Y	Y	Y	Y
Sweet Vernal Grass	Y	Y	Y	Y	Y
Yorkshire Fog	Y	Y	Y	Y	Y
Wildflowers					
Autumn Hawkbit	Y	Y	Y		Y
Betony	Y		Y		Y
Bird's-foot Trefoil	Y		Y	Y	Y
Black Knapweed	Y	Y	Y		Y
Burnet-saxifrage		Y	Y	Y	Y
Cat's-ear		Y		Y	
Common Sorrel	Y	Y			Y
Cowslip	Y	Y	Y	Y	Y
Devil's-bit Scabious	Y		Y		Y
Dropwort			Y	Y	Y

	Clay and damp soils	Sandy soils	Chalky soils	Spring meadow	Summer meadow
Field Scabious		Y	Y		Y
Greater Knapweed (above)		Y	Y		Y
Hoary Plantain	Y		Y	Y	Y
Kidney Vetch			Y	Y	Y
Lady's Bedstraw	Y	Y	Y	Y	Y
Lady's Smock (plant as plugs)	Y			Y	
Meadow Buttercup	Y	Y	Y	Y	Y
Meadow Vetchling	Y	Y	Y	Y	Y
Ox-eye Daisy	Y	Y	Y	Y	Y
Pepper-saxifrage	Y				Y
Ragged Robin	Y			Y	
Red Clover	Y	Y	Y	Y	Y
Ribwort Plantain (above left)	Y	Y	Y	Y	Y
Rough Hawkbit		Y	Y	Y	Y
Salad Burnet			Y	Y	Y
Self-heal	Y		Y		Y
Small Scabious			Y		Y
White Clover	Y	Y	Y	Y	Y
Wild Basil			Y		Y
Wild Carrot			Y		Y
Wild Mignonette		Y	Y		Y
Yarrow	Y	Y	Y		Y
Yellow Rattle	Y	Y	Y	Y	Y

Making a Cornfield Home

A century ago, our cornfields were a visual feast because of all the beautiful 'weeds' among the corn, a treat for pollinating insects and rich pickings for farmland birds.

Then, just as in our meadows, things changed. New technology meant that weed seeds could be separated and destroyed from the cereal seeds before they were sown, and chemical herbicides knocked out most weeds that were left in the soil. All those wildflowers that once shone so brightly but had tainted the harvest could now be eradicated.

It's hard to imagine every farm ever having a reason to return to weed-filled crops, no matter how attractive or good for wildlife they are, so it is in our gardens where we have one of the best opportunities to revisit some of these lost glories.

KEY SPECIES
— The cornfield flowers themselves
— Finches
— Hoverflies
— Beetles
— Bees

The inspiration

These days you can find a few fields full of poppies, one of the few species that can be resistant to herbicides, but rarely **exquisite scenes** like this.

Most cornfield flowers are annuals. They germinate, grow, flower, set seed and die within a single season, their copious seeds tumbling back into the earth they came from.

Few perennial plants can tolerate the **regular upheaval** of land that gets ploughed each year.

Bees and other pollinating insects find food in the **wealth of flowers**. Even Grasshoppers can find a suitable home here.

Several cornfield flowers that were once prolific have now pretty much been eradicated from the British countryside, such as the Corncockle and the blue **Cornflower** (left).

At the end of summer, when the corn is harvested and the soil ploughed, many of the cornfield flower **seeds are buried** where they want to be, in the soil.

Those **seeds left lying on the soil** give seed-eating finches and buntings a field day, but enough weed seed is left for a new generation of flowers to bloom the following year.

How to make your cornfield garden: step by step

In simple terms, what you are going to do is scatter a load of flower seeds on a bare, prepared area of soil, water them, and let nature do the rest, giving you a gorgeous summer display. You are not creating a meadow, no matter what some seed packets will tell you! This is a bed of annual flowers. Check out Making a Wildflower Meadow (see page 146) for more about the differences between the two.

1. Choose a sunny site, as large or small as you like

It could be a large flower border, it could be a tiny corner, the choice is yours, but it should be in a place that gets lots of sunlight. The larger the area, the more wildlife is likely to find and use your cornfield but, as I will show you, you can get beautiful results in just a large plant pot. As a cornfield isn't a meadow, you don't need impoverished soil – in fact, some fertility is ideal.

2. Prepare your plot

Get ready for either an autumn (August–early October) or early spring (March–April) sowing. You're going to be scattering thousands of seeds, so they need ideal conditions for germination. That means a bed of lovely, crumbly, weed-free soil. Some people advocate using a glyphosphate weedkiller to prepare the seedbed, which kills weeds on touch but doesn't have a long term effect in the soil. I stick to organic methods, which are rather more labour-intensive, in which I dig or rotavate the soil and then hoe off any weeds that emerge. It's a bit of a bind, but a vital step. Once free of weeds, rake until the soil on the surface is a fine tilth.

3. Measure your area and buy your seed

You will need about 2 grams of seed per square metre. Look for those called 'cornfield annual mix' or something similar. One

seed packet is usually way too much for a pot, but you'll need to buy larger quantities for a large border.

4. Broadcast the seed

Sow your seed evenly. To help, mix the seed with silver sand (about 100 parts sand to one part seed is fine). When sowing a large area, I like to divide my plot up into equal sections and then I split my sand-seed mix into the same number of batches. Just take handfuls of the sand-seed mixture and swish them side to side across the sowing area: it's very satisfying! You don't need to rake the seed in; just walk across the surface to make sure it is in contact with the soil. Then water with a fine rose, and you will need to keep it watered in any dry periods.

5. Sit back and enjoy the summer spectacle

The plants should germinate quickly but it seems to take an age for them to spread a blanket of green across the plot. Then growth accelerates into summer and before you know it flowers are bursting out everywhere! Poppies tend to dominate from autumn sowings; Corn Chamomile, Corn Marigold and Corncockle come to the fore if you sow in spring. Seeds sown in autumn tend to flower from about June; those sown in spring flower after about 12 weeks. The main show should last about four weeks, but a few flowers may keep going until the frosts.

◄ If sowing a large area, divide your seed up into equal batches and likewise with your plot – you'll get a more even spread of seed.

▲ Note how there are no poppies flowering in this mix I sowed in spring; the photo might have been filled with red had I sown the same mix in autumn.

◄ Cornflowers are dominating the mix here, which is no bad thing as they are perhaps the best of the mix for pollinating insects, and intensely beautiful too.

6. In late August or September, scythe the crop down to about 5cm

Either leave the cuttings on the soil for a few days so that the new seed drops onto the soil, or lay it on a tarpaulin so you can collect the seeds that fall onto it. Then gather up and compost.

7. If you want a repeat show again next year...

It is possible to just lightly cultivate the soil in autumn, and all the seed that has dropped from this year's crop will provide you with the basis of next year's display. However, this often isn't as successful for two reasons. Firstly, unwanted 'weeds' may have crept in among your crop this year. Annual Meadow Grass, Nettle, Sow-thistles, whatever is abundant nearby may start to invade. Secondly, whichever of your cornfield flowers did well in Year 1 will have seeded well and so is likely to do even better next year, increasingly at the expense of those flowers that weren't so abundant. So few poppies one year will probably mean even fewer the next. If you want to be sure of a good performance next year, my best advice is that either to do a very thorough weed in autumn and replenish the seeds with extra of whatever flowers performed poorly, or start from fresh and go back to Step 1.

▶ Here's a standard cornfield mix I sowed in a large pot on 6 April (top). By 17 May, it was a fuzz of green seedlings (centre); by 6 July it was in full flower (bottom).

The key flowers of the cornfield

- **Common (or Field) Poppy** The signature plant of the cornfield for many people; just remember to sow in autumn for best results. A great plant for bees.
- **Corn Marigold** The large, daisy-like flowers are a vibrant yellow, and are great for hoverflies and solitary bees.
- **Corn Chamomile** Not a great plant for pollinators, but a welcome dash of daisy colours and plentiful seed.
- **Corncockle** The pink-mauve flowers with a white centre I find work best for pollinating beetles. The seeds are large.
- **Cornflower** The intensity of the blue is hard to match in the garden, and is probably the best of the bunch for bees and bumblebees.

◀ Corncockle came to Britain in the Iron Age, but became extinct as an arable weed in the 20th century. Gardeners are helping it make a comeback.

◀ A single Corn Marigold pokes out from a sea of Corn Chamomile. In my garden, Field Voles and Grass Snakes hunt under the dense cover of the stems and flowers.

To recreate the authentic cornfield effect, why not add some cereal seeds, such as wheat, barley and oats, which will then produce heads full of fresh seed for sparrows and finches. When sowing cereal seed, it is best to sow them first, rake them into the seedbed so they are covered, and then scatter the wildflower seed onto the surface.

There are several other flowers you might like to add to the mix which would also have turned up in cornfields in times gone by. Those with a long history in the UK include Field Pansy, Linseed (Common Flax), Scented Mayweed and Night-flowering Catchfly. White Campion is sometimes offered, but can be a bit robust. Some mixes even come with very rare plants such as Thorow-wax and Corn Buttercup.

Adding extra spice

It is thought that most cornfield annuals are archaeophytes, plants that were brought in by early settlers with cereal seed, some possibly as long ago as the Iron Age. It means that you needn't feel too guilty about being a 'modern settler' and adding a little bit of something more fanciful to the mix.

'Exotic' annuals are just as easy to grow as the conventional cornfield annuals, and some fantastic seed mixes have been developed to offer a long flowering season and different colour combinations. The seed merchants have turned to northern Africa for the vibrant Red Flax and Fairy Toadflax and to North America for Californian Poppy and the Midwestern Tickseed. Bee-magnets such as Scorpion Weed and Poached-egg Plant are definitely worth including, and your palette can include Opium Poppy, Cosmos, Larkspur and Bishop's Flower.

Cornfield annuals as the 'first act' for perennial meadows

You can, if you want, mix in cornfield annual seeds when you sow a perennial wildflower meadow (see page 146). Just mix the two types of seed together at the start. You will get a flush of colourful annuals in the first year that then quickly peters out as the perennials take over in subsequent years. Remember though to start with the infertile soil that the perennial meadows will need.

◀ The exquisite Cornflower is desperately rare in the wild, but easy to grow in gardens.

Making a Heathland Home

If you live somewhere where the soils are acidic and nutrient-poor, because they are either sandy or peaty, you have a choice when deciding what to do with your garden. You could bulk up your garden soil – repeatedly – with tonnes (literally) of expensive soil improver and lime to pretend that you live somewhere else. Or you can accept that your soils are like they are, and so select plants that can cope with it.

Most people adopt the back-breaking first option, but I urge you to consider the more adventurous 'leave the soil as it is' route. Nearby there is likely to be an area of natural habitat that will inspire you as to the kind of plants that can and will grow for you.

In southern, dry, lowland areas this habitat will be heathland; in the wet north and west it will be moorland or coastal heath.

Lowland and coastal heath are two of the world's rarest habitats, and all of these acid habitats support their own special wildlife including dragonflies, butterflies, moths, beetles and bees, some of which may then visit your garden.

KEY SPECIES

— Goldcrest
— Coal Tit
— Siskin
— Lesser Redpoll
— Common Lizard
— Slow-worm
— Solitary bees and wasps
— Many moth species
— Many beetle species
— Several ant species
— Dragonflies and damselflies
— Small Copper and Wall Brown butterflies

The inspiration

A few beautifully-shaped **Scots Pines** provide nesting, roosting and feeding places for specialist birds like Goldcrests and Coal Tits.

Plumes of **heathland grasses** emerge fresh green in spring and turn golden in later summer.

Glorious **beds of heather** include various native species such as Ling, Bell Heather and Cross-leaved Heath, and are a delight for the bees.

In **wetter flushes**, plants such as Cranberries and Cotton Grasses can grow.

Birches cast their light shade and fill with seed in autumn.

Acidic pools support dragonflies and damselflies.

The **woody heather stems** provide good shelter throughout the year.

On lowland heaths, the **dry, sandy soils** heat up quickly in the sunshine, a sunbed for cold-blooded reptiles and easy digging for burrowing insects.

How to make your heathland garden: step by step

1. Are you on the right soil?

If your soil is not already acidic, it is technically possible to add sulphur, iron sulphate or aluminium sulphate to increase acidity, or some texts still advocate absolute no-nos such as buying peat, but I strongly advise that you don't fight nature, you are unlikely to win. If your soil is already acidic, this is the section for you!

2. Go for open and sunny

Heathland and moorland habitats are typically open and exposed, and the baked and blasted plants tend to be low-growing. Try to replicate this kind of look.

3. Reduce the fertility

If previous gardeners have attempted to improve your soil, it is good to rake off the top layer of humus to expose poorer soil beneath.

4. Remember to include a wetland

Even dry sunny lowland heaths usually have areas that have poor drainage where pools develop, and these can be excellent for a host of unusual wildlife.

5. And then it is all down to choosing the right plants.

Despite the obvious differences between a baking sandy southern heath and a windswept rain-soaked upland moor, they share a surprising number of plants, showing how influential that poor, acidic soil is. It takes some special plants to survive all these strange deprivations and extremes.

Trees Birches, pines and rowans.

Shrubs Oregon-grapes, barberries, lavenders, brooms, gorses, bilberries and other plants in the *Vaccinium* genus, and junipers.

◀ There are several native species of heather to try, such as this gorgeous Cornish Heath *Erica vagans*.

Heathers Yes, they're small shrubs, but they're such an important part of the heathland garden that I'm giving them a paragraph of their own. The obvious choice is Heather itself, also known as Ling, for which there are dozens of interesting cultivars offering different flower and foliage colours, but there are several other native species such as Bell Heather and Cross-leaved Heath in the *Erica* genus, also with cultivars. All are great nectar sources for bees and other insects, and also tend to be well used by some moth caterpillars.

Grasses Purple Moorgrass and Tufted Hairgrass are very typical native heathland and moorland species that have been bred to offer dozens of attractive cultivars.

Herbaceous perennials If you want more than just the 'moorland' look of heathers, then try some of the typically Mediterranean species that can cope with the acidic conditions such as Lamb's-ear, Pot Marigold, *Allium hollandicum*, Honeywort, Teasel, mulleins and sea hollies.

Wetland areas Bogbean, Cotton-grass, Alternate Water-milfoil, Bog Pondweed.

Fruit and vegetables Raspberries, Blueberries, Carrots, Parsnips, Garlic and Onions.

▲ Heather gardens are somewhat out of vogue, but when you see one done well like this, who cares about fashion.

Making a Wetland Home

What a miracle-worker water is: life just seems to flourish in it. Hardly a day goes by when I don't go out to my pond and peer through the glassy surface into the parallel universe beneath. It is inhabited by a minibeast world of bulging-eyed monsters, tiny swimmers and rowers, and love-struck amphibians.

People clearly love and need water – think of all the pools, lakes, reservoirs, canals and fountains we have made everywhere. But at the same time we have had a monumental impact on our natural wetlands. We have drained huge – and I mean huge – areas of the countryside, while underneath our fields are hundreds of thousands of miles of land drains. Together with street drains, gutters and ditches, we seem to want to channel water away as fast as we possibly can.

Against this chequered background, garden ponds have become vital homes to many creatures. Individually they may be tiny, but collectively they are fantastic.

Ponds are a triple-winner for wildlife. First, they support those creatures, such as water lice and pond snails, that spend their whole life in water and would otherwise never get a look-in in your garden.

You will also see far more of those animals that spend part of their life in water, such as frogs and toads, dragonflies and damselflies. If you don't have a pond, they might still pass through your garden but won't have a reason to stop.

And just as exciting are those animals that don't live in water at all but benefit from the flush of food that ponds create, or turn to it as a vital drinking and bathing hole.

Making a wildlife pond of some sort is probably the single most effective thing you can do to boost the biodiversity in your wildlife garden, and everyone's got room to do something. The larger you can make your mini-wetland home, the more life it is likely to host. But even if all you have room for is a pond in a pot, life will still find it, and there are workable options, too, for families with small children who need to think safety-first.

KEY SPECIES

— Amphibians
— Grass Snakes
— Dragonflies and damselflies
— Birds (coming to drink and bathe)
— Bats (coming to catch insects and drink)
— Pond creatures (galore!)
— Many fly species
— Water plants

◄ Frogs are one of the best loved, and most easy to cater for, pond visitors.

The inspiration

It's hard to find a 'natural pond' in the countryside these days. Almost every pond out there has been made or modified by human hands. But we can nevertheless take inspiration from all sorts of larger ponds and lakes in the countryside.

Dense vegetation growing along the margins provides flowers and seeds, as well as perches for dragonflies and nesting sites for Moorhens.

A little bit of shade is useful so that creatures which like to stay out of the heat can do so.

Submerged aquatic vegetation is vital for the health of the pond, keeping the water crystal clear, while offering a hiding place and hunting ground for pond minibeasts.

Areas of shallow water warm up quickly and offer safe bathing for birds and mammals.

Flat open areas around the margins offer safe access to the water's edge for birds and mammals to drink and for dragonflies to sun themselves.

Areas of deeper water provide a sanctuary for underwater life during cold weather and safety from predators such as Herons.

Floating aquatic vegetation provides perching pads for insects, and places for dragonflies, damselflies and pond snails to lay their eggs.

Out of sight on the **pond-bed**, muddy sediments and gravels are a roving ground for some of the pond's cleaners which tidy up the debris that falls from above.

How to make your wetland: step by step

1. Choose the right site
The pond should get direct sunlight for at least some of the day. If you put it beneath trees, be aware that leaves will fall in and you'll either need to fish them out or they will rot, robbing the pond of oxygen and creating a right stink. I like to have a pond within view of the house, as it is such a focal point for wildlife.

2. Design it on paper
Don't worry if your drawing skills are ropey – it will be worth it. Devise its shape from above *and* also its cross-section. Include deep bits and shelves where plants can sit but most importantly include lots of shallows; this is vital to help wildlife get in and out of the pond. If you are planning to use a rubber-type liner, be aware that it won't do right angles.

The pond can be as small or large as you like, but just be aware that very small ponds are more difficult to plant and maintain, and the larger the pond the more wildlife of more species it is likely to hold. The pond I made, shown on page 165, was 3.2m x 1.4m, and I wished I'd been braver and gone even bigger!

In larger ponds, I like to make the middle at least 60cm deep; it isn't to stop it freezing solid (it would take a vicious winter indeed to do that to any UK garden pond that was 20cm deep!) but I find that amphibians love having the opportunity to escape into deeper water, and the pond will also hold a more stable temperature than one with less volume.

There are no hard and fast rules for shape – wavy edges increase the length of shoreline in relation to the area of the water surface, but if you want to go perfectly rectangular or circular, wildlife won't hold it against you.

I like to dig a 'U' shaped trench around the margin to create a planting pocket which I fill with gravel and which also helps anchor a rubber-type liner.

▼ Not many of you will have the space to create the astonishing wetland habitats that Ennis and Richard Chappell have crafted from scratch in their Gloucestershire garden, but that's not the point. The important thing is to take inspiration about how ambitious you can be with water.

It is essential that any creature that wants or needs to get in or out can do so. Use ramps and beaches so that anything that falls can easily climb out again. Make sure *you* can get close to it too!

3. Always think safety

Water can be dangerous, especially for children who love ponds but are incredibly prone to falling in. To create a wetland feature with safety in mind, try one of the following:

❀ Create a pond but fence it off with a secure gate
❀ Buy special metal grills to go over the top of the pond – they can be decorative
❀ Make a water feature in a pot.
❀ Or make a bog garden or rain garden (see page 166).

4. Choose a liner – and don't skimp!

There are a number of choices for making a pond watertight:

Concrete ponds either need a timber frame ('shuttering') as a mould into which the concrete is poured, or can be made from concrete blocks. It will need to be made waterproof with a special render and seal.

Clay is natural but expensive and liable to cracking.

Pre-cast fibreglass moulded liners can last well, but are quite expensive and you are restricted to the shapes available.

Stretchable synthetic rubber liner is the preferred option for most ponds, either **butyl** or **EPDM rubber**. It comes as heavy black sheets and you can usually order the exact dimensions you need. The size of liner to buy should be (greatest width + 2x greatest depth) by (greatest length + 2x greatest depth), so for example for a 10m x 5m pond that is 1.5m deep you will need a liner 13 x 8m. The liners come in varying thicknesses; 0.75mm is usually adequate for most ponds, but choose 1mm if you want a bit more durability. Just be aware that these liners are surprisingly heavy; when I made a pond that was 16m x 8m, the liner weighed 350kg!

5. Dig!

Feel free to make a pond at any time of year, but the going can get boggy in winter.

Mark out the outline on the ground using sand or a hosepipe, or use taut string if your design is geometrical. If fitting a

▲ Digging is the heavy-duty part of creating a pond. You'll be surprised how much spoil it creates.

◀ Hammer marked posts into the ground and use a spirit level to check that the pond edges will be level.

◀ Here, I've laid a layer of sand, and over the top are going sheets of fleece underlay held in place temporarily by bricks.

▶ The liner is heavy and needs to be pulled bit by bit into position.

▶▶ Here I've put underlay over the top of the liner, and then gravel over the top of that.

▶▼ The finished pond, six months after filling.

preformed pond, it is a good idea to make a template using cardboard of the shape of the rim to then guide you as you dig.

Then start digging. It creates mountains of spoil, so plan where it will all go (for example, you could create raised mounds and banks). Dig out an area at least 5cm deeper and wider than the size you want your pond to be.

Work hard to make the pond level in all directions – you'll feel like a muppet if you end up with one side of the pond sticking way out of the water. A spirit level is your greatest ally.

If using a rubber-type liner, it will easily puncture so remove every stone or hard root jutting out from the pit sides.

6. Line the pond

Even after removing all the rocks and roots you can see, others will work their way through the soil over time, so create a cushion for the liner using old pieces of carpet, soft builders' sand or pond underlay fabric, or all three! (hence the extra 5cm digging you did earlier).

7. Laying a liner

If using a rubber-type liner, roll the liner out across the pond (in your stockinged feet!) and push and pull it so that it is stretched as neatly as possible. You may need to pleat and fold it where it goes around bends. Anchor the outer edge with bricks or logs.

If using a preformed liner, try and make the hole as close a match to the 3D shape of the liner, plus a few centimetres extra. Then use soft builders sand to get a snug fit.

8. Edging the pond

To cover the edges of the liner, here are four options:

Turf offers wildlife a safe margin to crawl into, but it will need a deep layer of soil and the grass will suck up water like a sponge.

Paving slabs can be mortared around the edge as in the pond on page 165, with the liner sandwiched between them and concrete blocks below. With the slabs' surface angled very slightly towards the pond, rainwater will run into the pond helping to keep it topped up.

Large rocks, again mortared in place, make great hidey-holes for amphibians, but can make access to the edge tricky for you.

Gravel boards inserted vertically around the edge allow the liner to be neatly folded over the top; they will rot eventually but can serve you well for years.

9. Extra protection?

If there is a risk that larger wildlife such as Grey Herons, Foxes or deer may visit and damage the liner (or excited children for that matter!), consider adding a layer of fleece underlay over the top of a rubber-type liner. Be careful, however, that the fleece does not extend above the pond surface or it will wick up water.

10. Don't add soil

It can be tempting to fill the pond with a nice thick layer of rich soil to plant in. Don't! It will flush the pond with nutrients, prompting algae to bloom and the water to become murky.

Instead, either use very poor subsoil (put it in before you fill the pond) or just grow your pond plants in special mesh pots.

A bed of smooth pebbles is a great alternative for hiding the liner, while I like to use a thick bed of gravel and sharp sand which doesn't slump or roll down a shallow slope. Whatever you use, make sure you add nothing that will jag the liner.

11. At last, add water!

Wherever possible, use rainwater either from the sky or from a water butt. If that really isn't possible, then take it from the tap, but be aware that tap water contains nitrates and phosphates, exactly the thing to cause algal blooms.

12. Planting up the pond

Be very careful to only use plants that are right for the size of your pond, see my recommendations on page 248.

Avoid non-native invasive plants at all costs (see page 257). There are wild ponds all around the world that are clogged with alien plants that escaped from garden ponds.

Also avoid plants with needle-sharp roots that have been known to pierce pond liners — Bulrush and Lyme-grass are particularly problematic.

13. Stocking the pond with wildlife

Don't bring in frog or toad spawn from another pond – it risks spreading the terrible diseases that are currently afflicting amphibians.

You might be tempted to throw in a bucket of water or lump of mud from another pond to introduce some minibeasts, too, but this runs the risk of transferring fragments of invasive plants.

So the safest and most rewarding route is just to fill the pond and see what comes. Creatures that look incapable of life out of water, such as water beetles and pond skaters, are actually excellent flyers that habitually seek out new ponds.

Ensure that animals that fall in can get out. Steep-sided ponds in particular are a death trap for creatures such as Hedgehogs. A log angled into the water will often do the trick, but having shallows around the margins is even better.

14. Annual maintenance

If waterweeds are beginning to dominate the pond, lift out small amounts at a time, and leave them on the pond edge for a day or two before composting. This lets any creatures within the weed crawl back into the pond.

In autumn, keep the pond clear of leaves, either by covering the pond with netting or by fishing them out with a net once they're in.

15. Dealing with a frozen pond

When a pond freezes, wildlife beneath the ice has no problem surviving unless there is rotting vegetation in there, in which cases the gases are trapped and may poison the inhabitants. If you want to maintain a hole in the ice:

❀ Don't smash the ice, which can cause shockwaves through the pond.

❀ Don't bother with the oft-quoted 'trick' of floating a ping-pong ball on the surface.

❀ You can melt a hole through the ice by resting a saucepan of boiling water on top, but it does take an eternity to melt your way through (believe me, I've done it!).

Me? I just leave the pond as it is, frost is natural, after all!

▲ A finished pond is a constant source of delight. Even Kingfishers visit this superb pond in Sue Camm's Devon garden.

◀ As you lift weed out, give it a shake to encourage pond life to dive back into the water.

▶ It takes several visits back to the cooker to heat the saucepan and its contents back up to steam a hole in the ice.

MAKING A FORMAL WILDLIFE POND

These six pictures show how I made a formal pond that is still good for wildlife.

It is a 'brimming' pond, where the water surface is designed to be at the level of the slabs, making access into and out of the water easy for even small creatures.

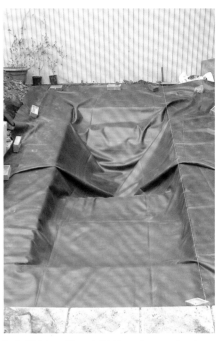

1. The pond is marked out using string and a spirit level – accurate horizontals are vital if the water surface is to sit flush with the edges.

2. The dug pond is bordered with concrete blocks and lined with a thick layer of sand. See how there are lots of shallows as well as a deeper area.

3. A thick butyl liner is laid into the pond and pleated into deeper areas. The weight of the water will help push it into shape.

4. Slabs are laid on mortar over the top of the liner along the lines of the concrete blocks and allowed to set.

5. The edges of the liner are brought up the outside of the slabs and cut off neatly (here hidden by shingle). The pond is filled with rainwater and plants.

6. The completed pond was home to frogs, toads, newts, dragons and damsels within a year.

Ponds and wildlife Q&As

Can I have a fountain or pond pump?

Ah, the gentle sound of water splashing into a pond. It adds oxygen, which creates a healthier home for most pondlife and helps keep the water clear. Unfortunately, pumps have a huge carbon footprint, with some using 500 watts of power. A well-made pond in a good position with a healthy community of plants and animals should look after itself without needing energy-guzzling solutions; if you do want a little fountain, use a solar-powered one.

Can I introduce fish?

Fish, whether non-native goldfish or wild species such as Three-spined Sticklebacks, aren't usually recommended for wildlife ponds because they will eat many pond creatures (including tadpoles and water fleas). But some natural ponds have fish, and a well-designed pond with shallows and hideaways can still host all sorts of creatures. It's your call.

How do I deal with blanket weed?

A problem that almost any pond will face at some point is the dreaded algae. Long green filaments spread through the water, or it turns into a green or brown soup. The simple solution is to wind it around a bamboo cane like spaghetti. You can also try bundles of barley straw, which appear to kill algae as they decompose. The key, however, is ensuring no nutrients are getting into the pond, be it tap water or garden run-off. And it if happens in Year 1, don't worry, that's totally normal while the pond ecosystem establishes itself.

The bog garden

There are places in nature where drainage is poor and the ground waterlogged, but there's rarely any standing water at the surface. These bogs, mires and quagmires may not attract all the dragonflies and aquatic creatures that a pond does, but they are home to all sorts of fantastic plants that like these conditions, such as Meadowsweet, Snake's-head Fritillary and Marsh Woundwort. In among their stems it remains lush and cool all summer, offering a perfect home for many damp-loving creatures to chill out.

To make your bog garden:

* Dig out a suitable area to a depth of at least 60cm and line the pit with a waterproof liner. Spike some drainage holes in the bottom, and cover the base with a layer of gravel.
* Then refill the hole with the soil you removed. You can then add water, or let rain do it.
* And get planting!

Making a pond in a pot

If you have a small garden or have concerns about children, why not make a container pond.

* Take a large glazed bowl, half-barrel or container. Reclaimed ceramic sinks are great (below left, raised on a brick den for frogs and toads).
* Seal up any drainage holes using a silicone sealant (below centre). If the pot is at all porous or if you're using barrels, paint on special pond waterproofing from a specialist shop. Alternatively you can use a rubber-type pond liner, but getting it to look neat within a round barrel can be hard.
* Place it where it only receives a little full sun each day, but not in deep shade or under trees..
* Create shallows and deeper areas, with submerged plants and marginals. But limit yourself – about three plants is as much as a small water garden can take (below right, with Hornwort, Water Mint and *Equisetum hyemale*).
* And a word of warning: the smaller the water area, the more difficult it is to establish a wildlife community that regulates itself and keeps the water clear.
* Ensure wildlife can get in – and out – easily.

Rain gardens

The term 'rain garden' has a rather magical air, don't you think? But what it is? Well, it's a solution to what you can do with all the water that lands on your house. For decades, the basic premise has been to send it as fast as possible into drains and soakaways. Of course, the problem is that, as a result, someone or somewhere further down the system gets flooded.

In contrast, nature – in its eternal wisdom – is very good at holding water back, thus spreading the impact. So what happens if we take nature's example and 'slow the flow', giving water places to linger along its route? Well, that's what rain gardens are, usually a depression in the ground filled with lush vegetation, where much of the water gets soaked up or drains away gradually, creating great new habitats for wildlife in the process. They are part of the modern idea called Sustainable Urban Drainage Systems (SUDS), which aims to create win-win solutions to flood risk in our towns.

You can create your own rain garden by digging a very shallow hollow either next to a paved area or by redirecting your downpipes into it. You don't line it and it will only occasionally – and temporarily – hold water, so it is quite different from a pond and easier to create. Aim for your rain garden to be about 30cm deep and cover about 10 percent of the area it is receiving water from. The plants you grow there must be able to cope with periods of dry as well of damp, so try native waterside species such as Hemp Agrimony, Meadowsweet and Yellow Flag. On clay soils work in some shingle into the base to ensure that it will ultimately drain and not overflow. It should work a treat.

◀ A rill is in effect a long thin pond. Plant-free, it is good for bathing and drinking; planted up would be even better.

Rills

Here is a cheap and simple way to bring some damp mini habitats to your garden. Basically, all you do is dig a shallow trench through part of the garden; it doesn't really matter where, and it can be straight or winding and as long as you wish.

Yes, you've sussed it out: effectively what I'm asking you to do is create a 'ditch'! I realise that doesn't sound very glamorous, so call it a 'rill' and I guarantee you will impress your friends and neighbours.

Unless you line it, it will probably not hold standing water very often, unless you are on clay or in wetter parts of the country. However, it will be appreciably damper than the surrounding areas, not much but enough for the vegetation in to be more lush and for wildlife to feel the benefit. It is exactly the kind of habitat used by Ringlet and Orange-tip butterflies, by Slow-worms, and by Song Thrushes.

I like to dig my rills about 30cm deep and with gently sloping sides and a very gentle gradient from start to finish. If you finish with a larger pond-like area, any flows will have somewhere to end up. You may find that plants such as Lady's Smock, Angelica and Meadowsweet grow better here than elsewhere in the garden.

▲ This is a type of rain garden on a new housing estate where excess water collects after heavy rain. You can create a mini version of this in your garden.

Making a Hot-rot Home

No hotel is complete without a sauna, and with a compost heap you can create your very own wildlife steam-room.

Composting only happens because of wildlife. Old bits of plant go in (right), something breaks it down, and out comes compost. That 'something' can be fungi, yeasts, worms, slugs, snails, woodlice or other small creatures, but bacteria do most of the legwork. The process creates lovely, crumbly, rich, brown fertiliser to go back onto the garden, and it creates heat, so much so that the centre of a well-made heap can be as high as 60°C.

The inspiration

Nature makes its own compost heaps. Autumn leaves blow into piles such as this, while rivers wash up damp mounds of flotsam during floods.

Natural compost heaps work for wildlife because they are **open and easy to access**. Creatures large and small can get into them easily, with the smaller 'detritivores' munching their way through the rotting vegetation and the larger animals rummaging through to find the smaller ones.

Frogs, toads, Hedgehogs and some birds such as Robins and Wrens all love the chance to probe through a bit of compost.

Compost is great at holding in **moisture**, and at the same time the process of decomposition often generates considerable heat. Many creatures love this moist, warm blanket.

Grass Snakes and Slow-worms are compost specialists. The Grass Snake uses piles of rotting vegetation to help incubate its eggs, while Slow-worms seem to like bearing their live young here.

It's possible to replicate nature by composting in free-standing heaps, but **using a container** is usually neater and the process is faster.

How to make your hot-rot home: step by step

1. Make your compost heap of slatted wood

It is nigh on impossible for most creatures to get into a closed plastic composter, while a wire mesh heap can allow too much heat to escape, so make it from something like old pallets. Size is important – it ideally needs to be at least 1m x 1m x 1m to allow the heap to heat up.

2. The heap should have an open bottom

Position it on soil rather than slabs so that soil creatures can work their way up into the compost. You can create your heap on a foundation of sticks if you wish – it will allow air into the base of the heap and offer hibernation sites for amphibians.

3. How to give it air without turning

Without oxygen, the compost won't rot properly and will pong. The usual advice is to turn heaps with a fork but this is a problem if Slow-worms and Grass Snakes are breeding in there. The trick is always to mix up your carbon and nitrogen and never to have deep layers of just one of them. Follow this rule and you will never have to turn your heap. Check out the table below for ideal materials.

4. Compost needs moisture

Don't drench it; just sprinkle on the contents of a watering can in dry weather.

5. Keep the heat in

Lay an old square of carpet or (even better) a corrugated, bitumen roofing sheet (see page 99) on top to keep in the heat – Slow-worms and amphibians will happily hide beneath it.

6. If you have the room, have two heaps or more

One can be your active pile, while the others are left undisturbed to finish rotting down.

What can go on the compost heap?

✔ carbon	✔ nitrogen	✘
Shredded non-glossy paper and cardboard (most printing inks are vegetable-based these days)	Grass clippings	Meat and bones
Hay and straw	Annual weeds	Cooked vegetables
Sticks and twigs, preferably shredded	Horse manure	Perennial weeds and their seeds
Dead leaves (including tea bags)	Vegetable peelings including orange peel	Bread, cooked rice, etc
Wood chippings	Chicken manure	Diseased plants
Eggshells		Pet waste

Hot-rot but rat-free

Rats and mice will probably visit most compost heaps from time to time, but if you follow the table above strictly, they are unlikely to stay. In the rare case that they do take up residence, don't add vegetable peelings either. Rodents also like to tunnel into the base of the heap, so exclude them when you build your heap by laying a fine wire mesh on the ground.

Gardening for Wildlife in a Large Garden

If you're lucky enough to have a large garden, you have so many opportunities when it comes to wildlife, including the chance to satisfy the needs of whole communities. What a privilege!

One approach is to create the widest range of habitats possible. By offering a bit of everything, you can certainly achieve the 'diversity' part of biodiversity.

Alternatively you could create a larger area of one particular habitat. This will allow you to support colonial species that need enough space for all their aunts, uncles and distant cousins!

If you create a large meadow area, for example, you might then be able to support self-sustaining populations of butterflies, such as Common Blues, Meadow Browns and skippers. Or, plant a spinney rather than just the odd tree and you have a greater chance of visits from Chiffchaffs and other warblers. You may also have a large enough garden to invest for the future by planting the types of trees that will eventually grow to be massive, opening up maximum extra storeys in the grandest of grand hotels.

Being bold with the size of your pond can bring all sorts of surprises. In particular, the number of dragonfly and damselfly species should increase, and even unusual birds, such as a Common Sandpiper or Snipe, might drop in on passage. But do be careful about the laws regarding water-bodies – in some instances, planning permission or licences are required if you want to hold huge volumes of water.

You flower borders can also be bigger and bolder, with repeated planting, such as these foxgloves in Sue Camm's Devon garden. Dramatic shows, such as *Verbena bonariensis* (below), are much preferred by most pollinating insects – they can just move from one colourful dinner plate to the next. You can also grow some of the giant herbaceous perennials that would dominate smaller gardens such as Cardoon, Joe-pye Weed, delphiniums and, if you're in a relatively frost-free area, *Echium pininana*.

You can fulfil the home needs of species that require a lot of space. Imagine knowing that your Robins or Wrens never have to stray beyond your garden boundary, that they have all the food, water, shelter, nesting and roosting sites they need, thanks to you.

You have more opportunities than most to leave undisturbed areas. For example, if you created a patch of scrubby woodland and then steered clear in spring and summer, it would give shy ground-nesting warblers such as Blackcaps and Willow Warblers the chance to breed – what a coup!

A large area of cornfield annuals will be heaven, not for the odd finch or sparrow but for whole flocks of them. They can settle themselves in for a good feast over a number of weeks. Why ship in bird food when you can grow your own?! Poppies and tickseed dominate this planting (above).

Gardening for Wildlife in a Small Garden

Though some of us might enjoy an acre or two to play with, many of us have the proverbial postage-stamp garden. Fortunately, that's no barrier to doing great things for wildlife.

It is often tempting to try to cram in as many different habitats as you can, but the smaller each one becomes the fewer the species that can survive. It's like us being offered a flat with only a bathroom when we need a bedroom and kitchen too. Your best bet is to focus on creating just a couple of key habitats.

Select plants that get absolutely smothered in nectar-rich blooms. Butterflies and bees prefer a profusion of flowers, which can be difficult in a small space. But if you choose plants that bear thousands of flowers or have a long flowering season, there is plenty for insects to tuck into. Flowering bushes can be some of the best, such as this Beauty Bush *Kolkwitzia* (below).

Fill every available space with plants – clothe your walls and fences; grow climbers up into trees so that two plants occupy one space, and train them over pergolas and pyramids; fill empty corners and line flights of steps with pots; put up hanging baskets (below) and window boxes; and give your shed and garage a 'green roof'. Your house has so much potential for wildlife (above).

Choose multi-tasking plants. These are ones that work for wildlife all year. Something like an apple (right) will have flowers crawling with wild bees, foliage that is eaten by some moth caterpillars, dense twigs where thrushes will nest, and then as a final flourish they will be decked with fruit in autumn. Other good plants include currants, hawthorns, and climbers such as honeysuckles and Ivy.

Give wildlife plenty of routes in and out of gardens. Many small gardens are so well fenced that they are like closed boxes which creatures can't get in or out of. Cut holes under gates or fences, use wire instead of timber or, best of all, plant hedges.

One habitat that still performs well, even when on a scale more fit for the Borrowers, is a pond (above). Newts, some damselflies and even a couple of the larger dragonflies will all take readily to a small garden pond that is only a metre or so across, and birds will happily drink there. But choose your plants carefully as many are too large and vigorous and will swamp your little water feature.

Where would you bring up a family in your garden? That's how wildlife has to think, but it constantly faces disturbance in a small garden because there are so many people around too. If you can create places of sanctuary where no gardener, cat or child bothers to go, creatures will learn that this is their safe haven. Thorny shrubs and climbers in particular offer all sorts of safe nooks and crannies.

Take a peek over your garden fence. Understanding what other habitats are in your area can help you decide what best to do in your own garden. On the one hand, you might choose to replicate neighbouring habitats so that existing wildlife communities can spread straight into their new extension. Alternatively, you might like to create a habitat that is in short supply in your area, offering something new to the marketplace.

Work with your neighbours. Inspire them, tell them what you're doing and why, and take cuttings from choice plants and share them. With their cooperation, your gardens will work together as one larger habitat.

Think carefully about light. So much wildlife thrives in bright sunshine, but it is easy to block it out of a small garden with badly thought-out trees or shrubs. Below, a well-planned butterfly garden has been designed facing south where butterflies can enjoy dawn-till-dusk sunshine.

Gardening for Wildlife in Pots

If your garden is little more than a balcony, roof garden, patio or window box, where there is no soil to plant directly into and often shade, wind and searing sunshine, you have the toughest job of all to successfully accommodate wildlife. The flip side is that every wild visitor who does come calling is a precious victory.

Sometimes these triumphs are so astonishing they make the rest of us swoon with envy, such as the Brighton family whose plant-trough on their high-rise flat's balcony was adopted by a pair of nesting Peregrines!

At other times, the successes may seem low-key but turn out to be very significant indeed. I will always remember my visit to a delightful lady living in a flat in central London. She had contacted the RSPB to let us know that sparrows were coming to her balcony every day. There she gave them seeds and water, and they collected Sage leaves from her pots of herbs, which they use as natural pest control in their nests. Effectively this lady

was fulfilling almost all of their home needs from one balcony. It turned out to be one of the very last populations of House Sparrows in that part of London.

Or how about Jenny Sweet's third-floor urban balcony garden (left) with choice plants for her select range of pollinator visitors.

Pit-stops for wildlife. There are very few species that will be able to set up permanent residence in a potted garden, so aim to be a café of choice rather than worrying about becoming an all-encompassing five-star hotel. Your aim is for them to learn that your mini establishment is worth dropping into on their rounds.

It is the more mobile species of wildlife that are most likely to visit gardens like these. So concentrate on catering for migrants and nomads. Try providing nectar for Red Admirals and white butterflies, for bumblebees and for moths including some of the hawkmoths.

Supplementary feeding is the easiest way to guarantee return custom from birds. In the past, we might have baulked at the idea of House Sparrows and Starlings taking the lion's share of the handouts, but these days they need our help more than almost any other garden birds.

Be creative. Turn big ideas in this book into small miracles. A deadwood area, bare ground, pond – all can be created in miniature on a balcony.

Planting in pots is often your best – or only – solution for providing as much greenery as possible. They can look really attractive (such as Chris Jones' Brighton garden (left), you can rearrange them to show off flowers as they peak, and there is *almost* no limit to what you can grow in them.

But you do need to be prepared for the challenges:

❀ Pots heat up quickly in summer, and then get very cold in winter.

❀ They often don't hold much soil, especially window boxes and hanging baskets, which can check plant growth and cause a shortage of nutrients.

❀ They dry out terribly, although paradoxically they can also suffer from poor drainage when there are inadequate holes in the pot base.

❀ And when several round pots are arranged together, the dark, damp gaps between are perfect hideaways for snails and slugs.

Don't be put off! Gardening for wildlife in pots is well worth the effort. Here are the golden rules:

❀ Choose containers that are as large as possible – you ideally need a good 30cm of soil depth.

❀ Use square troughs to maximise the soil volume and reduce the hidey-holes for snails.

❀ Make sure there is good drainage. Put a thick layer of crocks and gravel at the base, or use polystyrene packaging 'chips' underneath a piece of greenhouse mesh. If the pot is large, the polystyrene will also reduce the final weight of the pot.

❀ Include water-retaining gel in the compost to help reduce the amount of watering you will need to do.

❀ Mulch the top of the pot with gravel or bark to hold in moisture.

❀ Be prepared to water daily and feed weekly in the growing season. Organic liquid feeds are widely available, often based on fish or bonemeal, or – for vegetarians – seaweed.

❀ When you go away, use slow-release watering systems, such as the water spikes that screw in to plastic bottles.

❀ For perennials and shrubs, 'top-dress' the pot each year by removing a little of the topsoil and replacing it with rich compost, and be prepared to repot every couple of years.

All sorts of plants grow well in pots. If there is little soil, try houseleeks, stonecrops, annual bedding plants, small bulbs, rockery plants, heathers and herbs, which should all be able to cope with few nutrients and dry conditions. In larger pots, almost anything is possible, from climbers, such as jasmines and Ivy, to vegetables, such as trailing tomatoes and strawberries, and even trees (below).

When growing larger plants, choose them carefully. Select dwarf varieties unless you are going for that jungle look!

Low-maintenance Gardening for Wildlife

If you lead a busy life that doesn't leave much spare time or you have mobility or health problems, don't worry, gardening for wildlife is very much still for you. Just adhere to the Dos and Don'ts and your reward should be a good-looking garden full of wild creatures.

Do…

Plant a wildlife shrubbery. Unlike trees, they tend to have big billowy skirts that keep any weeds underneath firmly under control. You'll ideally want ones that don't need much in the way of pruning, but don't just settle for evergreen conifers – go for bushes that will flower and give you berries. Check out the Shrubs section (pages 208–214) for a range of excellent options.

Use wildlife-friendly ground-cover plants. These trail out across the ground, forming a mat of vegetation that suppresses weeds. Geraniums, Bugle, heathers, Ivy and dead-nettles are all great for this.

Plant a herbaceous border. Choose clump-forming perennials that come up year after year and all you'll need to do is mulch the bed well in early winter, cut back the dead stems and spent seedheads in late winter, and do the odd spot of weeding in spring and summer. The end result? Joyous flowers alive with bees and butterflies all summer.

Underlay bark or gravel paths with a fabric membrane to suppress weeds. Buy it from garden centres, or Google 'geotextile landscape fabric' or 'weed control fabric'.

Plant an informal hedge. It offers so much more for wildlife than a fence, will last for 50 years and won't need repainting. With its rambling natural look, you won't have to be out with the shears every weekend trimming it to spirit-level perfection. Instead an annual trim – one side one year, the other the next – is all it will need.

Mulch, mulch, mulch (above). Just a couple of days spent spreading a thick layer (10cm) of compost or bark will then suppress most of the weeds and feed the soil, and the worm community will dig it in for free.

Create a pond (left). It is not only one of the best wildlife features in the garden, but once made it will pretty much look after itself. The only maintenance is to pull out excess weed occasionally and to stop autumn leaves falling in it.

Turn your lawns into meadows. Two cuts a year with a mower, it's a dream!

Grow plants that can look after themselves without you having to mollycoddle them.

Put up nest boxes. Remember you will only help a few species this way, but for a quick visit to an RSPB shop or a few minutes online, and then ten minutes up a ladder, it has got to be worth it!

Provide plenty of dead wood. Dump your woody cuttings discreetly in shrubberies and flowerbeds.

Don't...

Take the easy route out and cover your garden with decking, concrete or gravel. It's not necessary, you'll end up having to paint it or weed it anyway, and from the point of view of most wildlife it's like wiping part of their world off the map.

Start a vegetable patch (below). It's a year-round task requiring a day a week, and at times in spring and summer it will need daily attention, especially for weeding and watering.

Grow too many plants in pots and containers. You'll be a slave to their demands to be watered, fed, top-dressed and repotted. Hanging baskets are the worst. Aim for all your plants to have their feet firmly in the soil where they can just get on with things.

Grow too many plants from seed. It is cheap and very rewarding, but it can be time-consuming, is prone to disasters and is mighty fiddly!

Try to maintain a formal lawn. You'll be out there with the mower each week, and then have to top-dress it, rake it and trim the edges.

Grow annual flowers in seasonal bedding schemes. Leave that to the gardeners in the local park who have five days a week to do it, *and* they get paid for the palaver!

Plant overexuberant plants. Some such as the mints can run riot, leaving you with a constant job of penning them in or pegging them back.

Try to grow demanding or difficult plants. Roses, for example, need careful pruning, a surveillance operation to check for pests and regular feeding, while tender plants have to be swaddled in sheaths of bubble-wrap at the first sign of frost and floppy tall perennials require supporting. It all takes time, which you don't have.

Gardening for Wildlife in the Function Zone

You'll remember that wildlife-friendly gardening is at its best when you incorporate it everywhere, no matter what other needs you have from your garden; all it takes is imagination.

Perhaps the last place you might think of doing things for wildlife is what I call the 'Function Zone', those dull bits such as paths, drives and sheds that allow us to move about the garden or store things. And yet, with a bit of creativity, they can be turned into useful features for wildlife too.

Driveways

Most people need somewhere to park their car (or three), and it is so easy to believe that you've got no choice but to sacrifice a big chunk of your garden (and its wildlife potential) under tarmac or paving.

Here are your wildlife-friendlier alternatives:

✿ Only your tyres really need to sit on something hard, so why not limit yourself to a two-track driveway with grass either side and down the middle.

✿ Or use one of the modern 'cellular paving' or 'ground reinforcement' systems, which are honeycombs strong enough to park on but where the gaps can be seeded with grass. Typical systems include grids of interlocking recycled plastic (below), while 'grasscrete' is a bed of concrete studded with holes.

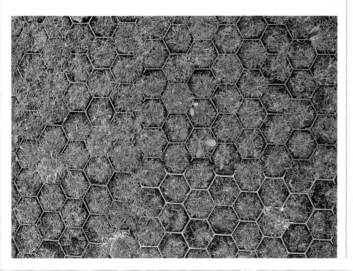

✿ Neither system will give you a perfect lawn but it will be green, hardwearing, kind on the worms and will dramatically reduce the area of your world lost to tarmac. And because the water can soak into the soil, it will also help reduce the risk of flash flooding. Isn't it about time that all new drives were like that?

Paths

So you've parked your car on your new cellular ground-reinforced drive, but you still need a good firm surface to get you to your front door and around the garden. The usual solution in most gardens is a continuous paved or concrete path, losing many more square metres of garden to hard landscaping.

Time for some more wildlife-friendly options:

✿ There are lightweight versions of cellular paving on the market to try, or create 'mesh-protected turf' (don't you just love all this jargon?). The mesh is made from tough plastic and is simply laid over existing grass, pegged down, and the grass grows through. It can then be mowed and cared for much like a normal lawn.

✿ In woodland areas, try a bark path instead of concrete or paving.

✿ If you must have concrete slabs, then don't butt them right next to each other but lay them as stepping-stones with grassy gaps in between (above) – that's more green space saved.

✿ Of course, where possible have grass paths – they are by far the best for wildlife.

Green and brown roofs

We tend to think of roofs as the things that keep our possessions and us safe and dry, end of story. Bar the odd bird singing from the gable end and a splattering of lichens, they don't seem to have much wildlife value or potential.

If we lived in somewhere like Denmark or Germany, we'd think very differently. There, an estimated 12 per cent of all flat roofs are 'green roofs' where insects and other wildlife can thrive. (In the definition of 'green roofs' I am including 'brown roofs' which have a substrate of rubble and pebbles and shells). Slowly, the number of buildings in the UK with green roofs is increasing, and the list of beetles and spiders that have been found on them is very impressive, showing what can be achieved.

Green roofs also intercept rainwater and help to insulate the house beneath. When you think how much of our landscape is taken up with our houses, you can't help thinking what a good idea this is.

There's no denying that retrofitting a green roof is not cheap or easy. Plants need something to get their roots into and that adds up to a lot of weight; some roofs just can't take it. But the technology is getting ever better, and green roofs are now available weighing about 55kg/square metre, which is within the load-bearing limit of most roofs. And green roofs don't need to be flat either – their slope can be as much as 45 degrees. At the very least, we all ought to consider a green roof for something like a new shed or flat garage roof.

Although it is possible to use grasses or wildflowers, the usual plant mix is of native and non-native stonecrops (sedums), which are evergreen, flower in summer and are great for bees (left and above). They are grown commercially as a 20mm-thick mat and laid over about 50–70mm of growing medium on top of a waterproof membrane. Stonecrops are the tough-nuts of the plant world, able to cope with just a little soil and all the exposure that our roofs have to endure. Green roofs then just require an annual check to ensure that no tree seedlings have taken root!

If you like the idea, follow the three golden rules:
❀ Ensure that the building beneath the roof can take the load
❀ Ensure that the waterproofing layer is waterproof
❀ And always take professional advice before you start.

Wildlife-friendly boundaries

Like so many creatures, we love to mark out our territories. We may not have scent glands that we rub against trees and we don't sing from prominent positions, but we make a pretty strong statement with all manner of vertical structures that clearly say, 'This is mine; keep out'.

However our boundaries can be a tragedy for wildlife, forming impenetrable, lifeless barriers. Think how challenging it would be for any species trying to navigate the housing estate in the photo below. What a nightmare!

Yet with a little imagination, boundaries can be homes, not assault courses. A hedge is by far the best option (see page 144), but if you are stuck with walls or fences, there are two key issues that will help wildlife: growing things up them; and making sure wildlife can get over, under or through them.

Making the most of garden walls

Whether made from brick or stone, the solidity of garden walls offers a great surface for training climbing plants. In fact the volume of vegetation you can get to cover them may almost match that of a hedge, offering plenty of nesting sites for birds and leaf fodder for some moth caterpillars. Don't forget to try espalier fruit trees as well as more obvious climbers.

Walls also create interesting microclimates. On the south side, it may be so warm and sheltered that you can grow unusual plants that would otherwise not survive.

A drystone wall is probably the best for wildlife (above right). They look fantastic, and the materials are often local. The different-sized gaps between the stones are magnificent for all sorts of wildlife from Common Lizards to invertebrates and even nesting Blue Tits, Wrens, Robins and Pied Wagtails, while lichens, mosses and ferns are all likely to colonise.

Covering fences

Ah, fences: not one of our finest inventions as far as wildlife is concerned. But if it is what you're stuck with, you might as well make the most of them.

❀ Try to ensure they are made from FSC timber (see page 195 – it will cost more, but save wildlife elsewhere).
❀ Train climbing plants all over them. Use batons to affix trellises a good 4–6cm from the fence to create enticing gaps where insects and Wrens can play hide and seek. Bring trellis supports down to ground level to add more stability to the fence.
❀ Put Robin and Wren nest boxes on the fence, hidden behind climbers.

Hedgehog highways

The problem with most walls and fences is that they block the path of any animal that needs to wander between gardens but can't climb very high or fly. It's a difficult problem to solve with an established wall, although growing climbers up them will at least offer 'wildlife ladders'. If you're building a wall from scratch, build in tunnels at ground level.

With fences, it is somewhat easier to create gaps along their bases to allow the free-flow of wildlife. Consider also having 'hit and miss' fencing, where adjacent slats are offset from each other, or picket fencing, both of which allow the wind and small creatures through. If not, take a saw to the base of a panel (it can be in a corner tucked out of the way) and cut a hole about 12cm square (above), fine for Hedgehogs but too small for most dogs or Foxes. Ideally put one in every 5m or so – but do check with your neighbours before that first cut!

House walls

The big vertical walls of our houses are like sheer cliffs, blank canvases crying out for a wildlife-friendly feature or two. Wonderful climbing shrubs such as wisterias (below left), climbing roses or honeysuckles can be trained up a stout trellis and don't interfere with the brickwork in the way that Ivy does.

Don't forget to put up House Martin and Swift nest boxes under the eaves, and house walls are also ideal for boxes for House Sparrows, Starlings, Spotted Flycatchers (place the box among climbers) and Robins (hide the box behind climbers).

Water butts

Watering your garden using rain collected in a butt is clearly environmentally friendly, but the butt itself can be a plastic eyesore and a no-go zone for wildlife.

So here is a challenge to you to come up with ideas for making them work harder for wildlife. Maybe it could be a frame that fits over them that allows climbers such as Hop to cloak them during the summer, which can then be cut away when the butt needs cleaning in winter? Maybe erecting trellis around the butts could do the same job?. Over to you to unleash your creativity…

Gardening for Wildlife in the Leisure Zone

We all need parts of the garden where we can relax, play, be sociable and snooze. It might be the lawn, or perhaps the patio or some benches. But that doesn't mean that nature has to be excluded. With a bit of imagination, wildlife can have a 'timeshare' in those places when you're not around.

Lawns

The biggest area we usually give over to leisure is our cherished lawn. Part sunbathing arena, part sports field, part stage for garden parties, they are nature's amazing, living, green carpet.

There are lots of creatures that will be longing to come and use it too. Unless you absolutely demand a perfect sward with immaculate rolled stripes, then a meadow option such as this unmown geometric block (below) will work wonders for wildlife such as meadow butterflies and beetles. Even just lifting the mower blades a notch compared to your usual mowing regime will give that bit of extra microhabitat and will also help your lawn cope with droughts. But whatever you do, don't blast it with chemicals. For full guidance, see page 150.

Patios

For those times of year when the lawn is too wet and uninviting, or in gardens where there is no lawn, the patio becomes our social hub in the garden. But did you realise it can almost do the same job for wildlife, too?

It's the perfect place for an array of pots (above) where you can tend bedding plants, climbers and even trees and vegetables. With a pergola or arbour built over the top, you could grow wisterias, honeysuckles or Hop overhead as a natural roof, creating sun-dappled areas on the patio.

If the patio is paved, you could go one step further and actually lift up the odd slab or two and plant up the gaps (below), maybe with something like low-growing thymes or Chamomile.

Seating

We all like to have somewhere to rest after an exhausting session in the garden, from where we can admire our handiwork. But could a seat be more than that?

Think laterally and it is possible to turn it into a place for wildlife, such as this one (above) where the back is made from dead wood, perfect for wood-boring insects.

Or use slabs to make a lichen-encrusted, dry-stone bench (below). Another idea for a seat is to create an arbour over the top, up which you can grow wildlife-friendly climbers. What could be more salubrious than being wafted with the smell of fragrant honeysuckle while relaxing in your bower?

Or what about a turf bench where insects and worms can live? They were popular in medieval times, and there are plenty of paintings that depict the Madonna on one. If it was good enough for her…

Child's play

As a child my garden was probably the place where I was happiest. My parents might have described it as 'most excitable'! Given free rein to be inquisitive, a garden full of wildlife can be a constant source of wonder and discovery for the young…and young at heart.

So don't content yourself with just putting in a metal swing and climbing frame. Be creative. Important aspects of play are exploring and creating imaginary worlds, so why not create a jungle den out of living willow or wildlife-friendly shrubs?

Give children the opportunity to grow wildlife-friendly plants themselves. They love anything that grows quickly and easily, has big, bold flowers or is edible. Ideal plants include:

- ❀ sunflowers (great for a growing competition)
- ❀ snapdragons (to watch bees climbing inside the dragons' jaws)
- ❀ Nasturtium (such a cheerful rambling plant)
- ❀ sweet peas (for the beautiful smell)
- ❀ Borage (just as the bees drink the nectar so the kids can eat the flowers)
- ❀ and strawberries (because they're scrummy, as any slug will tell you).

In addition, kids in general are far more inquisitive and excited about creepy-crawlies than adults are. Make a wildlife sunbed (see page 99) so they can enjoy discovering the world underneath, build log piles (see page 141), and mow a maze in your lawn allowing the grass in between to grow up long (see page 150).

And, of course, make some kind of pond. You will need to consider safety, but it will be the thing that fascinates them the most.

Gardening for Wildlife in the Production Zone

The vegetable patch isn't the obvious place to want to share with wildlife. This is where you grow the food for you and your family, not to send it straight down the neck of some hungry beastie.

Indeed, some of your time here will undoubtedly be spent actively countering the species that are intent on destroying your crops, such as Carrot Flies, slugs, snails, Rabbits, mice, caterpillars and Woodpigeons.

But on the other hand, many of your crops would be nothing without nature. You need all those helpful pollinators in order to produce many of the subsequent luscious fruit and seed crops. And you can also turn to wildlife in your war against pests. As with all parts of the garden, it is not a matter or 'vegetables or wildlife'; with your guiding hand they can be happy bedfellows.

One of the most productive crops you can grow that works for us and for wildlife is orchard fruit. Apple, pear and plum trees offer nectar for pollinating insects, foliage for caterpillars, a great structure for birds to sing from and sometimes to nest in, bark where lichens can grow, and you can also sow a meadow beneath the trees.

There will be parts of the vegetable garden you will want to net (below left), probably the brassicas and soft fruit, so that birds can't ravage the crop. Make sure the netting is firmly anchored all around the base to stop birds and larger mammals, such as Hedgehogs, getting in and then getting trapped, and check daily just in case.

Planting a herb garden is a great way of growing produce for yourself and benefiting wildlife at the same time. One species you will almost certainly encounter is the Small Purple and Gold Moth *Pyrausta aurata* which flies by day around many herbs, and with Gatekeepers coming to Marjoram flowers, bees to the Chives, and all sorts of hoverflies, flies and solitary bees coming to Coriander, Dill and Fennel, it can be a busy wildlife area.

Many root vegetables if allowed to flower and set seed are adored by insects. Try leaving the odd carrot, onion (below right) or parsnip to grow on, and you may also be able to harvest your own seed for the following year.

It is true, too, that some companion flowers lure in hoverflies with their nectar; it is then only a short flight onto your aphid-infested crops nearby for them to lay eggs and for the resulting hoverfly larvae to then eat the greenfly: nature's own pest control.

When you think about it, the old cottage garden technique of growing veg scattered in amongst flowers (technically called 'polyculture') has to be better than serried ranks of the same crops, which are surely an open invitation to pests.

Here, then, are some commonly recommended companions you might like to try and which I believe will bring wildlife value:

* Beans with marigolds (below).
* Cabbages with Borage, Chamomile, Dill, geraniums, Hyssop, marigolds, Marjoram, Nasturtium and thymes.
* Carrots with Chives, Flax and Hyssop.
* Cucumbers with Borage, Dill, marigolds, Nasturtium and Tansy.
* Onions with Chamomile and Dill.
* Potatoes with marigolds.
* Radishes are helped by Chervil, lettuces, Nasturtium and peas.
* Raspberries with Tansy.
* Strawberries with Borage.
* Tomatoes with Borage, marigolds, Marjoram and Nasturtium.

Companion planting

Probably the best way to incorporate some welcome wildlife into your vegetable patch is to adopt the technique known as companion planting.

People have claimed for a long time that if you grow certain types of plant in among your crops, they will not only boost your harvest but they also have the power to ward off pests or they attract insect predators that feed on the pests. This technique gained a bit of a reputation for being based more on blind faith than fact, but some scientific research has now suggested that there may indeed be some science behind it.

The explanation is beautifully simple. Many crop pests are the larvae of insects; their parents hunt for their preferred plant species on which to lay their eggs, but are only satisfied if they find large areas of the host plant growing together. So if they find their target plant and think 'Hoorah!' but with the next hop find themselves on a different, unsuitable plant, they may conclude this isn't the nirvana they were looking for, and move on.

Gardening for Wildlife in the Aesthetic Zone

I travel a lot by train and can't help but have a good gawp through the window into the many gardens I pass. What is clear is that many people put in a lot of effort to make their gardens look presentable.

I think it's a basic human trait, a mix of pride in ourselves and our homes, combined with the more abstract pleasures of being artistic and of enjoying good-looking things. Some people even make gardening competitive (another human trait) at the very popular flower shows where gongs are handed out to show gardens and plant growers based on largely visual appeal. Most of us can only aspire to a gold medal for our gardens.

The desire for a good looking garden is not at odds at all with gardening for wildlife; it is perfectly possible to incorporate creatures' home needs into your artistry and orderliness, and some of the best looking gardens are brilliant for wildlife.

▼ It's a mass of colour, but how good is it for wildlife? Well, the osteospermums at the back and the petunias at the front are nigh on useless; only the single-flowered Dahlia 'Roxy' cultivar in the middle has nectar on tap for bees.

Choice of plants is an important part of wildlife-friendly gardening. Therefore, by electing to work mostly with plants that are known to attract wildlife, you can still use all of your artistic flair and have the best of both worlds.

Unfortunately, many bedding plants have little value for wildlife (left). From the look of their big gaudy blooms you'd think that pollinating insects would adore them, but they have been selectively bred and hybridised for petal size, colour, longevity and ease of growing. Many no longer produce nectar and pollen, or it is unobtainable inside a frilly blouse of petals.

One compromise you may have to make is in the search for perfect foliage. A garden where nothing gets nibbled is no good to wildlife, so tolerating the odd perforated leaf is essential. Most wildlife gardeners get to the point where they cheer if something is getting a full belly thanks to them!

Clipped hedges and topiary aren't out of the question. The last thing you want to do is disturb any birds that might be nesting in there, but you can get away with a single late-summer trim of formal hedges such as Yew, Hornbeam or Beech. But if you can enjoy the more rustic charm of an informal hedge, then all the better because it is more likely to flower and fruit freely.

Art and wildlife can mix well. The innovative log fence below was in a RSPB Show Garden at the Chelsea Flower Show, and the blue pond edging (right) was recycled plastic. Or why not drill a pattern of holes in a piece of driftwood as nesting sites for solitary bees? It's just a matter of being creative.

Do you like things to be 'just so'? Don't worry, that's OK (with certain caveats). The tidying gene is not one that I was blessed with (if you could see my desk you'd scream), but many gardeners do have it. Now here I want to make a fine distinction: if your tidiness is to do with orderliness and geometry, no problem; however, if it means that every flower is deadheaded, every leaf cleared away and every spent stem chopped to the ground, then we have a problem. Instead, learn to appreciate the beauty (and value) in leaving seedheads standing over winter or in using leaves as patterned mulches on the woodland garden floor. Tidiness does not have to mean that you have to leave things sterile for wildlife.

There is no harm in making a pond neat and geometric if that's the visual style you are looking for. It might be at the expense of wild, woolly margins, but it may allow you to bring your pond centre-stage, into a sunnier position and to make it bigger which will be great for wildlife.

Massed planting can both look good and provide a 'piled dinner plate' for wildlife. It allows bees and other pollinating insects to concentrate their feeding time instead of having to invest energy searching between each few sips.

A wildlife-friendly flower border can look simply stunning. Pick your favourites from the Top 500 Plants (pp 209–248) and you can achieve beautiful combinations with shrubs, herbaceous perennials and annuals. These photos show how it can be done.

(Above left) Soft pastels of eryngium, white foxglove, anchusa and lavatera; (above right) a bolder display of *Geranium* x *magnificum*, astrantia and single rose; (below) billowing prairie planting of persicaria, coneflower, Sedum 'Matrona' and eupatorium with perennial grasses.

Leave the seedheads standing. If there's one key thing to do in a flower border for wildlife, it is to take a deep breath and resist the urge to clear everything away once the last flowers fade. Yes, there will be times over the winter when it may look a little tired and bedraggled, but on the other hand during frosts and snow it will look way more glorious than an empty bed.

Birds then have a chance to probe for seeds throughout the winter, while all manner of wildlife will enjoy the cover. Ladybirds may hibernate among the dried seed cases, insect eggs may be tucked in among the old leaves, and the soil will have more protection from the elements. (Below left) *Phlomis russeliana*; (below right) *Achillea*; (bottom) *Eryngium giganteum*.

Gardening for the Planet

Conservation

It is easy to think that wildlife conservation can only happen on big nature reserves, but you can actually make a real contribution in your own garden.

These aren't just empty words. There may not be any internationally rare species in your garden, but there is every chance that you are visited by widespread ones that are nevertheless of 'conservation concern' because they are declining alarmingly. It is only in the past few years that we have realised what a crucial role gardens have to play in the conservation of birds such as House Sparrows (below), Starlings, Swifts, Song Thrushes and Spotted Flycatchers. You have every chance to do your bit to aid their recovery, and there is plenty of other wildlife in peril whose conservation you can genuinely help too.

You may think that any efforts you make are trivial – what good is it if you help your one pair of sparrows increase to two? The point is that things only change if everyone plays their part. As Gandhi said, 'Whatever you do may seem insignificant, but it is most important that you do it.' There are more than 20 million households in the British Isles, so it would only take one per cent of these to increase their garden sparrow population by one for the number of sparrows to increase by a whopping 200,000. It makes you want to be part of that one per cent, doesn't it?

In my garden, the key species of conservation concern are Stag Beetle, Common Frog, bats, House Sparrow and Song Thrush, so that's where I plough a good bit of effort. Fortunately, much of what I do for them benefits many other creatures, too, so I get the best of both worlds.

A few lucky people are able to help truly rare species in their gardens. One gardener I know has a small garden on a housing estate, but is near to good habitat for the rare and enigmatic Brown Hairstreak butterfly. By planting Blackthorn, the only foodplant of the caterpillars, she now has them breeding in her garden.

The key, as we have seen with all wildlife gardening, is knowledge. If you make the effort to get to know which species you can best help and how to go about it, you'll make a real difference.

Peat

Lovely, crumbly, warm, brown peat: it is so tempting to use it because plants love growing in it. But it comes at a cost – a big, unsustainable cost – to the environment and to wildlife.

The problem, as is now widely appreciated, is that in order to satisfy our desire for it, peat bogs have to be destroyed. They only exist in some of our wettest wild places where mosses, grasses and sedges grow on waterlogged ground. These plants only partly decompose in the oxygen-deficient conditions, which is how the peat is formed, accumulating millimetre by millimetre. A metre of peat can take 1,000 years to form but just a few seconds to dig up.

If you haven't been to see a peat bog, you must. At first sight (right) it is rather barren and featureless, but get up close and you'll find all sorts of rare and wonderful things living there. Unusual dragonflies flit over the pools and insect-eating sundews just a few centimetres high grow out of the moss. They are the breeding grounds for declining birds such as Curlews.

It is the peat from lowland peat bogs, composed largely of sphagnum moss, that are most suitable for use in gardening. And boy, have we plundered them! Of the original 95,000 hectares of lowland peat bog in the whole of the British Isles, fewer than 5,000 hectares are thought to remain in good condition. Almost all the peat that has been extracted has gone into horticulture, and about two-thirds of that went into domestic gardening.

What can gardeners use instead of peat?

The horticulture trade tested peat extensively over many years, so we know exactly how to use it and get great results from it. In contrast, peat-free composts are a bit scary: they're all rather new, and we haven't yet learnt either how to get the best from them or how to trust them.

But we must be brave. The National Trust recognised that we can't just go on destroying whole habitats and, in 2001, went peat-free, avoiding peat (bar exceptional circumstances) for the plants it grows and sells. The Royal Horticultural Society (RHS) aims to use 90 per cent non-peat products in its gardens. If they can do it, so can us gardeners. In fact, the RHS has done excellent trials that show that bark- and wood-fibre-based mixes produce just as good results as peat.

There's more experimentation that needs to be done, better labelling on products, and in particular better peat-free seed composts need to be developed. But we must all use our consumer power to demand these things. There is just no excuse any longer for using peat. Curlews need it; we don't!

Climate change and energy

The science of climate change is incontrovertible – put more carbon in an atmosphere and it will warm up. We're doing just that, and it is causing the climate to change faster than it would naturally.

Those of us in the developed world and in temperate climes probably won't see the worst of it – in fact we might see some benefits such as fewer frosts and lovely warm springs and autumns. But we mustn't let this distract us from the bigger picture. There will be profound implications for the world and for wildlife. The home needs of many creatures and the plants they depend on will no longer be met in the places they currently live. They will all have to adapt or move, and many won't be able to do either. The big question is whether we have the courage to do something about it, and that includes in our gardens.

Gardening I would claim is one of the most climate-friendly pursuits. We grow things rather than destroy things, and we don't travel anywhere to do it. In terms of carbon footprints, gardening is what the world needs.

But we mustn't rest on our laurels. Some gardening methods still burn up fossil fuels, which is ironic for a pastime that is based on plants harnessing the power of the sun. Every time you plug something in – a hedge-trimmer, lawnmower, shredder or pond pump – you're contributing to climate change. Suddenly that one-cut-a-year meadow in place of your repeatedly mown lawn (see page 146) seems all the more necessary – it is a winner for wildlife locally and globally.

So don't switch off your mind when climate change is mentioned; switch off at the socket!

Reduce, reuse, recycle

As well as using electricity in the garden, there are other hidden energy costs where we can easily turn our garden into a drain on the planet instead of an asset.

The problem is all the things we import into the garden. The use of hard landscaping – gravel, concrete paving, brick, stone, timber, and metals – has proliferated in gardens. Garden makeover shows have tempted us with new cool materials to try; we've wanted to create lots more off-road parking, patios and decking; and we've had the cash to make it all possible. Hidden behind all this are the environmental costs of extraction, production and transport. It's what is called 'embedded carbon'.

Take concrete. For each person on the planet, the Environmental Literacy Council (ELC) estimates that two tonnes of concrete are used each year. Making cement in order to make concrete is an energy-intensive process, and the ELC estimates that one tonne of carbon dioxide is released for every tonne of cement produced.

In the case of gravel, every year in the UK alone we extract some 275 million tonnes of aggregates (sand, gravel, etc.). Most is destined for the building and road industries, but a fair few tonnes end up in our gardens. These have to be extracted and shipped around the country, with consequent carbon emissions. That's not to deny that the aggregates industry doesn't do wonderful work reinstating gravel pits for the benefit of wildlife. But do you really need tonnes of it in your garden?

We also have a tendency to accumulate 'things': a sculpture here, a colourful pot there, a mirror, or a bit of garden furniture. Gardens can even become the victim of fashion where you're 'no-one' if you don't have the latest wrought iron obelisk, crushed glass mulch or ceramic pedestal. They, too, have embedded carbon.

It's no accident that 'reduce' comes first in the good old sustainability mantra of 'reduce, reuse, recycle': it urges us always to ask ourselves 'Do I really need this?'

It's the same with gardening equipment. Isn't it amazing that even those of us with a tiny garden often have a complete shedful of it? Does every few square metres of lawn really need its own lawnmower? The obvious answer is to share our tools, be it with friends, relatives or colleagues. We don't, but we should. Give it a go and earn maximum greenie points.

When you are sure that you have reduced all you can, then is the time to concentrate on the 'reusing' and the 'recycling'. Many of you will be past masters at this and will know it is largely about being creative. Common tricks include:

❀ Turning old pallets into compost heaps
❀ Converting old sinks into mini-ponds
❀ Using yoghurt pots as plant pots and plastic drink bottles as mini-cloches
❀ Creating home-made sculptures out of driftwood and 'rubbish'.

There are a million other ideas out there. Share them; be proud of them. You may not see wildlife benefiting, but it will, for you will have reduced your burden on the planet.

Organic gardening

We're all used to seeing organic produce on supermarket shelves, and we know that it means that no chemicals have been used, but is there more to organic gardening than that, and is it an important part of gardening for wildlife?

Well, organic gardening does indeed mean that no artificial pesticides, herbicides, 'genetically modified organisms' or 'synthetic growth promoters' have been used at any point during the growing of produce or rearing of livestock. In the agricultural business there are very rigorous inspection, certification and labelling processes to ensure that if it says organic, it is organic.

However, organic gardening in practice is more than just an absence of man-made chemicals. It requires crops to be rotated to prevent the build up of pests, and green manures to be planted to nourish the soil. It involves growing plant varieties that are resistant to disease to stop you having to reach for the chemical bottle in the first place. And it aims to work in harmony with natural systems, encouraging a healthy balance of pests and predators.

While there have been few rigorous scientific studies to prove one way or the other its effect on wildlife in a garden, there is something about the whole organic ethos that chimes well with gardening for wildlife. Organic gardening is 'gardening with nature'; gardening for wildlife is 'gardening for nature' – pretty comfortable bedfellows, I'm sure you'll agree!

Organic gardening is often talked about in reference to crop production, but the philosophy can be extended across the whole garden, including what you paint your fences with (if you still haven't planted that hedge). Going 100 per cent organic is difficult. Just aim to do your best and go to bed each night with a clear conscience.

Green manure

One important organic technique in the vegetable patch is to use green-manure cover crops. You sow these in between crops so that they carpet the ground with foliage and flowers. This helps to protect the soil surface and stops nutrients being leached away, and when you want to plant a crop you dig them in, adding to the fertility of the soil. Some even 'fix' nitrogen from the atmosphere.

There are different cover crops for different seasons. Many are in the pea and bean family, and Mustard is widely used, but two that are brilliant for pollinating insects are Scorpion Weed (*Phacelia tanacetifolia*) (right) and marigolds (*Tagetes*). You can even grow them on bare plots in summer or autumn where they will flower to the benefit of bees and hoverflies.

A nice pot of comfrey tea

A great way to produce a homemade fertiliser – no chemicals required – is to use comfrey leaves (above). As the flowers of comfrey are useful for Honeybees and bumblebees, it is a great plant to have in the garden anyway, although it can be a bit rampant.

Pick a bundle of fresh leaves, put them in a bucket of water, weigh them down with a brick and cover the bucket. (If you do it in an open bucket, it will stink to high heaven!) Three weeks later you will have a dark liquid fertiliser that should be diluted yet further before being used as plant feed.

Crop rotations

Growing the same crop in the same bed year after year allows pests to build up. Keep one step ahead of them by using the well-established rotation system of growing peas and beans in year one, brassicas in year two, root vegetables in year three, and onions and leeks in year four.

Water-wise gardening

For several decades, we have gardened as if we have a right to use as much water as we like in order to achieve the lush, perfect, green gardens we desire.

Those times are a-changing. Climate change and an ever-growing human population mean that water can no longer be taken for granted. It is a limited commodity, to be cherished and cared for. The sprinkler has had its day.

The problem for wildlife is that a lot of our water supplies come from aquifers and rivers. In many places we have abstracted so much of this water that it has damaged wetlands and reduced the natural flow of rivers, and hence we are hurting the wetland wildlife that needs it.

Ways to make water go further

Harvest rainwater It's amazing how much rain falls on our sheds, greenhouses and house roofs, water that normally gets channelled straight into the drains. Direct it into water butts (plural) joined up with lengths of hosepipe, or even into an underground tank.

Don't pull the plug after a bath Let the water cool and then bucket it (or if you're clever siphon it) onto flowerbeds. (It's best not to use it on vegetables, and don't put too much detergent or bath salts onto the garden.)

Hold moisture in with mulches It is amazing how much water can be locked safely in the soil using a protective blanket of compost, leaf-litter or bark.

Use plants that like it dry Many plants have evolved to thrive in drought conditions. Try lavenders, hawthorns, hedge veronicas, California lilacs, hollies, jasmines, wisterias, pyracanthas, geraniums, catmints, Iceplant, globe thistles, Sea Kale, woundworts, thymes, alliums and sages.

Beef up the soil Adding plenty of organic material to sandy soil ensures that water doesn't run away; adding it to clay soil allows plant roots to get at water more easily.

Water in the evening If you water in the heat of the day it will evaporate before it can get to where it is needed.

Ditch greedy plants Avoid species such as cypress trees that suck the soil dry.

Be tolerant In periods of drought, lawns will go yellow, but they quickly green-up again when the rains come – it's what they're designed to do.

Raise the mowing height a notch, too, as the longer grass will shade the ground surface better.

Sustainable timber

It would be a cruel irony if you put up a Blue Tit box to help your garden birds but it was made from timber from a wood that had been chopped down and was not going to be replaced. How can you tell whether or not this is the case, and for any other wooden products you might use in the garden?

The answer is to always look for the FSC logo. The Forest Stewardship Council is an independent, not-for-profit organisation that ensures that the timber we use comes from places that have been audited annually for the highest social and environmental standards.

It is a logo you can trust – if you don't see it, don't buy it.

THE TOP 500 GARDEN PLANTS FOR WILDLIFE

This topic absolutely fascinates me, and I've been immersed in it for over 15 years now. Like many gardeners, I love growing plants and I think they're endlessly fascinating, but I want to fill my garden with those that I know are going to do great things for wildlife as well as look wonderful.

But I have a confession – there is no such thing as the 'top however many plants for wildlife'. A plant that is favoured by one species is often pretty useless for another and vice versa. It means that making the case as to why one plant is better than another in general wildlife terms is quite difficult.

There is another problem. The RHS lists some 70,000 or so different types of garden plant in cultivation in Britain. To research the wildlife value of each of those would take decades. In fact, the number of scientific studies that have been done so far is tiny, and when it does happen it tends to focus on those most visible and popular wildlife groups such as butterflies or – in recent years – bees.

Even those studies that have been done, great though they are, would need to be replicated in other parts of the country and on other soils and conditions to be sure that the results are reliable.

It means that almost no research has been done, for example, into the value of garden plants for moths (whether adults or caterpillars). We also don't know the relative value of native trees versus related non-native species grown in gardens. And we're not even sure which garden plants produce the best or most nutritious seeds for birds. As the Wildlife Gardening Forum has so eloquently set out, there is more that we don't know about garden wildlife than we do.

But I'd like to think that I haven't lured you here under false pretences. What I've tried to do is select those plants that will offer you visible, exciting results. Inevitably, the list often veers towards plants that are

enjoyed by those groups of species we are naturally drawn to and can readily observe, such as birds, butterflies and bees, but I've also included plants for moths, beetles, weevils, hoverflies... Some 'less appealing' creatures might take issue with my plant choices, but I'll just suffer their indignation.

I have also concentrated on those plants that most people actually want to grow, ones that look great and behave nicely as well as having appeal for certain creatures. But I did finally capitulate and include some garden 'weeds' that, while aesthetically leaving something to be desired, are guaranteed winners for plenty of wildlife. If you can find somewhere suitable to let them grow, then great, even if they might make some gardeners wince.

Almost every plant listed is one for which I've had personal experience, based on my visits to dozens of gardens across the country. I'm also greatly indebted to Marc Carlton, creator of The Pollinator

▲ Ringlet on a white marjoram; butterflies are one of the most conspicuous diners in your hotel restaurant.

◄◄ Single Michaelmas Daisies, such as this Aster (*Aster amellus*) 'Rudolph Goethe', come into their own as a pre-hibernation nectar plant of choice for Red Admiral butterflies. Look at all those blooms to choose from!

Garden website and fellow Trustee of the Wildlife Gardening Forum, who has commented on all of my recommendations. But there are definitely more plants out there doing more great things for wildlife that neither Marc nor I have yet discovered. If you have suggestions, I'd love to hear from you.

I have listed plants alphabetically by their vernacular names if they are in common usage, even though their scientific name might also be widely used. For those who love Latin and Greek, don't worry, every name is listed in the index.

I've also indicated where plants come from to help those who would like to plant flowers local to them. You will see some species listed as archaeophytes – these are plants that aren't strictly native but which arrived in the British Isles before AD 1500, and many probably arrived with early settlers thousands of years before that. Turn to pages 14–15 for more explanation of why 'native' is often but not always good, and why 'non-native' can sometimes be just as good – I adore my non-native, wildlife-friendly plants!

'Double' flowers like this dahlia might look nice, but if you were a bee you'd be wondering where the food is. The answer? There isn't any!

Star rating

★ You'll see that some of my choices are starred. These are plants that have some key wildlife species associated with them or that appeal to a wide range of creatures, such that no garden should be without them (if there is room of course!).

Quantity as well as quality

When choosing which plants to grow for wildlife, it is just as important that you consider how many you are going to grow, and how you assemble them into 'habitats'. Just as one house doesn't make a town, so one tree doesn't make a wood and one daisy doesn't make a meadow. Many types of wildlife don't just search for a particular type of plant – they will only move in if you've got a glut of them.

It means that planting in drifts is definitely 'in' as far as wildlife is concerned, whereas 'dot' plants – just one of each – won't usually cut the mustard. Even for bees or butterflies feeding on nectar, they are going to be much happier if they can step from flower to flower rather than having to search for every sip: if you want to be a five-star hotel, provide a banquet, not 'nibbles'.

Singles vs doubles

You may have heard the 'rule' that single flowers (those with a single ring of petals) are good for wildlife but 'doubles' (those with double rings or more of overlapping petals) are not. There's quite a bit of truth in this, but there's a bit of nuance, too. You see, I could name you lots of 'double' flowers, such as various dahlias and Michaelmas Daisies with double rings of petals, that

you could grow and are likely to be full of pollinating insects.

So here's the problem. Flowers tend to have a structure based on circles: in general, in the middle is a ring of female parts, surrounded by rings of male parts (where the pollen is made), then a ring of petals, then a ring of sepals on the outside. A 'double' flower is one where breeders have selected plants where one or more rings of sexual organs are replaced by petals. If you think that each petal is replacing a structure that would have produced food, then you can see why the more rings of petals mean the worse the flower is for wildlife.

Hybrids – beauty or beast?

You may have heard it said that hybrid plants are no good for wildlife. This 'fact' is definitely mired in detail. Again, I could name you all sorts of hybrids that have very clear value for wildlife. For example, one of the features of some hybrids is that they are sterile (they don't set seed), meaning that the plant endlessly flowers because it hasn't had the signal to stop and produce seeds. But you might then spot a problem: while such plants are good for pollinators, the seed-eaters go hungry. In summary, hybrids are a mixed blessing, but the best can still have plenty of wildlife value; it is more the plants that have been highly modified by selective breeding which tend to have lost their wildlife value.

The law and wild plants

The basic situation is that it is illegal in the UK to intentionally uproot any wild plant without the permission of the landowner. You are not breaking the law by collecting their seed, although you should only take a few and leave plenty. However, there are a few species that are so rare it is also illegal to pick the flowers or take the seed. If you want to Google them, the Joint Nature Conservation Committee lists them online as 'Schedule 8 plants'.

Large trees

If you've got the space to grow a large tree (or several), they bring such a wealth of habitats and such a volume of food and living spaces that they are a must. Just be careful to consider the space they (and their roots and shade) will ultimately occupy – most of these trees in this section are for large or very large gardens only.

★ Alder *Alnus glutinosa* ▲

Native throughout the British Isles, a medium-sized, upright tree to 28m that likes wet ground. The leaves are eaten by caterpillars of many garden moths including the May Highflyer. Alder is also important for the Parent Bug, which is unusual in that it cares for its young. Alder flowers are wind-pollinated and the resulting 'cones' contain vital winter seeds taken by finches, especially Siskins, Lesser Redpolls and Goldfinches. Unfortunately, some Alders succumb to a deadly water-borne disease, *Phytophthora*. Avoid the invasive Italian Alder *A. cordata*.

Ash *Fraxinus excelsior* ▼

Since the first edition of this book, the terrible ash dieback disease (Chalara) has swept across parts of Britain, meaning that you won't be able to buy Ash trees, probably until a proven disease-resistant strain is available. However, you may well still have existing Ash trees in your gardens. Healthy, this deciduous tree can reach 30m with a rather open structure; it is native throughout the British Isles and found on most soils. The caterpillars of a few moths such as Ash Pug, Lilac Beauty, Dusky

Thorn and Tawny Pinion eat the foliage. The fruits – hanging bunches of 'keys' – are taken by Bullfinches and Greenfinches. Ash is late to come into leaf, allowing a long spring-flowering season on the ground below, and it can be coppiced to keep it to a manageable size.

Beech *Fagus sylvatica* ▲

An imposing and spreading deciduous tree to 40m, best known for its beautiful autumn colours, native to south-east England but widely planted elsewhere. The seeds (beechmast) are highly desirable to many mammals and birds, especially Great Spotted Woodpeckers, Great and Coal Tits, Nuthatches, Jays, Blackbirds, Siskins, Chaffinches, Bramblings and Woodpigeons. Beech trees only start to produce seed at about 40 years old, and the

size of the crop varies year on year. Some insects are associated with the tree, including the caterpillars of September Thorn and Barred Sallow moths. However, the dense summer foliage of a mature tree means that little can grow beneath it. They can be pollarded but not coppiced. (Also see Hedges on pages 144–145.)

★ Birches *Betula* ▲

Many different species are grown in gardens for their attractive white bark. **Silver Birch** *B. pendula* (above) and **Downy Birch** *B. pubescens* are both native across most of the British Isles, with Silver preferring better-drained soils and Downy able to cope in the wet. They grow tall, but are slender and airy, and can be coppiced if necessary. The soft timber is perfect for Great Spotted Woodpeckers to excavate holes. The foliage is eaten by many moth caterpillars including the Poplar and Lime Hawkmoths, Scorched Wing and Canary-shouldered Thorn. Other munchers include beetles, bugs and Birch Shieldbug and Birch Sawfly larvae, and then the seeds are eaten by many birds including Lesser Redpolls, Goldfinches and Siskins. The light shade they cast means that plants can be grown beneath their canopy, and you may even be lucky enough to have some of their associated fungi appear, the most famous being the Fly Agaric. Many other birches are available for sale, with **Himalayan Birch** *B. utilis* var. *jacquemontii* with its gleaming white trunk and **Paperbark Birch** *B. papyrifera* being especially popular. However, quite how they measure up in wildlife terms to our natives isn't well known.

Handkerchief Tree *Davidia involucrata* ▲

Here's a novel option to try that will be a talking point in spring. From China, it is a spreading deciduous tree that grows to 15m or more, and is hardy across much of the British Isles. In spring, its nectar-less flowers have two large and curious drooping white bracts, making the tree look as if draped with handkerchiefs, also giving it its alternative name, the Dove Tree. I include it partly because the tree's structure makes for good perches, but mainly because the brown, plum-sized fruits (above) stay rock hard into the winter and are often still in place ready for when Fieldfares come to visit in hard weather.

Cypresses *Cupressus* and their hybrids ▲

These evergreen conifers have scale-like leaves and small cones, and are grown widely for hedging and screening. In fact, they can be so tall, fast-growing, moisture-hungry and shade-casting as to cause many an un-neighbourly dispute. But I feel I must include them, in part because they are so widely available – ubiquitous, even – and also because they provide good cover for birds, including as a favourite nesting site for Greenfinches. The foliage harbours a few small insects, teased out by Goldcrests, while the caterpillars of the Cypress Pug, Cypress Carpet and Blair's Shoulder-knot moths feed on the leaves. Big trees may be used by roosting Greenfinches and Blackbirds or by a noisy mass of Starlings. However, I wouldn't advocate the infamous Leyland Cypress x *Cupressocyparis leylandii* which lives up to its brutish reputation, grows faster than you'll be able to keep on top of, and then blows over by the time it gets to about 30 years old. There's a problem, too, with the equally common Lawson's Cypress *Chamaecyparis lawsoniana* which is now on Schedule 9 of the plant species to be avoided. So seek out something such as one of the slow-growing cultivars of **Monterey Cypress *Cupressus macrocarpa***, such as the encouragingly named **'Goldcrest'**. In other words, don't dismiss cypresses as useless for wildlife (they're usually much better than no cover), but choose them carefully and grow them responsibly.

Elms *Ulmus* ▲

I debated hard whether to include the elms, given the tragedy of Dutch Elm disease. An introduced fungus (originally from Asia, not Holland!); it swept across the British Isles during the late 1960s and 1970s, infecting an estimated 30 million trees that were once such a glorious and prevalent species across large parts of Britain. In **English Elms *Ulmus minor***, the roots survive, sending up lots of young saplings from suckers before they, too, are knocked back by the disease; the **Wych Elm *Ulmus glabra*** also often survives as young trees, enough to set seed. While the wind-pollinated flowers and winged seeds offer little value to wildlife, Elm leaves are the only food of the White-letter Hairstreak butterfly as well as many species of moth. Moves are afoot to develop disease-resistant strains of Elm, and it is now possible to buy saplings to try.

Maple, Norway *Acer platanoides* ▲

Although not native to the British Isles, the Norway Maple is widely planted, very hardy, and originates across a large swathe of Europe including parts of France. It grows quickly, and can reach 30m tall. The acid-yellow flowers emerge in early spring before the leaves and fill the tree with zingy early colour; they are excellent for early pollinating insects. A number of small insects are also associated with the leaves and bark, but the winged seeds don't offer much wildlife value, so see it as an interesting alternative to Sycamore.

Hornbeam *Carpinus betulus* ▼

Tall deciduous tree, to 25m, native to south-east England but planted widely throughout much of the British Isles. The wind-pollinated flowers are of little wildlife value, but the clusters of seeds with their papery bracts (on mature trees only) are taken by birds such as Chaffinches, Bramblings, Great Spotted Woodpeckers and Nuthatches, although you'll have to cross your fingers hard if you hope to be visited by the real Hornbeam aficionado, the Hawfinch. The corrugated leaves turn

yellow in autumn but are only eaten by a few moth caterpillars. It will, however, grow in most soils, and it coppices well. (Also see Hedges on pages 144–145.)

Larch (European) *Larix decidua* ▼

I have retained this in the list, but the critical thing to understand is that it is now at risk of the *Phytophthora ramorum* pathogen, which you may have heard by the name of 'Sudden Oak Death'. Larch had been introduced to Britain by 1629 and is now widespread; it is a fast-growing, deciduous conifer to 40m, native to the Alps, with a straight trunk and graceful, drooping branches. The wind-pollinated flowers have little value for wildlife, but the seeds within the small cones are favoured by Lesser Redpolls, Siskins, Goldfinches, Bramblings and Chaffinches, while the foliage is eaten by the Larch Pug moth. The needles turn golden in autumn, and the fresh spring growth is an energising fresh green. If you are thinking of growing it, check on forestry.gov. uk for the latest disease advice, and certainly don't plant **Japanese Larch *L. kaempferi***, which has been shown to host fewer insects than the European species.

Limes *Tilia* ▲

The **Small-leaved *T. cordata*** and **Broad-leaved *T. platyphyllos*** **Limes** are natives of England and Wales, and their hybrid, the **Common Lime *T. × europaea***, is rare in the wild but widely planted. All are big, domed trees, up to 46m high in the case of Common. The July flowers smell glorious and are pollinated by insects. The leaves are eaten by several moth caterpillars, including the thorn family and Lime Hawkmoth, and also by masses of aphids, producing lots of honeydew that is then drunk by various creatures. The fruit is a hard nut occasionally taken by a few birds such as Greenfinches. The trees can be pruned repeatedly and hard.

★ Oaks *Quercus* ▲

The oaks have an impressive reputation for wildlife, and quite rightly so. Growing up to 38m, these mighty trees offer countless homes for wildlife and mountains of palatable leaves and acorns. They are slow to grow, but see them as an investment for future generations. The two common species are **Pedunculate Oak *Q. robur*** and **Sessile Oak *Q. petraea*** (above), both native across almost all the British Isles, with the Sessile preferring acidic soils. Acorn lovers include Jays, Woodpigeons, mice, Badgers and the Acorn Weevil, while caterpillars of dozens of moth species feed on the foliage including the Oak Hook-tip, Oak Lutestring, Oak-tree Pug and Merveille du Jour. Plagues of Winter Moth and Green Oak Tortrix moth caterpillars offer rich pickings for tits, Treecreepers and Nuthatches. The acres of deeply-fissured bark offer homes to all sorts of bark beetles, weevils and spiders, while gall-forming midges, mites and wasps disfigure leaves and acorns, and Great Spotted Woodpeckers drill nesting holes. Avoid **Turkey Oak *Q. cerris*** from southern Europe and Asia, whose catkins support a species of gall-forming wasp which then goes on to affect the acorns of our native oaks. Avoid, too, the evergreen **Holm Oak *Q. ilex***, which is proving to be invasive.

Poplars *Populus* ▲

Two species of poplar are native to the British Isles: the widespread and rather wispy **Aspen *P. tremula***, found on many soils and growing to 20m, whose small leaves tremble in the slightest breeze, and the mighty but rare **Black Poplar *P. nigra***, native to much of lowland England, Wales and parts of Ireland, growing to 38m, usually near water. However, the **Lombardy Poplar *P. n. 'Italica'*** (above), a slender Asian variant of the Black, plus various hybrids, are more widely grown. Lots of moth caterpillars use the trees including the Red Underwing, Herald, Poplar Hawkmoth, Puss Moth, Poplar Kitten, Poplar Grey and Chocolate-tip, plus leaf beetles and gall wasps, while finches eat the seeds. Don't grow near buildings because of their invasive roots.

★ Scots Pine *Pinus sylvestris* ▲
A tall tree to 40m, native to small areas of the Scottish Highlands, but planted almost everywhere and self-seeds in abundance on sandy soils. If you live near the native pine forests of Scotland, you can collect and plant local seed, knowing you may be helping rare local wildlife including moth caterpillars, weevils, beetles and the Pine Cone Bug, and of course Red Squirrels. Elsewhere in the country, a garden Scots Pine is still likely to be visited by Goldcrests and Coal Tits, plus Pine Beauty and Pine Carpet moths, while the seeds are eaten by Goldfinches, Great Spotted Woodpeckers and Siskins. There are plenty of other species of pine, but the beautiful Scots is worth sticking with in a large garden.

Spruces *Picea* ▼
This is perhaps one of the most desirable groups of conifers to have in the garden, with one to suit every situation and size. One of their biggest benefits is that birds seem to like the dense sprays of firm needles for nesting, and Goldcrests and Coal Tits do make a beeline for them. The **Norway Spruce *P. abies*** (once sold widely as Christmas trees, although replaced these days by types of fir) is for large gardens only, as it can grow to a

whopping 50m. Much more suitable for smaller gardens is the **Blue Spruce *P. pungens***, (above) with its glaucous foliage, growing to less than half the height.

Sycamore *Acer pseudoplatanus* ▼
A very familiar deciduous tree, to 30m, native to south and central Europe but possibly — contentiously — also to the British Isles. It is much maligned but deserves a break! It may not accommodate as many insects as the oaks, and the helicopter seeds aren't flavour of the month for wildlife, but it has

its worth. Mature trees support thousands of aphids, which are food for birds and provide honeydew for butterflies. In addition, the leaves are eaten by several moth species, such as the well-named Sycamore moth, and its bark is one of the best for lichens. As for birds, Collared Doves and Chaffinches nest in the branches, passage warblers such as Chiffchaffs and Willow Warblers favour it for feeding, and tits glean plenty of food from it too. It grows well in seaside locations and has several cultivars with attractive leaves, and, yes, it self-seeds furiously but I happily give it space in my garden.

★ Yew *Taxus baccata* ▲
A spreading evergreen tree to 25m, and faster growing than you might imagine, Yews ultimately develop mammoth trunks and have dense foliage that casts a black-as-night shade in which little can grow. It grows well on chalk and is native to most of the British Isles although it is rare in the north and only scattered in Ireland. Several birds such as Greenfinches and Mistle Thrushes avidly eat the red berry-like fruits (drupes) on the female plants, despite Yew being toxic to most creatures. It can offer a great nesting site for birds. Yews can be endlessly shaped and trimmed, unlike most conifers, making them even more suitable for gardens. The **'Irish Yew' *T. b.* 'Fastigiata'** is useful in smaller gardens as it grows as a column. (Also see Hedges on pages 144–145.)

Small to medium trees

One of the questions I get asked most is 'Which trees can I plant in my small garden?' Here, then, is a selection of those whose ultimate height won't look out of place or cause problems for you or your neighbours, but will do wonders for wildlife.

★ Apple, Crab *Malus* ▲

Right up there near the top of my list of brilliant wildlife plants, the native **Crab Apple M. sylvestris** is a small tree to 9m, native to much of the British Isles. There are many other crab apple species around the world, and they and their hybrids seem to have much the same benefits for wildlife. The white or pink spring blossom is enjoyed by bees and Bullfinches, the foliage is eaten by many moth larvae, while the small sour fruits in autumn are taken by all the larger thrushes. Indeed, many crab apples will hang onto their fruit long enough for the Redwings and Fieldfares to get a look-in. With attractive autumn foliage too, these trees are all-round garden-worthy winners. I recommend 'Evereste', 'Golden Hornet', 'Red Glow' and 'Sentinel' but you might also like to try **Hupeh Crab M. hupehensis**, **Japanese Crab M. floribunda**, **Sargent's Crab M. sargentii** or **Siberian Crab M. baccata**, all of which I've seen doing a similar good job for wildlife.

★ Apple, Eating *Malus pumila* ▲

Thought to derive from just one species native to Asia and parts of Europe, there are many apple varieties to choose from, including famous names such as Granny Smith and Cox's Orange Pippin. All offer rich nectar for bees in spring, the foliage supports many common moth caterpillars such as the Chinese Character and Eyed Hawkmoth, and the bark is great for lichens. It's up to you whether you eat all the fruit, or you leave them for thrushes, Blackcaps, Starlings and Badgers, or you share them! There are also lots of ways of growing apples, from giving them space to develop into a medium-sized tree to growing them in a pot. An espalier or cordon trained against a wall or fence probably offers the best nesting opportunities for birds. Any apple tree you buy is likely to be grafted onto a rootstock that will help determine the ultimate size of the tree: MM106 is a semi-vigorous rootstock producing fairly big fruit trees, M26 is slightly smaller, and M9 is a dwarfing rootstock for smaller gardens.

★ Buckthorns ▲

If you live in the right areas, these are two small trees that should be high on any wildlife gardener's wish list. **Alder Buckthorn Frangula alnus** (above) and **Purging Buckthorn**

Rhamnus cathartica are deciduous trees, native to southern parts of the British Isles. They are essential for Brimstone butterflies, which only lay their eggs on these two plants. Both also have berries taken by birds such as thrushes and Blackcaps. Purging Buckthorn is found on chalk and rarely grows above 10m, with tiny flowers followed by a few black berries (the 'purging' part of the name is what happens if you eat them!). The scarcer Alder Buckthorn is a small shrubby tree, usually to only about 5m, growing mainly in acidic woodlands. It has simple leaves, and clusters of tiny green flowers that absolutely abound with bumblebees. A mature tree can hum loudly! The flowers are followed by a final bonus – a scattering of small red berries.

★ Cherries and Plums *Prunus* ▲

A huge family of deciduous trees and shrubs, some of which are very useful for wildlife. Many have wonderful nectar-rich blossom in early spring (if the buds haven't been taken by Blue Tits, Bullfinches and House Sparrows), foliage that some moth caterpillars eat including The Lappet and Clouded Silver, and succulent fruits in mid to late summer much favoured by many birds including thrushes.

One of the most abundant species in the countryside is **Blackthorn P. spinosa**, native throughout and thriving on most soils, forming dense spiny thickets. Although the fruits (sloes) aren't much favoured by wildlife, the mass of early April blossom is visited by bumblebees and some butterflies (see page 82). Many birds find safe nesting places at the heart of a bush, and the foliage is well eaten by many common moth caterpillars.

Bird Cherry *P. padus* is native to the northern half of the British Isles in moist woodland and along streams, and grows to 14m. It has white flowers in later spring and then small black cherries. **Wild Cherry** (or Gean) *P. avium* (above) usually grows to 12m, so is for medium or large gardens, and is native throughout most of the British Isles and likes rich, heavy soil. It has big leaves, white flowers in April and cherries by midsummer, and it can really pack in the bees in spring. Or why not go for a **Plum** *P. domestica*, including subspecies *insititia* (**Bullaces** and **Damsons**) and subspecies *italica* (**Greengages**), which grow to 10m and have been cultivated in the British Isles for probably a thousand years. For a small garden, try **Sour (Morello) Cherry** *P. cerasus*, from south-eastern Europe but grown here for several hundred years. In contrast, the widely available Japanese and Chinese flowering cherry cultivars rarely form cherries, and many have double flowers and much reduced nectar.

Lightly prune the cherry family after flowering rather than in winter to avoid the disease called silverleaf. And be prepared that most are prone to suckering, sending out roots that then sprout. A Blackthorn hedge, for example, can suddenly turn into a Blackthorn thicket, so you need to get out the loppers once in a while.

with small but heavily scented white flowers in June followed by a few small black berries taken by some birds, especially thrushes. The foliage is eaten by some moth caterpillars such as Mottled Pug and Yellow-barred Brindle, and turns attractive red colours in autumn, while the stems can really glow warm in winter, especially the cultivar **'Midwinter Fire'**. The **Cornelian Cherry** *C. mas* (below) is a widely grown, drought-resistant small tree from southern Europe. The yellow flowers appear in late winter, and it occasionally forms red elongated berries. Personally, I'm a fan of the **Strawberry Dogwood** *C. kousa* (above) from Japan and China, with bold flowers in spring, each formed of four creamy bracts, followed by strawberry-like fruit that my Blackbirds love.

Elder *Sambucus nigra* ▼
Everyone knows this fast-growing, rather unruly small tree, which grows to 10m and is native across almost all of the British Isles. The leaves smell pretty rank, it's not the most elegant of shapes, the big plate-sized fragrant clusters of flowers in June can seem empty of insect life and few moths eat the leaves. So is there a saving grace? Yes! The huge harvest of black berries in September is adored by Blackbirds, Starlings, Woodpigeons, Blackcaps and Spotted Flycatchers. The various cultivars with purple (below) or cut leaves are pleasing on the eye and flower and fruit quite well. An

alternative to try is the **European Red Elder** *S. racemosa*, which has really attractive cut foliage and then clusters of red berries.

Dogwoods *Cornus* ▲▼
The **Common Dogwood** *C. sanguinea* is native to England, Wales and parts of Ireland and is a small deciduous shrubby tree to 10m

Escallonia, White *Escallonia bifida* ▲
I include this because sometimes it is nice to grow something unusual, and few gardens have this one. Evergreen and growing to 8m tall, it is native to South America, and in autumn it can be smothered in fragrant white blossom that is a magnet for Red Admiral and white butterflies, and for bumblebees and Honeybees. It needs a very sheltered spot to do well.

of the understorey in woodland, although it can actually grow to a 20m monster if left unchecked. Perhaps its most well-known inhabitant is the Holly Blue butterfly, whose spring caterpillars eat the flowers and developing berries. Thrushes, too, are fond of Holly berries, but note that male and female flowers are on different plants so you will need a male nearby if you want berries on your female plant. Holly responds well to pruning, provides great dense cover (my Goldfinch flock roosts safe within my largest Holly) and there are plenty of variegated cultivars to choose from if you want a bit of variety.

★ Hawthorns *Crataegus* ▲

Brilliant trees for wildlife, the **Common Hawthorn** *C. monogyna* (above) is native throughout the British Isles, the **Midland Hawthorn** *C. laevigata* more restricted to south, east and central England, preferring clay soils. Both are very similar small deciduous trees to 15m at most, creating a mass of thorny branches and twigs perfect for many nesting birds such as thrushes and Dunnocks. The froth of white 'May' flowers appears just after the fresh green leaves have unfurled and is much loved by bees and other pollinating insects, plus some spring butterflies. The foliage is eaten by many moth caterpillars and bugs, including the Hawthorn Shield Bug, and the prolific red berries are a staple winter food for the thrush family – and Waxwings, if you're lucky. There are some red- and pink-flowered cultivars of Midland available, but most have double flowers and are not as suitable. However, one excellent cultivar with dark red and white single flowers, attractive to bumblebees, is 'Crimson Cloud'. This forms a manageable slow-growing small tree, is not spiny, and produces red berries in autumn. There are American types of hawthorns readily available, but with the British species being so good, why look elsewhere? (Also see Hedges on pages 144–145.)

★ Hazels *Corylus* ▼

European Hazel *C. avellana* is a small deciduous tree to 15m, native across almost all of the British Isles on all sorts of soils. It is often found in hedges or as an understorey in woodlands, where the leaves are eaten by moth caterpillars such as the Large and Little

Emeralds and the July Highflyer. The wind-pollinated catkins elongate in early spring and become conspicuous; they can be a bit hit and miss, but occasionally they can be alive with pollen-collecting bees. By autumn, the hazelnuts are eaten by Red and Grey Squirrels, Dormice, Wood Mice, Great Tits, Great Spotted Woodpeckers, Nuthatches and the Nut Weevil. If you cut a Hazel to its base every 7–15 years (known as coppicing), it throws up multiple new stems, and you can use the cut stems as poles around the garden. Also widely planted and probably as useful for wildlife is the purple-leaved **Purple Hazel *C. maxima* 'Purpurea'**.

★ Holly *Ilex aquifolium* ▲

A familiar shrub and small-to-medium sized tree, evergreen and painfully prickly, Holly is native to almost all of the British Isles as part

Magnolias *Magnolia* ▲

I'm sure that some people will be surprised to see these on the list, being such ornamental and showy trees, mainly from east Asia. Don't plant one expecting lots of pollinators because the large white, pink or yellow blooms are rather primitive and pollinated by beetles. Instead, I have found that the large, deciduous magnolias are great for birds – tits and finches especially. In fact, as I write this, I am being distracted by a Firecrest and two Long-tailed Tits busy in mine! The spreading structure clearly makes fine perches, and I suspect there are small insects that use the bark and flower buds, and tits then also eat the fruits. It shows that you shouldn't always discount the exotic!

Maple, Field *Acer campestre* ▼

Common small tree of hedgerows, to 9m tall, native across much of England and Wales, especially on moister soils. I've not

found the flowers to be especially attractive to pollinators, but moth caterpillars that feed on the attractive lobed leaves include Maple Prominent, Barred Sallow and Sycamore. The winged fruit aren't popular with birds, but this is a tree still worth growing. Several cultivars have been bred for both enhanced foliage colour and for different growing habits, but even the 'bog standard' species turns a glorious yellow in autumn.

Pears *Pyrus* ▲
Lovely, slightly raggedy fruit trees with white blossom that emerges in April (before the apples) and is enjoyed by many types of bee. **Wild Pear** *P. pyraster* is a rare native of southern and central Europe and possibly of southern Britain with small, rock-hard fruit, dense twigs and spiny young shoots, but you

are far more likely to find types of **Cultivated Pear** *P. communis*, which are grafted onto a dwarf quince rootstock. They probably started as a hybrid but have been grown for more than 1,000 years. Pear foliage is eaten by some moth caterpillars, and birds such as thrushes will peck at ripe or windfall fruit. Plant it in a sunny position with a good well-drained soil, and always have two trees if you want them to cross-fertilise to bear fruit.

★ Rowans *Sorbus* ▲
The native **Rowan** or **Mountain Ash** *S. aucuparia* is a pleasant, airy, deciduous tree with great autumn colour, native throughout the British Isles, liking lighter acid soils and hating shade. It grows to 15m, with plates of white flowers in spring that aren't especially favoured by pollinating insects, but the big clusters of red berries in autumn are simply gorged upon by Blackbirds, Mistle and Song Thrushes and Starlings. Even young trees will produce berries. It is the Waxwing's favourite berry, but few are left by the time they get here in winter. There are various cultivars, including the large-fruited **'Rossica major'** and the upright **'Sheerwater Seedling'**, suitable for smaller gardens.

There are lots of other rowan species, mainly from Asia, including ones with berries in white, pink or yellow. While there is good evidence that birds prefer red berries, what this means is that those with alternative colours are often left uneaten well into winter, offering a surprise bonus when flocks of Redwings, Fieldfares or even Waxwings come calling in cold snaps. It means that I'm a huge fan of the bright pink-berried **Vilmorin's Rowan** *Sorbus*

vilmorinii, the yellow-berried *Sorbus* 'Joseph Rock' (with stunning red autumn foliage), the white-berried *Sorbus cashmiriana* and the baby-pink-berried *Sorbus hupehensis*. In fact, they are often better trees for smaller gardens.

Snowy Mespil (Juneberry)
Amelanchier lamarckii ▲
A useful small, slender-branched, multi-stemmed tree for smaller gardens, native to Canada and growing to 10m at most. It is beautiful in spring when covered in delicate white flowers, although these don't appear to be especially well used by pollinators. The recommendation is more for the subsequent crop of small dark berries by the end of June, which are swiftly polished off by Blackbirds and Song Thrushes. With a splash of good autumn colour, too, this is a tree with good 'kerb appeal'.

Spindle *Euonymus europaeus* ▼
This widespread but thinly spread small deciduous tree of hedges and the woodland edge is native to most of England, Wales and Ireland. The flowers are inconspicuous but are nevertheless rich in nectar, visited mainly by flies but also by some bees. The autumn fruits are delightful although poisonous, a pink lobed berry that splits to reveal bright orange seeds. A few birds such as Robins will eat them, plus a micro-moth called the Spindle Knot-horn. The leaves are eaten by the Scorched

Carpet and Spindle Ermine moths, and they turn bright red in autumn, especially so in the widely available cultivar 'Red Cascade'.

Whitebeam, Common *Sorbus aria* ▲

Probably a British native only in southern England but widely grown elsewhere, this deciduous tree grows to about 15m and is easy to spot in spring when the young leaves are held upright showing off their silvery, felt-like undersides. It then produces bouquets of white flowers followed in autumn by sprays of rather chunky red berries. It is a neat tree, and very attractive in a garden, and those berries will be much enjoyed by your Blackbirds and Woodpigeons and, if you're lucky, Mistle Thrushes too.

Strawberry Tree *Arbutus unedo* ▲

This evergreen tree, slow-growing to 8m with small, serrated leaves, is native to the Mediterranean and south-western Ireland. It bears creamy bell-flowers in autumn, pollinated by bees, at the same time that the previous year's fruit ripen. These look a little like strawberries and are taken by Blackbirds and Blackcaps. The tree does offer some nesting and roosting opportunities for birds too. It needs full sun on a fertile and well-drained soil with some shelter in exposed places.

★ Willows *Salix* ▲▼

With 400 species of willows, several of which are native to the British Isles, and loads more cultivars, there's likely to be at least one suitable for your garden. Many have separate male and female trees. **Goat Willow (Sallow)** *Salix caprea* (below) is probably the most important species for wildlife. It is a brilliant medium-sized tree, native to most of the British Isles, growing to 20m at most. The male flowers are furry and golden ('pussies'); females have silvery-green spiky flowers. They provide early food for insects including bumblebees and some butterflies (see page 82) and many of the quaker moths, and the foliage is eaten by many moth caterpillars including the Eyed Hawkmoth, Puss Moth, Sallow Kitten and The Sallow. Willows also host all sorts of aphids, gall mites and other insects, and the seeds are taken by finches. For small gardens, **'Kilmarnock Willow'** is a 'weeping' cultivar of Goat Willow that only grows to 2m, and be careful not to plant large willows too near buildings because of their vigorous roots.

Other species of willow offer similar benefits for wildlife. **Grey Willow S.** *cinerea* is almost as widespread as Goat but likes wetter places and is bushier, to only 15m. **White Willow S.** *alba* is a European native long planted in the British Isles on riverbanks and lake edges. Here it is often pollarded, forming good nesting sites for Mallards and insect-rich corridors for small birds, but it can become a very big tree. (See Shrubs for smaller-growing species.)

Shrubs

For wildlife, shrubs are often as good as trees in the garden setting. They are normally on a scale that means they don't cast long shadows, letting the all-important sunlight reach into the corners of the garden, yet at the same time they support such a mass of foliage and stems that they offer shelter, safety and food in abundance. There is also a greater variety to try, with many offering massed nectar-rich flowers and copious amounts of berries. For hedging plants, see also pages 144–145.

you'll need to keep it in a pot in colder parts and bring it into a cold greenhouse in the winter or take cuttings.

Abelias *Abelia* ▲
Although there are several species of Abelia, the evergreen hybrid of two Chinese species, *A. x grandiflora* (above), is probably the most widely grown. It is a rather lax shrub to 1.8m, with glossy green leaves topped with little sprays of pinkish, tubular, fragrant flowers in late summer through to autumn, visited by some bees. If you can find it, however, I rate the deciduous *A. chinensis* more highly, with much better pulling power for butterflies. Give Abelias a sheltered spot in sunshine.

Ageratina, Privet-leaved *Ageratina ligustrinum* (syn. *Eupatorium ligustrinum*) ▼
This twiggy evergreen bush from Central America grows to 2.5m. The flat heads of small white flowers, produced late in the season, are good for pollinators, including bees plus some butterflies such as Small Tortoiseshells and Red Admirals. Give it a sheltered, sunny spot, but beware that it is frost sensitive so

Barberries *Berberis* ▲
A large family of shrubs, most garden varieties having small, shiny leaves with spiky margins, dangling clusters of little, yellow, stalked flowers favoured by bumblebees, and then dark bluish berries taken by birds such as thrushes and Blackcaps. **Barberry B.** *vulgaris* is possibly native to England and Wales but at the very least has been grown here for hundreds of years; its berries are red. Much easier to buy are the evergreen **Thunberg's Barberry B.** *thunbergii* from Japan, **Darwin's Barberry B.** *darwinii* (above) from South America, **Mrs Wilson's Barberry B.** *wilsoniae* from China and **Hedge Barberry B. x** *stenophylla*, a South American cross. You may also find *B. julianae* with ferocious thorns and 'mini-rose' yellow flowers. Grow any of these and you'll have a chance of hosting a population of the Scarce Tissue moth, whose caterpillars feed almost solely on barberries.

Brooms *Cytisus* and *Spartium* ▲
Airy, stiff-stemmed, evergreen shrubs with tiny clover-like leaves, mainly native to Europe, and covered in sunshine-yellow pea flowers in early summer. **Common Broom C.** *scoparius* grows to 2m and is native throughout much of the British Isles on poor, often sandy, slightly acid soils in sunny positions, and is good for bumblebees, but a bit prone to snail damage. The Grass Emerald and The Streak moth caterpillars feed on it. Garden centres tend to sell cultivars of the hybrid **Cytisus x praecox**, a mix of two western Mediterranean species, some of which still seem to be enjoyed by bumblebees. **Spanish Broom Spartium junceum** (above) is also worth a try, visited by some bumblebees. Keep brooms in good condition by nipping off spent flowers and pruning back some old stems straight after flowering.

★*Buddleja x weyeriana* ▲
You may have noticed one plant that is prominent by its absence from the list – the uber-common Butterfly Bush *B. davidii* from China, so familiar from gardens and railway embankments and even poking out of brickwork everywhere. Yes, it's a magnet

for many butterfly species, but its capacity to spread invasively is a major concern. That's why I'm suggesting that you make that extra effort to find *B.* x *weyeriana*, a sterile hybrid of *B. davidii*. It may not be as well known as its famous parent but it deserves to be so, with panicles of yellow flowers that start blooming late and go on and on until the first frosts, and no seeds to invade the countryside. It is visited by bumblebees as well as butterflies.

There is work underway, especially in the USA, to develop sterile versions of *B. davidii*. I shall be so pleased when that happens and I can start promoting them again, for they are such an easy plant to grow, so beautiful in flower, and so adored by butterflies and Hummingbird Hawkmoths. Research has even shown that its foliage is palatable to many species of moth, so the sooner those proven new varieties are on the market, the better.

In the meantime, you might also like to try **Orange-ball Buddleia** *B. globosa* from South America, with yellow pompoms in June, which is good for Honeybees and bumblebees. I also like **Fountain Buddleia** *B. alternifolia* from China, a bit unruly but flowering in May, offering nectar for Honeybees and spring butterflies. There is a very strong chance that you already have *B. davidii* in one of its many forms in your garden. If so, you are best advised to deadhead religiously once they flower to stop all that seed spreading.

of blue flowers visited by Honeybees and bumblebees. Garden centres usually only stock hybrid cultivars, which I have found quite variable in their wildlife value. Try '**Dark Star**' and '**Gloire de Versailles**', but with so many cultivars out there, do let me know if you find another good one. They like well-drained soil in sun. To maintain, cut out dead wood in spring and then prune lightly after flowering.

Daphnes *Daphne* ▲
We have two native members of this genus: the evergreen and widespread **Spurge-laurel** *D. laureola* and the rare and deciduous **Mezereon** *D. mezereum* (above). Both are useful in that they are neat, 1m tall shrubs that will tolerate some shade, especially the Spurge-laurel. While I haven't found that either are particularly big hits with pollinators, Mezereon has beautiful pink flowers in early spring borne along the stems, and they both produce good numbers of berries, black in Spurge-laurel and red in Mezereon. The latter in particular may be harvested enthusiastically by Greenfinches.

In the garden, you may be just as likely to grow one of the non-native shrubs, favoured for the beautiful scent of their very early spring flowers. *D. bholua* from the Himalayas and *D. odora* from Japan and China are perhaps the most frequent, and are visited by early pollinators, including a few spring butterflies.

their droves over the masses of simple, pink-rimmed flowers. Honeybees and solitary bees also visit. Growing to about 2m tall, it basically looks after itself and so I cherish it greatly! Other single-flowered Deutzias can be just as good, and indeed a Polish study found that *D. scabra* var. *watereri* had more nectar and pollen than any other, but sadly most of those you'll find on sale are frilly doubles, which may get some bee action but much less than if the plant breeders had left them alone!

California Lilacs *Ceanothus* ▲
Several species of small evergreen shrubs, most native to California, growing to about 3m and usually hardy. They typically have densely branching stems that are too slender for nesting birds but get covered with clusters

★ Deutzias *Deutzia* ▼
Deciduous shrubs from Asia that become absolutely decked in flowers in mid-spring. Of all the flowering shrubs in my garden, *D.* x *hybrida* '**Strawberry Fields**' (below) is the best of all for bumblebees, which crawl in

Flowering Currant *Ribes sanguineum* ▲
A nicely compact, spine-free, hardy shrub to 3m tall, native to the western USA, with several cultivars. In April they are covered with clusters of delicate reddish-pink or white flowers, useful for some pollinating insects, set against fresh-green, lobed leaves. There are just a few black fruits in autumn that will be

taken by birds such as thrushes. It can be used as an attractive informal hedging plant, and will tolerate dry shade and clay soils.

Germander, Shrubby
Teucrium fruticans ▲

A small shrub, 1m tall at most, hailing from south-western Europe. It develops a tangle of branches with small, rather grey, felt-like leaves typical of plants that need to cope with hot dry summers. The pale blue, hooded flowers are rather similar to those of Rosemary, and are regularly visited by bumblebees and other pollinators. Give it a free-draining soil in full sun for best effect and a long flowering season.

Gorses *Ulex* ▲

Familiar, dense, spiny shrubs from coastal cliffs and sandy soils that get covered in yellow pea flowers, some even in winter. Caterpillars of Grass Emerald and July Belle moths specialise on gorse, as do various beetles and bugs such as the Gorse Shield Bug. The flowers aren't well visited by insects but can be good for solitary bees, although you'll need to ensure that you get the wild, single-flowered species. The thicket-like structure offers shelter, support for spiders' webs, and nest sites for Wrens and Dunnocks.

Grevilleas *Grevillea* ▲

Although somewhat tender, I include this to show that something that comes from Australia can still have some wildlife value in a British context. There are many species, but here the most reliable are some of the hybrids, such as **'Canberra Gem'** (above), which are rather loose, rounded shrubs up to 2m high, their leaves a little bit like a conifer, and with strange, red flowers like curly spiders that are rich in pollen for some bees. Given a sheltered spot, the hybrids can survive perfectly well and can go on flowering for months on end.

Guelder Rose *Viburnum opulus* ▲

I include this separate from the main entry for Viburnums because it deserves its spot in the limelight. A widespread native in the British Isles, growing to about 4m high at most, it is deciduous with attractive tri-lobed leaves. The heads of white flowers are rather like a hydrangea with fertile inner flowers and large sterile bracts around the outside. It's the dangling bunches of succulent red berries that are its best asset, devoured by Bullfinches. The other native Viburnum in the British Isles is the southern English **Wayfaring Tree** *V. lantana*, fine in itself but the berries are rather tough and unattractive to wildlife. Both have a range of small insects associated with them, including the Viburnum Midget moth.

★ Heathers *Erica* and *Calluna* ▲

The mainstay of the heathland garden, heathers both look good and also work well for wildlife, even if they are a bit out of fashion. Most are dwarf shrubs to only about 60cm high, with a tough framework of woody stems and tiny evergreen leaves that offer good cover for insects and hanging places for spiders and their webs. Many common moth caterpillars eat the tough leaves including the Fox Moth, Beautiful Yellow Underwing, Yellow-line Quaker and True Lover's Knot. Perhaps its best-known wildlife value is as a nectar source for bees. There are two main genera: Calluna contains just one species, **Heather** or **Ling** *C. vulgaris*, our common heather of moors and heaths, native to acid soils across the British Isles, and now with hundreds of garden cultivars. The pink-purple flowers (or white in some cultivars) are a delight in late summer. Avoid those with double flowers. The other genus, *Erica*, has 750 species! On acid soils, try **Bell Heather** *E. cinerea* (above) or the bog-loving **Cross-leaved Heath** *E. tetralix*, native on heaths and moors throughout the British Isles, or **Cornish Heath** *E. vagans*, native to The Lizard in Cornwall. For those of us on non-acid soils, however, I heartily recommend **Winter Heath** *E. carnea* from the Alps, or **Darley Dale Heath** *E.* **x** *darleyensis* which is Winter Heath crossed with Irish Heath, both of which flower in late winter and are ideal for early and late bumblebees and butterflies. Plant all in full sun, and prune after flowering.

Hedge Veronicas *Hebe* ▲

Often known by their Latin name, these are densely-packed evergreen shrubs, to 2m at most, from New Zealand. There are several species and many cultivars and hybrids, some not fully hardy, with different varieties for different seasons with spikes of pink, purple or white flowers. They tend to all get touted as being good for pollinating insects, but in my experience some are brilliant, some are good and many are poor. Try *H.* **x** *franciscana* with its rather fleshy leaves and short flower spikes, or *H.* 'Great Orme' and *H.* 'Midsummer Beauty', while the tall *H. salicifolia* is good for butterflies such as Small Tortoiseshell, Speckled Wood and Green-veined White. Grow them in full sun, take cuttings in late summer and prune after flowering. And if you see one packed with insects in a friend's garden, beg a cutting or two!

★ Hyssop *Hyssopus officinalis* ▼

A semi-evergreen shrubby perennial to 60cm, native to southern and eastern Europe but hardy in the British Isles, with small aromatic leaves and dense spikes of two-lipped violet

or blue flowers in late summer and autumn adored by Small Tortoiseshell butterflies and bees. It needs a sunny well-drained soil, and can form a nice low hedge like lavenders. Cut back hard in spring.

Juniper *Juniperus communis* ▲

A conifer that has berries? What a brilliant way of adding year-round structure to a garden and offering something for wildlife! This is an evergreen shrub or small tree to 7m, with a scattered native distribution in the British Isles on southern downland, northern moorland and some heathland. The caterpillars of Juniper Carpet, Freyer's Pug and Juniper Pug moths feed on the needle-like foliage, as does the Juniper Shieldbug, while the fruit slowly ripen to black (over three years) and are eaten by many bird species. Note that male and female flowers are on different plants. The dwarf 'Compressa', to only 75cm, will struggle to fruit but is good for small gardens, while for mid-sized gardens you might like the upright 'Hibernica'.

★ Lavenders *Lavandula* ▲

Familiar, low, evergreen shrubs, with small, hard, aromatic leaves and long thin flower stems that are topped with small lilac flowers much visited by bumblebees, Honeybees, many butterflies (see page 82) and Hummingbird Hawkmoths. A garden favourite is **English Lavender** *L. angustifolia*, which isn't native to England at all but comes from the Mediterranean and flowers from June to August. Finches may visit to take the seed in late autumn if left untrimmed. There are loads of cultivars to try, and research has shown that *L.* **x** *intermedia* may often be the best for pollinating insects, but being sterile it is unlikely to set seed, reducing its value for birds. **French Lavender** *L. stoechas* with its purple 'rabbit's ears' at the top of the flower spike is not quite so good for bees, but still pretty effective. Larger lavenders seem to be better than the small cultivars such as 'Munstead' and 'Hidcote'.

Grow Lavenders in hot, dry places with a very well-drained and rather poor soil. Prune hard after flowering and then clip the tips again in spring. They are easy to propagate from cuttings too, important as they don't live long and can become leggy.

Myrtle (Common) *Myrtus communis* ▲

Evergreen shrub, up to 5m tall at most, native to the Mediterranean and well able to tolerate winds and dry summers. It has small, aromatic, glossy leaves, and the white early-summer flowers with sprays of long stamens provide pollen for bumblebees. Blackbirds take the astringent, dark berries in late winter. It can be used as hedging, but give it a sheltered spot if you are in an area prone to hard winters.

Oregon-grapes Mahonia ▲

Several species and cultivars in this family of rather straggly bushes, growing to about 2m, with holly-like leaves. Structurally they are not dense enough or strong enough to offer nesting sites for birds, and the leaves are only palatable to a few insects, but their saving grace for wildlife are the sprays of yellow flowers, often in midwinter, that give nectar (and colour) at a time when little else is flowering. Late- or early-flying bumblebees make good use, as do winter flies. The flowers

then turn into little pointed blue or purplish berries, taken by some birds such as thrushes. Commonly available are **Oregon-grape** *M. aquifolium*, native to North America, and the similar *M. japonica* from Japan. They can be planted as an informal hedge, preferring shade or half-shade in fertile soil.

Pieris *Pieris* ▲

At their very best, these can be fantastic shrubs for spring pollinators, at times heaving with bumblebees, solitary bees and flies. Given that they are also beautiful, with their cascades of mini-lantern creamy or pinkish flowers and often with bright red fresh foliage, they make a very garden-worthy plant. My recommendations are larger varieties of *P. japonica*, and its hybrid *P.* 'Forest Flame', both of which can reach up to 3m tall but don't need much care at all. Give them a well-drained soil and a position with a bit of shade but enough sunshine during the day to give the pollinators every excuse to visit.

Privet, Wild *Ligustrum vulgare* ▼

A fine hedging shrub to 3m, semi-evergreen, and native to most of England and Wales. It creates enough cover for some birds such as Blackbirds to nest and for House Sparrows to gather for a natter. The leaves are eaten by moth caterpillars such as Waved Umber, Privet Hawkmoth, Yellow-barred Brindle, Lilac Beauty and Small Blood-vein. The dense spikes of overpowering white blossom in June and July are visited by various pollinating insects, including some butterflies and moths, and in autumn the little black berries are eaten by Blackbirds, Robins and Blackcaps. Be aware

that privets suck moisture and nutrients from the ground around them to the detriment of other plants. Avoid the invasive but readily available Garden Privet *L. ovalifolium*.

Rosemary *Rosmarinus officinalis* ▲

At home in the flowerbed or the herb garden, this evergreen aromatic shrub, to 2m at most, is from the Mediterranean. It has thin, tough leaves on usually upright stems, dotted with small, lilac-blue flowers that are much visited by Honeybees and bumblebees. There are plenty of cultivars, including some spreading forms for walls and rock gardens. Give it a well-sheltered position in sun, and prune back in spring after frosts have damaged the tips. It can be used as a low informal hedge.

★ Roses *Rosa* ▼

This huge family of ever-popular plants is grown mainly for their pretty flowers and sweet scent. Those thousands of big-bloomed, heavily pruned cultivars in a rose bed aren't what we're interested in; we want those that offer nectar and pollen and

will target roses. Finally, the hips are eaten by Greenfinches and thrushes, plus Waxwings. Non-native roses to try include April-flowering **Incense Rose** *R. primula*, great for early solitary bees, and the shrub rose **Lyda Rose** (left). Just avoid the invasive Japanese Rose *R. rugosa*. (Also see Climbers page 215.)

Sea Buckthorn
Elaeagnus (Hippophäe) rhamnoides ▲

An exceedingly spiny shrub, to about 8m at most, it grows in poor soil and on sand and is tolerant of salt, and hence is popular in coastal areas. The fierce structure is great cover for wildlife. It is native to the English east coast, but a non-native invasive plant away from its native range and should be avoided in Ireland and along the British west coast. The leaves are silver-green, the twigs dark and the acidic berries bright orange, not a favourite of birds until harsh weather forces them not to be so picky! Note that you'll need two plants for berries to be produced.

Stranvaesia ▲
Stranvaesia davidiana, syn. *Photinia davidiana*

Closely related to the very common hedging plant Photinia 'Red Robin', Strenvaesia is well worth seeking out because its many simple white flowers, dotted among the leaves, can be bumblebee magnets. This large evergreen shrub from China, which can grow up to 8m tall, has rather leathery leaves that I suspect aren't that palatable to insects, but it does have red fruit after flowering.

Sweet Pepper Bush *Clethra alnifolia* ▲

A hardy deciduous shrub to 2m, native to North America, with oval, dark-green leaves and upright spikes of fragrant white flowers in late summer and autumn visited by bees, and by butterflies such as Peacocks. It grows best in half-shade and moist, lime-free soil, and benefits from some shelter.

Tamarisks *Tamarix* ▼

Rather untidy, deciduous shrubs to 4m, but with attractive featheriness due to the tiny bluish-green leaves on the fine stems. However, it is for the many slender plumes of baby-pink flowers that they are included here, which are visited by bees, and which bloom for a long season from spring onwards. They are also useful for their hardiness, being some of the best shrubs to grow in exposed coastal locations where they can cope with high winds and salt spray. Most frequently grown

succulent fruit (hips), which are usually the single-flowered older varieties and species roses. There are plenty of natives to try, including the vigorous **Dog Rose** *R. canina* growing to 3m, with pinkish flowers, and native to much of the British Isles. The shorter, rather weaker **Field Rose** *R. arvensis* is native to much of England, Wales and Ireland with white flowers, while the scrubby little **Burnet Rose** *R. pimpinellifolia*, native to much of our coastline, has lovely white flowers and black, round hips.

I'm a total convert to simple, single-flowered roses. Some attract heaps of pollinators, with *R. moyesii*, for example, being absolutely amazing and with the most intense red flowers on what is a large, vigorous shrub with arching stems. Among the thousands of hybrid roses, there is a small but growing group of single-flowered cultivars that are being recognised as very attractive to pollinators. In addition, rose foliage is eaten by many moth caterpillars including the Shoulder-stripe, The Streamer and Barred Yellow. Roses are also used by gall wasps (including the one that makes the Robin's Pincushion), leaf beetles and, of course, aphids (and hence ladybirds and hoverflies), while leaf-cutter bees

is **T. gallica** from the Mediterranean but there are several other very similar species. Prune them hard after flowering.

Vaccinium ▲

This genus of low-growing, even prostrate, small woody shrubs in the heath family is most associated with upland areas and acidic soils, the foliage often turning attractive reds in autumn. Most have pinkish bell-flowers pollinated by bees followed by red, bluish or black berries popular with many birds and small mammals. Familiar on uplands and heathlands throughout the British Isles is the native **Bilberry V. myrtillu**s, up to 30cm high

and with rather rounded pink flowers and black berries. In its wild habitats, dozens of moth species feed on the leaves as caterpillars, including the Fox Moth, as well as various sawflies and bugs. Somewhat easier to buy is **Cowberry V. vitis-idaea**, native to most of our high peat moorlands, but with several cultivars on the garden market. It also grows to 30cm, but has soft-pink bell-flowers and red berries. Most widely available is the North American **Blueberry V. corymbosum** (above) for your fruit garden, a taller bush up to 1.5m.

Viburnums Viburnum ▲

Several garden species and cultivars of mostly evergreen shrubs, to about 2–4m, with clusters of white or pinkish flowers, sometimes visited by Honeybees and hoverflies, and followed in some by mainly blackish berries taken by some birds such as thrushes. The ubiquitous but rather uninspiring **V. tinus** is native to the Mediterranean, growing to 3m and coping well in shade, although the spring flowers will be borne more freely in sun. I much prefer **V. x bodnantense** (above), a hybrid of two Chinese species, which is especially useful in that it flowers through the winter on the bare branches, offering nectar to bravely venturing Red Admirals. **V. x hillieri** is a pleasant small evergreen bush that in a sunny location will be visited by some butterflies as well as Honeybees.

★Willows Salix ▼

As well as the larger trees in the *Salix* genus, there are some smashing low-growing species that are great for smaller gardens and top notch for bumblebees; indeed they can be a mainstay for early-emerging species. My favourites are: **S. aegyptiaca** which can grow to 5m but can be cut back to 30cm or so

every couple of years; the **Halberd Willow S. hastata**, which grows to about 1.5m with purple stems; the fiery-stemmed *Salix alba vitellina* (above) and the well-named **Woolly Willow S. lanata**. For living willow domes and structures, use **Common Osier S. viminalis**.

Winter Honeysuckle
Lonicera fragrantissima ▲

Quite different from the typical climbing honeysuckles (see opposite page), this and its hybrid **L. x purpusii** are thin-stemmed shrubs from China. They bear rather inconspicuous but powerfully scented white flowers in winter and early spring that offer much-needed nectar in warm spells to bumblebees, honeybees, hoverflies and flies.

Climbers

subtle charms of the small-flowered types, focusing on ones such as *C. cirrhosa* for winter bumblebees, and *C. heracleifolia* and its hybrid *C. x jouiniana* for moths. The **Orange-peel Clematis** *C. tangutica* isn't a write-off for pollinators, but my absolute favourite is *C. rehderiana* (above), which becomes decked in autumn in cream-coloured bells that can be crawling with bees and other pollinators. Also *C. flammula* and its hybrid *triternata* will form a thicket, and will attract flies and other small pollinators. The early season *C. alpina* cultivars don't grow very big and will attract some bumblebees. For those that like to grow native plants, try **Wild Clematis (Old Man's Beard)** *C. vitalba* (below). A deciduous woody climber, it is native to most of southern England and coastal Wales, usually on limey soils, but planted further north and across Ireland. It trails up to 30m over bushes and hedges, with low-key, cream-coloured flowers in July to September followed by fluffy white seed heads lasting throughout winter. It isn't regularly offered as a garden plant, but it helps create a useful tangle of vegetation for spiders, and the foliage is eaten by the caterpillars of Small Emerald, Least Carpet, Small Waved Umber and The Fern moths.

spotted Quaker and Early Grey. The clusters of red berries that follow are eaten by birds such as finches, Blackbirds and Blackcaps, and Dormice use the bark in their nests. There are several species sold in garden centres, but it is probably best to stick to this native species, of which there are some excellent free-flowering cultivars to try such as 'Graham Thomas' and 'Belgica'. Grow them in a fertile and moist soil, preferably with their roots in the shade.

Boston Ivy *Parthenocissus tricuspidata* ▲
A superior alternative to the invasive Virginia Creeper (which should be avoided). It climbs using tendrils, and will happily cover a half-shaded wall with its 'dinosaur footprint' three-lobed leaves, which turn into the most glorious show of autumnal colour. It can be kept trimmed to shape, but the density of foliage makes it great for nesting birds such as Robins, Blackbirds and even House Sparrows; it even bears some berries.

Clematis *Clematis* ▲
Choose carefully from this familiar group of climbers, because some have been so interbred for their more showy blooms that they have lost their value for pollinators. The ubiquitous 'montana' types, in particular, are very poor. Instead, be content with the more

★**Honeysuckle** *Lonicera periclymenum* ▲▼
Strong, easy-to-grow climber with rather exotic-looking, sweet-smelling flowers much used by bumblebees and Honeybees and also by some moths such as the Burnished Brass and The Shark. Native to almost every part of the British Isles, it grows to 7m, twining around trunks or trellises. Plenty of moth caterpillars feed on the deciduous foliage that emerges by late winter including Small Blood-vein, Early Tooth-striped, Lilac Beauty, Twin-

★**Hop** *Humulus lupulus* ▲
Perennial climber, native to well-drained soils across much of the British Isles except the far north, clambering rampantly to 8m each year around posts and over hedges using strong rough stems. It then dies back completely

in winter. The leaves are large and palm-shaped, and the tiny greenish female flowers develop into the dangling golden 'cones' that were once used in beer production. This is a good plant for the caterpillars of the Comma butterfly, while those of Currant Pug, Pale Tussock, Twin-spotted Quaker and Dark Spectacle moths also eat it. 'Aureus' is a readily available golden-leaved version.

Just be careful if growing it up house walls as you will struggle to remove the unsightly roots. There are all manner of cultivars and some related species to try, but many don't flower as well as the original species.

are others to try such as the orange-blossom scented R. 'Wedding Day', 'Kew Rambler', the yellow-flowered R. helenae and the very vigorous R. filipes 'Kiftsgate'.

★ Ivy *Hedera helix* ▲

One of the workhorses of a wildlife-friendly garden. A familiar, evergreen, woody climber native to almost all of the British Isles, it climbs quickly up walls – even north-facing ones – and tree trunks, clinging with its short dense roots, and it will also carpet shady ground. The arrow-shaped, glossy leaves are eaten by a few moth caterpillars such as the Least Carpet, Yellow-barred Brindle and Willow Beauty, and the flowers by the caterpillars of the Holly Blue butterfly. Ivy also offers great cover for insects, encouraging visits by hunting tits and Wrens. The network of stems provides nesting sites for Robins and Spotted Flycatchers, and roost sites for many other birds. But it is when you encourage Ivy to grow into sunlight that it will shine the most, for only then will it flower. It is a superb autumn nectar source for butterflies (see page 82), wasps, bees (including being the sole food of the Ivy Mining Bee), many moth species and flies. The subsequent hard berries, super-rich in fat, are a staple winter food of Woodpigeons and Mistle Thrushes.

Mistletoe *Viscum album* ▲

One of Britain's most curious plants, this is an evergreen perennial forming balls of lime-green foliage high up in apple, poplar, hawthorn or lime trees where the roots tap into the food supply of the host tree. It is native to lowland England. The flowers are tiny, but the white berries in autumn and winter are eaten by many bird species, including of course the Mistle Thrush. In fact, the plant relies on birds transferring seeds to the bark of another tree in order to spread.

Nasturtium – See Flowers.

★ Roses *Rosa* ▼

As well as the shrub roses on page 185, I urge you to grow one of the single-flowered climbing or rambling varieties that will scramble up into a tree or over a trellis. The best not only have reams of gorgeous, simple flowers and arrays of small tasty hips but also help create a tangle of structure that may offer nest sites or at the very least safe lodgings for many creatures. Perhaps the very best is 'Francis E. Lester' (below), but there

★ Wisterias ▲

Two similar species are grown in gardens: Japanese Wisteria W. floribunda and Chinese Wisteria W. sinensis. Their whippy stems wander up walls and over arches, thickening over time into a network of trunks. Their long leaves are divided into leaflet pairs, and the summer flowers are borne in beautiful cascades, loved by bumblebees and Honeybees. While not much wildlife feeds on the foliage, the branches form wonderful platforms for nesting birds such as Blackbirds, Robins and Spotted Flycatchers.

Bulbs

Flowers that grow from bulbs are typically one of the joys of spring but they are a mixed bunch when it comes to wildlife, with some appearing to offer very little value at all. However, a few are gems so here is my pick of the bunch.

★ Alliums

A large family of bulbous perennials, including garlics, leeks, onions and their cultivars, typically with white or pink flowers in a dramatic, spoked globe at the top of a bare stem, much visited by bumblebees. The familiar herb **Chives** *A. schoenoprasum* is native to a few areas of Cornwall and mid-Wales on limestone and has pink pompom flowers emerging from the clump of grass-like leaves. Talking points for flowerbeds include *A. rosenbachianum*, *A. hollandicum* and *A. cristophii* which have giant, airy spheres of star flowers, or let a leek or onion go to flower and it will be just as successful. The one I think beats them all, however, is the **Round-headed Leek** *A. sphaerocephalon* (above), which can seem alive with bees. Just be aware that some of the heavily cultivated Alliums, such as 'Globemaster' or 'Giganteum', seem to have lost much of their attractiveness to wildlife.

Bluebell (English)
Hyacinthoides non-scripta ▲

A carpet of Bluebells is a glorious spring sight (and smell). A spray of basal leaves emerges in early spring, followed by the nodding, one-sided head of blue bells. It might seem a bit naughty that it has slipped into this list, because little wildlife actually uses it. There's a little moth called a Bluebell Conch that might visit if you live near a bluebell wood, and Brimstone butterflies and mason bees may sip a bit of nectar from them. But this perennial bulbous plant is extra special because it is native only to western Europe including most of the British Isles, and is classified as 'globally threatened'. So this is something you grow for the plant itself, not what life it supports. Only buy bulbs from reputable suppliers and, whatever you do, don't grow Spanish Bluebells *H. hispanica* (see page 257).

Crocuses *Crocus* ▼

Plant these bulbs in a rather shady spot in the garden and they will disappoint and rarely open; give them a glorious and sheltered sunny location, however, and they will enthusiastically spread their pink, purple and lilac petals wide, welcoming bumblebees, Honeybees and hoverflies from as early as February in mild winters. Crocuses may not be native to the British Isles, but they haven't come far, such as the ever-popular **Dutch Crocus** *C. venus*, originally coming from mainland Europe, and the rather more chunky *C. tommasinianus* from south-eastern

Europe. Try **C. angustifolius** (above) from Russia for a splash of golden yellow. In the right place, it's hard to go wrong with any Crocuses, especially when they are left to naturalise among the grass of a lawn left to become a spring meadow.

Daffodil, Wild
Narcissus pseudonarcissus ▲

You're very lucky indeed if you see a large insect visiting a daffodil flower – they just don't seem interested in them at all. However, turn back a flower head and you may find the inside dotted with tiny black beetles – pollen beetles. If you can, grow the rather delicate native species rather than the cultivars.

★ Fritillary, Snake's-head
Fritillaria meleagris ▼

A beautiful bulb for naturalising in a spring meadow. The large pendulous bells with their pink chequerboard markings are exquisite,

Snowdrop *Galanthus nivalis*   ▲

I can't claim that this ranks as one of the best plants for pollinators, but given that the pendulous white flowers bloom as early as January, it can really come into its own during those freakish mild spells in midwinter when some bees stir and have little else to turn to. Snowdrops are best planted 'in the green' after flowering – dig up clumps and replant in smaller groups that can then spread.

held on slender stems and dangling a few inches above the grass. They are one of the best bulbs for bumblebees.

Grape Hyacinths *Muscari*   ▼

Mainly from the Mediterranean, this is quite a large group of easy-to-grow bulbous perennials and their cultivars, familiar in spring with bluebell-like leaves and tight little spikes of blue flowers barely 10cm high. These are a valuable early-spring nectar source for bees, especially solitary bees, with lots of varieties to try. Plant the bulbs in autumn in sunny spots that aren't too damp.

★ **Sicilian Honey Garlic**
Nectaroscordum siculum   ▲

This, I think, is my favourite bulb for bees. A native of France and Italy, it sends up a tall slender stem in spring, from which a dozen or so pink-veined bells, each on its own fine stem, push upwards until they bend over under their own weight and dangle, inviting bees to enter from below. The seed heads are also attractive, and it's the kind of plant that you can dot through and among other plants in the border.

Squill *Scilla*   ▲▼

Although we do have some native species of Squill that are typically found on coastal clifftops around the British Isles, it is the **Siberian Squill** *S. siberica* that is most frequently planted in gardens. Barely rising 10cm above the clump of strap-like leaves, the nodding flowers are small and an intense blue, but the petals are spread more widely than a Bluebell and, grown en masse, they can be a useful food source in March for bees. They can be naturalised in a sunny woodland garden, where they get their moment in the limelight before the canopy closes over.

Flowers

Growing beautiful flowers has long been a bedrock of gardening, and it is one of the key ways of helping wildlife. In flower borders, freed from the shackles of growing among grasses, they can flower in profusion and set seed too. If you choose the right plants, pollinators, herbivores and their predators can thrive. Just remember to grow them in swathes rather than just ones and twos. Below is my selection of herbaceous perennials, biennials and annuals for flowerbeds, pots and planters. For further species for the wildflower meadow, see page 146, and for the cornfield garden, see page 152.

Agapanthus ▲

Sometimes called African Lilies, but almost always known by their Latin name, these are rather lush-looking perennials, native to southern Africa, and their hybrid cultivars. Their splays of long, strap-like leaves radiate from ground level, from which the flower stems emerge to 100cm in late summer topped with a firework burst of blue or white bells; only a few cultivars seem to work well for pollinators, so snap up any that you witness being visited by bumblebees or Honeybees. Grow in well-drained soil, in sun or part-shade, and they will flower well if the roots are constrained. You may need to provide frost protection in colder areas.

★ *Agastaches* ▼

An excellent genus of attractive and aromatic short-lived perennials and their cultivars, native to North America. Many look great in the flower border, forming compact or upright plants to 120cm with nettle-like (stingless!) leaves, topped with multiple spires of colourful summer flowers that are well-

liked by bumblebees and Honeybees, and may be visited by butterflies such as Small Tortoiseshells and Painted Ladies. Try species such as **Anise Hyssop** *A. foeniculum*, with pink or purple flowers, **Purple Giant Hyssop** *A. rugosa*, with short purple flower spikes, and **Mexican Giant Hyssop** *A. mexicana* with pale lavender flowers. Just as good are some of the readily available and compact hybrids such as the excellent *A.* 'Black Adder' and *A.* 'Blue Fortune'. Most like a sunny position on well-drained soils, although you may need to replenish from seed each year.

Alexanders *Smyrnium olusatrum* ▲

Native to the Mediterranean, this perennial was introduced to Britain by the Romans for cultivation and is now common around southern coasts. A flush of fresh, rather pungent leaves emerges in midwinter, followed in March–May by big yellow-green umbels of clenched-up little flowers on top of hollow, metre-tall stems. These are visited by many insects, especially solitary bees and flies. It isn't an obvious choice for the flowerbed, but it's not unattractive – just rather green! It self-seeds easily, but is easily controlled by deadheading or weeding.

★ Alkanet, Green

Pentaglottis sempervirens ▲

This boldly spreading perennial is really great for bumblebees and Hairy-footed Flower Bees. It is also one of the few flowers that Holly Blue butterflies seem to get stuck into. It is native to south-western Europe but long established in Britain. Very easy to grow and reaching about 60cm tall, it has rather rough oval leaves, above which bright blue flowers with a small white centre emerge from pink buds, flowering from spring into summer. Because of its invasiveness, restrict it to wilder parts of the garden and lightly shaded places such as hedgerow edges.

Anchusa *Anchusa azurea* ▼

A member of the Borage family (which is always a good start as far as pollinators are concerned), this is a fine-looking herbaceous

gigas (above) from eastern Asia with reddish flowers, or **A. archangelica**, the tall biennial culinary herb which likes sunny well-drained positions where *A. sylvestris* will not thrive.

★Bedstraws *Galium* ▲

This family is little cultivated, but there's definitely a place in gardens for them. Typically the different species form long trailing stems with whorls of tiny leaves and a froth of small, star-like, usually white flowers. Especially good is the rather delicate and low-growing **Lady's Bedstraw** *G. verum*, native to meadows throughout the British Isles, and unusual in its yellow flowers. It is the food plant of Hummingbird Hawkmoth and Elephant Hawkmoth caterpillars, among others. The more robust **Hedge Bedstraw** *G. mollugo*, native of lowland Britain but not Ireland, is good for sprawling through hedges, and is also used by the hawkmoth caterpillars above, plus those of Cream Wave, Small Scallop, various carpet moths and the Small Elephant Hawkmoth. Bedstraws are also eaten by the Bloody-nosed Beetle.

perennial from the Mediterranean, rather similar to Green Alkanet but with much richer purple-blue flowers, like large forget-me-nots. Grow in well-drained soil in a very sunny position for best effect, where bumblebees in particular are likely to visit regularly.

★Anthemis ▲

The stand-out species in this genus is the perennial **Dyer's Chamomile A.** *tinctoria* (above). It is a clump-forming short-lived perennial from mainland Europe to 90cm tall, with finely cut leaves above which are masses of large-centred yellow daisy flowers that bloom over a long season. Solitary bees and tiny wasps delight in the flat-topped flowers. Hardy, easy to grow and quick to flower, it's great for a herbaceous border, especially on light soils, and there are several good cultivars to try.

★Angelica (Wild) *Angelica sylvestris* ▲

Bold biennial or short-lived perennial up to 2.5m tall, native throughout the British Isles on rich, moisture-retentive soils in sun or part-shade. Large, shapely leaves emerge from great pin-striped sheaths, and the purple stems are topped with big loose umbels of whitish pompoms, June–September, a magnet for a wide range of insects including solitary bees, flies, hoverflies and beetles. Every umbel can be chock-full of life. Try also the cultivar **A. sylvestris 'Purpurea'** (also known as 'Vicar's Mead') with purple foliage, the even larger **Korean Angelica A.**

Aubretia (Purple Rockcress)
Aubrieta deltoidea ▲

A native perennial of southern Europe, commonly grown to spill over rockeries and low walls in a mat of small leaves. These are studded in March–June with hundreds of pink to magenta flowers visited by Honeybees, bumblebees, hoverflies, flies, Bee-flies and butterflies such as Peacocks. It and its many hybrid cultivars like full sun and a well-drained soil.

Bee Balm (Bergamot) *Monarda* ▲

This is – as its name suggests – a staple plant in the bee-friendly border. It is a herbaceous perennial from North America, throwing up clumps of serrated-edged leaves in spring.

Then in late summer it is topped with rather spidery flower heads in reds and pinks, each one a whorl of individual tubular flowers clustered around a domed head of short bracts. There are plenty of cultivars to choose from, and I have yet to find one that doesn't attract at least some bees, with the added bonus of Small Tortoiseshell and other large butterflies. However, it can be temperamental! It doesn't like wet winters, yet also doesn't like to dry out in summer.

★ Bellflowers *Campanula* ▲

Including some of Britain's most beautiful native flowers, these perennials are insect pollinated, some by bees, and are also used by Campanula-specialist pollen beetles, gall-forming mites and gall-flies. **Nettle-leaved Bellflower** *C. trachelium* is native to much of southern England on dry, base-rich soils, with a beautiful flower spike, up to 80cm, of purple-blue bells in June–September. The nettle-like leaves are eaten by the Campanula Pug moth. **Giant Bellflower** *C. latifolia* is native from the English Midlands up into Scotland. The flowers are even larger than Nettle-leaved on an even taller stem. Both prefer to grow in shade or along a hedgerow, **Milky Bellflower** *C. lactiflora* (above) is a good garden substitute.

Betony *Stachys officinalis* ▲

Growing to 75cm at most, and native in hedgerows, woodland rides and unspoilt grasslands throughout much of England and Wales, this perennial bears heads of

small, claret-coloured, hooded flowers in midsummer. It can be grown in flowerbeds or in meadow areas, and there is also a lovely white form 'Alba' to try. Some butterflies such as Brimstone and skippers visit it, as well as bumblebees.

★ Bird's-foot trefoils *Lotus* ▲

Top wildlife marks for these must-grow, low-growing relatives of the clovers, native perennials across much of the British Isles. The commonest are **Common Bird's-foot Trefoil** *L. corniculatus* (above) of dry meadows and **Greater Bird's-foot Trefoil** *L. pedunculatus* from damper grassy places. Both have clover-like trefoil leaves and heads of yellow pea flowers carried over a long season. They are essential as the caterpillar food plants of the Common Blue butterfly and various moths including burnet moths and the Burnet Companion, while adult Common Blues and short-tongued bumblebees will nectar from the flowers. Common Bird's-foot Trefoil works well in lawns, forming mats of cheerful yellow if the mower is lifted a notch, or even in stone walls.

Bistorts *Persicaria* ▼

I think it's fantastic that some native plants are sold by garden centres, unaltered, for flower borders, and this knotweed family includes one of them, **Common Bistort** *P. bistorta*. It looks great in high summer, with candyfloss-pink drumstick flower heads the size of a cocktail sausage on slender stems held up above the carpet of green leaves. It doesn't appear to have many insects associated with its foliage, but no matter, for it is excellent for bumblebees and some other pollinating insects. Left to spread in damp or even boggy ground, it will create good ground cover, reducing your need to weed! Another two to try are from the Himalayas, one called

P. amplexicaulis, the other *P. affinis* 'Donald Lowndes' (above). The former includes a range of cultivars, often with much redder, more slender flower heads than Common Bistort, and also rather taller. The latter I think is great for the front of a border, barely taller than 20cm high, with a mat of slender leaves. Again, they are good bee plants.

★ Blackroot/Culver's Root
Veronicastrum virginicum ▲

Closely related to the speedwells and part of the foxglove family, this perennial is magnificent for bumblebees and Honeybees. From north-eastern America, it grows to 1.2m, topped with an array of the slenderest pointed candles of flowers borne July–September, which depending on the cultivar can be pink, white, purple or lavender blue. They need a good sunny position, and will be a star at the back of a border.

Blanketflower *Gaillardia* x *grandiflora* ▲
From America, this is like a flower as drawn and coloured-in by children, the large daisy flowers with (usually) bold red centres and yellow tips. Growing about 30–60cm tall, it is a short-lived perennial and probably underused in the wildlife-friendly garden, given that they have a very long flowering season and can attract butterflies and all manner of bees, especially bumblebees. Single-flowered seed-raised strains are the best. It needs a light, well-drained soil or it will not get through the winter.

Bugbane *Actaea simplex* ▲
Sometimes listed as *Cimicifuga*, Snakeroot or Baneberry, its tall flower stems grow to 2m from the deeply cut purple foliage and bear dense spires of tiny white flowers in late summer and autumn. These are adored by Red Admiral and Comma butterflies and by bumblebees. It needs moist soil, and does best in a little shade, but is prone to slug and snail damage when young. Cultivars to try include 'Brunette' and 'James Compton'.

hugging bronzed foliage. It is an excellent source of early nectar for Green-veined White and Orange-tip butterflies and for bees. It prefers moist soils in semi-shade, spreading vigorously using runners. Several cultivars are available, mainly for flower and foliage colour. It can be grown in a damp lawn in a 'spring meadow' regime.

Burdocks *Arctium* ▲
A small group of closely related species, native to most of the British Isles, with **Lesser Burdock** A. *minus* the most widespread. They are herbaceous perennials of woodland and hedgerows, with broad basal leaves. The flower stems are up to 90cm tall, and bear rounded hook-covered flower heads topped with small, purple thistle-like flowers loved by Honeybees, bumblebees and butterflies such as Peacocks, Commas, Red Admirals and Painted Ladies. The burr-covered seed heads persist all winter and are visited by Greenfinches and Goldfinches. Grow them in moist, rich soil in semi-shade in wilder parts of the garden. They self-seed effectively; just be aware that the burrs can be a problem for livestock, pets or woolly socks!

★ **Borage** *Borago officinalis* ▲
An annual, native to the Mediterranean but widely naturalised in British lowlands, this is a bushy hairy plant growing to 90cm, with attractive (and edible!) bright blue flowers, May–September, where bumblebees flock! There is an attractive white-flowered form. They do best in a moist, rich soil and are very easy to grow from seed.

★ **Bugle** *Ajuga reptans* ▲
Scrambling hardy perennial, an essential plant for the woodland garden, and native to most of the British Isles. Spikes of blue flowers in April–May poke 10–20cm above the ground-

Calamints *Clinopodium*
(also known as *Calamintha*) ▼
Excellent for bees, **Common Calamint** *C. ascendens* (*Calamintha sylvatica*) is a perennial herb native to base-rich soils in southern Britain, but more familiar in gardens is the paler-leaved **Lesser Calamint** *C. calamintha* (*Calamintha nepeta*), found naturally in just a few parts of East Anglia and good on dry, stony soils. Both grow to about 60cm, with

bumblebees also visit. My favourite is **Red Campion** *S. dioica* (above), growing to 1m tall, with intense pink flowers borne mainly April–June but some flowering until November. It is native to almost all the British Isles, and enjoys the light shade of hedgebanks and open woodland. Expect to see noctuid moths nectaring at dusk; caterpillars of the Rivulet moth also feed on it. It self-seeds readily.

White Campion *S. latifolia* is an archaeophyte throughout most of the British Isles, flowering May–October often on sunny field margins. It can be used in a cornfield mix as an annual but another archaeophyte, the **Night-flowering Catchfly** *S. noctiflora* is often a better choice. The perennial **Bladder Campion** *S. vulgaris*, good for long-tongued bumblebees, grows to 1m in dry, grassy places throughout the British Isles, and the similar but shorter **Sea Campion** *S. uniflora* is found right round our coast on cliffs and shingle. Both have white flowers, the petals emerging from an inflated papery case, and the latter is the food plant of the Netted Pug moth caterpillar. **Ragged Robin** *Lychnis flos-cuculi* is a familiar perennial of wet meadows and ditches, growing to 75cm, with deeply cut pink petals. It is native throughout the British Isles and lovely in a damp garden meadow.

Cardoon (Globe Artichoke)
Cynara cardunculus ▲

Dramatic perennial from the Mediterranean, whose large purple-topped thistle flowers crawl with happy bumblebees and other insects, but you'll need a big garden for it not to look out of place. The flower stems grow to 2.5m in a season, and the thistle-like leaves can spread just as wide. It needs full sun and well-drained soil, and can be propagated by seed or division in spring.

rounded mint-scented leaves and small pink flowers with maroon spotting, borne in loose whorls up the stems. Also in the genus is **Wild Basil** *C. vulgare* (above), a native perennial to much of the British Isles although absent from uplands, growing to about 30cm with whorls of pink flowers up the stem and small, downy leaves with a soft aroma. It is found in hedges, coastal areas and downs, usually on alkaline soils, and is similarly enjoyed by bumblebees and also skipper butterflies.

Candytufts *Iberis* ▲
Some candytufts are visited by butterflies, including Red Admiral, Painted Lady and Small Tortoiseshell. The annual **Candytuft** *I. amara* is a British native but only to the Chilterns. It likes bare ground in full sun, preferably on chalk, and is short lived with white flower heads, May–August. Grow from seed. Several related species and their cultivars from southern Europe are commonly grown in gardens, including *I. umbellata* in shades from white to pink to purple, and the evergreen *I. sempervirens*, which is like a tiny shrub. They can be a bit hit-and-miss, but are worth a try.

★**Campions** and **Catchflies**
Silene/Lychnis ▲
Moths are the primary pollinators of this group of plants, especially from the *Hadena* genus whose caterpillars also feed on campion foliage and their seeds. Weevils, bugs and some

★**Catmints** *Nepeta* ▲
A brilliant genus of hardy perennial plants for Honeybees and bumblebees – almost every variety I have seen works. Most have a haze of bluish or mauve flowers from June onwards on spreading clumps of rather glaucous

foliage. **Catmint** *N. cataria* is an archaeophyte on southern English chalk, bushy to 90cm at most with a strong mint smell and small white flowers flecked with pink that are much appreciated by Honeybees; however, cats like it even more and will trash plants by rolling deliriously all over them! Instead, my cat-resistant favourites include *N.* x *faassenii*, a hybrid of two Caucasian species; it and its widely available cultivars 'Six Hills Giant' (above) and 'Walker's Low' are great for edging a border. **Hairless Catmint** *N. nuda* from southern Europe isn't quite so hot for bees, but is a lovely airy plant growing to 120cm; *N. subsessilis* from Japan grows to 90cm with tighter heads of larger purple-blue flowers and is liked by bumblebees; and *N. nervosa* from Kashmir has upright spikes of flowers, rather like Bugle. Catmints generally like hot, sunny positions in a free-draining soil.

Chicory *Cichorium intybus*   ▲
Hardy perennial growing to 1m, native to southern Europe but long since naturalised throughout much of southern Britain. The flowers are a little bit like blue dandelions, but held on tall, branched stems; they are visited by hoverflies, Honeybees and some solitary bees and bumblebees. It will grow in poor soil thanks to its deep tap root and likes a sunny position. Finches will eat the seeds if you grow en masse.

★ **Clovers** *Trifolium*   ▼▶
'Trifolium' means three leaves, a familiar feature (unless you're very lucky and find one with four!) of these grassland plants that

gardeners often want to eradicate from their lawns; you'll hopefully want to encourage them instead. Two perennial species stand out by being native to almost every corner of the British Isles and for having flowers that are a favourite of bumblebees and Honeybees. **White Clover** *T. repens* (above) can grow to 50cm if unchecked, with rounded heads of whitish flowers; there are many different strains used in agriculture, but look for seeds listed as 'wild White Clover'. It can be mixed with a hard-wearing grass seed mixture to add life to a new lawn. It can boost the nitrogen in a lawn, helping the grasses, so you might prefer to go for **Red Clover** *T. pratense*, which is a bit more robust than the White, with rounded heads of pinkish (not red) flowers. Both don't mind being trampled or cut. The foliage is eaten by Narrow-bordered Five-spot Burnet, Shaded Broad-bar, Common Heath, Mother Shipton and Burnet Companion moth caterpillars, plus clover sawflies and several weevils and gall midges. For bees, just allow the clovers to spread across a lawn and give them a chance to flower by holding off with the mower in summer. My favourite clover of all is **Zigzag Clover** *T. medium* (below) – its name is great, the larger flowers are a deeper, richer pink than Red Clover, and I find them more reliable for attracting butterflies.

★ **Columbine (Granny's Bonnet)**
Aquilegia vulgaris   ▲
It is hard to believe that such an exquisite blue flower is native to most of the British Isles. It grows to 90cm, the flowers dangling above delicate triple-leaved foliage in May–June. It is visited by long-tongued bumblebees while aphids feed on the stems, attracting ladybirds. It has been the plant breeder's dream, producing all manner of gaudy colours, but stick to the simple, gorgeous original and definitely avoid doubles. It prefers a rich, well-drained soil in sunny woodland, and self-seeds readily.

★ **Comfreys** *Symphytum*   ▲
Several species of vigorous clump-forming perennials, all rather coarse and best kept to more informal parts of the garden, where their

leaves can be harvested to make home-made liquid fertiliser. Their drooping bell-flowers are superb for bumblebees, and various flea beetles and weevils feed on them too. **Common Comfrey** *S. officinale* is probably native to most lowland areas of the British Isles, growing to 1.5m with crimson, mauve or white flowers from May to July, and preferring damp, ditch-side conditions. **Russian Comfrey** *S. x uplandicum*, a garden hybrid, can grow even taller and in drier conditions, with purple flower buds opening to deep blue. It is well established in Britain having once been a fodder crop. **Tuberous Comfrey** *S. tuberosum* is less in-your-face, growing only to 60cm with pale yellow flowers, and is native to much of lowland Scotland. **Creeping Comfrey** *S. grandiflorum*, from southern and eastern Europe, only grows to 40cm high, and is good for ground cover; although not especially pretty, it does flower from early in spring. However, top of my list for looks are the powder-blue comfreys such as 'Hidcote Blue' (above), which is an early flowerer and great for Hairy-footed Flower Bees.

★ Coneflower *Echinacea purpurea* ▲
Clump-forming perennial, growing to 120cm, native to the eastern American prairies, the roots being used for the herbal medicine you might recognise from the Latin name. It has dramatic flowers with pink outer petals (rays) and a dense mound of orangey central florets, especially enjoyed by bumblebees but also well used by other bees and many butterflies (see page 82). The seed heads form attractive 'cones' offering seeds for finches and Blue Tits. Grow in full sun and well-drained, fertile soil but keep well watered in summer. There are several cultivars with varying ray colour and shape that are worth growing, but I heartily recommend the gorgeous and simple original species. To propagate, divide in spring or autumn.

Coral Bells *Heuchera* ▲
The sheer explosion in the number of cultivars of these North American perennials in the Saxifrage family has been astonishing. All have that basic characteristic of a neat mound of lobed leaves from which grow several slender flower stalks topped with sprays of very small pinkish or red flowers. Heucheraholics love them for the sheer profusion of leaf colours and patterns, from acid greens to purples. I was ready to dismiss them as worthless, but actually the flowers have proven to be great for some bees. I find that those with larger, red flowers such as 'Firefly' tend to do best, and be aware that those with green leaves will cope better in shadier conditions.

Cornflowers See Knapweeds and cornflowers

Corydalis solida ▼
I don't think anyone really knows this by the name Fumewort, so I'm sticking to the Latin name for this delicate perennial that originates from mainland Europe and is a good bumblebee plant early in the spring when little else is in flower. Above the ferny foliage, the shoals of flowers (for I think they look like little fish!) are pink with a hint of blue (in the photo above with Scilla) and are unusual in that they point downwards, with the long spurs at the rear pointing skywards.

Cosmos *Cosmos* ▼
Bees enjoy these three Central American plants and their cultivars, widely grown in gardens for their open, gaudy flowers. **Chocolate Cosmos** *C. atrosanguineus* (below) is a tuberous perennial, up to 60cm, with deep-red flowers and a scent that does have a touch of chocolate about it. It will struggle in cold winters. Frost-tender annuals to easily grow by scattering seed on prepared soil or in a large pot are *C. bipinnatus* with very feathery leaves and *C. sulphureus* with more simple leaves, which grow to 90cm. Cosmos generally like full sun and a moist, well-drained soil, and may need staking.

Cowslip *Primula veris* ▲

With its nodding head of yellow flowers, this native of lowland meadows of the British Isles is much planted on road verges, although it is rare in the north. It is pollinated by early bees such as the Hairy-footed Flower Bee. It can sometimes cope well when added as plug plants to a lawn, and once it settles in and starts to self-seed, it can create a wonderful spring display.

★ Cranesbills *Geranium* ▲▼

A fantastic family of mainly sprawling or semi-erect perennials, adored by bees. Don't confuse them with pelargoniums, which are often sold as Geraniums but are something different altogether! Of the many species and cultivars of true Geraniums, most are usually less than 80cm high, have palmate leaves and are covered in delightfully simple, open, five-petalled flowers. Key species to look for include: **Dusky Cranesbill** *G. phaeum*, native to the Alps and Pyrenees, which has the most saturated dark maroon flowers; **Meadow Cranesbill** *G. pratense*, with large blue-mauve flowers, one of our most beautiful native plants, found on road verges and meadows in most of inland Britain (but not Ireland); the exquisite **Bloody Cranesbill** *G. sanguineum* which is a sprawling native to some of our coastal cliffs, dunes and northern limestone areas; and one of my favourite flowers, **Wood Cranesbill** *G. sylvaticum*, coping in half-shady positions and with pinkish flowers with a white centre.

There are also dozens of cultivars to choose from, such as **'Mavis Simpson'** (left); in fact, it's hard to find a bad one for bees if you stick to those with single flowers. The hybrid *G.* x *magnificum* (above) is especially good – it just keeps on flowering, and soon your local bumblebee population will learn that it is a plant that never stops giving. Geraniums tend to be happy in most soils, except those that are very wet, and most like sun or semi-shade. However, *G.* x *macrorrhizum* can cope even in almost full shade and spreads well, extending the family's value even further.

Dahlias *Dahlia* ▼

Most readily available in this large genus are hybrid cultivars of *D. coccinea* and *D. pinnata* from Mexico, with big showy flowers in reds, pinks, oranges, yellow and whites. Take care! Only the single-flowered varieties and some of the 'collerettes' and 'doubles' will do – all the hundreds of 'pompom', 'cactus' and

other extravagantly petalled cultivars are at the expense of the all-important nectar and pollen. Find the right ones, however, and they can be simply brilliant for pollinators, from bumblebees and Honeybees to hoverflies and even a few butterflies. Good varieties include 'Yellowhammer', 'Twyning's After Eight' and 'Moonfire', while the widely sold 'Bishop of Llandaff' and 'Bishop's Children' do well too; personally I adore the 'Happy' series (above). Dahlias will flower from midsummer right through to the first frosts. They take some effort – they are prone to earwig, slug and snail damage and mildew, often need staking, and most need to be lifted in winter to avoid the frosts. But if you have the time to care for them, they are well worth the effort.

Dame's Violet (Sweet Rocket)
Hesperis matronalis ▲

Slightly ungainly cottage-garden perennial, growing to 1m, with sweetly scented four-petalled flowers in pink, white and mauve borne over a long flowering season. It is a favoured drop-in for white butterflies and particularly for Orange-tips. It is widely established across much of the British Isles, originating in southern Europe, and prefers slightly shady hedgebanks and streamsides.

★ Dead-nettles *Lamium* ▲▼

This group of ground-cover plants has big-hooded, open-mouthed flowers much loved by bumblebees, and includes two common but attractive 'weeds', the **Red Dead-nettle** *L. purpureum* and **White Dead-nettle** *L. album* (above), both of which are archaeophytes found across most of the British Isles. They flower March–November. The Red is an annual of fertile, turned soils, sometimes persisting in lawns. It grows to 40cm, with purple-red whorls of flowers and round soft leaves that are often red-tinged. The White is a neat perennial of hedgerows growing to 60cm and with pure white whorls of flowers. Funny then how we ignore the 'boring' weeds and grow similar plants from garden centres, such as *L. maculatum* (below) from southern Europe and its cultivars. Fortunately, they're still great for bumblebees, and they cover the

ground well in shady – even dry – spots. Other insects use dead-nettles, too, including many generalist moth caterpillars, pollen beetles, the Pied Shieldbug and the Wool Carder Bee.

Delphiniums ▲

Although the delphinium family includes several species of hardy perennials native to North America, Asia and parts of Europe, most grown in gardens are hybrid cultivars. They produce spikes densely packed with blue, mauve or pink flowers, the tallest (at over 2m) requiring staking. Most are enjoyed by bees, especially the larger bumblebees, and the foliage is eaten by the caterpillar of the Golden Plusia moth. What you may struggle with are slugs and snails, which love them even more – swap to Larkspur if that is the case. Grow delphiniums in rich soil in a sunny position, keep them well watered and avoid the doubles.

★ Fennel *Foeniculum vulgare* ▲

Tall hardy perennial in the carrot family, growing to 2m, probably native to the Mediterranean but grown as a herb in Britain since Roman times and now naturalised in southern coastal areas. Broad umbels of small yellow flowers attract all manner of insects, including hoverflies, flies, soldier beetles, parasitic wasps and solitary bees, the kind of insects poorly served by many garden flowers. It self-seeds readily but is easy to control. 'Purpureum' is an attractive cultivar with bronzy foliage.

★ Fleabane, Common
Pulicaria dysenterica ▲

Native herbaceous perennial of damp grassy places in most of the southern half of the British Isles, spreading to form stands of rather furry leaves. These are topped with loads of golden composite flowers from July to September, with large centres and rather short ray petals. It's not a plant you'll find in most gardening catalogues (so you'll need to go to a wildflower supplier or collect seed), but it is so good for butterflies (see page 82) that it should be! It also supports several micro-moths, plus leafhoppers and leaf beetles.

★ Foxgloves *Digitalis* ▼

The **Common Foxglove** *D. purpurea* is a gloriously showy, short-lived perennial or biennial of woodland glades, native throughout the British Isles. The familiar flower spike, growing up to 2m, is produced June–August, with dangling deep-pink bells into which long-tongued bumblebees clamber, while the Foxglove Pug (moth, not dog!) feeds on the leaves. Common Foxgloves prefer acid soils, moist and rich, and do well in light shade, self-seeding well. A white version 'Alba' is widely

which many tight spikes of pink flowers bloom from late summer to autumn. Bumblebees, Honeybees and some butterflies such as Brimstones eagerly visit. It likes a moist soil in sun or partial shade, and there are several cultivars including those with white and dark-purple flowers.

available, and I'd select those over most of the various cultivars. However, think about growing some of the more subtle perennial species, too, such as **Large Yellow Foxglove** *D. grandiflora*, **Yellow Foxglove** *D. lutea*, which is good for woodland areas, and **Rusty Foxglove** *D. ferruginea* (above), best in dry sunny places; the latter two are great for small solitary bees. Perhaps the best I've found so far for pollinators is '**Goldcrest**', a hybrid between *D. obscura* and *D. grandiflora*, which seems to draw in bees from miles around.

Geums ▲

Instead of the rather unspectacular and persistent garden weed, Herb Bennet *G. urbanum*, which can be a bit troublesome, gardeners have the choice of a range of hybrid cultivars with their attractive and numerous individual red, yellow or orange flowers. Most tend to grow to around 60cm tall, and are a fine addition to the flower border. I admit that I find them quite variable in their attractiveness to pollinators, so definitely avoid the doubles, but a good single like '**Totally Tangerine**' should do the trick, and there are few orange-coloured varieties to match it.

Gayfeather *Liatris spicata* ▲
A herbaceous perennial, growing to 90cm, from eastern North America, surviving all but our hardest winters as a fattened root. In spring it forms a clump of grass-like leaves above

★ **Globe thistles** *Echinops* ▲
An eye-catching part of the herbaceous border and one of the very best plants for bumblebees, the spiky spherical flower heads the size of tennis balls are carried from midsummer to early autumn on 2m stems. Most are perennials native to southern Europe. Popular in gardens are *E. ritro*, to 1.2m, with lilac-blue flower heads, and the similar *E. bannaticus* '**Taplow Blue**', both of which are also visited by butterflies such as Commas. *E. sphaerocephalus* is native to southern Russia with whitish flowers. All have thistle-like foliage.

Goat's Rue *Galega officinalis* ▲
Honeybees and bumblebees love this rather rambling hardy perennial, which grows to 1.5m and is native to central and southern Europe but is hardy further north. The white, pink and lilac pea flowers are borne in profusion June–August. It prefers sunny grassy places, and will do perfectly well on poor soil.

Ground-ivy *Glechoma hederacea* ▲
Sprawling, furry perennial native to most of the British Isles on sunny road verges, hedgerows and open waste ground. Its purple flowers in

April–June, on stems up to 20cm tall but often held close to the ground, are loved by bees, bee-flies and spring butterflies such as Small Tortoiseshell and Peacock, while the small kidney-shaped leaves are often used by gall wasps.

Hellebores *Helleborus* ▲

The late-winter flowering season of several of these perennials offers early nectar for queen bumblebees. The multiple stems, up to 60cm, have simple, five-petalled, large nodding flower cups in whites, greens, pinks and even blacks, with a central cluster of big yellow stamens. Two types in particular stand out for the garden – **Christmas Rose** *H. niger*, native to central Europe, and *Lenten Rose H. orientalis*, native to the Black Sea area. But don't discount the more subtle charms of green-flowered **Green Hellebore** *H. viridis* or the red-rimmed green bells of **Stinking Hellebore** *H. foetidus*, not quite as showy but both native to parts of south-western England and Wales and still enjoyed by bumblebees. All are great for the spring woodland garden in rich soil.

★ Hemp-agrimonies *Eupatorium* ▼

Top plants for butterflies, bees and hoverflies, our own **Hemp-agrimony** *E. cannabinum*, native throughout much of the British Isles although rare in Scotland, is a brilliant place to start. See page 82 for the butterflies that visit its pale pink froth of flowers in July–September. It grows to 1.5m, spreading and setting seed readily, preferring damper soils and doing fine in light shade. Avoid the double-flowered variety found in garden centres. The American **Joe Pye Weed** *E. purpureum* (below) (now renamed *Eutrochium purpureum*) grows even

taller, to 2m (subspecies *maculatum* is a little smaller), and has red stalks and flowers that are flushed deep pink. It is just as good for butterflies, and is best placed at the back of the border where it needs a good moisture-retentive soil.

Hollyhock *Alcea rosea* ▲

Originally from Asia, this dramatic plant, usually grown as a biennial, has large-petalled open flowers that bloom in sequence up the 2m stem. The flowers are pink in the original species and purple, maroon, white or yellow in cultivars. Inside, bumblebees wallow in yellow pollen, while caterpillars of the Mallow moth eat the large-lobed leaves. Avoid the doubles, grow in a moist but well-drained soil, and stake if necessary.

Honesty *Lunaria annua* ▲

This easy-to-grow biennial, native to southern Europe, has heart-shaped leaves and delightful spring flowers in purple, magenta or white on stems up to 75cm tall, followed by disc-like translucent seed pods much used in flower arranging. The jury is out as to quite how good they are for wildlife, but Orange-tip and Green-veined White butterflies will certainly nectar and lay eggs there. It enjoys half-shade on moist but well-drained soils, and will self-seed.

Honeywort *Cerinthe major* ▲

Hardy annual or biennial native to southern Europe, its triangular, fleshy, bluish leaves topped with nodding plum-coloured flowers are much visited by bees, especially long-tongued bumblebees. Easily grown from seed, it needs a light, well-drained, fertile soil, preferably in sun. Deadhead to prolong flowering.

★ Iceplants *Sedum* ▲

Sedum spectabile stands out as one of the very best flowers for autumn garden butterflies. A hardy perennial native to eastern Asia, best grown on poor soils in full sun. It forms an evergreen clump of fleshy blue-green leaves above which the flower stems grow up to 60cm and open into flat-topped, massed clusters of hundreds of tiny pink stars. This is a feeding table in late summer and autumn for some of our showiest butterflies (see page 82), but make sure you grow several plants together for best results. Bumblebees and Honeybees love it too. Cultivars include white-flowered '**Iceberg**', pink '**Brilliant**' and deep-pink '**Indian Chief**'. You might also like to try **Orpine** *S. telephium*, probably native to many parts of the British Isles on woodland edges, but widely grown in gardens, too, where it works well for bees. Its plum-coloured cultivar '**Matrona**' looks great in a border. The ubiquitous hybrid *S. spectabile* x *telephium* (above), marketed as S. '**Herbstfreude**' or '**Autumn Joy**', is sold everywhere as being good for butterflies but isn't; it is fine for Honeybees but otherwise can be quite a disappointment.

★ Inulas *Inula* ▼

Tall perennials, most from eastern Europe and Asia, forming clumps of big broad leaves with tall flower stems topped with broad yellow daisy flowers. These are visited by several butterfly species, especially Peacocks, Commas, Red Admirals and Brimstones, but also whites and browns, and by bumblebees

and Honeybees, and then by Goldfinches once the seeds have set. **Elecampane** *I. helenium* (above), from western Asia but now naturalised in Britain, grows to 2.5m with a flower up to 9cm across, and *I. magnifica* from the Caucasus is almost as big. As you can guess, they need plenty of space. Smaller gardens might suit *I. hookeri* from the Himalayas, only 75cm tall with flowers 3cm across. Inulas will tolerate some shade but they like rich, moist soil.

Jacob's Ladder *Polemonium caeruleum* ▲
A clump-forming hardy perennial, its fairly long leaves are divided neatly into opposite pairs of pointed leaflets. Multiple flower stems up to 90cm are topped with cup-shaped, mauve-blue flowers loved by Honeybees. In the British Isles it is native but only to steep

limestone screes in the Pennines, whereas in gardens it grows best in fairly fertile soils. Several other species and cultivars are grown, including the similar **Abscess Root** *P. reptans* from the eastern USA and **Boreal Jacob's Ladder** *P. boreale* from the High Arctic.

★ Knapweeds and cornflowers
Centaurea ▲▼

A fantastic genus for bumblebees, bees, butterflies and birds, with flowers beautiful enough to be centre stage in the flower border. **Common (Black) Knapweed** *C. nigra* is native to the whole of the British Isles, **Greater Knapweed** *C. scabiosa* (above) to much of lowland England and Wales. Found in unimproved downland and meadows, they have stems up to about 80cm from which they bear pink-purple, thistle-like flowers on top of a firm, swollen head covered in bracts. See page 82 for all the many butterfly visitors. The foliage is eaten by a whole host of leaf beetles, gall-flies and leaf-miner flies, and Goldfinches like the seeds. Grow them in poor soil as they may get too tall and floppy in a compost-rich border.

The cornflowers include the annual **Cornflower** *C. cyanus*, an archaeophyte that was once a problem weed of arable crops but is now rare in the wild. It has the purest of blue flowers, visited by Honeybees and hoverflies, and is ideal for your cornfield mix, but avoid the doubles. Just as good as the native species, at least for pollinators, are **Perennial Cornflower** *C. montana*, a native of the mountains of central Europe with large blue flowers, and **Mealy Cornflower** *C. dealbata* (below) from the Caucasus with pink flowers. For something different, try *C. macrocephala*, also from the Caucasus but with big yellow

a close relative of the delphiniums. It has finely cut leaves and tall stems lined with open flowers in purples, blues and pinks that are great for bees, especially bumblebees, and its foliage is food for the caterpillar of the Golden Plusia moth. Avoid all the widely available doubles and hunt down the simple singles. Grow in sun and a well-drained soil, maybe as part of an annual seed mix, but be prepared for major slug and snail damage. Taller cultivars may need support.

Lavatera, Annual See Mallows

flowers, or for deep intense purples go for **C. 'Jordy'**, a hybrid of C. montana and C. jacea but no less good for pollinators for that. Full sun and light soils suit most Centaureas.

If you are on clay, I'm a big fan of the closely related **Saw-wort** *Serratula tinctoria*, a rather slender plant that grows to 70cm with tight little knapweed flowers, loved by skippers and brown butterflies, and a delight in summer meadows. It is native to much of England and Wales, especially the south and west.

★ **Lamb's-ear** *Stachys byzantina* (syn. *S. lanata* and *S. olympica*) ▲
Growing to 50cm and native to the Caucasus, the little pink flowers of this clump-forming perennial are a big draw for various bees. However, its prime attraction is for the Wool Carder Bee, which harvests the soft, white hairs off the leaves to form its nesting chambers. It is fascinating to see one of these feisty bees determinedly guarding a clump, fending off intruders. Grow in a well-drained or even poor soil in a sunny position, and make sure you buy the flowering form rather than the non-flowering variety sold as ground cover.

Lithodora *Lithodora diffusa* ▲
Perhaps best regarded as a sub-shrub, given that it is evergreen rather than herbaceous, but it barely reaches more than 15cm high as it creeps over rockeries and the front of borders. It hails from as close to Britain as France, although it never made it to the British Isles under its own steam. The most widely available cultivar is called **'Heavenly Blue'**, and the simple, star-like flowers are indeed of an intense blue and are wonderful for attracting all sorts of pollinators from late spring through much of the summer. You will need to grow it in acid soil with good drainage, and it does like sun.

★ **Lady's Smock (Cuckoo-flower)**
Cardamine pratensis ▲
Delicately beautiful perennial that grows up to 60cm and is native throughout the British Isles and much of northern Europe in damp, even boggy, grassy places and ditches. It bears pale pink flowers of great simplicity, each with four petals, a sure sign of spring. It is essential as one of the two food plants of caterpillars of the Orange-tip butterfly, and is also used by those of the Green-veined White, and the adults of both species will nectar at the flowers in April–May. We need more gardeners to grow it.

Larkspur *Consolida ajacis* ▲
An annual, growing to 90cm (some cultivars are larger), native to the Mediterranean and

★ **Lungworts** *Pulmonaria* ▼
I love these plants! On a springtime woodland garden floor, they form little clumps of white-spotted leaves, and hungry bumblebees, Honeybees and bee-flies thrust themselves deep into the throat of the blue tubular flowers. One species, the **Narrow-leaved Lungwort** *P. longifolia*, is native – if you live in parts of Dorset, Hampshire or the Isle of Wight, that is. Plain, simple **Lungwort** *P. officinalis* from Europe has been widely grown here for hundreds of years, and these days you can also buy *P. angustifolia*, *P. rubra*

and *P. saccharata* (the latter with red flowers), plus lots of cultivars. All are perennials, up to about 20cm tall at most, enjoying partial shade and a loamy or clay soil.

Lupins *Lupinus*   ▲

Dramatic, short-lived perennials, mainly available to buy as Russell lupins, which are a group of hybrid cultivars based on the North American species **L. polyphyllus** and the shrubby Tree Lupin **L. arboreus**. Even the hybrids tend to be good for bumblebees, Honeybees and mining bees, with their showy 1m high spires of carefully and densely arranged pea flowers in whites, yellows,

pinks, reds and purples. Most are hardy but are prone to slug and snail onslaught. Grow in full sun in a fairly fertile soil, either sowing from seed in autumn or taking cuttings in spring. Just be aware that some lupins can be invasive, including Tree Lupin which is causing problems in some coastal sites, so compost all spent plants at home.

Lysimachia *Lysimachia clethroides*   ▲

Although there is an English name of Gooseneck Loosestrife, it is rarely marketed as such, so I'm sticking to the scientific name. It is a herbaceous perennial native to China and Japan, which produces heads of white flowers in a spike up to 1m tall, which in form are rather like those of buddleja but the tips habitually nod. It should quickly form a clump, and with dozens of nodding flower heads lined up, you can see the resemblance to a flock of farmyard geese. Given a sunny position, I think it is much undervalued as a nectar plant for butterflies, and it isn't bad for bumblebees either.

Mallows and lavateras

Malva and *Lavatera*   ▼

Two closely related genera of mainly perennials with large open pink flowers, often with notched petals, that look pleasant in the herbaceous border. All are visited by some bumblebees and Honeybees. **Musk Mallow M. moschata** is my favourite, a native beauty to almost all of England and Wales growing to about 80cm. It has fine-cut leaves and pale pink summer flowers, with an exquisite white version 'Alba'. It likes sheltered edges with a bit of shade but will do fine in the open. **Common Mallow M. sylvestris** is a bit of a straggler with stems up to 1m, and

is hit-and-miss with pollinators, but its deep-pink summer flowers are beautiful. It is the food plant of the Mallow moth, and there are some well-behaved cultivars to try. It is an archaeophyte across almost all lowland areas of the British Isles except the far north.

Bees seem to prefer the warmth-loving **lavateras** (above), sometimes called the 'shrubby mallows'. We do have a couple of native species in the British Isles, but it is hybrid cultivars that are most widely grown, rising to 1.5m at times yet rarely needing support. There is also the lush annual **L. trimestris** from the Mediterranean. Mallows and lavateras like a well-drained soil and can cope with a little shade; most will self-seed.

Marigolds *Tagetes*   ▲

Widely grown in gardens, **French Marigolds T. patula** and **African Marigolds T. erecta**, both native to Mexico (work that one out!), have a neat mound of foliage and many daisy-like flowers with orange or yellow rays around the outside and a mass of tiny florets in the centre enjoyed by some pollinating insects, especially hoverflies and solitary bees. All are fast-growing half-hardy annuals and perfect for summer bedding, flowering in summer and usually 20–50cm tall, but you'll need to search hard to avoid the double and pompon cultivars that are readily available but have had much of their goodness bred out of them. Good French Marigolds to seek include the single flowers of the 'Disco' series, 'Naughty Marietta' and 'Cinnabar', while African Marigolds include 'Tangerine Gem' and 'Lemon Gem'. Grow them in a sunny position in a good, free-draining soil, or as companion plants to cabbages, cucumbers, potatoes and tomatoes.

Marigold, Corn *Chrysanthemum segetum,* syn. *Glebionis segetum* ▲
One of the staples of the cornfield garden, long since present in the British Isles although not originally a native here. It's very easy to grow, and the large, daisy flowers are a joyous deep golden yellow. The open flowers make fine feeding for some solitary bees and hoverflies.

Marigold, Pot *Calendula officinalis* ▲
An easy-to-grow garden favourite, native to southern Europe and 30–60cm tall, depending on the cultivar. It is a hardy annual covered in lots of yellow or orange daisy flowers, which, if you avoid all the many double-flowered varieties and stick to the simplest varieties, will be visited by hoverflies and some solitary bees. Grow them in a sunny position in a well-drained soil, and you can easily extend the flowering season by deadheading.

★ Marjorams *Origanum* ▲
A must! Marjoram *O. vulgare* (above) is a perennial native growing to 50cm in dry grassy places throughout much of the lowland British Isles, although it is rare in Scotland. The clusters of small pink flowers open from deep red buds and are irresistible to Gatekeepers and many other butterflies (see page 82), but are also one of the very best bumblebee magnets. I have found the subspecies *hirtum* to be particularly effective (see photo page 7). There are also several other species and cultivars to try, such as **Sweet Marjoram** *O. majorana* from the Mediterranean.

Masterwort *Astrantia major* ▼
Hardy, clump-forming perennial, native to central and southern Europe, growing up to 60cm and great in the herbaceous border. Its little pincushion flowers in a ruff of white or pinkish papery bracts can be popular with Honeybees, bumblebees, flies, hoverflies and beetles, especially when grown in drifts. They flower from summer to autumn, the individual blooms on upright branched stems. The cultivar 'Rubra' is deep red, and there are several others to choose from. Grow in fairly fertile soil, preferably in sun.

★ Meadowsweet *Filipendula ulmaria* ▼
Native and still common throughout the British Isles on riverbanks and in fens, it is easy to dismiss this herbaceous perennial as not worthy of the garden, but if you have wilder, damper parts of the garden in full sun or light shade, it can make a dramatic show, heavy with scent. It quickly forms a clump, with long, strongly ridged, pinnate leaves. The flowers individually are tiny but combined in the large, irregular flower heads they form a creamy-white haze. After all the bee-friendly flowers in the list, it's nice to recommend one that is great for flies (remember, many of your birds need flies!), and the plant itself is associated with a huge range of moth caterpillars, sawflies, bugs and beetles.

their ancestry. Varieties include the British archaeophyte **Spearmint** *M. spicata*, the widely grown **Peppermint** *M.* x *piperita* (*M. aquatica* x *spicata*) and **Applemint** *M. suaveolens*. They prefer rather moist habitats, with the small pink flowers borne in whorls up the stem or in terminal short spikes, visited by bees and some butterflies such as the whites. The 'Buddleia' group of cultivars of **Horse Mint** *M. longifolia* is said to be especially good, although more research would be welcome. Mints spread like the clappers so be prepared to contain them.

★ Michaelmas Daisies

Aster and *Symphyotrichum* ▲

These flowers keep the memory of summer alive, with massed daisy flowers on tall stems, mainly in pinks and purples, that bloom from September onwards. The best of them prove irresistible to autumn butterflies (see page 82), while Honeybees and hoverflies also visit some varieties in droves. Most are 80–120cm tall, sometimes needing some support. Key species, of which there are dozens of cultivars, are **New York Aster** *S. novi-belgii* and **New England Aster** *S. novae-angliae* from North America with big showy flowers, **Heath Aster** *S. ericoides*, another American studded with smaller leaves and smaller pastel flowers, and **Blue Wood Aster** *S. cordifolium*. They have only recently been reallocated into the *Symphyotrichum* genus, but feel free to still call them Asters – I do! However, choose your cultivars carefully. Research at the National Collection in Malvern showed that only a small proportion of the varieties available shine for pollinators, with *A. novi-belgii* 'Alice Haslam', 'Alderman Vokes' and 'Dandy' coming out top. As a general rule, definitely avoid those where the flowers are all petal and no 'middle'.

A. amellus from Europe, especially 'Grunder', can be good for butterflies, and has been shown to be great for hoverflies, but I am yet to be convinced by its hybrid, *A.* x *frikartii* 'Mönch', which is popular because it starts flowering in July and is less prone to mildew than others.

Grow Michaëlmas Daisies in a moisture-retaining soil in a sunny position, and divide in spring to propagate.

Mignonette *Reseda lutea* ▲

Biennial or short-lived perennial native to much of England and some lowland areas of Wales and Scotland in rather sparse grassy areas and especially on alkaline soils. It has deeply cut leaves and multiple narrow spikes of lime-yellow flowers up to 75cm during June–September, visited by various bees including the yellow-faced (*Hylaeus*) solitary bees and by soldier beetles. It is rarely grown in gardens, despite the flowers making an attractive foil for gaudier blooms. Plant in a sunny position. Two alternatives from the Mediterranean include **White Mignonette** *R. alba*, similar but with white flowers, and the widely grown *R. odorata* with fragrant flowers.

Mints *Mentha* ▲

Group of familiar aromatic perennials, most growing to 75cm, that have been much hybridised, with many having a bit of native British Water Mint somewhere in

Monkshood *Aconitum napellus* ▲

Native perennial to parts of south-western England and southern Wales, and naturalised in other parts of the British Isles. The summer flowers, in a spike up to 1.5m, have unusual purple-blue helmets visited by bees, especially long-tongued bumblebees. It enjoys rich soil in sunshine or the semi-shade of an open woodland, especially near water. There is also a beautiful white form. Be aware that the plant is highly poisonous.

Motherwort *Leonurus cardiaca* ▼

The whorls of small pink flowers around the 1m stems reveal this to be in the Mint family. Native to south-eastern Europe, it was once grown in Britain as a herb. The leaves are rather like the shape of a duck's foot, and it forms an interesting feature in a herbaceous border, where it can be very popular with a range of insects including bumblebees and

hoverflies. It isn't as invasive as the mints, and will do fine is a stony, poor soil, so is definitely one to consider.

Mulleins *Verbascum* ▼

The most prominent creature to use these dramatic plants is the Mullein moth, whose warning-coloured caterpillars feed openly on the large rosettes of leaves. Most mulleins produce a tall, slender flower spike studded with yellow or white flowers visited by hoverflies, solitary bees and bumblebees. The plants are also nibbled by various flea beetles and weevils. The biennial **Great Mullein V. thapsus**, up to 2m high, is a widespread native of lowland British Isles, with leaves like soft, pale-green felt. Similar garden plants, although more branched, are **V. olympicum** from Turkey and **V. bombyciferum** (below) from

Asia. The perennial **Dark Mullein V. nigrum** is native to grassy places in central, southern and eastern England and has green spikes of purple-centred yellow flowers. **V. chaixii** from central Europe is just as effective for insects, and feel free to try some of the many hybrid cultivars. Grow mulleins in sunshine in a free-draining soil.

Nasturtiums *Tropaeolum majus* ▲

It is absolutely pot-luck, it seems, whether any pollinators will find your nasturtiums – sometimes the bumblebees seem to go a bundle on them, sometimes the flowers remain resolutely empty. However, I include them more as a great plant to grow with kids, for these annuals, originally from Central America but now in a range of cultivars, grow incredibly quickly, clambering and in some cases climbing, and soon bearing lots of gaudy red and yellow flowers. On the rounded leaves, Large and Small White butterflies lay their eggs, and they make a great place for studying a butterfly's life cycle, up close and without ruining your cabbages!

Pachysandra terminalis ▲

From Japan, an evergreen perennial (some might consider it a sub-shrub) that is useful in

the garden because it will grow in dense shade and, indeed, doesn't like too much sunlight. It grows by sending out runners, from which grow neat, 25cm high stems with whorls of leaves topped by insignificant clusters of spring flowers. However, these are sweet and rich in nectar, and in a woodland setting before the canopy closes, they can be a good food source for spring butterflies and bee-flies.

Pansies and Violets *Viola* ▲

Most people love the simple, colourful flowers of this big family of low-growing plants, several of which are native to the British Isles. Wildlife doesn't flock to them in gardens, but Honeybees, bee-flies and smaller bumblebees will sometimes visit, and some violets form excellent ground cover in the woodland garden. Avoid the rather coarse and insect-free garden varieties and stick to the 'small is beautiful' native species. **Sweet Violet V. odorata** is a perennial of lightly shady places throughout lowland England and Wales and parts of Ireland; the violet, pink or white flowers are indeed sweet-smelling, and it spreads well. **Common Dog Violet V. riviniana** is a native perennial to almost the entire British Isles, mainly in woods; the small lilac flowers have a pale yellow spur at the back. **Wild Pansy or Heartsease V. tricolor** (above), with exquisite purple and yellow flowers, grows on acid soils often in the mountains and sometimes persisting as a perennial. And **Field Pansy V. arvensis** is an annual for the cornfield garden. Sadly, Garden Pansies, which are complex hybrids, rarely seem to deliver any wildlife value whatsoever and are another of those garden plants that might as well be plastic.

an upright stem, often in blues and purples, into which bumblebees readily crawl. Some bumblebees also learn to pierce the base of the bell from the outside to get at the nectaries – so-called nectar-robbing. Cultivars of the species *P. heterophyllus* are especially good, but you're more likely to find hybrid cultivars for sale, which are hardier. Rock-garden varieties grow to about 20cm and herbaceous ones, which may need staking, up to 1.2m. They like full sun or light shade and a moist, well-drained soil.

Parsnip, Wild *Pastinaca sativa* ▲

The smaller bees and hoverflies do need rather different flowers than the heftier, longer-tongued bumblebees, and that often means members of the carrot family. However, something as widespread as Cow Parsley rarely seems to deliver, and in the absence of robust studies into non-native members of the family sold by flower catalogues, I think it is well worth considering Wild Parsnip, a native biennial of English and Welsh verges and grasslands on chalky soils. It does have rather a pungent smell, but I think the pinnate leaves look good and while the umbels of flowers aren't dramatic, the yellowy hue is quite unusual and they can come alive with all sorts of insects, from flies to true bugs, that you just don't see on other flowers.

Penstemons *Penstemon* ▲

From North America, this fairly large group of species is related to the foxgloves and has smaller, more numerous, trumpet flowers on

Peonies *Paeonia* (singles) ▲

For a long time I saw no value in this group of herbaceous flowers until I realised how good some of the single-flowered varieties could be for a wide range of bees, which appear to be drawn in for the pollen. They only flower for a short time in the summer, and need to be in fertile deep soil and out of the blazing afternoon sun, but for the size and beauty of the bloom and as something for the bees away from the main sunny borders, they will be much admired.

Phlomis ▼

Evergreen perennials with whorls of simple, heart-shaped leaves growing at intervals up the 1m stems which cup the hooded flowers,

yellow in the case of *P. russeliana* (above) and lilac-pink in *P. italica*. Long-tongued bumblebees visit for nectar, but added value is the chance of finches taking the seed, plus the seed heads are very attractive indeed so you'll be happy to leave then standing over winter, providing a sanctuary for various insects.

Phlox, Perennial *Phlox paniculata* ▲

There are over 100 cultivars of this North American herbaceous perennial, with simple, five-petalled pink, purple and white flowers. Plants quickly develop into a clump, and even though the flower stems can be 1m or more tall, they rarely need staking. The flowers hide a deep tube down to the nectar, so this is a plant either for butterflies, especially the Brimstone, or for hawkmoths including the Hummingbird Hawkmoth. The foliage can be prone to mildew, and you are best to plant it in deep rich soil that holds moisture well, especially if well mulched.

Poached-egg Plant
Limnanthes douglasii ▲

Very easy to grow, a hardy annual, native to north-western USA, its flowers having yellow centres (the 'yolk') and white tips. Sow it in March directly into prepared ground where you want it to flower or in pots, ideally in a sunny position. It will grow quickly and is good for solitary bees and Honeybees, flowering in June–August. It will self-seed.

Poppies *Papaver* ▲▼

Much loved and deeply symbolic, most poppies also provide a good source of pollen as well as a little nectar for Honeybees and bumblebees, although there is little other insect life associated with them. Birds such as Goldfinches take the copious seeds. The red poppies we see in cornfields are several different species, the commonest being **Common Poppy** *P. rhoeas* (above) and **Long-headed Poppy** *P. dubium*. Both are annuals, growing to about 60cm, and are archaeophytes in most lowland areas of the British Isles.

There are some cultivars of Common Poppy – the so-called 'Shirley Poppies' – which can be just as good, but avoid the doubles. **Opium Poppy** *P. somniferum* (above), despite looking so exotic, is also an archaeophyte, again widespread and annual, growing to 120cm; its large lilac flowers have a purple blush at the centre. Again, avoid the blousy doubles and 'peony-flowered' cultivars. You can also try **Oriental Poppy** *P. orientale*, an Asian perennial, with its vermilion papery petals. All these poppies prefer sunny positions in rather dry cultivated ground. For shadier areas, you can't go wrong with the yellow **Welsh Poppy** *Meconopsis cambrica*, native to western areas of the UK, which should self-seed freely.

Primroses *Primula vulgaris* ▲

There are lots of garden primulas but, for wildlife, stick to evergreen **Primrose** *P. vulgaris* (above) and avoid the useless hybrid primulas and polyanthus. Native almost everywhere in the British Isles, its foliage is eaten by caterpillars of dozens of moth species, especially the various species of yellow underwing and the *Xestia* genus including Setaceous Hebrew Character. The beautiful lemon flowers are also visited by bee-flies, although be aware that it is not a flower that buzzes with insect activity.

Rattle, Yellow *Rhinanthus minor* ▲

As well as being the crucial ingredient in the summer wildflower meadow because of its ability to suppress vigorous plants like grasses (see page 149), this is a plant that has the added benefit of being enjoyed by bumblebees. It is a short annual, usually 20–30cm tall, with yellow, hooded flowers. If you live near to large meadows full of Rattle, you may be visited by the Grass Rivulet moth whose caterpillars feed on the ripening seeds in their inflated dry pods. Sow in autumn.

Red-hot Pokers *Kniphofia* ▼

Attention-grabbing perennials from southern Africa with dense heads of red or yellow flowers in June–September on a 1m stem above a rosette of spiky foliage. House Sparrows, Blue Tits and Great Spotted Woodpeckers have learnt to visit them for nectar, getting their heads covered with pollen in the process. Some are great for Honeybees and bumblebees, and are also enjoyed by wasps, while the clump of evergreen leaves

provides a winter refuge for ladybirds and other beetles. The many species and hybrid cultivars like a sunny position in moist, well-drained soil, and do well in coastal gardens.

Rudbeckia ▲

I've stuck with the Latin name for this herbaceous perennial as the sometimes used English name, Black-eyed Susan, is also used for the climbing plant *Thunbergia*. It is really easy to grow and soon clumps up into a tall swathe of large deep yellow daisies, ideal for the prairie garden, with a domed black disc of florets at the heart of each flower. Two key species to try are **R. fulgida** (including the cultivar 'Goldsturm' (above)) and **R. hirta**, both of which are moderately attractive to some butterflies and bees, but I include them as much for the seed heads, which if you're lucky will be found by flocks of Goldfinches.

★Sages and claries *Salvia* ▲

One of the very best groups of plants for bees, with a whole host of native and foreign species and cultivars, and all good looking, too. Most are clump-forming perennials, with spikes of flowers somewhere on the purple spectrum, each tubular flower having a tall hood and a large landing pad. For a native beauty, go for **Meadow Clary S. pratensis**, a very rare plant in the wild in Britain, with 1m stems of vibrant deep-blue flowers. A good filler for borders is **Balkan Clary S. nemorosa** and a whole host of hybrids based on it, often under the names **S. x sylvestris** and **S. x superba** (above), whose spikes packed with deep-purple flowers are great for bees. **Whorled Clary S. verticillata** and its cultivars are also good for bees, while the herb **Sage S. officinalis** forms a low evergreen bush, but still sporting good spikes of bee-friendly flowers. Most salvias need full sun and a well-drained soil, but **Bog Sage S. uliginosa** from South America likes a moist soil where it will grow to 2m tall and delight bumblebees that visit the large sea-blue flowers. Even some of the heavily cultivated Salvias, such as **S. x jamensis** 'Hot Lips' can, on occasion, be good for pollinators, but the bedding cultivars of *S. splendens* tend to be lifeless.

Sainfoin *Onobrychis viciifolia* ▼

A perennial in the pea family, with pleasing diamond-shaped heads of pink pea flowers above rows of paired leaflets. It is possibly native to southern England chalklands as a dwarf form and was then developed as a fodder crop; it is now most regularly seen on road verges. It produces nectar and pollen, a bounty for large pollinating insects, especially bumblebees, which can open the flowers with their weight. It is also a food plant of the Narrow-bordered Five-spot Burnet moth.

★Scabiouses *Scabiosa/Knautia/Succisa* ▼

Three closely related genera of mainly perennial plants, simply brilliant for nectaring butterflies (see page 82), burnet moths, bees and other pollinating insects, and for finches that feed on the seeds. My garden wouldn't feel complete without them! Most have lilac 'pincushion' flowers held on slender wiry stems. **Field Scabious K. arvensis** is native to most lowland areas of the British Isles although rare in Scotland, growing to 1m tall in unimproved sunny grasslands. It flowers July–October if deadheaded regularly. **Small Scabious Scabiosa columbaria** is like a petite version, native to chalk and limestone soils in England, and has a pale yellow version, **S. c.**

var. *ochroleuca*. Devil's-bit Scabious *Succisa pratensis* has smaller, deeper-coloured pompons in autumn (great as late nectar for butterflies), and is native throughout almost the entire British Isles. All will look fine dotted among other perennials. If you want something from further afield, **Sweet Scabious Scabiosa atropurpurea** from southern Europe is much like Small Scabious but with deep crimson flowers. It is often grown as an annual; avoid the widespread doubles. *Knautia macedonica* (above) from central Europe grows to 75cm and has scarlet flowers. Give all Scabiouses a well-drained soil, preferably alkaline.

★ **Scabious, Giant** *Cephalaria gigantea* ▲
I've kept this separate from the other Scabiouses as it is in a different genus and you'll need to site it carefully as it does grow over 2m tall! It can be blooming marvellous for bumblebees; in fact, at times they cluster on the pompon cream flower heads as if deliriously happy. It is a perennial from the Caucasus and, as you can imagine from the height and the 1m spread of the large clump of basal leaves, this does need a bit of space at the back of the border.

★ **Scorpion Weed** *Phacelia tanacetifolia* ▼
Sometimes called Fiddleneck, this is a stand-out plant for pollinators and is easy and cheap to grow. An annual grown from seed, it is a little straggly with fine-cut leaves and coiled heads of lavender flowers that unfurl over a long season. Bees and hoverflies of many

species visit large patches of Scorpion Weed in their droves, such as when it is planted as a green manure crop and allowed to flower. You can sow Scorpion Weed in spring or autumn, and it will freely seed.

★ **Sea-hollies** *Eryngium* ▲
Several species of spiky-leaved perennials, most with a dense cone of blue-tinged flowers borne from mid to late summer in the middle of ruffs of thorny bracts. **Sea-holly Eryngium maritimum** is native to shingle beaches and dunes in the southern half of the British Isles and grows to 60cm. Common garden plants in the family include: *E. giganteum* (above) from the Caucasus, which reaches 1.5m, including the dramatic silvery cultivar '**Miss Willmott's Ghost**'; *E. planum* from central Europe, the least spiny of the bunch; and

E. bourgatii from the Pyrenees, growing to 40cm with blue flowers. They're brilliant for adding texture to borders, and the flowers are well visited by bumblebees, solitary bees, Honeybees and some butterflies such as Gatekeepers. For something more unusual, try **Agave-leaved Sea-holly E. agavifolium** from Argentina and **Rattlesnake Master E. yuccifolium** from America, both with fierce leaves and with smaller, green, spiky flower heads on branched flower stems up to 1.8m, adored by soldier beetles and many other pollinating insects. Give all sea-hollies a free-draining soil in full sun, and they even cope well with drought.

Snapdragon *Antirrhinum majus* ▲
From south-western Europe, the original species has been turned into a mass of cultivars grown as half-hardy annuals in bedding schemes everywhere. Most have been tweaked too far and lost their wildlife value, but those that have retained their worth provide us with the entertainment of watching as bumblebees fly onto the 'landing pad' at the mouth of the flower, their weight opening the dragon's mouth so that they can reach the nectar. Low-growing varieties for small gardens include '**Floral Carpet**', barely 25cm tall, but some cultivars retain more of the character of the wild species and grow up to 1.5m tall; look out for those growing semi-wild on walls and collect the seeds! Avoid the doubles, go for old varieties, and grow them on a hot sunny site, deadheading through the season.

often annual, but the rare *Spiked Speedwell V. spicata* (above) is a perennial native to parts of East Anglia and forms clumps of foliage topped with 60cm high spikes of bright blue flowers. It has several garden cultivars in reds, pinks and whites. *V. longifolia*, native to mainland Europe, is similar but even taller, again with cultivars. For sheer native charm, the **Germander Speedwell** *V. chamaedrys* may have small flowers but they are the most intense blue and produced in profusion, and it creates a wonderful mat of ground cover in semi-shady spots and hedgebanks.

grow up to 45cm, bear little white tubular flowers dotted among colourful purple bracts (or various other colours in cultivars), and are enjoyed by several butterfly species.

Sneezeweeds *Helenium* ▲

Wonderful clump-forming perennials that will add a blaze of colour to any flower bed. Native to North America, they were once used by native Indians to make snuff, hence the name. The species *H. autumnale* grows to 1.5m, with lovely, sunshine-coloured, large daisy flowers, the central florets in raised cones that are visited by all sorts of bees, often in excellent numbers. However, you are far more likely to be able to get hold of the many hybrid cultivars, which tend to be shorter with orange or red petals or cones – try something like 'Sahin's Early Flowerer' or the old variety 'Moerheim Beauty'.

Spurges *Euphorbia* ▲

A huge genus of plants, with some 450 species or more worldwide including many cactus-like succulents. However, here in the British Isles we're much more familiar with either those annual weeds of the vegetable patch such as **Sun Spurge** *E. helioscopia*, the native knee-high **Wood Spurge** *E. amygdaloides* found in ancient woodlands, or the range of non-native species available for herbaceous borders. The latter tend to get grown for their architectural feel, many having neat whorls of leaves above which the acid-green flowers are like a cluster of cups held above ruffs of green bracts. I won't deny they are a bit hit-and-miss as far as pollinators go, but the best can be great, especially for solitary bees, flies, hoverflies and ants. The top choice I have found is *E. cornigera* (above) from the Himalayas, which is a beautiful perennial with white midribs to the leaves. Avoid the invasive *E. amygdaloides* var. *robbiae*, and just be careful of the poisonous sap of spurges when handling.

Stock, Night-scented
Matthiola bicornis ▲

In the cabbage family, this is a rather weedy-looking annual from Greece growing to only 30cm tall with narrow grass-like leaves. Its wildlife value is that its simple, four-petalled, pale pink flowers open at night, releasing a glorious scent that draws in night-feeding moths.

Stonecrops *Sedum* ▼

Ground-hugging perennials forming bobbly carpets of bulbous little leaves in inhospitable places such as gravel, walls and cliffs. Their little starburst flowers, often densely packed, are good for bees of all sorts. Several species are used on 'green roofs' (see page 179); typical (and desirable) in the mix are **Biting**

Speedwells *Veronica* ▲

Large genus of flowers including some very attractive native species. In the British Isles, most wild speedwells are low-growing weeds,

Statice *Limonium sinuatum* ▼

A Mediterranean version of Sea Lavender, much grown in gardens as a half-hardy annual for flower arranging, and is ideally suited to dry free-draining soils. The winged stems, which

Stonecrop S. *acre*, native throughout much of the British Isles except the Scottish Highlands, with yellow-star flowers, and **White Stonecrop S. *album***, possibly native to parts of Devon but at the very least an archaeophyte almost everywhere in lowland areas of the British Isles. One of the best I have seen for attracting insects is the yellow **Kamchatka Stonecrop S. *kamtschaticum*** (above), but try **Spanish Stonecrop S. *hispanicum*** and **Reflexed Stonecrop S. *reflexum*** too. See also Iceplant for larger Sedums.

Strawberry, Wild *Fragaria vesca* ▲
A tiny version of the garden strawberry, this low-growing perennial with little, three-toothed leaflets spreads out through semi-shady glades by slender runners. It has small, open, white flowers which turn into strawberries barely a centimetre across. These fruits, while just a morsel for us, are greedily snapped up by Blackbirds, mice and Foxes. Many weevils and good numbers of

generalist moths eat the foliage, and mining bees visit for nectar. Let this undemanding plant cover the ground in a woodland area – it is easy to weed out if necessary.

★ **Sunflowers** *Helianthus* ▲▼
Most of us at some stage must have grown a sunflower from seed – and I bet it was one of the giants! Any plant that grows almost as fast as Jack's beanstalk is a great introduction to gardening for kids. The late summer flowers are much appreciated by bumblebees, and you may be able to harvest some home-grown birdseed from them, too. Originally from North America, some cultivars can reach 4m or more in a season, and all tend to have golden rays and a large disc of dark brown florets in the centre, sometimes to 30cm across. Avoid the doubles and the 'chrysanthemum' series, and try shorter varieties to avoid having to stake them, such as 'Taiyo' which only grows to 120cm.

Most are annuals, but if you fancy one that comes back year after year, try the perennial *H.* x *laetiflorus* 'Lemon Queen' (above), which grows as a spreading clump and bears large daisy-like flowers in the purest of yellows and is great for bumblebees and Honeybees. However, the best for butterflies in my experience is another perennial *H.* x *multiflorus* 'Capenoch Star'.

Sunflower, Mexican
Tithonia rotundifolia ▲
Here is a really easy to grow annual flower that will brighten up any sunny flower border. Within the one growing season, it can reach 1.5m tall, with a mass of branches and large, spear-shaped leaves, but it is the many 5cm-wide daisy-like flowers that draw the eye. The ring of large ray petals is coloured the most vivid orange as if from a child's paintbox. You can expect bumblebees and hoverflies, but this is also a great flower for butterflies which, considering there are so few flowers they will regularly visit, make this a real winner from a very reasonably priced seed packet in spring.

Sweet William *Dianthus barbatus* ▲
Part of the large family of pinks, Sweet William is a half-hardy perennial from southern Europe, usually grown as a bedding annual,

and reaching 40cm. The massed heads of open, tooth-edged flowers have petals neatly marked with red, pink and white rings, and some varieties are moderately successful for butterflies, with Red Admirals, Small Tortoiseshells, Peacocks, Painted Ladies, whites and even skippers visiting. Sow early indoors, and plant out once the risk of frost has passed in a sunny position at the front of a border.

★ Tansy *Tanacetum vulgare* ▲

Aromatic (OK, slightly smelly!) perennial, probably native across much of Britain although thought to be introduced in Ireland. It grows to 120cm, with pretty, fine-cut leaves eaten by more than a dozen species of micro-moths. The yellow button flowers, produced June–August, are very popular with insects, including butterflies, hoverflies, pollen-eating beetles, solitary bees and wasps, ants and more, while the seeds are taken by Greenfinches. It likes sun and a fertile soil, often on riversides and other damp locations. Propagate by division in spring, or just allow it to spread by its creeping roots.

★ Teasel *Dipsacus fullonum* ▼

Familiar throughout much of lowland Britain, although scarce in Scotland and Ireland, this native biennial is a rather robust plant with large, coarse basal leaves and then a spiny hollow stem topped with spiky 'hedgehog' flower heads. The small purple flowers open in hoops around the heads, and are visited by bumblebees and butterflies such as Peacocks. Once the flower heads have dried, Goldfinches cling eagerly to extract the seed. Easy to grow, even in semi-shade, it will then set seed as it pleases!

Thistles *Cirsium* and *Onorpordum* ▼

It is easy to dismiss thistles as prickly, troublesome weeds – and some are indeed unsuitable for all but the wildest of gardens – but their purple crowns of flowers are some of the very best for bees, butterflies, beetles and a whole host of other insects, and the seeds are snapped up by Goldfinches. A great garden compromise is the trendy *C. rivulare* 'Atropurpureum' (below), a perennial from central Europe growing up to 1.5m, less prickly than most, with tall, branched flowering stems from June to September, great for bumblebees and some butterflies such as Small Tortoiseshell and Large White. *C.* 'Mount Etna' also appears to be good and

C. japonicum from eastern Asia is similar. For a wilder, woodland area of the garden, try **Marsh Thistle** *C. palustre*, an upright perennial native to the entire British Isles, which grows up to 2m with many little purple flowers on small side branches favoured by butterflies (see page 82). For a large herbaceous border, an option is the mighty *Scotch Thistle Onopordum acanthium*, actually a native of southern Europe; a biennial, it forms a spiny, woolly rosette of leaves in year one and then goes bananas in year two, throwing up 2m fiercely-spiked stems topped with large purple flowers which are loved by bees and larger butterflies. Perhaps my favourite is the immaculate and non-spiny **Melancholy Thistle** *C. heterophyllum*, which looks much happier than the name suggests and whose flowers will be rummaged endlessly by your bumblebees.

★ Thymes *Thymus* ▲

This large family of herbs form aromatic, low-growing mats of tiny, evergreen leaves, which become topped during May–July in equally small pink or purple flowers loved by bees and other pollinating insects. They grow well in full sun on steep banks and in troughs and are invaluable in gaps in paving, struggling if they face competition from other plants. **Wild Thyme** *T. polytrichus* is a common native across much of the British Isles, even in the mountains, and on downs, cliffs and heaths. In garden centres you are more likely to find **Large Thyme** *T. pulegioides*, native to southern England, and the very rare East Anglian native **Breckland Thyme** *T. serpyllum*, but there are plenty of other species and cultivars to try too.

Tickseeds *Coreopsis* ▲

Most members of this genus of flowers from North America are quite bushy if delicate perennials to about 60cm, with attractive open daisy flowers in summer. The sunshine-gold outer petals often have serrated edges, and the small knot of florets at the centre is much visited by bees and some butterflies (see page 82). Three perennials to include in herbaceous borders are **C. lanceolata**, **C. grandiflora** and **C. verticillata** (above), the latter with especially fine-cut foliage. Annuals to try include **C. tinctoria**, usually with a band of chestnut at the base of the petals, and **C. drummondii**. Avoid double-flowered cultivars. Give Tickseeds a position in full sun in free-draining, even poor, soils; some may need staking.

Toadflaxes *Linaria* ▲ ▼

Related to snapdragons, these attractive flowers are designed for bees, whose weight opens the mouth of the flower to get at the nectar and pollen inside. The best for pollinators is **Purple Toadflax** *L. purpurea* (above), native to Italy but long since grown

in the British Isles and widely naturalised. It is a hardy, upright, rakish perennial growing up to 1m and looking fine among other perennials in a sunny border; it self-seeds freely. The small purple or pink flowers in June–August are fantastic for bumblebees. **Common Toadflax** *L. vulgaris* is a native perennial of unimproved grassy places throughout much of the British Isles, especially on chalky soils, but is rare in Scotland and Ireland. It is usually quite short, with delightful yellow flowers July–October with orange 'headlights' to guide in bumblebees. Toadflax Pug moth caterpillars feed on the foliage. **Fairy Toadflax** *L. maroccana* is an annual, as the Latin name suggests from Morocco, only growing to 30cm, with grass-like leaves and lots of small flowers in yellows and reds. Visited by solitary bees, it is ideal for the cornfield garden (see page 152). **Ivy-leaved Toadflax** *Cymbalaria muralis* (below, with Painted Lady) is native to southern European mountains but has been grown here for hundreds of years, and is now naturalised almost everywhere on old walls, where it roots into tiny gaps. The tiny flowers are visited by tiny bees!

Tobacco Plant (Flowering Tobacco)
Nicotiana sylvestris ▼

Native to Argentina, this rather ungainly annual (sometimes perennial in sheltered places) grows quickly to 120cm, topped in summer with immensely long and thin white tubular flowers releasing their heady fragrance at night. Only something with a very long tongue can reach the nectar, and

that means hawkmoths, and in particular the migrant Convolvulus Hawkmoth with its 10cm wingspan. Grow in a well-drained but fertile soil in a warm position. There are other tobacco plants to try, such as the much shorter cultivars of **N. alata**, also known as Flowering Tobacco or sometimes Jasmine Tobacco, native to South America, but avoid the scent-free *N. x sanderae*.

Valerian, Red *Centranthus ruber* ▲

Easy-to-grow, slightly fleshy, evergreen perennial, up to 1m, native to southern Europe but widely naturalised in northern Europe, especially in coastal areas on shingle and walls where it can be a problem for rare native shingle flora (so avoid it in such places). The loosely massed heads of pink or scarlet flowers (or white in the form 'Alba') bloom May–August and can be visited by several butterfly species (see page 82). It is also an important nectar plant for moths including the Hummingbird Hawkmoth, and some bumblebees also check in. It will grow in very poor soils, preferring plenty of sun, and self-seeds readily.

★ Verbenas ▲

From this big family, of which a few species are frequently grown in gardens, the best by far is *V. bonariensis* (above) from South America, the airiest and trendiest foil for all sorts of herbaceous border plants. It has thin but self-supporting stems, up to 1.5m, topped with flat clusters of small, pink-purple flowers. Some bumblebees visit, but it is even better for butterflies (see page 82) and Hummingbird Hawkmoths. It self-seeds well, and it is easy to take cuttings in autumn. **Vervain** *V. officinalis* is thought to have been in Britain since Neolithic times and has a subtle charm (ie very small flowers!) but is still quite popular with butterflies. *V. rigida* from South America, growing to 90cm or less, and *V. hastata* from the USA are readily available and can satisfy some bees and butterflies. Grow all verbenas in sun in well-drained soil.

Vetches *Vicia* ▼

Group of plants in the pea family, which clambers using tendrils. Despite not being typical garden centre plants, they look great in the garden, especially **Tufted Vetch** *V. cracca* (below), which is native to almost every corner of the British Isles. It scrambles

up to 2m, draped over other vegetation, with rich-purple flowers in a one-sided spike visited by bumblebees, some butterflies such as skippers, and in particular by burnet moths. The foliage is the food plant of The Blackneck moth caterpillars. Another perennial, again a widespread native here, is **Bush Vetch** *V. sepium* (below), with small clusters of mauve flowers, the leaves eaten by Cream Wave moth caterpillars. **Common Vetch** *V. sativa* is an annual, native everywhere except the far north and rare in Ireland, with paired pink flowers. *Vicia* vetches are also eaten by other generalist moth caterpillars, gall midges and leaf-miner flies.

★ Viper's buglosses *Echium* ▲

Great name; great wildlife! The stems of these perennials and biennials are usually covered in glass-like hairs and are topped with spikes of often blue flowers, popular with bees and many other insects. **Viper's Bugloss** *E. vulgare* (above) is a fine-looking biennial of dry grasslands and coastal habitats, native to much of lowland Britain except the far north, growing to 60cm. Soldier beetles and burnet moths nectar at it and many garden moth caterpillars feed on it including the Orange Swift. However, if you want something even showier and you live in the sheltered south, go for one of the giants from the Canaries or Madeira, such as the 3m tall biennial *E. pininana*, the shrub-like perennial *E. fastuosum*, or my favourite flower of all, the scarlet flame-flowered *E. wildpretii*. For the front of flower borders, the annual *E.* 'Blue Bedder' is just as good as all the wild species.

Wallflowers *Erysimum* ▼

The familiar **Wallflower** *E. cheiri* from southern Europe, also sold as *Cheiranthus cheiri*, and the similar **Siberian Wallflower** *E. allionii* are useful spring bedding plants with fiery flowers, the best of which are visited eagerly by bumblebees, but they are rather variable when it comes to insects. So focus if you can on the hybrid cultivars based on *E. bicolor* from the Canaries, in particular *E.* **'Bowles' Mauve'**, which is widely

acknowledged to be the best for pollinators including bees, bumblebees and especially many butterfly species. It is a perennial but quickly turns leggy, so take cuttings from them to keep a stock of fresh young plants.

Willowherb, Rosebay
Chamerion angustifolium
(syn. *Epilobium angustifolium*) ▲

This native perennial of open woodlands, railway embankments and waste ground across most of the British Isles, forms dense stands. The flower stems, up to 1.5m tall, have pink spikes of flowers June–August opening from the base up, turning to curly pods of white fluff. It is an excellent nectar plant for moths and some bumblebees and

a food plant for the caterpillars of Elephant and Small Elephant Hawkmoths. Some bees will also visit. A superb white-flowered form, **'Album'**, looks great in borders. Plant from seed in autumn; just beware you may need to keep it in check once established.

Wood Sage *Teucrium scorodonia* ▲
Native throughout much of the British Isles, this adaptable, patch-forming perennial grows up to 50cm high in woodland glades, hedgerows, shingle beaches and dunes. It forms a modest flower spike of lime-yellow flowers with a large lower lip, a source of nectar for the Shears and Tawny Shears moths, while the soft, rounded leaves are the sole food plant of the day-flying moths Speckled Yellow and Golden Pearl. Look out, too, for **Caucasian Germander** *T. hircanum*, which has dense spikes of tiny purple flowers visited by bumblebees. The **Wall Germander** *T. chamaedrys*, a rare native of Sussex, is a small plant for a dry sunny situation that is a magnet for bumblebees.

Yarrows *Achillea* ▲
It is likely that your lawn already contains **Yarrow** *A. millefolium*, a native weed throughout most of the British Isles and the origin of a whole suite of garden cultivars. It is a perennial growing to 75cm, mainly in grasslands where its feathery foliage can be inconspicuous in cut grass. If allowed to flower, the flat densely-packed flower heads are white or tinged pink and offer easy access for solitary bees and solitary wasps, while a whole host of beetles and generalist moth caterpillars feed on the foliage, including the Tawny Speckled Pug. Plant breeders have been able to draw out flower colours from bright yellows to fiery reds, which I often find every bit as good for insects. *A. filipendulina* from Asia, rather taller up to 1m, has even larger 'table tops' of often bright yellow flowers that are great for short-tongued pollinating insects. Yarrows like a free-draining soil in full sun.

Yellow Archangel
Lamiastrum galeobdolon ▲
Closely related to the dead-nettles, this is a beautiful native of moist woodland in southern Britain, often in ancient woodlands, where it forms patches up to 30cm high, spreading via long runners. The whorls of bright yellow, hooded flowers during April–June are visited by bumblebees and larger solitary bees such as the Hairy-footed Flower Bee. The subspecies *L. g. argentatum* is a widely planted cultivar with silver patches on the leaves but is highly invasive and should be avoided.

Grasses

So often dismissed as 'just grass', there is so much more to it than that. In gardens, lawns tend to be sown with a very restricted range of cultivated species, often dominated by various rye grasses and fescues, but there are actually dozens of different wild species, including ones adapted to woodland, heathland and dry grassland. These wild grasses can also be incredibly beautiful in an understated way, such as **Quaking Grass** *Briza media*. Many of the wild species, such as **Yorkshire Fog** (right), bents and wild fescues are vital food for the caterpillars of several meadow butterflies as well as for various moth caterpillars, grasshoppers and bugs including the Tortoise Bug and the Turtle Bug.

There are then also lots of ornamental grasses, which have had something of a boom in popularity due to the trend for prairie planting. Often quite tall and with a 'tufted' habit (growing up from a central point), they are increasingly being recognised as a fabulous place for beetles and other small creatures to snuggle into, especially for the winter. They often produce lots of seeds, too, which can then be devoured by sparrows and finches.

One of the key things with any grasses, as far as wildlife is concerned, is letting them grow unchecked rather than mowing them constantly. This then offers wonderful cover for all sorts of wildlife, including Hedgehogs, and the tussockiness is used by voles and carder bees.

See page 146 for those grasses to plant in a wildflower meadow, and page 156 for heathlands. Anything you can do to choose grasses other than those used in cultivated lawn mixes gets you a giant tick where wildlife is concerned.

Ferns

The lush green foliage of ferns makes them pleasing additions to the moist, shady parts of the garden where few other plants survive. I have to be honest, their wildlife value is somewhat compromised by their lack of flowers or fruit, and few creepy-crawlies seem able to eat the foliage either. Nevertheless, they offer cover and microclimates that might otherwise be absent, often year-round in the case of evergreen species, and there are some micro-moths and leaf-mining flies that will use them. Why look further afield than our beautiful natives?

Three common evergreen species of walls and rocks: **Common Polypody** *Polypodium vulgare*, growing to 20cm, often on mossy tree trunks; **Wall-rue** *Asplenium ruta-muraria*, up to 10cm, with fans of little clover-like leaves; and **Maidenhair Spleenwort** *Asplenium trichomanes*, with delicate weak stems lined with square leaflets.

Three deciduous species that form familiar 1m high shuttlecocks in woodland with deeply cut leaves: **Lady Fern** *Athyrium filix-femina*, **Male Fern** *Dryopteris filix-mas* and **Broad Buckler Fern** *Dryopteris dilatata*.

Hart's-tongue *Phyllitis scolopendrium*, an unusual fern with its simple clump of leathery strap-like leaves, which grow to 30cm.

Hard Fern *Blechnum spicant*, common on acid soils in the wetter west, growing to 40cm, with leaves divided neatly into 'fingers'.

Wall-rue

Maidenhair Spleenwort

Hart's-tongue

Common Polypody

Male Fern

Ostrich Fern (*Matteuccia struthiopteris*)

Pond and bog plants

The range of plants to use in a pond is small compared with what you can grow in flowerbeds. Their wildlife value is as much for the varied cover they offer as what might take pollen, nectar or feed on the leaves. Avoid the non-native invasive species at all costs (see page 257), buying only from the most reputable suppliers, but also avoid those plants that will be just too vigorous for the size of your pond – I've seen too many ponds where something like a White Water-lily has not only covered the entire surface but is actually busting out from the banks.

Avens, Water *Geum rivale*   ▲
Waterside flower of poorly drained soil native throughout much of Britain, especially the northern half. It has nodding, understated bell-flowers on long stems, the petals and cup of sepals a deep, shady red-pink. It will grow in semi-shade quite happily, where it is visited by bumblebees.

Bogbean *Menyanthes trifoliata*   ▼
One of the most distinctive water plants, with sprawling stems up to 1.5m long from which rounded trefoil leaves poke up through shallow water as a dense crowd of foliage. They are joined in late spring by flower spikes with pink buds opening to a head of white star flowers with frilly edges, visited by some bees and other pollinating insects such as flies. Grow in larger ponds only.

Bulrushes *Typha*   ▼
Everyone knows the head-height **Bulrush** *T. latifolia* (sometimes called Reedmace) that grows tall and dominant in large ponds and canals with its giant, chocolate-brown sausage seed heads. It is native to most of the British Isles but rare in Scotland. You may also know **Lesser Bulrush** *T. angustifolia* (below), rather more slender but often as tall and with thinner sausages; it is a scattered native mainly in England. Both have several beetles that use them and a few moth caterpillars such as the Bulrush Wainscot, and their seed heads are probed by Blue Tits and Chiffchaffs in search of insects hiding within them, as well as by Reed Buntings for seeds. However, they are vigorous plants that can choke small ponds quickly and their roots can puncture pond linings, so only plant it if you are sure your pond can cope with it. Avoid Dwarf Bulrush *T. minima* which is an invasive non-native species.

Flowering Rush *Butomus umbellatus*   ▲
One of the most attractive wetland plants native to most of lowland England, preferring fertile soils in alkaline waters. It is a perennial that likes to have its feet permanently in shallow water. The leaves are thin and grass-like, but the flowering stems grow to 90cm with an umbrella of pink flowers at the top in summer. It reproduces by rhizomes, is not especially rich for wildlife, but the slender stems are ideal for emerging dragon- and damselflies to cling to, and it certainly looks good!

Frogbit *Hydrocharis morsus-ranae* ▲
A free-floating plant of still, shallow water, with leaves (borne in summer only) like miniature lily pads, this is a rather scarce native of scattered locations in England and Ireland. It sports charming three-petalled white flowers just above the surface. Its wildlife value is as a place for damselflies to alight and for pond snails to lay their eggs.

★ Hornworts *Ceratophyllum* ▲
An invaluable waterweed, including for the smallest of ponds. The common species is **Rigid Hornwort C. demersum** (above), native to still and slow waters throughout much of southern Britain, where it lives mostly submerged and free floating, forming dense masses without getting out of control. It is eaten by Moorhens and Mallards, and provides wonderful hiding places for aquatic life such as freshwater shrimps and tadpoles. It is also used by many dragonflies and damselflies as places to secure their eggs.

Irises ▼
What beautiful flowers water irises are, with their strap-like leaves and large elegant flowers, but select carefully for the size of your pond. The glorious **Yellow Flag** *Iris pseudacorus* is native to almost the entire British Isles, with sunshine-yellow lily heads, but is too aggressive for a small pond or bog garden; however it will form a dramatic clump of 1m tall strap leaves along a large pond margin. If the flowers are en masse, Bumblebees will

visit, and Moorhens will find plenty of places to hide among the leaves. For small ponds, there are two brilliant irises to try: **Japanese Iris** *I. laevigata*, or the equally beautiful *I. veriscolor*, both of which are typically a blue-purple colour.

★ Loosestrife, Purple *Lythrum salicaria* ▼
One of our most beautiful wildflowers, with elegant flowering stems up to 1.5m topped

with a long head of magenta flowers loved by bees (bumble, Honey and solitary) and Brimstone butterflies. It is native to most of lowland British Isles, growing in clumps in damp soil or even with its feet in water. Some generalist moth caterpillars feed on the foliage, as do various leaf beetles and weevils. There are over a dozen cultivars of the species, with many spreading well in a moist herbaceous border where they are just as good for bees. For medium ponds and larger.

★ Marsh Marigold *Caltha palustris* ▲
Native throughout the British Isles, growing to 60cm at most, a glorious deciduous perennial of water margins and wet meadows, with large kidney-shaped leaves. In April–June, it is decked with large yellow buttercup flowers, visited by various pollinating insects such as hoverflies, flies and solitary bees but sometimes by Small Tortoiseshell and Peacock butterflies. It will happily grow in 10–20cm of water and is well behaved, even in quite small ponds. Avoid the doubles, usually called 'Flore Pleno' and 'Monstrosa'.

★ Mint, Water *Mentha aquatica* ▼
A native perennial to almost the entire British Isles with scented foliage, growing along water margins and around ponds, even with its roots fully submerged. It is 90cm high at most, the flowers clustered in pompons at the top of leafy stems where they are visited by butterflies, especially the whites, Small Tortoiseshells and Peacocks. Easy to grow, but

flowers. Both **Broad-leaved Pondweed** *P. natans* (below) and **Bog Pondweed** *P. polygonifolius* have floating, heart-shaped leaves up to 12cm long, ideal resting places for damselflies and egg-laying spots for pond snails. The former is native to most of the British Isles, the latter to acid waters in the west, north and on heaths. Different in habit are **Curled Pondweed** *P. crispus* and **Perfoliate Pondweed** *P. perfoliatus*, both scattered natives in lowland areas of the British Isles, with upright submerged leaves.

just be aware that, like most mints, it will put plenty of its energy into spreading, so if using in a small pond be prepared to need to keep it in check.

Pondweeds *Potamogeton* ▼
There are many species of pondweeds in the *Potamogeton* genus, many growing up to 4m long under water, and so are only suitable for larger ponds. Here they help form the underwater landscape for pond creatures. Fleshy flower spikes emerge above the surface with clenched, lime-green, wind-pollinated

Reed *Phragmites australis* ▲
Wetland grass native across almost all lowland areas of the British Isles where it spreads quickly to form the familiar monoculture swathes of swaying, golden-topped stems in fens and marshes. Growing up to 3m high in a year and spreading by rhizomes, it is for large ponds only! It is also said to puncture pond liners. It does, however, provide wonderful cover, and even a few square metres of it may host some of its specialist moths, such as those in the wainscot family. Moorhens may nest among the stems, warblers and tits hunt for insects and Reed Buntings may drop in for the seeds, so if you have a pond large and robust enough it is certainly worth planting. Bundles of the cut stems are useful for adding to solitary bee boxes.

Rush, Soft *Juncus effusus* ▼
Native across almost all the British Isles and common in damp areas, it forms a clump of sharp cylindrical leaves up to about 60cm tall. Its wildlife is a rather unspectacular entourage

of micro-moths, leafhoppers and leaf-mining flies, but the fascinating form of the plant called '*spiralis*' twists all over the place and makes an unusual addition to the pond, while the upright structure of the basic species is ideal for damselfly nymphs to clamber up as they emerge. Can be used in a small pond.

Spearworts *Ranunculus* ▼
These two species of aquatic buttercup, both native to the British Isles, are useful in ponds to add marginal cover, although the flowers and foliage are not especially favoured by insects. **Greater Spearwort** *R. lingua* (below) is a deciduous perennial, up to 1m tall, a scattered native to lowland areas, much declined in the wild but popular as a pond plant and able to spread quickly on long runners. The open

yellow flowers are up to 5cm across. **Lesser Spearwort** *R. flammula* is more suitable for small ponds, usually no more than 30cm high, with flowers 2cm across, and native throughout the country.

Water Crowfoots ▲
Ranunculus subgenus *Batrachium*

There are about a dozen species of this very variable, floating, aquatic buttercup, some of still water, some of fast-flowing. They often bear a mat of floating leaves plus a tangle of thread-like submerged ones; those on the surface become studded with a mass of white, five-petalled flowers. The leaves are eaten by Mallards and Moorhens, and pond creatures hide and lay eggs among the underwater leaves.

Water-lilies *Nymphoides/Nymphaea* ▼

Choosing the right water-lily for the size of your pond is crucial. If you have a very large pond (one that most of us might call a small lake!), then try **White Water-lily** *Nymphaea alba* or **Yellow Water-lily** *Nymphaea lutea*, both probably native across much of the British Isles in large pools, lakes and slow rivers. Both are vigorous perennials, each large lily pad up to 25cm across offering wonderful vantage points for damselflies, while pond snails lay their eggs on the undersides of the leaves. The rootstock is huge. For smaller ponds (those still maybe 4m or more across), try **Fringed Water-lily** *Nymphoides peltata*, a native perennial to parts of the East Anglian fens and the Thames Valley but widely planted elsewhere. The leaves are 8cm across at most; the flowers up

to 3cm, the whole plant spreading no more than 2.5m. For small garden ponds, you will need to choose carefully, selecting something like **Pygmy Water-lily** *Nymphaea pygmaea* from Europe and its hybrids, which are not known to be invasive.

Water-milfoils *Myriophyllum* ▲

These are perennial waterweeds, more feathery than the hornworts, with long stems up to 1m and fine-cut leaves in distinct whorls. In summer, the tiniest of reddish flowers poke above the surface. There are two widespread species native to the British Isles – **Spiked Water-milfoil** *M. spicatum* from lowland and eastern areas and **Alternate Water-milfoil** *M. alterniflorum* from more upland, western and acidic waters. They have some semi-aquatic weevils associated with them, but arguably

their greater wildlife value is for all the pond creatures that hide among their fronds. In my pond, it tends to be where the Emperor dragonflies lay their eggs. Both are fine for small ponds.

Water-plantain ▲
Alisma plantago-aquatica

Native throughout much of the British Isles except the far north, this perennial likes growing with its feet in the mud beneath a few centimetres of water. It has immaculate, broad, pointed leaves held clear of the surface, and then flowers on an incredible, slender candelabra, up to 90cm tall, each branch ending in a small, three-petalled, pale pink flower. OK, so the leaf-mining beetles, flies and the micro-moth that use the plant aren't going to set your wildlife world alight, but it is a nice native pond plant to have, and is dainty enough for small ponds.

Water Plaintain, Lesser ▼
Baldellia ranunculoides

I include this separately from Water Plantain as it is in a separate family and looks very different. Instead of the erect leaves and wiry candelabra of its cousin, the Lesser forms a spreading clump of inch-long leaves in shallow water, with a sprinkling of dainty, palest-pink flowers over the top.

It is the kind of plant that can get rather lost in a large pond, but is perfect for a small pond where so many other plants would be thuggish. The cover it offers, rather than its palatability or nectar, is what makes it a useful addition for wildlife.

Water Speedwells *Veronica* ▼

There are three main species to try, all attractive and all found in pond margins and sunny ditches, sprawling to about 50cm, with typical four-petalled speedwell flowers. Few large insects are associated with them, and their value is more for the cover and microhabitat they bring to the water's edge. **Brooklime** *V. beccabunga* is native throughout most of the British Isles, with rich blue flowers, fleshy purplish stems and rounded leaves. **Blue Water Speedwell** *V. anagallis-aquatica* and **Pink Water Speedwell** *V. catenata* are both annuals, less fleshy and with longer leaves than Brooklime. The Blue is native to much of lowland British Isles, the Pink more restricted to England and Ireland. All look great in a small pond.

Water Soldier *Stratiotes aloides* ▼

This plant is something of a curiosity, which many gardeners love to grow in their ponds. It is perhaps best described as a floating crown, for each plant is a whorl of spiky, saw-edged leaves. In autumn, each 'crown' sinks under the surface, then rises again in late spring, its stiff leaves emerging like synchronised swimmers sticking their legs in the air.

In the UK, it may be native only to East Anglia, but can be grown in most sheltered, mild areas. Interestingly, there are no male Water Soldiers in Britain; our all-female population can have simple three-petalled flowers in summer. Its value for wildlife is in the cover, shade and damselfly perches it offers.

Woundwort, Marsh *Stachus palustris* ▼

This downy perennial is far better behaved and prettier than its cousin, Hedge Woundwort. It is native in damp places throughout the British Isles, rarely grown as a garden plant but a fine addition to bog gardens and damp pond margins. The whorls of pink flowers up a 1m strong stem are excellent for bumblebees, especially Common Carder Bees.

Given enough damp soil or mud to colonise, it should quickly clump up into an attractive stand. However, avoid the hybrid between Marsh and Hedge Woundwort, however, which is a brute. Use alongside medium ponds and larger.

Water-starworts *Callitriche* ▼

It took me a long time to come around to the virtues of this group of understated aquatic plants. Individually, the paired leaves are small and insignificant; as for the flowers, blink and you'll miss them. But it is when the plants create a dense mass of fresh-green leaves, whether in still water or flowing, that you sense its value as underwater cover for a whole host of pond life. There are seven species native to the British Isles, but you'll need to find a specialist grower of native pond plants to be able to purchase a clump or two.

Vegetables and soft fruit

These are some of the crops you can grow that will feed you and your family but at the same time benefit wildlife. I'm not including plants such as cabbages where, if you took a deep breath, you might be able to tolerate a few Large White or Small White caterpillars chomping through your dinner. Nor do I mean those plants that, if sacrificed and allowed to go to seed, are good for wildlife too, although remember that onions, leeks, parsnips and carrots are great for that. No, this is very much about 100 per cent win–win situations.

Bean, Broad *Vicia faba* ▲
Although they don't necessarily need insects to pollinate the flowers – they can do that themselves quite happily and still produce pods full of beans – some fascinating research almost 50 years ago showed that if you do encourage pollinators, especially bumblebees, your crop will increase quite dramatically.

Bean, Runner *Phaseolus coccineus* ▼
A star plant for bumblebees and Honeybees, the scarlet flowers also look wonderful in the flower border or large pots growing up a wigwam of canes. Grow in sheltered spots, even lightly shaded, give them deep, rich soil,

water regularly, and remember they are frost-tender so start them off indoors in spring. A cultivar such as 'Butler' has masses of flowers; just pick regularly to keep the flowers coming. Dwarf cultivars can be as little as 40cm tall. Note that French Beans *P. vulgaris* are self-pollinated – it's 'runners' you want for wildlife.

★Currants *Ribes* ▲
You may not want birds gorging themselves on the berry crop, but there is still a chance for wildlife to enjoy the bushes earlier in the year if you hold off netting until the crucial season. There are three main species, all of

which are widely naturalised in the British Isles: **Redcurrant** *R. spicatum* (which may actually be native), **Blackcurrant** *R. nigrum* (which has aromatic leaves) and **Gooseberry** *R. uva-crispa*. The latter two are both thought to be European in origin. All grow to about 1.5–2m tall, enjoying light shade and rather moist ground. Their small flowers look insignificant, but bumblebees love them and research has shown that you will get a better crop if you allow bees access to them. The foliage is also eaten by caterpillars of the Phoenix, the Spinach, Currant Pug and the V moths.

★Raspberry *Rubus idaeus* ▲▼
A native of woodlands and scrubby areas throughout almost the entire British Isles, it has since been cultivated to produce summer- and autumn-fruiting varieties offering bigger fruit and a heavier crop. The list of insects, from sawflies to moths, that feed on the foliage is huge, and although Raspberries can be self-fertile, the number of berries produced is higher if there are good numbers of bumblebees and other bees to pollinate them.

Weeds

There are some native plants that are so unruly or bland or coarse that I think I'd struggle to convince all but the most dedicated gardeners to plant them on purpose, but which are likely to pop up anyway in your garden because they are so successful and ubiquitous. These are your out-and-out, bona fide weeds! However, they have some considerable virtues for wildlife, so if you have a corner where you can just let them be, wildlife will certainly benefit.

★Bramble *Rubus fruticosus* ▲

Although not compulsory, Bramble is an undeniable wildlife all-rounder of the highest standard, offering tasty foliage for many moth caterpillars including Buff Arches and Peach Blossom, and for Speckled Bush-crickets. They produce ample nectar for many butterflies (see page 82) and bumblebees, and the berries are eaten by Dormice, mice, Foxes and birds such as Greenfinches, while many autumn moths get merry on the overripe berry juices. In addition, its thorny, thickety nature creates ideal nest sites for birds such as Wrens and hideaways for Hedgehogs. Maybe you can find a space for it in wilder parts of the garden or train it over a log pile?

Charlock *Sinapis arvensis* ▲

This is one of several widespread species in the very useful wild cabbage family (crucifers). It is a coarse annual, usually growing to 50cm, with four-petalled, bright yellow flowers in any month April–November. An archaeophyte across most of the British Isles in arable fields and waysides, it provides valuable seeds for finches, and a fine breeding ground for various leaf beetles, weevils, pollen beetles, thrips and generalist moths, as well as Large and Small White butterflies.

Chickweed *Stellaria media* ▲

I bet this extremely common but incon-spicuous annual weed is probably in flower somewhere in your garden right now. Native almost everywhere in the British Isles, its tiny, starburst, white flowers appear in any month. It can churn out three generations of plants a year, producing lots of seeds for finches and buntings. Its foliage also seems eminently palatable, with caterpillars of dozens of moths munching happily on it. All Chickweed needs to flourish is a bit of disturbed fertile soil. It is easy to weed out, so just leave it be where you can.

Coltsfoot *Tussilago farfara* ▼

A low, spreading perennial, up to 15cm tall, Coltsfoot has dandelion-like flowers from January onwards that appear before the leaves. It is this early source of seeds that marks it out as an important plant for finches and sparrows just at the point when resources are often low. It also provides food for Triangle Plume and Coltsfoot Bell moth caterpillars.

Dandelions *Taraxacum* spp. ▼

Surely one of the best-known native wild-flowers, there are over 230 microspecies in the British Isles of this perennial, all looking rather similar to all but the few experts. A field full of Dandelions is a joy to behold, such is the intensity of the sunshine-yellow flower colour; strange, then, that we make such an effort to remove them from our lawns. Left in place, they are especially good for solitary bees, some butterflies will visit them, and the leaves that are so beloved of Rabbits are also one of the best for a wide range of moth caterpillars.

★ Garlic Mustard (Jack-by-the-hedge)
Alliaria petiolata ▼

This biennial may even get a place in your borders for its wonderfully fresh-green, heart-shaped leaves, but it becomes dried and withered by July. It is a key food plant for Orange-tip and Green-veined White caterpillars, and for the Brassica Bug.

Goosefoots and Oraches
Chenopodium/Atriplex ▼

It is hard to claim that these are attractive plants, but they are important for the amount of seeds they produce, which are eaten by finches, sparrows and buntings. Plenty of insects feed on the foliage, too, including caterpillars of Dark Spinach and the Nutmeg moths. Key plants in the group include **Fat Hen** *C. album*

and **Common Orache** *A. patula*, both of which are native throughout the British Isles except in the Scottish Highlands, wherever the soil has been turned. In a garden, let them do their thing in a fallow plot and watch the little birds flock in! They are really easy to weed out with a quick tug if you need to. However, I do rather like the perennial **Good-King-Henry** (cracking name!) *C. bonus-henricus* (above), which is an uncommon perennial found on rich soil around farmyards and, in my view, rather stately.

Groundsel *Senecio vulgaris* ▲

Ubiquitous annual weed wherever the soil is turned, native throughout the British Isles. The stems are reddish, to 30cm max, flowering in any mild spell of weather where the little flower heads are like clenched baby dandelions quickly turning to seed-clocks. Its value for wildlife comes from its commonness, the palatability of all those seeds for finches, and the fact that the leaves are edible to dozens of moth caterpillars and leaf beetles. If you don't need to yank it up, leave it be.

Hedge Woundwort *Stachys sylvatica* ▼

Rather coarse weed with unpleasantly scented leaves (I warn you: don't rub them!), native to most of the British Isles and spreading quickly along hedges and in light shade using rhizomes. It sends up flower spikes to 1m at most, with whorls of sparse, pink-purple, lipped flowers that are fabulous for bumblebees, while the Bronze Shield Bug feeds on the furry foliage. It can be invasive, but in a grassy hedgerow margin it is possible to tolerate it.

Hogweed *Heracleum sphondylium* ▲

A coarse, hairy, deep-rooted perennial growing up to 2m, with large umbels of white flowers, native to almost the entire British Isles in woodland glades, hedgerows and grassy places. In a sunny position, it can be a magnet for all sorts of hoverflies, solitary wasps, longhorn beetles and flies that you'll rarely see on other flowers. With all sorts of gall midges, leaf beetles and micro-moths using the foliage too, it is insect paradise. It can be grown in semi-shade, and self-seeds easily.

Knotgrass *Polygonum aviculare* ▲

Understated little annual, native throughout the British Isles, one that you'd step on and not know it, and yet eaten by dozens of moth caterpillars. It can trail up to 1m across the ground or through sparse grass, with small, simple leaves and minute flowers that are slightly pink (if you get up close!). It flowers June–November, and the prolific seeds are enjoyed by birds such as sparrows and buntings.

★Nettles *Urtica* ▼

Stinging or **Common Nettle** *U. dioica* is a native perennial throughout almost the entire British Isles, forming dense stands on fertile ground. Hairs on the stems and leaves snap at a slight touch, injecting the chemical cocktail that causes the pain. The flowering stems can grow to 2m, with insignificant wind-pollinated flowers but copious seeds eaten by Bullfinches and Dunnocks. The foliage is eaten by brave caterpillars of Burnished Brass, the Spectacle and Dark Spectacle, the Snout, Mother of Pearl, Small Magpie and the very common Nettle-tap moths. Nettle also has its own weevil and ground bug, and many other insects find excellent cover here.

However, it is as a food plant of the caterpillars of Peacock, Small Tortoiseshell, Comma and Red Admiral butterflies that it is perhaps best known. What isn't so well understood is that they are rather picky about how and where the Nettles are growing. Unless you have large, sunny beds of them, your chances of success are quite slim, but if you have room I'd still say give it a go because a garden filled with those four butterflies is paradise.

Small Nettle *U. urens* is a rather neat annual archaeophyte of disturbed ground in much of lowland Britain, but rare in Ireland, growing to 60cm and offering some of the same benefits as its big cousin.

Plantains *Plantago* ▲▼

If you aim for a perfect lawn, you probably spend hours trying to winkle these fellas out. Native to almost every part of the British Isles, **Greater Plantain** *P. major* is particularly adept at coping with being crushed underfoot, throwing out a suffocating low rosette of broad leaves, while **Ribwort Plantain** *P. lanceolata* (above) has much more slender leaves and is a common and rather attractive plant of grassy meadows. The foliage of both is eaten by lots of generalist moth caterpillars. Both have hard, plain flower heads with a ruff of shaggy stamens, the result of which is more seeds for more birds such as finches and sparrows. Try **Hoary Plantain** *P. media* (below) in wildflower meadows (see page 146).

Redshank *Persicaria maculosa* ▼

Yes, a weed with the name of a bird, this is an annual, with stems up to 80cm or so tall but which usually sprawls across cultivated or damp ground. The lance-shaped leaves are easy to spot, each with a dark smudged 'V' across them, and are eaten by various sawflies and weevils. The flowers are borne in a tight, pinkish spike, producing abundant nutty little seeds for birds such as Greenfinches.

Sorrels *Rumex* ▼

I stopped short of recommending the rather coarse and vulgar docks, despite how much seed they produce, but the closely related sorrels are just as good as a seed source for birds such as Greenfinches, *and* they are the food plant of caterpillars of the Small Copper butterfly and Blood-vein moth. Both **Common Sorrel** *R. acetosa* (below) and **Sheep's Sorrel** *R. acetosella* are native throughout the British Isles in grassy places, the former growing to 80cm in pastures and downland, the latter only 20cm tall at most and preferring acid soils and short vegetation. The small red flowers are held in dangling clusters. Grow in a meadow area, where they can look beautiful against the light.

Plants to avoid

Considering what *not* to plant is perhaps more important than all of the species you might like to try.

We grow thousands of garden plants from all corners of the globe, and most of them are wholly benign and 'behave' themselves. However, a few have run riot. They are called 'invasive non-native species' or INNS. They can have a devastating impact on native wildlife, and can be very expensive to control.

The plants in this section are all on Schedule 9 of the Wildlife and Countryside Act, which means it is illegal to plant them in the wild, and in gardens it is expected that 'reasonable measures will be taken to confine them to the cultivated area so as to prevent their spreading to the wider environment'. As of 2014, five are also banned from sale in England and Wales, and the Wildlife and Natural Environment (Scotland) Act 2011 brought in new provisions governing the introduction of non-native species in Scotland.

The list of invasive species is unfortunately growing, and more work is being done to 'horizon scan' to see whether others are likely to cause a problem in the future: it is far better to nip something in the bud now rather than wait until the horse has bolted. Those identified as being 'Critical' for investigation have not been included in the main list of recommended plant species, and include these very familiar species:

❀ Butterfly Bush *Buddleja davidii*
❀ Pampas Grass *Cortaderia richardii*
❀ Bay *Laurus nobilis*
❀ Tree-of-heaven *Ailanthus altissima*
❀ False-acacia *Robinia pseudoacacia*
❀ Portuguese Laurel *Prunus lusitanica*
❀ Firethorn *Pyracantha coccinea* and *P. rogersiana*.

What harm do Invasive Non-native plants cause?

Freed from the natural factors that control them in their homelands, some non-native plants have spread like wildfire into our native habitats. They out-compete native plants, which has a knock-on effect on the wildlife that lives in UK habitats. For example, invasive non-native water plants choke waterways and ponds with dense mats of vegetation. This cuts out light from the water, reducing oxygen levels and increasing the nutrients, meaning far fewer water creatures survive. They can even increase the risk of flooding.

If you have any of the invasive species in this section, do try to control and destroy them, but **don't put them in green waste bins**. With some species such as Japanese Knotweed and Giant Hogweed, it is best to seek advice from professionals.

Cotoneasters ▼

Sadly, for a groups of shrubs that were excellent for berry-eating birds, it appears that **Holly-berry Cotoneaster C.** *bullatus*, **Wall Cotoneaster C.** *horizontalis*, **Himalayan Cotoneaster C.** *simonsii*, **Entire-leaved Cotoneaster C.** *integrifolius* and **Small-leaved Cotoneaster C.** *microphyllus* are becoming invasive shrubs in the countryside, and dozens of other varieties may be following suit. Their seeds are spread by birds, so they are best avoided.

Bluebell, Spanish
Hyacinthoides hispanica ▲

This bulbous perennial native to Iberia, grown widely as a garden plant, has 'escaped' into the wild where it grows strongly and interbreeds with the **English Bluebell H.** *non-scripta*, threatening to dilute our native species. In flower, the 'bells', which can be blue, pink or white, are fragrance-free, surround the stem rather than being in a single spike, and don't 'nod' like ours do.

Hogweed, Giant
Heracleum mantegazzianum ▲

A giant biennial, up to 4m tall, from the Caucasus and once used as a border plant, it has immense leaves that block out native vegetation. Take great care if you come across it as the sap can cause a violent skin reaction lasting years, and removal of the plants needs to be done with full protective equipment. With one plant capable of producing 100,000 seeds, control is proving difficult.

Himalayan Balsam/Indian Balsam

Impatiens glandulifera   ▲

A waterside annual introduced to Britain for its attractive pink-purple flowers. These are enjoyed by bumblebees, but don't let that lessen your resolve! They grow to 3m in one season, and form explosive seedpods that catapult seeds up to 7m. Pull it up before it seeds to stop it spreading.

Hottentot Fig *Carpobrotus edulis*   ▲

A fleshy trailing species from South Africa with showy flowers, a single plant can be 50m across. Mainly found on southern cliffs, it smothers native vegetation, and when it is removed it leaves the exposed soil vulnerable to erosion.

Knotweed, Japanese *Fallopia japonica*   ▲

Introduced from Japan in the 19th century for its creamy-white flowers, this is a brute that can grow through tarmac and floorboards, and can regenerate from a fragment of root. Removal involves a horribly costly process of chemicals and burial of contaminated soil.

Parrot's Feather (Brazilian Water-milfoil)

Myriophyllum aquaticum (M. brasiliense)   ▲

Widely available, with delicate fresh-green feathery leaves in whorls of four to six, the 2m stems swamp ponds. Control is by chemicals or repeated pulling.

Pennywort, Floating

Hydrocotyle ranunculoides   ▼

From North America, with attractive lobed leaves on top of the water, it can grow at a rate of up to 20cm a day. It is causing huge problems, all the more alarming as it was first found in the wild in Britain only in 1990. Control is very difficult, best done by repeated and careful hand-pulling.

Pondweed, Canadian *Elodea canadensis* and
Nuttall's Pondweed *Elodea nuttallii*   ▼

From North America, these submerged pondweeds, similar to native Hornwort, can fill the water column with long stems lined with whorls of leaves. Control by hand-pulling.

Pygmyweed, New Zealand (Australian Swamp Stonecrop)

Crassula helmsii   ▼

An innocuous-looking bruiser first grown in English gardens in the early 20th century, and now found in more than 2,000 wild locations. It is a low-growing, rather fleshy plant with whorls of little pointed leaves on pinkish stems and small white flowers with four triangular petals. Control is very difficult, and often requires chemicals.

Rhododendron
Rhododendron ponticum ▼

Oh dear, this one particular type of rhododendron is such a problem plant, despite such beautiful flowers. It shades out native plants, changes the chemical composition of the soil making it difficult for other plants to germinate, spreads quickly and is host to the tree-killing disease *Phytophthora*. Fortunately, if you love rhododendrons there are plenty of types other than *R. ponticum* to grow.

Rose, Japanese *Rosa rugosa* ▼
I've seen this widely grown shrub with its large pink flowers marching out of control across sand dunes and sea cliffs. No matter that birds like Greenfinches enjoy the hips and bees visit the flowers – the damage it does to other wildlife outweighs this.

Water-fern
Azolla filiculoides and *A. caroliniana* ▲
Creating a reddish mat of floating, tiny, lobed leaves that block the light from ponds, control requires painstaking removal with a net.

Waterweed, Curly
Lagarosiphon major/Elodea crispa ▼
This submerged pondweed from southern Africa with long stems is similar to Hornwort but the whorled leaves curl tightly around the stems. Control by hand-pulling.

Virginia Creeper
Parthenocissus quinquefolia ▼
Yes, even familiar species like this are now on Schedule 9 of the worst offenders, so although the autumn colour as it cloaks walls is delightful, go for something like Boston Ivy which has the same visual effect but without known invasive tendencies.

Water-hyacinth *Eichhornia crassipes* ▼
From tropical America, this free-floating plant has violet flowers plus fleshy leaves that act like sails. It is one of the most invasive water plants in the world but has yet to establish itself in the wild in the British Isles – the situation needs to stay that way!

Rhubarbs, Chilean
Gunnera tinctoria and *G. manicata* ▼
The huge leaves are magnificent – unless you're another native plant shaded out by them. They produce thousands of seeds, which are spread by birds.

GARDENING FOR WILDLIFE CALENDAR

If you're like me and have a head like a sieve, this next section is a simple month-by-month aide-memoire that will help ensure you don't miss key gardening dates.

In it I cover not only those activities that are specific to gardening for wildlife but also other gardening jobs because, as we've seen, the two should be inseparable.

As activities go, gardening is forgiving enough to give you a little bit of flexibility so, if one season you're a little late or early with a job, you can probably get away with it in most cases.

To start you off, below is a quick ready-reckoner of the most important and time-specific wildlife gardening jobs throughout the year.

▼ In the table below, dark lilac shows the prime time to complete the activity, pale lilac is not as ideal but I reckon you'll get away with it!

	J	F	M	A	M	J	J	A	S	O	N	D
Trees and shrubs												
Plant bare-rooted trees, shrubs, hedges and roses	■	■									■	■
Prune deciduous trees, fruit trees, late-flowering shrubs and shrub roses, and coppice hazels	■	■										■
Prune spring-flowering shrubs			■									
Prune hedges	■	■							■	■	■	■
Prune trees in the cherry family (plums, cherries, etc)						■	■	■				
Prune winter- and spring-flowering shrubs as they go over					■	■	■					
Take cuttings from shrubs							■	■	■			
Tie in climbers					■	■	■					
Flowers												
Divide herbaceous perennials			■	■					■	■		
Sow beds of annuals / cornfield mixes				■	■							
Plant spring bulbs									■	■		
Clear herbaceous beds of last year's seedheads		■	■									
Sow biennials for next year						■	■					
Lawns and meadows												
Sow or lay lawns				■	■				■	■		
Repair any damage to lawns				■					■	■		
Sow meadows				■				■	■			
Mow spring meadows							■	■	■	■		
Mow summer meadows			■	■								
Ponds												
Clear out excess weed							■	■	■			
Nesting boxes												
Put up bird boxes	■	■								■	■	■
Clean out used bird boxes									■	■	■	
Supplementary food and water												
Feed garden birds	■	■	■	■	■	■	■	■	■	■	■	■
Provide fresh water for birds	■	■	■	■	■	■	■	■	■	■	■	■
Feed Hedgehogs			■	■	■	■	■	■	■	■	■	

January

If it wasn't for the feverish to-ing and fro-ing of birds at your feeders and bird tables (and hopefully also at some of the seedheads you've left standing), winter gardens might look very lifeless indeed. It's a miracle that insect-eating birds, such as Goldcrests and Long-tailed Tits, survive at all and, for them, every waking moment is spent seeking sustenance.

Periods of snow and ice are especially difficult for garden birds. The shelter that evergreens such as Ivy and Holly now offer is a lifesaver over the long winter nights, while Blue and Great Tits will have laid claim to nest boxes for roosting.

Given the short, cold days, you'd think that there wasn't much to do for your garden. Oh, you'd be so wrong!

Essential jobs

• Planning is priceless: make a sowing plan for the year ahead and design new features, then order seeds, seed potatoes and onion sets.
• Take part in the RSPB Big Garden Birdwatch on the last weekend in January and help the RSPB measure how garden birds are faring.
• Get creative: January is a great month to beaver away indoors making nest boxes for birds, bats and bees...

Trees and shrubs
• Continue to plant bare-rooted trees, shrubs, fruit trees and bushes during frost-free periods, and transplant shrubs or saplings (from now until mid March).
• Prune established apple and pear trees (until the end of February), removing dead, diseased and damaged wood, and opening up the centre of the tree.
• Prune shrub roses (from now until April), taking stems back by half and getting rid of dead and crossing stems.
• Knock snow off shrubs to stop it damaging stems and buds.

In the vegetable and fruit plot
• Prune Gooseberry and currants bushes (now and into February), opening up the middle of the bush.

• Finish digging beds and borders – improves drainage and opens up the soil so your plants can send down their roots, while exposing seeds and minibeasts for the birds.
• Take particular care not to disturb Hedgehogs that could be hibernating in log piles and compost heaps.
• Keep birdbaths ice-free during freezing weather, but use warm water, never salt or de-icer.
• Get in the experts to do any major tree surgery.

Indoors
• Sow in warmth, such as in a heated greenhouse or propagator: French beans, leeks, lettuce, mustard, onions, radishes, tomatoes.
• Check stored dahlia tubers – feel for any soft parts, which indicate rot and will need cutting out.
• Wash pots ready for the sowing season, to reduce the risk of disease.

At the feeding station
• Keep bird feeders topped up at all times and, as importantly, keep them clean. Clear up spilled seed from the ground beneath feeders if it's causing a problem, but don't put it on compost heaps.

February

Although this is often the coldest month in the UK, bulbs are already beginning to poke through the soil, signalling welcome changes afoot. On warm days later in the month, Frogs can start to become active in ponds, even laying the first spawn, and a Brimstone butterfly or queen bumblebee might be lured out of hibernation. There aren't many native flowers that bloom in February, so the bees may turn to winter heathers, Winter Honeysuckle, daphnes and *Viburnum* x *bodnantense*.

February can be a lean time for birds, especially during snow, and those bird feeders become essential to help see them through cold days and long, even colder nights.

Essential jobs

• Ensure you've put up any new bird boxes – prospective owners will be checking them out soon.

• This is the best month to prune wildlife hedges, if all the berries have been taken. Cut hedges over a 2-year cycle, alternate sides each year.

• Get ready for sowing – check you have a good supply of clean pots and plenty of peat-free potting compost because sowing season is about to kick off.

Trees and shrubs

• Prune winter-flowering shrubs, such as Winter Jasmine and *Viburnum* x *bodnantense*, once the blossom is over (now until April), taking out old stems and thinning new growth.

• Hard prune climbers like wisteria and late-flowering clematis and also overgrown honeysuckles.

In the flower border

• Mulch borders with a good, thick layer of compost.

• Tease out old leaves from ornamental grasses before fresh growth starts.

In the vegetable and fruit plot

• Have you got all the compost bins you need? Slatted ones are better for wildlife.

• Plant willow whips (now and into March), to create imaginative dens and screens.

• Continue to keep birdbaths clear of ice.

• Clean water butts of leaves and debris, which will otherwise will rot and pong!

• Lift, divide and replant snowdrops 'in the green' (i.e. with leaves on) – they will spread more quickly that way.

• Make sure all your tools are in good working order.

• Do a final preparation of vegetable beds, lightly forking them over and raking.

• Late in the month, start to sow broad beans, carrots, lettuces, onions, parsley, parsnips, early peas, spring cabbage and turnips in sheltered places or under cloches.

• Lift and store parsnips.

Indoors

• Start to sow seeds of flowers like dahlias, snapdragons, sweet peas, Tobacco Plant and verbenas in heated propagators.

• Sow broad beans, cauliflowers, French beans, leeks, early lettuces, onions, radishes, sprouts and tomatoes.

• Start off dahlia tubers in warmth in trays or pots of compost.

• Chit potatoes and place in a warm, bright place till they sprout.

March

This month can start so cold, yet can soon seem full of hope: there's an undeniable sense that nature is stirring all around. On a still, sunny day, hibernating butterflies start to emerge and, by month's end, the first Chiffchaffs have returned and are singing. Blackbirds and Robins crack straight on with their first brood.

Daffodils and primroses begin to brighten up the place, but of greater value to wildlife is the sallow blossom and the first lungworts, both magnets for early bees. But don't be lulled into thinking that birds must now be having it easier – this is still a difficult time for them as all the natural winter supplies become exhausted.

Essential jobs

• Try to complete all hedge pruning early in the month ahead of the bird breeding season – that will be it then, until September.

• Prepare the ground and sow your area of cornfield annuals (now until early May).

• Sow herbaceous perennials indoors in clean compost, watering with tap water to avoid diseases.

• Sow hardy annuals in pots indoors, and prepare flowerbeds ready for sowing them outside.

• Cut back the dead seedheads of last year's herbaceous perennials. If you think they may still be harbouring seeds or insects, just leave them in tidy piles in the garden rather than putting them straight to compost.

Trees and shrubs

• Prune elders, lavateras, caryopteris and *Buddleia* x *weyeriana* back to 30–60cm stems.

• Check that saplings haven't been root-rocked by the winter storms; tie them back to their stake if necessary.

In the flower border

• Plant out perennials (now into May) such as scabiouses, sweet peas and wallflowers.

• Take cuttings of delphiniums and lupins.

• Lift and divide herbaceous perennials (between now and April), including herbs and 'sensitive' ones, such as asters, catmints, delphiniums, red-hot pokers, scabiouses and sneezeweeds.

• Trim winter heathers (now until May).

In the vegetable and fruit plot

• Continue to fork over the soil when weather allows.

• This is the main month for sowing vegetables and their companion plants. Almost all of them can be started off this month.

• Plant out Chives and mint that you kept indoors in winter.

• You can sow a green manure crop, such as Field Lupins or Crimson Clover, for a few weeks to carpet bare ground.

Lawns and meadows

• Do an early cut or two of your lawns if you are going to manage them as a summer meadow.

Indoors

• Sow cucumbers, French and runner beans, sweetcorn and tomatoes (now and into April).

April

April is so exciting; prepare to be busy. There can be real warmth from the sun on some days, even while there is still frost on some nights. Plants put on a growth spurt with many more coming into flower. There's a blanket of Blackthorn blossom in the hedge-rows, Marsh Marigolds illuminate ponds, spring meadows come into their own, and it's all go on the woodland garden floor.

You know spring is officially here when the first Swallow passes over and when the weeds start to germinate! The latter is your cue to sow seeds directly into the soil. But this can often be a hard time for seed-eating birds, just at the point when male birds need to defend a territory and females need to lay eggs, so keep up the supplementary feeding.

Essential jobs

• You should be kept very busy sowing vegetables, potting on seedlings, and transplanting and nurturing young plants. When watering seeds in pots and trays, use tap water to reduce the risk of the dreaded 'damping off' fungal disease.
• Get on top of weeds. Dig out perennial weeds carefully (and compost them separately) and hoe annual ones.
• Sow annuals outside into prepared ground, such as Pot Marigold, Candytuft, Cornflower, California Poppy, Annual Lupin, Poached-egg Plant, Larkspur, scorpion weeds and Annual Sunflower.
• Divide herbaceous perennials as they start to show signs of life, especially those that will flower in late summer. Replant the divisions separately, well spaced, to create drifts of colour and insect food later in the year.

Trees and shrubs
• This is the best time to plant or transplant evergreen shrubs (now until May), just as they come into full active growth.
• Prune Flowering Currant and other early flowering shrubs (usually to within three buds of old wood) as soon as the blossom is over.
• Take tip cuttings of Hop, inserting into free-draining compost but watering often.

In the flower border
• Prune an inch off the tips of lavenders to promote healthy, bushy growth.

In the vegetable and fruit plot
• Finish planting maincrop potatoes.
• Start sowing broccoli and maincrop peas, and continue sowing other vegetables: little and often will give you a succession of crops.

In the pond
• Divide aquatic plants, replanting in baskets using peat-free, low-nutrient compost.
• Be patient if there is a flush of algae – if you have followed the rules it should soon clear.

Indoors
• Sow hardy perennials in clean pots and trays.
• Plant up hanging baskets but keep them inside for now.

At the feeding station
• Switch from dried to live or soaked mealworms, make sure peanuts can't be taken whole by birds and cut out homemade fat foods, which tend to go off quickly as temperatures rise.

May

What a glorious month this is! Nature has moved to full throttle, temperatures are rising (although late frosts are possible), and there's a buzz of insects in the air. With everything so fresh and vibrant, it makes you want to get out there.

The breeding season for birds is in full swing and latecomers, such as Swifts and Spotted Flycatchers, return. Many garden residents are already introducing their first brood of youngsters to the delights of your garden.

In the pond, tadpoles and 'toadpoles' are growing fast and the first damselflies are on the wing, while in the woodland garden Bluebells grab their moment before the canopy closes over.

Essential jobs

• Continue to prune flowering shrubs as they go over, taking out a few old stems to encourage new growth ready for next year – they will flower on this summer's growth.

• Mulch fruit bushes such as currants and raspberries with manure or compost.

• Be a Miss Marple with your breeding birds and work out where they are nesting – then give them a wide berth.

Trees and shrubs

• Tie in climbing roses to encourage sideshoots.

• To rejuvenate Rosemary, prune back hard to new shoots.

• Take heel cuttings from lavender, pulling a side shoot down off the main stem and potting in sandy compost.

In the flower border

• Plant out 'unstarted' dahlia tubers at the start of the month.

• Plant out hardy annuals that you raised in trays in March, and thin those sown directly into the soil to 10–15cm apart.

• Put up wigwams and supports and train sweet peas; take softwood cuttings of fuchsias and verbenas, and sideshoot cuttings from Wallflower 'Bowles' Mauve'.

In the vegetable and fruit plot

• Hoe out weeds.

• 'Chelsea chop' perennials that flower in later summer, removing the top third of growth, to keep them shorter and bushier.

• Keep newly planted perennials, trees and shrubs well watered.

• If you sowed a meadow the previous autumn, mow it now to 5cm and remove the clippings.

• Sow outside: beans (broad and runner), beetroot, cabbage, cauliflower, Chives, lettuces, onion sets, parsley, peas, sweetcorn; and plant out early sown brassicas and leeks.

• Earth up potatoes and stake peas.

• Pinch out the tips of broad beans as soon as the lowest pods begin to set, to help curb blackfly, and nip out strawberry runners.

• Put card collars around young brassicas to prevent Cabbage Root Fly.

Lawns and meadows

• Sow lawns or re-seed bare patches, and lay new turf.

Indoors

• Pot on seedlings.

June

After the frenetic spring, there is more of a feeling of calm as you wander around your garden attending to rather more routine jobs, such as hoicking out the stubbornly shooting weeds or starting to deadhead flowering plants.

Things can seem much quieter on the bird front, but they're unobtrusively getting on with raising their young and, for many, starting the next brood. It's a genuine lull for adult butterflies before late summer's rush of species, but bumblebee colonies are beginning to build up in strength, and there should be many solitary bees on the wing, taking advantage of all the flowers including your cornfield patch at its colourful peak.

Essential jobs

- Tie in climbers to direct them where you want.
- Stake top-heavy perennials with hazel and willow twigs saved over the winter.
- Make 'comfrey tea' to feed pot plants.

Trees and shrubs
- Prune spring-flowering Broom, taking out three-quarters of the length of flowering stems.
- Thin out apples and pears to get a good crop.

In the flower border
- Lift out spring bedding plants, such as wallflowers and forget-me-nots, and sow next year's in seed drills in the vegetable patch, plus foxgloves and Honesty.
- Lift, divide and re-plant Primroses.
- Sow more hardy annuals directly into the borders.
- Harden off bedding plants by putting them outside by day in a sheltered, sunny position and bringing them in at night. After a couple of weeks, they're ready to plant outside.
- Move hanging baskets outside.

In the vegetable and fruit plot
- Plant out tomatoes, marrows and cucumbers.

- Deadhead flowers as they go over to prolong the flowering season until you are ready to let them go to seed.
- Keep on top of weed seedlings.

- Transplant brassicas from nursery beds into the main vegetable plot.
- Sow beetroot, carrots, cauliflowers, courgettes, cucumbers, French beans, lettuces, marrows, peas, runner beans, spinach and sweetcorn.
- Mulch peas and beans to keep in the moisture.
- Earth up potatoes and lift early varieties.
- Put straw around strawberries to stop soil splashing onto the fruit and spoiling them.

In the pond
- Remove excess weed, a small amount at a time leaving it for a day on the pond edge for creatures to crawl back. Once it has begun to dry out, simply compost it.

At the feeding station
- Reduce the amount of seed you put out, never letting food lie uneaten for days at a time.

July

The heat of summer brings a bustle of butterflies and bees, moth traps reveal that the night-time garden is even busier, and dazzling dragonflies patrol the airways over ponds. There can be apparent calm on the bird front, but they are soldiering on with second and third broods under the cover of summer's dense vegetation.

Flower borders are now riotous, thick with brilliant reds and oranges that match the fieriness of the season. The woodland garden is refreshing in its deep shade, and the summer meadow is rising to a flowering peak. Pots and hanging baskets are at their best, and there are delicious scents of Summer Jasmine, honeysuckles and stocks on the light breeze.

Essential jobs

• There'll be plants demanding water daily, but butts are likely to be running low, so conserve limited supplies by watering in the cool of evening or early morning, and water right to the roots of those that need it most such as pots and hanging baskets, cucumbers, potatoes, beans and tomatoes.

• Keep birdbaths topped up – this is the time when birds need it the most. Take the opportunity to give the bowls a good scrub to keep them hygienic.

Trees and shrubs
• Remove suckers around trees and shrubs, such as cherries and plums, from now through to autumn.

In the flower border
• Deadhead annuals and bedding plants to prolong their flowering season.
• Arrange the pot garden, bringing those at their best to the fore for their star turn.

Lawns and meadows
• Mow the spring meadow for the first time, keeping the blades quite high to start with, and then every few weeks thereafter.

• Take semi-ripe cuttings of almost any shrubs and climbers, from dogwoods to honeysuckles, Rosemary to roses: cut a non-flowering shoot just below a leaf node, remove the lower leaves and plant in gritty, free-draining compost; water with tap water, cover with a clean, clear plastic bag and place in a shady warm position. In a couple of weeks, rooting should have started and you can remove the bag and allow the new plants to grow on.

In the vegetable and fruit plot
• Harvest currants and Gooseberries, and give the bushes a booster mulch.
• Harvest strawberries and onions.
• Continue sowing beetroot, carrots, lettuces, radishes and salads.
• Finish planting courgettes, marrows, sweetcorn and leeks.
• Earth up potatoes.
• Pinch out the sideshoots of tomatoes.
• Late in the month, give the annual prune to trained fruit, such as espaliers and cordons of apples, redcurrants and Gooseberries, reducing sideshoots to three leaves.

August

Hot days can still be upon us, formal lawns can look rather exhausted, and your summer meadow is turning to yellowing hay, but flower borders continue to pack a punch. Butterflies such as Peacocks, Painted Ladies, Red Admirals and Brimstones are in evidence, and the heathland garden is a purple haze.

Pond levels can drop dramatically, but bear with it – summer storms should bring levels back up quickly. It's a good month to see plenty of dragonflies and bats, and Hedgehogs may bring youngsters to snuffle around flower borders and meadows. Watch, too, for the synchronised emergence of flying ants from under paving.

Essential jobs

• Keep deadheading, but remember to leave some flowers to go to seed and roses to turn into hips.
• Keep watering those plants that need it, using 'grey water' from washing the veggies or even from your bath. Continue to keep birdbaths topped up with clean water.
• Keep feeding pot plants and hanging baskets little and often – they soon exhaust their natural supplies.
• Late in the month, scythe down the cornfield garden.
• If, and only if, you are absolutely sure there are no late bird broods, from late in the month prune evergreen shrubs and privet, Beech, Hornbeam and cypress hedges.

Trees and shrubs
• Summer prune wisterias, taking off long shoots to encourage more flowers next year.

In the flower border
• Dry weather can cause mildew – cut afflicted plants back to the base and water well.
• Collect seed for sowing this autumn or next year.

In the vegetable and fruit plot
• Harvest beans regularly to keep the crop coming; harvest onions once the tops have died down; harvest blackcurrants, cherries and plums, leaving a few for the wildlife!
• Keep celery and leeks well watered and earth up.
• Sow late beetroot, lettuces, French and runner beans, plus winter and spring cabbages.

• When they have finished fruiting, cut summer raspberry canes back to the ground, and thin new growth to 10cm apart, tying in to supports.
• Cut off all strawberry leaves and runners to force the plants' energy into next year's flowers.

Lawns and meadows
• Sow new lawns.

Indoors
• Order spring bulbs.

At the feeding station
• Apart from squabbling House Sparrow families or Starlings, feeders can often be eerily quiet now. Don't worry – there is plenty of natural food for the birds at the moment. Only put as much food out as is getting eaten.

September

Warm September sunshine may lull you into thinking that summer will never loosen its grip, but nature knows better. It senses that nights are eating rapidly into day length, and for much wildlife it is time to start shutting up shop, with summer migrants heading south in droves.

Enjoy the butterflies and bees that cling on in numbers, relishing the fading glory of the herbaceous border that still shows off with beauties such as Coneflower, achilleas and *Verbena bonariensis*. Some butterflies also turn to windfall fruit, as do drunken and slightly touchy wasps.

Essential jobs

- Feed your Hedgehogs to get them into good condition for winter.
- While the soil is warm, divide and replant perennials that have finished flowering, avoiding sensitive souls such as scabiouses, asters, delphiniums and red-hot pokers.
- Thin out pondweed and divide aquatic plants.
- Plant out evergreen shrubs and relocate established ones if you need to (now until November).
- Lightly cultivate the cornfield garden mid month to prompt germination of what will be next year's display; ideally, remove weeds and replenish those areas with fresh cornfield annual flower seeds.
- Sow a new wildflower meadow.
- Plant daffodil and other spring bulbs (see November for tulips).
- Your compost bins are probably filling – shred or use a lawnmower to break up material and get the decomposition really motoring.

Trees and shrubs
- Prune rambler and climbing roses now through to November, once flowering is over, by taking back sideshoots on climbers and taking out a third of old stems to ground level on ramblers. Take rose cuttings.
- Trim lavenders after flowering, either with secateurs or shears, never going into old wood.

In the flower border
- Now until November, plant out herbaceous perennials not in flower.
- Take cuttings from snapdragons and verbenas.
- Divide irises.

In the vegetable and fruit plot
- Harvest beetroot, carrots, marrows, onions, potatoes, sweetcorn and tomatoes.
- Harvest and store pears and apples.
- Prune fruiting canes of blackberries and summer raspberries down to ground level, and tie in new growth to wire supports.
- Don't let flowers set on tomatoes, as new fruit now will not ripen.
- Sow lettuces, spring cabbages and winter spinach.

Lawns and meadows
- Mow (or scythe!) summer meadows for the first time, leaving the hay lying a while to drop seed before removing.

October

Every month in the garden is special in its own way, but this one just pips it for me. You've got berry-laden bushes, dew on the spiders' webs, Red Admirals clustering around Ivy flowers, an explosion of fungi, and the last fling for the herbaceous borders with Michaelmas daisies putting on a defiant show. Blackbirds clamour over the windfalls, Robins sing their melancholy autumn song, and Redwings and Fieldfares begin to pass overhead.

And I haven't even mentioned the stunning backdrop as the autumn leaves flush with fire and then fall. If there was a bit more of a poet in me, I'm sure I could make something of all the mists, mellowness and fruit out there.

Essential jobs

• Net ponds to prevent leaves from falling in, and collect them from here and from flowerbeds and lawns. Give them a quick run-over with the mower to speed up decomposition and then put them in a wire cage to create leaf mould.
• On the other hand, see if you can leave leaves (so to speak) lying naturally in woodland gardens for beetles and autumn caterpillars to hide among and for the Blackbirds to turn over.
• Don't tidy up herbaceous borders more than you need to – leave those seedheads in place.
• This is the best month to clean out bird boxes.
• Put up new nest boxes – birds may use them for winter roosts.

In the flower border
• When the first frosts turn dahlia leaves brown, lift them, hang upside down for a few days under cover, and bung them in a box of sand in a dry, cool place for the winter.
• Plant spring-bedding wallflowers and forget-me-nots (now until December) into their flowering position for next spring.
• Pot up perennials such as fuchsias and herbs, and bring them and tender pot plants into the greenhouse or conservatory.

In the vegetable and fruit plot
• Clear out and compost any spent crop vegetation.
• Harvest beetroot, carrots, potatoes, swedes and turnips; gather and store apples and pears.
• Sow broad beans and peas for standing overwinter. Plant autumn onion sets, and sow late lettuces and spring cabbages.

• Take hardwood cuttings of currants and Gooseberry from now into November.
• Start winter digging.
• Plant raspberry canes in soil enriched with plenty of compost.
• On vacant patches, sow green manures, such as *Phacelia*, winter tares and ryegrasses. In the spring it can be dug in to add nutrients straight back into the soil.

Lawns and meadows
• If you have a formal lawn rake out any moss, scarify (using a machine that cuts deep slits into it) to get into the thatch and give the turf air, and then top dress with a loam-based compost and grit. Sow seed onto bare areas. This is also the last chance to create new lawns from seed or turf.

November

There's no holding out any more – winter is on its way. The Ivy gives a brave last stand offering nectar for late insects, but the trees are now losing their last leaves and herbaceous plants are dying back.

It's a month when the temptation to tidy is often strong, like clearing the table of the crumbs after a hearty meal. You don't need to deny the urge completely – just tidy creatively, enjoying the effect of dead stems and seedheads and a kickable carpet of leaves wherever you can.

Essential jobs

• Take extra care on 5th November that no Hedgehogs have clambered into the bonfire you've just built.
• Time to start digging! On an established plot, dig in manure as you go or cover the surface with a thick layer of compost mulch and let the worms continue the job.
• Begin planting deciduous trees and shrubs including fruit trees, roses, soft fruit and hedges,

Trees and shrubs
• Chop back the long stems of honeysuckles (now until February) to as little as 30cm if necessary, though it's really just to keep them under control.
• Collect tree seeds, extracting them from berries if necessary; sow them in pots and stand outside over the winter.

In the flower border
• As annuals die in the border, remove and compost them once they have shed seed.
• Mulch herbaceous borders around the dead stems of the perennials, preferably with leaf mould.
• Plant tulip bulbs.

In the vegetable and fruit plot
• On a new plot, dig carefully, removing all weeds.

• Take hardwood cuttings (now until January) of roses and many deciduous shrubs and climbers such as brooms, elders, Flowering Currant, honeysuckles and willows. Cut a 30cm stem with a bud top and bottom, and insert 15cm into a slit in the ground, adding a little sand to the slit if your soil is heavy. Give the plants a year to get going before you transplant them.

• Mulch fruit bushes and fruit trees.
• Harvest beetroot and carrots.
• Clear out the dying foliage of tomatoes and cucumbers.
• Sow hardy broad beans and peas for an early summer crop.
• Prune autumn raspberries right down to the ground.

Indoors
• Take root cuttings of herbaceous perennials with fleshy roots such as Coneflower, mulleins, phlox and hardy geraniums (now through to March).

At the feeding station
• Even when we feel the cold, there are still lots of insects, seeds and berries in the countryside so don't panic if there aren't many birds in your garden. By late November, as the birds return, put out more supplementary food.

December

There's barely anything left in flower in the garden now, and any bee or butterfly abroad is brave or foolish. Winter Jasmine and Oregon-grapes are two of the few shrubs that offer welcome nectar, although there is little around to take advantage of it.

Evergreen shrubs really come into their own to hold your garden design together against the bare background of the borders, but wild animals are more interested in whether they've got any berries on them.

It's down to the birds to keep us entertained, hopefully gorging on food that you and your garden produced as well as what's in your feeders.

Essential jobs

• It's the start of the main pruning season, keeping fruit trees open and airy, renovating old and tired shrubs, and sometimes even removing trees if the garden is becoming too overgrown. And that means it's the season for creating log and stick piles, as artistically as you like.
• Dig some more of the vegetable and annual-flower borders when the soil isn't too wet, with your friendly neighbourhood Robin by your side grabbing grubs from the turned soil.
• Coppice willows and Hazel between now and February, saving the stems for some home weaving, pea-sticks or herbaceous-perennial supports.

Maintenance
• Fit water butts to catch rain from the gutters of your house, shed, conservatory and garage.

Trees and shrubs
• Winter prune wisterias (from now until February), cutting again those whippy shoots that you dealt with in summer, taking them back to only about 3cm now to encourage flowering next year.
• Plant bare-rooted trees, shrubs, roses and hedging whips (from now until early March), rehydrating their roots in a bucket of water before planting and getting them into the ground as soon as possible.
• Prune back trees and shrubs if they are in the way of paths or views, adding the branches to log piles.

• Give protection in frosts to tender shrubs such as Olives.
• Winter prune apple and pear trees (now into January) if they are heading skywards.
• Check that tree ties and stakes aren't chafing the bark.

In the flower border
• Lightly clip old flowers off autumn heathers.

In the vegetable and fruit plot
• Harvest sprouts, starting at the bottom.
• Prune Gooseberry sideshoots back to about 5cm.

Indoors
• Sharpen tools, wash pots, clean canes and tidy up after all the months of frenzy and distraction.
• Send off for seed catalogues.

Measuring Success

It's always reassuring to know that the things you do are having the effect you desire, and with gardening for wildlife that means doing some kind of recording.

Some of us have a natural tendency to want to catalogue, compare and analyse what is going on – if so, this section is right up your street. Even if you are normally allergic to surveys, I hope you'll try some of the quick ideas in the starter level, because the benefits of monitoring are huge.

Not only can it give you confidence and satisfaction that things are improving under your watch, but you can also contribute your data to national surveys. It is through these that we have been able to spot changes in garden wildlife populations – such as the decline of Song Thrushes, Starlings and House Sparrows – and so do something to remedy them.

I've recorded my garden wildlife pretty assiduously for 16 years now, and the results have amazed me. What is most revealing is how flawed my memory is! Where I might previously have sworn that a species was now commoner or rarer than before, I find the data often tells a very different – and I now realise a far more accurate – story.

Starter-level monitoring

✿ Take photos of your garden, if possible from the same place each time, to visually monitor the changes. You'll be astonished at the differences over time.

✿ Take part in the annual RSPB Big Garden Birdwatch. For one hour only during the last weekend in January, count the maximum number of each species that visits your garden, and enter your results online along with half a million other people.

✿ Keep an annual list of the species of birds and butterflies that visit your garden.

✿ Keep a wildlife gardening diary and write about what you've seen and how you feel.

Intermediate-level monitoring

✿ Try the British Trust for Ornithology's Garden Birdwatch. There's a small annual fee, and each week you record the maximum number of each species that you see in your garden. You then enter your records online or send them in, and it gives the BTO (and you) a fascinating insight into how birds use gardens year-round.

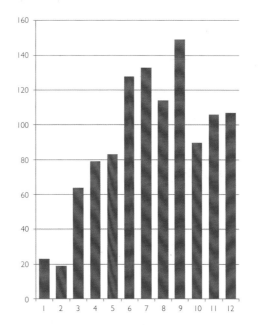

◀ My recording sheets just sit on the windowsill. Every time I see a bird, butterfly or dragonfly, it takes only a second to scribble it in. Over time, the sheets become a fascinating record of the changing visitors to my garden.

◀◀ Trail cams are a great way of revealing what is using your garden under cover of darkness.

◀ The graph shows butterfly numbers in my garden recorded over a 12-year period. The totals are the maximum number of each species seen each week, added up for each year. Numbers rose quickly at first after I planted the right flowers, then dropped a little as my garden became shadier.

Advanced-level monitoring

Moth trapping

You will have noticed that many moths are attracted to light with what looks like a death wish. Why they do it is still poorly understood, but it is part disastrous (they are distracted from mating and feeding by all our street and house lights, and they get picked off under them by enterprising bats) and part fortuitous (because we can use special light traps to monitor which species are about and measure how well they are doing).

With a moth trap, the moths fly towards the light then are deflected into a collection area, where they hunker down in special resting bays (egg boxes). 'Moth-ers' (not to be confused with mothers) then either identify and count them at night using a torch or wait until the following morning, after which the moths are released unharmed. You'll be amazed by what you catch!

Two types of light are widely used: a fluorescent (actinic) tube that only gives off a vague blue light to human eyes and a more powerful mercury-vapour (MV) bulb that will illuminate half a street but will quadruple the number of moths you catch. There are three main types of trap:

* The Heath Trap uses a vertical actinic light, in the middle of three perspex 'wings' that guide moths into a collecting basin.
* The Skinner is a square wooden trap with either an actinic or MV light and two sloping perspex panels to guide the moths into the heart of the trap.
* The Robinson trap is a robust round 'bin' with a perspex collar and an MV light.

Bat detectors

Bat detectors convert a bat's squeaks into clicking sounds we can hear and show what frequency the noise is. Because different species squeak at different frequencies, we can then work out what species is nearby. Well, it's almost that simple! Those who like gadgets will love it, and in the absence of you holding a bat licence for inspecting roosts and bat boxes, it's one of the few ways to get a better understanding of your garden's bats. Prices will vary depending on the model.

Pitfall trapping

To trap monsters on the prowl, try this minibeast version of the jungle explorer's bear trap. Take a plastic drink cup, skewer some holes in the base, sink it into the soil so that its lip is level with the soil surface and cap it with a flat stone raised a couple of inches on some pebbles to keep the rain out. Unsuspecting beetles that scuttle past drop in and can't get out. Check your catch early each morning before some of your captives eat each other!

Bird ringing

This is really specialist territory now. Bird ringers need to train for years under the guidance of a guru to get a licence before being let loose. Bird ringing involves slinging a very fine, vertical mist-net across a well-used flight path and waiting for birds to fly into it. Birds are carefully extracted, have a uniquely numbered metal ring put on one of their legs, then are aged, measured and logged before being released.

The hope is that someone somewhere else at some future date will re-trap the bird, allowing us to see how far it has moved and how long it has lived. Data collected in this way has been jaw-dropping. It is only through ringing, for example, that we know British Swallows winter in South Africa and our wintering Blackcaps come from Germany. Check out www.bto.org for more information on how to become a ringer.

▲ Moth trapping is a great activity to take to friends' gardens as an after-dinner entertainment. In my experience, they are always amazed when a previously hidden world of wildlife is revealed in their own backyard.

▶ Bird ringing brings physical contact with birds that you don't normally get which, when the bird is something such as this Sparrowhawk, is especially exciting.

▼ With a night-vision trail cam, you can get an idea of what secret activity takes place under cover of darkness in your garden.

Acknowledgements

My huge thanks to all those who have supported me in the writing of this book.

In particular, my thanks to Julie Bailey at Bloomsbury for having the faith to support me through two editions.

To the book's designer Julie Dando and its illustrator Marc Dando for doing such a grand job on the creative side.

To all those who bravely let me into their wonderful gardens: Malcolm Berry, Richard Brown, Adrian and Glen Bury, Sue and Barry Camm, Ennis and Richard Chappell, Caroline Clarke, Simon Dannatt and Mark Taylor, Mike Dilger and Christina Holvey, Carol Goulden and Sarah Ingle, Margaret Harbidge, Chris Jones, Roy Lovell and James Dawson, Duncan Macdonald and Pieter Wessels, Sue Makin, Cheryle Sifontes, Jenny Sweet, Alessandra and Steven Towell, Sue and Darren Vallier, and Jim Woolley.

To Marc Carlton for his expertise on wildlife-friendly planting.

To the Royal Horticultural Society and The Royal Parks, whose gardens have offered me wonderful opportunities to study garden plants and the wildlife used by them.

To Wendy and David at the inspiring Merriments Garden in East Sussex, where many of the photos were taken. And extra thanks to David for modelling so gallantly.

To all those in the RSPB who did such a wonderful job of proofing sections of both editions of my book: John Day, Sarah Eaton, Mark Gurney, Ian Hayward, Sarah Niemann and Kirsi Peck.

To Mum and Dad for allowing their garden to be a testbed for some of my ideas, and where my gardening interest was able to first emerge. This book is in Dad's memory.

And especially to Peter Francis for supporting me throughout.

Recommended reading

If you would like even more wildlife-gardening advice than is contained here, I recommend the website of the Wildlife Gardening Forum – www.wlgf.org – where there is information about the topic from every conceivable angle, written by many of the authorities on the subject (and me!)

And do check out No Nettles Required by Ken Thompson (Eden Project Books, 2006) – a laugh-out-loud read that contains the science that informed much of this book.

If you would like to find out about specific groups of species, the following are all excellent:

RSPB Handbook of British Birds Fourth edition, Peter Holden and Tim Cleeves (Bloomsbury Publishing, 2014).

Britain's Butterflies, David Tomlinson and Rob Still (WILDGuides, 2002). .

Field Guide to the Dragonflies and Damselflies of Great Britain and Ireland Fifth edition, Steve Brooks and Richard Lewington (Bloomsbury Publishing, 2002).

Field Guide to the Bees of Great Britain and Ireland, Steven Falk and Richard Lewington (Bloomsbury Publishing, 2015).

Field Guide to the Moths of Great Britain and Ireland, Paul Waring, Martin Townsend and Richard Lewington (Bloomsbury Publishing, 2016).

Field Guide to the Micro-moths of Great Britain and Ireland, Phil Sterling, Mark Parsons, Richard Lewington (Bloomsbury Publishing, 2012).

Britain's Hoverflies: A Field Guide (2nd Ed), Stuart Ball and Roger Morris (WILDGuides, 2015).

Complete Guide to British Insects, Michael Chinery (HarperCollins, 2009).

Insects of Britain and Western Europe, Michael Chinery (Bloomsbury Publishing, 2007).

Complete Guide to British Mushrooms and Toadstools, Paul Sterry and Barry Hughes (HarperCollins, 2009).

Wild Flowers of Britain and Ireland Second edition, Marjorie Blamey, Richard Fitter and Alastair Fitter (Bloomsbury Publishing, 2013).

RSPB Handbook of Garden Wildlife Second edition, Peter Holden and Geoffrey Abbott (Bloomsbury Publishing, 2017).

Index

Photo credits

Bloomsbury Publishing would like to thank the following for providing photographs and for permission to reproduce copyright material. While every effort has been made to trace and acknowledge all copyright holders, we would like to apologise for any errors or omissions, and invite readers to inform us so that corrections can be made in any future editions of this book.

Where more than one photograph appears on a single page the credits are listed from top to bottom and left to right.

All photographs in this book are © the author, Adrian Thomas, with the exception of those listed below:

The RSPB

Many people know the RSPB for its high profile projects – looking after great swathes of nature reserves, battling to save flagship species like albatrosses or Red Kites, or knocking on the doors of government to remind our politicians that nature matters.

But the RSPB is also deeply interested in those little oases we call gardens. No wonder – the total area of all those gardens in the UK is estimated to be about 400,000 hectares. That's about three times the size of all the land the RSPB manages. So imagine if just one in three gardens were looked after with wildlife in mind – it would effectively double the area of our nature reserves.

Now gardens will never be important places for Capercaillies or Bitterns, those charismatic species that need wild and rare habitats. Nor will gardens ever support Skylarks and Corn Buntings, which is where the RSPB's championing of a healthy countryside comes in.

But that doesn't matter. Gardens are proving to be important habitats in their own right that, if managed well, can be a perfect home for declining birds such as House Sparrows and Starlings.

Much as we'd like to, the RSPB can't deploy real-life wardens into all those gardens. But we can do the next best thing and provide you with all the advice you need. That's where this book comes in, and also our *Give Nature a Home* campaign, our online advice service. To find our more about RSPB *Give Nature a Home*, or to register to get your free online advice, go to rspb.org.uk/homes or visit www.rspb.org.uk/plan to get tailored advice for your garden.

You can help us too through Big Garden Birdwatch. Half a million people each year count their garden birds for an hour in the last weekend in January, giving us a powerful snapshot of how they are faring.

And there are now some lovely RSPB gardens to visit on some of our reserves, such as the Chris Beardshaw-designed garden at Saltholme, or the tranquil visitor centre garden at Rainham Marshes.

The RSPB is what it is because of its members – over a million voices for nature. With your support – as members, as campaigners, as customers of our bird care products, and, of course, as wildlife gardeners – together we can give nature a home.

Martin Harper, Director of Conservation

If you would like to know more about The RSPB, visit the website at www.rspb.org.uk
or write to: The RSPB, The Lodge, Sandy, Bedfordshire, SG19 2DL; 01767 680551.

The RSPB and SITA Environmental Trust's prize-winning garden at the RHS Chelsea Flower Show, which was designed to provide great homes for wildlife.